Reading-Based W

Stephen McDonald
Palomar College

William Salomone
Palomar College

Wadsworth Publishing Company
I(T)P ® **An International Thomson Publishing Company**

Belmont • Albany • Bonn • Boston • Cincinnati • Detroit
London • Madrid • Melbourne • Mexico City • New York • Paris
San Francisco • Singapore • Tokyo • Toronto • Washington

English Editor: Angela Gantner Wrahtz

Editorial Assistant: Royden Tonomura

Developmental Editor: Angela Gantner Wrahtz

Assistant Editor: Rebecca Deans Rowe

Production Service: Carol Carreon Lombardi

Print Buyer: Barbara Britton

Interior Design: Christy Butterfield

Copy Editor: Judith Abrahms

Cover Design: William Reuter Design

Composition: Fog Press

Printer: Malloy Lithographing, Inc.

Printed in the United States of America
1 2 3 4 5 6 7 8 9 10

This book is printed on acid-free recycled paper.

Library of Congress Cataloging-in-Publication Data
McDonald, Stephen.
    Reading-based writing / Stephen McDonald,
        William Salomone.
        p.   cm.
    Includes index.
    ISBN 0-534-20094-x
    1. English language—Rhetoric. 2. English
language—Grammar. 3. College readers. I. Salomone,
William. II. Title.
PE1408.M267   1996
808'.0427—dc20   95-33217

**For more information, contact
Wadsworth Publishing Company:**

Wadsworth Publishing Company
10 Davis Drive
Belmont, California 94002, USA

International Thomson Publishing Europe
Berkshire House 168-173
High Holborn
London, WC1V 7AA England

Thomas Nelson Australia
102 Dodds Street
South Melbourne 3205
Victoria, Australia

Nelson Canada
1120 Birchmount Road
Scarborough, Ontario
Canada M1K 5G4

International Thomson Editores
Campos Eliseos 385, Piso 7
Col. Polanco
11560 México D.F., Mexico

International Thomson Publishing GmbH
Konigswinterer Strasse 418
53227 Bonn, Germany

International Thomson Publishing Asia
221 Henderson Road
05-10 Henderson Building
Singapore 0315

International Thomson Publishing Japan
Hirakawacho Kyowa Building, 3F
2-2-1 Hirakawacho
Chiyoda-ku, Tokyo 102, Japan

Dedication

With love to
George and Joan McDonald
and to
Kathryn and Michelle Salomone

Contents

Readings Listed by Rhetorical Mode

Articles that illustrate several modes may appear more than once.

ILLUSTRATION

CAUSE-EFFECT

ARGUMENT AND PERSUASION

Preface

The premise of *Reading-Based Writing*, as its title suggests, is that it is nearly impossible to write well without also reading well, that college courses today demand not only that students write clearly and read accurately but also that they write effectively *about* what they have read. *Reading-Based Writing* is designed as an introductory text to academic writing, the type of writing based on the careful, deliberate reading and the clear, critical thinking demanded of students throughout their college careers.

The Reason for This Text

Writing in Response to Reading. College courses outside of our English departments rarely ask students to write personal experience essays, nor do they ask students to write papers on topics *similar* to those they have read in some textbook. Rather, such classes more often ask that students write papers and essays in direct response to ideas they have encountered in assigned reading. Such writing assignments demand careful reading and clear summary. They demand that students be able to recognize and respond to specific points in the material they have read, to synthesize ideas from several reading selections, and to evaluate and to argue about the ideas they have found in their reading material. *Reading-Based Writing* introduces students to these and other skills they will need to write successful college-level papers.

Using Personal Experience. Although *Reading-Based Writing* introduces students to academic writing, it does not at all ignore the importance of their personal experiences, nor does it fail to recognize that writing about themselves is often the best way for writers to find their own voices and to discover that they do indeed have something to say. For this reason, the assignments throughout *Reading-Based Writing* ask students to use personal experience to respond to the material they have read in the text when it is appropriate to do so. Chapters 1–4 in particular emphasize personal responses. Then, when the students are writing more directly *about* what they have read in Chapters 5–8, optional assignments allow instructors to assign personal experience responses when they want to do so.

About the Text

Reading-Based Writing integrates reading, writing, sentence combining, and editing. Its writing instruction is kept simple and clear, and its reading selections consist of over sixty short articles, most of which are both recent and timely in their subject matter.

Organization

Part One: The Reading-Writing Conversation. Part One, consisting of the first four chapters, introduces students to the reading and writing processes and to the concepts of unity, coherence, and development. Each of these chapters contains a variety of reading selections to illustrate the points being made and to provide material that students can respond to using their own personal experience. In these first four chapters we want students to become comfortable with the writing process and familiar with the elements of well-written paragraphs and essays. At the same time, we want students to become careful readers and to recognize that accurate reading is an integral part of clear thinking and good writing.

Part Two: Writing about Reading. Part Two consists of four chapters that introduce students to ways of writing *about* what they have read. We start Part Two with a chapter on how to write brief summaries, extended summaries, and summary-response essays because so often students have trouble doing much more than identifying the central idea of what they have read. Writing the summary gives them practice in recognizing and expressing both the central idea and the supporting points of a reading selection. We then move to a chapter on evaluating the effectiveness of material they read. In this chapter students must read accurately as well as explain why they have or have not found a selection convincing, persuasive, or effective. In the next chapter, students synthesize the issues involved in several reading selections. Here, students must not only summarize what they have read but also recognize connections among reading selections and explain those connections in their papers. The final chapter of Part Two asks students to argue from several reading selections, using material from a number of brief articles to support their positions.

Part Three: Editing Skills. Part Three of *Reading-Based Writing* is meant to act as a supplement to the primary instruction provided in Parts One and Two. It serves as a brief handbook for those students who need help with grammar, punctuation, or usage problems, and it allows the instructor to cover such material as needed. We have arranged it as a separate part of the text rather than spreading its material throughout each chapter so that the student can quickly and conveniently use it as an aid in the editing process.

Part Four: Additional Readings for Writing. Part Four includes nineteen reading selections for the instructor to use in addition to those in the body of the text. The first nine selections cover a variety of topics appropriate for the writing assignments in the first six chapters. The remaining ten selections are then grouped into three specific topic areas so that they can be used as synthesis and argument topics in Chapters Seven and Eight. All of the reading selections reflect the criteria discussed below.

Features

The Reading Selections. In choosing the reading selections for *Reading-Based Writing*, we have kept several criteria in mind. First, we wanted most of the selections to be relatively brief since this text is, after all, an introduction to academic writing. For that reason, the majority of the selections are only a few pages in length. However, we also wanted our students to have to "stretch" their mental muscles at times, so we have included some longer, more complex articles for instructors to use as they see fit. Second, we wanted the reading selections to be both timely and interesting, appealing to as wide a range of students as possible. To achieve this end, we have chosen articles that challenge the students to think about who they are as well as about how they fit into our increasingly multicultural world. Titles ranging from "Go Ahead, Try to Define Your 'Self' in One Descriptive Word" to "A Generation of Bigots Comes of Age" to "The Changing Face of America" reflect the variety of topics to be found in this text. Finally, to allow for the kind of synthesis and argument that *Reading-Based Writing* is meant to encourage, we have included several articles grouped around common topics, such as "Should Drugs Be Legalized?" "Competition: How Does It Affect Us?" "Flag Burning and Free Speech" and "English as the 'Official' Language of the United States."

Evaluating Student Models. In addition to writing instruction and brief reading selections, each of the chapters in Parts One and Two includes a section on evaluating sample student papers. This section has two purposes. First, it is designed to provide students with "models" of successful papers that can be used to discuss what is expected of well-written paragraphs or essays. Second, it is meant to teach students to distinguish between successful and less successful papers so that they can better evaluate the effectiveness of their own writing.

Sentence Combining. Each chapter in Parts One and Two includes a section on sentence combining. Since so many student writers rely primarily upon compound and relatively brief complex sentences, the sentence combining sections are designed to give students practice in writing sentences that move beyond the patterns they are most comfortable with. Beginning with simple exercises in recognizing when modifiers in one sentence can easily be "embedded" within another sentence, these sections gradually introduce more difficult sentence structures involving the use of coordination, parallelism, subordination, participial phrases, appositives, and sentence variety.

Group Work. Throughout the text, exercises and writing assignments encourage students to work together, discussing the reading selections, comparing their responses to those selections, and helping each other develop their papers. While individual instructors will, of course, use such group work as they see fit, we have found it to be an invaluable teaching device, helping students to clarify their own thinking as they work with those around them.

Support Material

The Instructor's Manual for *Reading-Based Writing* provides suggestions for teaching the course on a chapter-by-chapter basis and offers comments about the reading selections. It will also include answers to all exercises in the text.

Acknowledgments

We thank our friends and colleagues in the English Department at Palomar College for their advice, encouragement, and support. We particularly thank Jack Quintero and Brent Gowen, whose thoughtful suggestions helped to shape this text.

At Wadsworth Publishing, we extend our thanks to Angela Gantner Wrahtz, whose enthusiasm got this project off the ground; to Carol Carreon Lombardi, whose hard work kept the text moving along; and to the entire Wadsworth team for their efforts during the development and production of this text.

We are especially grateful to the following students, who graciously allowed us to use their work as models for evaluation: Rosemarie Tejidor, Amy Duran, Sherrie Kolb, Kevin Farrar, Christapher Quintero, Daisy Faeldon, Jung Yun Park, Petra Guiland, Tami Jacobs, Elizabeth Jackman, Juan Alcantar, Dennis Amrhein, Jill Wilson, Tracy Thornton, and Louise Homola.

We are also very grateful to the following colleagues for their input during the creation of this book: William Bernhardt, College of Staten Island; Linda J. Daigle, Houston Community College; Dianne Gregory, Cape Cod Community College; Kathleen M. Krager, Walsh University; and Milla McConnell-Tuite, College of San Mateo.

Stephen McDonald
William Salomone

Reading-Based Writing

PART ONE

The Reading-Writing Conversation

Have you ever talked to someone who wouldn't listen or listened to someone who just rambled on and on without making a clear point? Probably you tried not to have many more conversations with that person. After all, in a conversation, both listening well and speaking clearly are important, and a poor listener or a confusing speaker is not a very enjoyable person to talk to.

Writing and reading are very much like speaking and listening. When you read, you *listen* to what someone else has to say; when you write, you *speak* your own ideas. Together, reading and writing make up a conversation between the reader and the writer, and either a poor reader or a poor writer can pretty much spoil that conversation.

As students in college classes, you will be asked to participate in this reading-writing conversation by writing in response to what you read. Depending on the instructor or the class, you might be asked to summarize the ideas you have found in textbooks, to analyze topics after reading about them, to evaluate opinions expressed by a writer, to define concepts discussed in several articles, or to respond in any number of other ways to what you have read.

Obviously, to *write* clearly and accurately in response to what you have read, you need to *read* clearly and accurately too. Part One of this text will help you work on both activities at the same time—clear and accurate reading and writing.

The curse of "artist's block"

The Writing Process

Writing is a messy business. It is full of stops and starts and sudden turns and reversals. In fact, sometimes writing an essay can be one of the most confusing, frustrating experiences a college student will encounter. Fortunately, writing does not have to be a horrible experience. Like almost anything in life, writing becomes much easier as you become familiar with the "process" that makes up the act of writing.

Writing is often called a *recursive* process. This means that the many steps to writing an effective paper do not necessarily follow neatly one after the other. In fact, often you will find yourself repeating the same step a number of different times, in a number of different places, as you write a paper. For example, you might jot down notes on scratch paper before you start writing your first draft, but at any time while you write, you might stop to jot down more notes or to rethink what you are writing. To help yourself understand this writing process, think of it as divided roughly into three stages: **prewriting, writing,** and **rewriting**.

Prewriting involves anything you do to help yourself decide what your central idea is or what details, examples, reasons, or content you will include. Freewriting, brainstorming, and clustering (discussed below) are types of prewriting. Thinking, talking to other people, reading related material, outlining or organizing ideas—all are forms of prewriting. Obviously, you can prewrite at *any* time in the writing process. Whenever you want to think up new material, simply stop what you are doing and start using one of the techniques you will study in this chapter.

The **writing** stage of the process involves the actual writing out of a draft. Unfortunately, many people try to start their writing here, without sufficient prewriting. As you may know from firsthand experience, trying to start out this way usually leads directly to a good case of writer's block. During this stage of the writing process, you should be ready to do more prewriting whenever you hit a snag or cannot think of what to write next.

Rewriting consists of revising and editing. You should plan to revise every paper you write. When you *revise*, you examine the entire draft to change what needs to be changed and to add what needs to be added. Perhaps parts of your paper will need to be reorganized, reworded, or thoroughly rewritten to express your ideas clearly. Perhaps your paper will need more examples or clearer explanations. Unfortunately, people pressed for time often skip this stage, and the result is a very poorly written paper. Finally, after you have revised your work, you must edit it. When you *edit*, you correct spelling, grammar, and punctuation errors. A word of warning: Do not confuse editing with revising. Merely correcting the spelling, grammar, or punctuation of a poorly written paper will not make much difference in the overall quality of the paper.

Prewriting: From Writer's Block to Writing

Have you ever had a writing assignment that absolutely stumped you? Have you ever found yourself *stuck*, staring at a blank sheet of paper for fifteen minutes (or thirty? or sixty?), wondering what in the world you could write to meet the assignment?

If you have not had this experience, you are a lucky person. Certainly almost everyone knows the frustrated, sinking feeling that comes as minute after minute passes and nothing seems to get written. In fact, for many writers, *getting started* is the most agonizing part of the entire writing process.

What we're talking about here is **writer's block**, a problem as common to professional writers as it is to student writers. Because it is so common, you need to learn how to get past it quickly and painlessly so that you can get on with your assignment. Here are a few prewriting techniques to help you.

Freewriting

Since writer's block means that you aren't writing, one of the quickest ways to get around it is to write anything at all. You can write whatever you are thinking, feeling, wondering about, or trying to get *out* of your mind—just start writing. The only rule here is that you must *not* stop to correct spelling, grammar, punctuation, or other parts of your writing. Set a time limit for yourself—five or ten minutes—and just keep writing.

Let's say you were asked to write a paragraph or an essay explaining your reaction to the Gary Larson cartoon on page 2. To help yourself get started, you might try freewriting first. Here is how some freewriting might look:

> Okay—time to start writing—but what to write?? The cartoon is funny, but so what? What could I possibly write about this? I really don't know. What a frustrating assignment! I thought it was funny, but I don't really know why. And I'll bet some people think it's stupid. What could I write? Maybe I could—no. Why do I think it's funny? Well, partly because I've been stuck just like the guy in the picture. I guess I kind of relate to him. But it's also funny because of the cow. I mean, anyone knows what a cow's head looks like, so why is this guy confused? Maybe that's why it's funny. He really shouldn't be confused. And he doesn't have a clue! He hasn't even thought of a cow's head yet. It would really be funny if he ended up thinking of a different head. Also, I think the guy's appearance looks pretty strange. He's really freaking out—bug-eyes—and he's just an overall strange-looking guy.

As you can see, freewriting is very informal. Notice that the above freewriting moves from questions that express general frustration ("What could I write?") to answers that the writer might be able to use in a paper ("I've been stuck just like the guy in the picture." "But it's also funny because of the cow." "He's really freaking out—bug-eyes"). This movement—

from searching for ideas that you might use to focusing on specific details—is very common in freewriting.

Brainstorming

Brainstorming is like freewriting in that you write down whatever comes to mind without stopping, but it is different because it looks more like a list of ideas than a string of sentences. Here's an example, again about the Gary Larson cartoon:

> How I reacted—laughed—why?
>
> Funny—what's funny here?
>
> —cow with no head
> —man stuck—can't think of cow's head
> —bug-eyes
> —look of panic
> —frustration—hands by head
> —even his body
> —fat stomach—scraggly beard
>
> Maybe he'll use wrong head!
>
> Funny because I've felt same way (Why is that funny?)

This writer has a number of specific observations about the cartoon that she could use in a paper, but she did not waste time staring at a blank page. Instead, she just started making a list.

Clustering

A third technique to help you generate ideas is called clustering. It differs from brainstorming and freewriting in that what you write is almost like an informal map. To *cluster* your ideas, start out with a topic or question and draw a circle around it. Then connect related ideas to that circle and continue in that way. Look at the following example of how the brainstorming material might look if it were clustered.

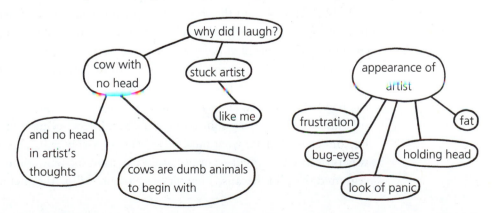

As you can see, clustering provides a mental picture of the ideas you generate. As a result, it can help you to organize your material as you think of it.

Freewriting, brainstorming, and clustering are only three of many techniques to help you get past writer's block. When you use them, you should feel free to move from one to the other at any time. And, of course, your instructor may suggest other ways to help you get started. Whatever technique you use, the point is to **start writing**. Do your thinking on paper (or at a computer), not while you are staring out the window. Here's something to remember whenever you have a writing assignment due: **Think in ink**.

Readings

Read the following articles. Then practice your prewriting techniques by responding to the questions at the end of each article.

Without Emotion

G. GORDON LIDDY

Squirrel hunting was a popular sport in West Caldwell in the 1940s. I loaded my homemade rifle, cocked the spring, and waited on the steps of the porch. A squirrel was in the top of the pear tree. I raised the rifle. The movement startled the squirrel and he jumped to the oak tree and froze as I stepped off the porch. I sighted along the side of the barrel, aimed for the squirrel's head, and fired. [1]

I missed the squirrel's head and gut-shot him. Bravely, he clung to the tree as long as he could, then started to come down, clutching piteously at branches as he fell, wounded mortally. [2]

I didn't know it, but the shot alerted my mother. She watched the furry creature's descent until it fell to the ground and I shot it again, this time through the head at point-blank range, to put it out of its suffering, then cut off its tail to tie to the handlebars of my bicycle as an ornament. [3]

When I came into the house my mother told me reproachfully that she had seen from the kitchen window the suffering I had caused. I went off and wept. The dying squirrel haunted me. I kept seeing it fall, clutching and clawing from what must have been a terribly painful wound. I was furious with myself—not because I'd caused the pain, though I regretted that, but because I hadn't been able to kill without emotion. [4]

How could I expect to be a soldier in the war? I had to do something to free myself from this disabling emotionalism.

I cast about for an idea and found it across the street. Bill Jacobus's father, to help combat the wartime food shortage and to supplement rationing, had built a chicken coop in his backyard. He and his son used to butcher the chickens, then drain, scald, pluck, and clean them for sale.

I asked young Bill if I could help kill the chickens. He was glad to have the help. He showed me how to grasp the bird in such a way as to have control of both wings and feet, lay its neck on an upended stump, and then decapitate it with one chop of an ax held in the other hand. Bill explained that the shock made the corpse convulse and, if I let go, the body would run about, wings flapping, and bruise the meat. I'd need to control the corpse until the shock wore off and the limp body could be hung up by the feet to drain the remaining blood. I should wear my old clothes.

Using the ax tentatively rather than making a bold stroke, I made a mess of my first chicken kill; it took me a number of chops to get the head off. The bird slipped out of my grasp and half flew, half jumped about, blood spurting from its neck all over me and everything else in range. Bill was good about it and gave me another chance.

I got better at it, and over a period of time I killed and killed and killed, getting less and less bloody, swifter and swifter, surer with my ax stroke until, finally, I could kill efficiently and without emotion or thought. I was satisfied: when it came my turn to go to war, I would be ready. I could kill as I could run—like a machine.

© 1980 by G. Gordon Liddy. Reprinted with permission.

Prewriting Practice

1. Freewrite for five minutes (or for a time specified by your instructor) to react to Liddy's article in any way that you want. Write whatever comes to mind.

2. Discuss your freewriting with other members of your class. Did they have similar responses?

3. Now respond to one of the following questions by using the prewriting techniques of freewriting, brainstorming, and/or clustering:

   a. Did your feelings or thoughts change as you moved from the start of this article to the end of it? Is so, what parts of the article caused them to change?

   b. Have you ever had to act "without emotion"? Describe any times you can remember when you had to repress or ignore your emotions.

4. Discuss your responses with other members of your class. Did they develop ideas that had not occurred to you?

The Cautious and Obedient Life

SUSAN WALTON

Little herds of people mill around intersections in the morning, wait- 1
ing for the lights to change. Washington is full of traffic circles, so
sometimes you have to wait through several lights, standing on narrow
islands of concrete while traffic comes at you from unexpected directions.

Not everyone waits. Some people dash, even when they see the No. 42 2
bus bearing down on them or some squirrel of a driver running every red
light for blocks. The particularly daring ones make the cars stop for them.

I seldom walk until the light turns green. It is part of being obedient, a 3
manifestation of the misbegotten belief that you must do what people
tell you to do, and if you do, you will be rewarded. This syndrome of
behavior is characterized by a dedication to form at the expense of spontaneity and substance. It is turning papers in on time and expecting to
receive better grades than those who turn them in late, even if theirs are
superior. It is believing your mother—who probably didn't believe it herself—when she says that boys prefer nice girls. This toe-the-line mentality is not confined to women; men, too, lie awake wondering how things
ended up so wrong when they so carefully did everything right. Which is
exactly the problem.

Some people are born to follow instructions. They are quiet children 4
who always finish their homework, are never caught being bad, never
sneak off and do undetected wicked things. They never figure out that it
is possible to ignore what others want you to do and do whatever you
like. The consequences of deviation are usually minimal. Nobody really
expects you to be that good. If you are born this way, you acquire a look
of puzzlement. You are puzzled because you can't figure out how or why
these other people are doing outrageous things when the rules have been
so clearly stated. Nor do you understand why people are not impressed
with your mastery of those rules.

Puzzlement may turn to smugness. At first, when people asked me 5
whether I had completed an assignment, I was surprised: of course I had;
didn't the teacher tell us to? After I realized that punctuality was not all

that common, I became smug. Yes, of course I turned my paper in on time. I did not see that the people who got noticed were likely to be erratic and late, rushing in explaining that their thesis had not fallen into place until 4 A.M. of the third Monday after the paper was due. Us punctual types did not wait for theses to fall into place. Whatever could be knocked into shape in time was what got turned in. The thing was due, wasn't it?

The message did not sink in for years, during which I always showed up for work, double pneumonia and all. I wandered into a field—journalism—mined with deadlines and populated by more missed deadlines, per capita, than any other. I repeated the process—first the assumption that you had to make the deadline, or why did they call it a deadline? Then I realized that this behavior was not universal. By the time I began working for a weekly, I had deluded myself into thinking that reliability was the way to success.

6

And it was, sort of. At this job, however, I encountered one of those people apparently sent by life as an object lesson. For every deadline I made, he missed one. Stories that everyone was counting on failed to materialize for weeks, as he agonized, procrastinated and interviewed just one more person. Everyone was annoyed at the time, but when the work was completed, mass amnesia set in. Only the product mattered, and the product, however late it was, was generally acceptable.

7

We advanced together, but what I gained with promotion was the opportunity to meet more deadlines per week and to hang around waiting to edit the copy of those who were late. What he got was the opportunity to linger over ever more significant stories. In my case, virtue was its own punishment. The moral of this story is that you should stop to think whether being good is getting you anywhere you want to go.

8

The most common and forgivable reason for the cautious, obedient life is fear. It is true, something terrible could happen if you stray. Something terrible could also happen if you do not stray, which is that you might be bored to death. Some people are lucky; what they are supposed to do is also what they like to do. They do not need to muster their nerve. I do not consider myself a nervy person. Rather, I think of myself as a recovering coward. Cowardice, like alcoholism, is a lifelong condition.

9

The James boys, William and Henry, are instructive on the subject of following too narrow a path. William James wrote in a letter to Thomas Ward in 1868 that the great mistake of his past life was an "impatience

10

of results," which, he thought, should not be "too voluntarily aimed at or too busily thought of." What you must do, he believed, is to go on "in your own interesting way." Then the results will float along under their own steam. Henry left the classic record of the unlived life in "The Beast in the Jungle." It is the story of a man convinced that fate has something momentous in store for him, and he sits around carefully waiting for it to arrive. Consequently, his fate turns out to be that of a man to whom nothing ever happens. Better for him had he not listened quite so earnestly to the inner voice murmuring about fate. Better had he been distracted from his mission.

Be bold, my graduate school adviser, Mr. Ragsdale, used to say—his   11
only advice. I see now that he was right. Think again of your future self: the little old lady sitting on the porch of the old folks' home. When she thinks back on opportunities, will she regret the ones that passed unused?

Or find some other device. Myself, I keep a dumb postcard in my desk   12
drawer. It is light purple, with a drawing of a cowering person standing on the edge of a diving board. Beneath the drawing it says, "If you don't do it, you won't know what would have happened if you had done it." Think about the possible headline: "Cautious Pedestrian Squashed by Bus While Waiting on Traffic Island—Should Have Jaywalked, Police Say." Then look both ways, and go.

Prewriting Practice

1. Freewrite for five minutes (or for a time specified by your instructor) to react to Walton's article in any way that you want. Write whatever comes to mind.

2. Discuss your freewriting with other members of your class. Did they have similar responses?

3. Respond to one of the following questions using the prewriting techniques that follow them:

   a. Explain in what way Susan Walton's description of the "cautious, obedient life" applies to your own life.

   b. Susan Walton says that not everyone is so cautious and obedient. Do you know people who are not? Describe any you can think of.

   c. Are you a "cautious and obedient" person, or do you follow the advice of Susan Walton's adviser to "be bold"? Describe some situations that illustrate your acting one way or the other.

4. Ask people you know or members of your class whether they consider themselves to be bold or cautious and obedient. Ask them to give you examples in which they act one way or the other.

Writing the Preliminary Topic Sentence or Thesis Statement

Once you have developed some ideas by using the prewriting techniques discussed so far, you are ready to decide on the **central idea** of your paper. Everything that you write or read has *some* kind of central idea. In academic writing (the kind of writing that you will be expected to produce in college classes), the central idea of a paragraph is expressed in its **topic sentence**, and the central idea of an essay is expressed in a **thesis statement**. Your ability to write clear topic sentences or thesis statements can determine whether or not your readers will understand and be able to follow the points you want to make. In college classes, that ability can make the difference between a successful paper and one that is barely passing (or not passing at all).

Perhaps the first thing you need to know is that topic sentences and thesis statements *develop* while you write. They do not usually spring from your mind fully formed and ready to go. Unfortunately, you may have been taught in the past that you should not even *start* writing until you know what your topic sentence or thesis statement is—and you may have found that such advice led you right back to a good case of writer's block. Certainly it would be convenient if you could simply sit down, think up a perfect topic sentence or thesis statement, and start writing—but the process of writing is just not that neat and orderly. So how *do* you write a topic sentence or thesis statement? To answer that question, we first need to define what such sentences are supposed to do.

- **Topic sentences and thesis statements state the topic of the paragraph or essay.** In academic writing, deciding on the *topic* of your paper is often not very difficult because it is assigned by your instructor. You may be asked to write about child abuse or a piece of literature or a particular political issue—but rarely (if ever) will your assignment simply be to "write about something." Of course, many times you may be asked to choose your own topics, but even then you will know which topics are appropriate and which are not. (For example, in a class studying the history of the Arab–Jewish tension in the Middle East, you probably would not choose state lotteries as the topic of your paper, right?)

- **Topic sentences and thesis statements identify the central idea to be explained, argued, or developed about the topic.** This is where many student writers get stuck. The problem is not "What is my topic?" but "What should I be *saying* about my topic?" For example, if you were asked to write a paragraph explaining why the Gary Larson cartoon on page 2 causes many people to laugh, you would know what your topic was (the cartoon), but you might not have *any* idea why people laugh. To put it another way, you wouldn't know what your *central idea* was, so how could you possibly write a topic sentence or a thesis statement?

How do you decide what your central idea is? Here are two suggestions.

1. First, look at your prewriting to find a preliminary central idea. (A preliminary central idea is one you will probably improve on as you write your paper.) For example, in the prewriting on pages 4–6 about the Gary Larson cartoon, you might notice that there seem to be several different reasons that people may laugh at the cartoon. Your preliminary topic sentence or thesis might look like this:

   preliminary central idea
   People might find the Gary Larson cartoon funny <u>for several different reasons</u>.

2. Another way to locate your central idea is just to start writing your first draft. Sometimes you may not know how to word your topic sentence or thesis statement, but you do have details or ideas you know you want to write about—so just start writing about them. As you write, you will clarify what you are thinking and will begin to see what your central idea is.

■ **Topic sentences and thesis statements should not make statements that are too vague, broad, or general to be supported within the length of the paper assigned.**

When you choose a topic and a central idea, **limit** your choice to something that can be covered in detail. For example, here is a topic sentence that is too vague:

Gary Larson's cartoon about "artist's block" is interesting.

Here the topic, "Gary Larson's cartoon about 'artist's block'," is limited well enough, but the central idea—that the cartoon is "interesting"—is much too vague and noncommittal. Here is a topic sentence that is too broad (that is, it tries to cover too much):

Gary Larson's cartoons are funny.

This sentence commits the writer to discussing *all* of Gary Larson's cartoons and to explaining *all* of the ways they are funny—a big job indeed!

■ **Topic sentences and thesis statements should not merely state a fact. They should make a statement that demands explanation.**

Because a central idea demands some explanation, argument, or development, a simple statement of fact will not work as a topic sentence or thesis statement. For example, this sentence would *not* be a satisfactory topic sentence or thesis statement:

The Gary Larson cartoon shows an artist trying to paint a cow.

As you can see, this sentence merely states a fact. It does not need any explanation.

EXERCISE   Examine each of the following sentences. If the sentence would be an effective topic sentence or thesis statement, underline its topic once and its central idea twice. If the sentence would not be an effective topic sentence or thesis statement, explain why not.

EXAMPLES

Two weeks ago, the Beach Boys gave a concert at the stadium.
(Not effective because it merely states a fact.)

Current movies are very enjoyable to watch.
(Not effective because its topic and central idea are too general.)

<u>*Attending Marine Corps boot camp*</u> *was* <u>*the most challenging experience of my life*</u>.
(Effective because the topic is quite limited and the central idea demands explanation and support.)

1. I have played on our college basketball team for two years.

2. My first job taught me how rude some customers can really be.

3. My family consists of some of the most obnoxious people you will ever meet.

4. Last January, a friend and I skipped work and went to the mountains.

5. This paper will be about affirmative action.

6. If people listened to all the warnings about eating sugar, fat, caffeine, or cholesterol, they would never have any fun at all.

7. Many food labels today are both confusing and misleading.

8. I love watching the seagulls and listening to the waves at the beach.

9. Although I don't approve of lying, sometimes a lie is both necessary and ethical.

10. If we are going to advance as a democracy, we need to improve our society.

EXERCISE

Reread the prewriting you did in response to the prewriting questions at the end of "Without Emotion" or "The Cautious and Obedient Life." Using that material, write a sentence that you could use either as a preliminary topic sentence for a paragraph or as a preliminary thesis statement for an essay.

Compare your results with those of other members of your class to determine which sentences contain specific topics and clear central ideas.

Preparing a Rough Outline

If you have ever been required to turn in a complete outline of a paper before the final paper was due, you know how difficult—even impossible, sometimes—it is to predict exactly what you will include in a paper, much less what *order* it will follow. So rest easy—although preparing a *rough outline* is part of the prewriting process, it is not at all the same as writing a complete, perfect, formal outline. Instead, it involves looking at what you have written so far in your prewriting, deciding what ideas you *may* use, and listing those ideas in the order in which you will *probably* use them. Essentially, you are trying to give yourself some direction before you start writing the first draft.

Let's use the Gary Larson cartoon again as an example of how to write the rough outline. The first step is to look at the prewriting on pages 4 and 5 and group together any details that seem related. (You might notice, by the way, that the clustering example has already grouped some of them.) They could be organized this way:

A	B	C
appearance of artist	cow with no head	artist is like me
bug-eyes	no cow head in artist's	artist's block = writer's block
look of panic	thought	I've felt same way
fat stomach	cows seem dumb	
scraggly beard	anyway	
holding head		

Once you've grouped the details that you want to include, you need to decide in what order you will discuss them. A common way to organize material like this is to save the most effective or important group until last, but you have to decide which one would seem most important to you—and you may change your mind as you write your paper.

EXERCISE

Using the prewriting you did for "Without Emotion" or "The Cautious and Obedient Life," group the ideas or examples that you have developed so far into a rough outline. If you need to, do more prewriting to develop more details.

Writing: The First Draft

If you have a preliminary topic sentence or thesis statement and have prepared a rough outline, you have everything you need to write your paper. So now is the time to sit and write. However, now is still *not* the time to worry about whether everything is spelled exactly right or worded perfectly. If you try to write your first draft and avoid all errors at the same time, you will end up right back where you probably started—stuck. Of course, you can correct some errors as they occur, but don't make revising or editing your primary concern at this point. What you want to do *now* is to write out your ideas. You can "fix" them later.

Here is the first draft of a paragraph about the Gary Larson cartoon.

I found the Gary Larson cartoon funny for a number of reasons when I first read it. First, the artist was feeling just like me when I have writer's block. I guess I just related to him—but I was laughing at myself as well as at him. As I did some freewriting about it, I realized there were other reasons the cartoon is funny. The overall appearance of the artist is ridiculous. There he sits. He has his head in his hands. His eyes are bugging out in panic, and his fat stomach is hanging over his belt. The whole thing is just really funny. The funniest part of the whole thing is that he hasn't even thought of a cow's head yet. (I think someone else showed me this.) I can just imagine him putting a crocodile's head on the cow. The cartoon really sums up how I feel when I'm stuck with writer's block. The whole situation is ridiculous and absurd.

You may notice that the above paragraph could also be used as the first draft of a short essay. Since it lists several different reasons, you could write each reason as a separate brief paragraph that you would later develop with more detail. Here is how it would look:

I found the Gary Larson cartoon funny for a number of reasons when I first read it.

First, the artist was feeling just like me when I have writer's block. I guess I just related to him—but I was laughing at myself as well as at him.

As I did some freewriting about it, I realized there were other reasons the cartoon is funny. The overall appearance of the artist is ridiculous. There he sits. He has his head in his hands. His eyes are bugging out in panic, and his fat stomach is hanging over his belt. The whole thing is just really funny.

The funniest part of the whole thing is that he hasn't even thought of a cow's head yet. (I think someone else showed me this.) I can just imagine him putting a crocodile's head on the cow.

The cartoon really sums up how I feel when I'm stuck with writer's block. The whole situation is ridiculous and absurd.

EXERCISE   Compare the material in the first drafts above to the rough outline on page 14.

1. How is the order of its material different from that of the rough outline on page 14? Why do you think the writer changed the order?

2. What details that appear in the rough outline on page 14 has the writer left out?

3. What is the preliminary topic sentence or thesis statement of this first draft?

4. What is the central idea in the preliminary topic sentence or in the preliminary thesis statement?

5. What idea in the final sentence of each draft could be used to improve the central idea of the topic sentence or thesis statement?

6. In the draft of the brief essay, each separate paragraph has its own preliminary topic sentence. What are those topic sentences?

Rewriting: Revising and Editing

Revising

As we mentioned at the start of the chapter, rewriting consists of two stages: revising and editing. Unfortunately, many people—especially if they are pressed for time—omit the revising stage and move directly to editing, often with disastrous results.

The problem is that editing will correct grammar, spelling, and punctuation errors *without* improving either the content or the organization of your paper—and these larger areas do need to be addressed before you submit your work. Now is the time to *read* what you have written, *think* about it, and *decide* what changes you should make.

Suggestions for Revision

■ **Refine your topic sentence or thesis statement.**

Usually, writing the first draft of a paper will help you become more specific about what your central idea really is. In fact, if you look at the concluding sentences of your first draft, you will often find a statement that sums up your central idea better than your preliminary topic sentence or thesis statement did.

The writer of the first draft about the Gary Larson cartoon (above) realized from her last sentence that the key to the humor in the cartoon is its absurdity. When you read the revised draft (below), note how she refined her central idea.

■ **Reorganize material.**

Perhaps you noticed that the material in the above first draft does not follow the order of the rough outline on page 14. In this case, the writer decided that she liked this order better because she wanted to discuss her sense of identification with the cartoon character first, then the appearance of the character, and then the character's thoughts.

■ **Add details.**

The first draft has left out several details from the rough outline. Note how the writer has restored them in the revised draft below.

■ **Reword sentences.**

Many times you will find that your original wording of sentences can be improved. Note the changes made in the middle of the revised draft below.

Here is a revised version of the above paragraph. Changes are shown in boldface.

Refined topic
sentence

  I found Gary Larson's cartoon about the painter with "artist's block" very funny because the situation it describes is so familiar yet so absurd. The first thing I noticed was that the artist was feeling exactly what I feel when I have "writer's block."

added details

His frustration and look of panic reminded me of myself, and I had to laugh because the situation really is ridiculous. I guess I just related to him—but I was laughing at myself as well as at him. As I did some freewriting about it, I realized that **the overall appearance of the artist is ridiculous. He's just sitting there, with his head in his hands, his eyes bugging out in panic, and his fat stomach hanging over his belt.** The whole thing is just really funny. **He's even dropped his paintbrush on the floor, as if he can't hold it any more—or maybe he's thrown it down.** Finally, the **most absurd** part of the whole thing is that he hasn't even thought of a cow's head yet. (I think someone else showed me this.) **He's thought of a bird, a duck, a donkey, a rhino, a hippo, even a crocodile—but no cow!** I can just imagine him putting a crocodile's head on the cow. The cartoon really sums up how I feel when I'm stuck with writer's block. The whole situation is **just absurd.**

reworded
sentence

added details

added details

reworded
sentence

Here is the same revision in essay form.

refined thesis
statement

I found Gary Larson's cartoon about the painter with "artist's block" very funny because the situation it describes is so familiar yet so absurd.

The first thing I noticed was that the artist was feeling exactly what I feel when I have "writer's block." **His frustration and look of panic reminded me of myself, and I had to laugh because the situation really is ridiculous.** I guess I just related to him—but I was laughing at myself as well as at him.

added details

As I did some freewriting about it, I realized that **the overall appearance of the artist is ridiculous. He's just sitting there, with his head in his hands, his eyes bugging out in panic, and his fat stomach hanging over his belt.** The whole thing is just really funny. **He's even dropped his paintbrush on the floor, as if he can't hold it any more—or maybe he's thrown it down.**

refined topic
sentence

added details

added details
refined topic
sentence

Finally, the **most absurd** part of the whole thing is that he hasn't even thought of a cow's head yet. (I think someone else showed me this.) **He's thought of a bird, a duck, a donkey, a rhino, a hippo, even a crocodile—but no cow!** I can just imagine him putting a crocodile's head on the cow.

added details

The cartoon really sums up how I feel when I'm stuck with writer's block. The whole situation is **just absurd.**

Editing

Now for the final step. You need to **edit** your draft before typing the final copy. *Editing* is the same as *proofreading*. Read your draft over carefully, looking for spelling, grammar, or punctuation errors as you do. If you are using a computer, be sure to proofread a printed copy of your paper, not just what appears on the screen. Once you have corrected any errors and are satisfied with the final product, prepare a clean copy (double-spaced) and submit it to your instructor.

Assignments

Writing with a Central Idea

Write a paragraph or a short essay, whichever your instructor assigns, in response to one of the following assignments. If you write a paragraph, be sure to include a topic sentence. If you write an essay, include a thesis statement.

1. After reading "The Cautious and Obedient Life," write a paper in response to *one* of the following suggestions.

   a. Explain in what ways Susan Walton's description of the person who is cautious and obedient applies to you. Give some examples to illustrate what you mean.

   b. Are you the type of person who follows the advice of Walton's graduate advisor to "Be bold"? Describe situations when you have acted boldly rather than cautiously and obediently.

   c. Discuss this article with your classmates or with other people outside of class. Find out in what ways they have ever acted boldly rather than cautiously and obediently. Give examples of what they have done and explain your reaction to those examples.

2. After reading "Without Emotion," write a paper in response to *one* of the following suggestions.

   a. If your reactions to G. Gordon Liddy or to the events in the article changed as you read it, explain which parts of the article caused your reactions to change.

   b. If you have found that at times you have had to repress or ignore your emotions, write a paper in which you describe specific situations that have caused you to do so.

   c. Interview other members of your class about this article. How did they react to it? Write a paper in which you explain the different types of reactions you discovered.

3. Write a paper in response to one of the articles in Part Four, as assigned by your instructor.

4. Read the following article by Lois Sweet. Use the writing process to develop a paragraph or short essay in response to one of the suggestions at the end of the article.

What's in a Name? Quite a Lot

LOIS SWEET

It was parents' visiting day. A week before, we'd waved goodbye to our   1
8-year-old daughter as she left on a bus for camp. We were dying to
see her again.

When we asked for her, we were told there wasn't anyone there by   2
that name. Our hearts stopped. What could have happened to her?

Well, said the counsellor, there wasn't anyone there by that *first* name.   3
There was a girl with that last name.

When we found her, she calmly announced that she'd changed her   4
name. No longer was she to be known by the name we'd given her at
birth—Dechinta. She had become Rachel, the girl of her middle name.

It may seem silly, but I take it seriously. Names are such statements,   5
such a form of self-identity, that any effort to change them has to be
considered.

Over the years, a lot of my friends have changed their names. A   6
number of them began to take an interest in their cultural backgrounds
and became horrified that their parents had anglicized their names in an
effort to deny cultural differences. To my friends, being pushed into the
great bland melting pot felt more like being drowned than saved. Their
culture was a source of pride and they demanded recognition for their
"ethnic" names.

Then there have been what seem like hundreds of friends whose   7
marriages ended. Having taken their husbands' names at marriage,
deciding which name to use when they split up was a problem. Some
argued that reverting to their birth names would create professional diffi-
culties. After all, they'd established reputations based on their husbands'
surnames.

Very Complicated

Others reclaimed their birth names, only to change again when they   8
remarried. It was very complicated. Whenever I wrote a letter to one of
them, I wasn't quite sure which name to put on the envelope.

A handful of friends changed their names when they discovered a life   9
cause. One person illustrated the seriousness of his newly found conviction with a modified name change. No longer could we call him "Russ."
He became "Russell," signifying that there was no room in the relationship for either casualness or false intimacy.

Still others chose to drop their last names completely in order to flag   10
their particular brand of radical feminism. Last names were a patriarchal
remnant, they said, created to establish male ownership.

Although it takes a lot of effort to remember what to call whom, I was   11
among those who forced such an effort on others. When I got married
15 years ago, it never occurred to me not to take my husband's name.
Ten years later, whose last name I was using became an issue.

I discovered that a married name is only an assumed name and that   12
reverting to my birth name involved neither lawyers nor bureaucracy.
Although the name Sweet had been a plague during childhood, it did
belong to me. I decided to reclaim it.

Open to Change

Everyone, except relatives, has been open to the change. Nevertheless,   13
the step was worth it. It might have been an old name, but it characterized a new me.

So what does a name change mean for an 8-year-old? Probably that   14
the child recognizes that her name reveals more about her parents than
about herself. The first name we gave our daughter (which, granted, is
unusual, but not made up), is an Athabaskan Indian word meaning self-
sufficiency. It says as much about our generation as the names Pearl or
Thelma said about our parents'.

Several years ago, when our daughter's kindergarten teacher sent home   15
a class list, we were struck with how much that generation of children
were stuck with the "counter-culture" influence. Moonbeam, Airborn
and names like them were in the majority. It's the unfaddish, un-made-up
Biblical names like Rachel, however, that wear like solid gold.

Changing names might be a bother for those who have to remember   16
to use the new name, but it obviously has significance for the person
who's insisting on the change. Rather than a new name bringing a new
personality, I think a new name is a sign of a new personality—or at the
very least, of a profound personality change.

A point not lost on countries, let alone people, is that the right to   17
name the world for yourself is a matter of great political importance.

If I can respect name changes in my friends—and vice-versa—I can   18
respect it in my daughter. After all, families should be democratic.

I just hope it doesn't happen too often.   19

From the Toronto Star Syndicate. Reprinted with permission.

a. Lois Sweet writes, "Rather than a new name bringing a new personality, I think a new name is a sign of a new personality—or at the very least, of a profound personality change." Have you gone by different names in your life? For instance, have you had nicknames? Have you ever used your middle name? Have you ever shortened your name? Describe your reactions to these different names. What do they say about you?

b. If you changed your name when you were married, how did you feel about the change? Describe your reactions in as much detail as you can.

c. Do you prefer to be addressed differently in different situations? For example, do you prefer that instructors call you by your first or last name? Describe situations in which you would expect to be addressed in different ways by different people.

Evaluating Sample Papers

At one time or another, most students have had the experience of turning in a paper they were *sure* they had done a good job on, only to have it returned a few class meetings later with a grade much lower than they expected. Even professional writers have the disappointing experience of having their manuscripts returned by editors with less-than-favorable responses. Perhaps you can *never* be 100% sure that your writing is perfect, but you can *greatly* improve the odds of submitting a successful paper if you learn how to judge the quality of what you have written.

One way to become a good judge of your own writing is to practice judging what others have written. You can get such practice by evaluating sample papers. In this text, each chapter will provide you with several student paragraphs and essays. Practice your judging skills by using the following checklist (or a format provided by your instructor) to determine which paper is the most effective one. If your instructor asks you to, use the same checklist to evaluate the papers of some of your fellow students.

Student Model Checklist

1. Thesis statement or topic sentence:

a. If you are reading an essay, underline the thesis statement and circle its central idea. If you are reading a single paragraph, underline the topic sentence and circle its central idea.

b. Can the thesis statement or topic sentence be more exact or specific? Is it too broad? Should the thesis or topic sentence be revised to incorporate a term used in the last few sentences of the paper?

c. Rank the overall effectiveness of the thesis statement or topic sentence:

1   2   3   4   5   6
(ineffective)   (excellent)

2. Support:

Look at the examples used. Do they refer to specific personal experiences and exact details, or are they general and vague? Rank the overall effectiveness of the examples:

1   2   3   4   5   6
(general and vague)   (specific and detailed)

3. Organization:

Can you tell where one idea or example ends and another begins? Rank the clarity of the organization:

1   2   3   4   5   6
(unclear, confusing)   (clear)

4. Spelling, punctuation, grammar:

Underline or circle any spelling, punctuation, or grammar errors that you find. Rank the effectiveness of the spelling, punctuation, and grammar:

1   2   3   4   5   6
(ineffective)   (excellent)

5. Rank the overall effectiveness of the paper:

1   2   3   4   5   6
(ineffective)   (excellent)

Sample Student Papers

The following paragraphs and essays were submitted as first drafts that would later be revised. To evaluate these papers, follow these steps:

1. Read the *entire* paper through before making any judgments about it.

2. Reread the paper to identify its topic sentence or thesis statement.

3. Identify the major sections of the paper.

4. Respond to the items on the checklist on pages 21–22 or to questions provided by your instructor.

Paragraphs

The students who wrote the following papers were asked to write a 250- to 300-word paragraph responding to one of the writing assignments on page 18.

Student Paragraph 1

After reading the article "The Cautious and Obedient Life," I can say that I would follow Walton's advice to "Be Bold." Life is a learning process and there is a first for everything. Those firsts have taught me how to deal with the world I live in. When I first came to America, I was curious about a lot of things and food was on top of my list. Now, I'm enjoying different kinds of food. I never imagine I would be eating food that looks weird. I guess whomever said "Don't judge a book by its cover" knows what he or she is talking about. Another instance that I can say I acted bold was my first month of driving. Taking different freeways, it took me an hour and half to find my way back home. On my way back home I discovered that freeways keeps going on and on without exit ramps, but I didn't mind because of the excitement of seeing the places I have been, even before I started driving, and to exactly find it on my own. Now every time my brother or my friends ask me if I know how to get to a certain place, I say that I know how to get there because I got lost there. Sometimes I just give the directions and let them figure out how I knew how to get there. Lastly, it is very irritating for me when people start to draw their own conclusions, and open their mouths to soon about certain people, places or circumstances; even before they hear both sides of the story. At first, it is hard for me to say what I really feel, but I have learned to tell people to mind their own business. It doesn't matter whether I'm up against my parents, older relatives or people with power in general. All I know is, if I know I'm correct, I fight for my right. I guess that's the only way people in general can advance and learn about life, to be bold and not to be afraid to take risks.

Student Paragraph 2

The article "Without Emotion" stirred up a few unpleasant feelings inside of me that I certainly was not expecting. When I first started this article and read about how the author went outside, lifted his rifle, and shot a small defensless squirrel, I felt very horrified and sad. Still, I was able to make it okay in my head because he was only a boy and all kids do mean things. Then he went on and wrote, that after his mother had told him it was wrong to kill things it made him cry. This made me feel very relieved to know that he didn't really enjoy causing pain to another creature. It was certainly a shock to me when I read that he wasn't crying because of the pain he had inflicted, but because he couldn't shoot the squirrel without feelings. I felt sick to my stomach at this point and I actually did not want to continue reading. My curiousity lead me to the next surprise which was him wanting to kill chickens so that he wouldn't feel anything. By this time the author could have said just about anything and it still wouldn't have shocked me. However, I did become a little scared and I was even more frightened when I read that he was able to kill and not feel bad. I wasn't only afraid of him doing the killing, but mainly of him <u>wanting</u> to do the killing. At the end of this horrible article I felt shivers inside of me and kept thinking of this person being out in the world with me. This article certainly did arouse quite a few negative feelings inside of me. It amazes me that such a short article could bother me so much.

Brief Essays

The students who wrote the following papers were asked to write a brief essay responding to one of the writing assignments on page 18.

Student Essay 1

In many aspects of my life I've wanted to do things my own way. I have taken short cuts and broken the rules, but sometimes I have to work at living by standards and playing by the rules to become an obedient person.

For example, driving, I would love to join a group of people zipping by me on the freeway at eighty miles an hour, but I've decided that I really have no need for a speeding ticket or higher insurance rate. There are many regulations to follow while driving and sometimes I find it unfortunate that I try as others give no regard for the laws.

In college I try to force myself to change into someone with priorities in order not to miss my homework deadlines. I've found that life is no longer like grade school, when my teahcer, with enough coaxing, would let me turn in assignments a week late due to my family problems or taking care of a sick puppy. My lack of effort now only results in failing grades, and I'm not getting a second chance in college unless I'm willing to pay to repeat the course.

When I was a child, I didn't do everything my mother told me to because I knew eventually that she would clean my room for me or let me do chores later and thus she was teaching me to be a procrastinator. Although as a result of my laziness my parents would restrict me from going to parties or school activites because they had control of my freedom. Their style of discipline began to sink in after a few weekends of boredom at home and I had to decide that doing my chores myself was well worth it.

Conforming to some of the rules in life is not always easy yet it is sometimes necessary if you want to enjoy life peacefully.

Student Essay 2

After reading Liddy's "Without Emotion," I was reminded of times in my own life that I felt I had to act without emotion. Many times I have had to repress my personal feelings just to make it through an unpleasant experience.

For instance, in 1984 I had to face the realization that a divorce was in order. I had no emotional or financial support, and I had an eleven-month-old son to take care of. It was a time when emotions had to be shelved, temporarily, and all of my attention directed toward how I would handle the more pressing issues. Those issues being: food, shelter, clothing, and a job. I struggled through the transition from marriage to solo living by remaining unemotional and methodical. There would be time enough to process feelings once the necessary tasks were taken care of.

A few years later, after the divorce was final and I was well settled into the daily living as a single parent, I was laid off from a typesetting position with a local newspaper. This time, also, I did not allow myself the luxury of feeling frightened, not even for a minute. I immediately busied myself with the task of finding a job. I didn't take time to feel sad or to feel sorry for myself; I just proceeded with what needed to be done, never once allowing myself to give in to everyone's barrage of "What if's?"

I think Liddy was trying to get to a point where he could kill without feeling emotion if he had to. He was aware of the "kill or be killed" probability that faced him as a soldier. For me, it was either conquer the challenges that had befallen me or be conquered by them.

Sentence Combining
Embedding Adjectives, Adverbs, and Prepositional Phrases

As you have worked through the writing process presented in Chapter 1, we hope you have discovered that good writing develops *as* you write. Many times, for instance, you will not know exactly what your central idea is until you have done a substantial amount of prewriting, and sometimes you may not know exactly how your ideas or paragraphs should be organized until you have tried one or two different organizations to see which works best. This willingness to make changes and to rethink material as you discover new ideas is at the heart of all good writing—and it works at the level of individual sentences as well as at the larger levels related to the central idea or the organization of a paper.

As you write the initial drafts of your papers, you will express your ideas in sentence structures that are comfortable to you because they reflect your personal style of writing. (You *do* have a personal style, even if you write very rarely.) However, as you become more and more proficient in using the writing process, you will find that you can improve your personal style. At the level of sentence structure, this improvement can include, among other things, recognizing when separate sentences contain related ideas that should be expressed in one sentence and learning how to use different types of sentence structures to express different types of ideas.

EXERCISE To illustrate what we mean, let's compare the following versions of a passage drawn from Lois Sweet's article on pages 19–20. One passage is just as Lois Sweet wrote it. The other is written as a beginning writer might have written it. Which is which? How can you tell?

> 1 Over the years, a lot of my friends have changed their names. 2 A number of them began to take an interest in their cultural backgrounds. 3 Their parents had wanted to deny cultural differences. 4 As a result, their parents had anglicized their names. 5 My friends were horrified. 6 They had been pushed into the great bland melting pot. 7 They felt more like they were being drowned than saved. 8 For them, their culture was a source of pride. 9 They demanded recognition for their "ethnic" names.

> 1 Over the years, a lot of my friends have changed their names. 2 A number of them began to take an interest in their cultural backgrounds and became horrified that their parents had anglicized their names in an effort to deny cultural differences. 3 To my friends, being pushed into the great bland melting pot felt more like being drowned than saved. 4 Their culture was a source of pride and they demanded recognition for their "ethnic" names.

As you can see, these two versions are quite different from each other, although they both express the same ideas. The first version uses nine sentences and eighty-two words. The second version uses nearly the same number of words (seventy-five) but only four sentences.

The second version is Lois Sweet's original. In it, you can see the ability of a professional writer to combine related ideas into sentences that are longer and more varied than those written by an inexperienced writer. In her version, Sweet has written in a single sentence (sentence 2) what it took three sentences (sentences 2, 3, and 4) for the first writer to express. And Sweet has written in two sentences (sentences 3 and 4) what the first writer expressed in four sentences (sentences 6, 7, 8, and 9).

Of course, combining related ideas is a skill all writers have to some degree, no matter how experienced or inexperienced they may be. For example, when you see that two or more ideas are related, you probably combine them without thinking much about it. Would you write this?

My brother is an auto mechanic. I asked my brother to fix my car. My car had not run properly for weeks.

Probably not. But you might express yourself any one of these ways:

My brother is an auto mechanic, so I asked him to fix my car because it had not run properly for weeks.

I asked my brother, who is an auto mechanic, to fix my car because it had not run properly for weeks.

Because my car had not run properly for weeks, I asked my brother, an auto mechanic, to fix it.

I asked my brother to fix my car, which had not run properly for weeks, because he is an auto mechanic.

My car had not run properly for weeks, so I asked my brother to fix it because he is an auto mechanic.

Which sounds better to you? Each of the above sentences might work in your speech or in your writing, depending on the situation. The point is that you already can and do combine related ideas in many different ways. And with practice, you will become even better at what you already do.

EXERCISE   To see what we mean when we say you already know how to combine related ideas, rewrite the sentences below. Join those ideas that seem obviously related into sentences that make sense to you. Don't worry about getting the "right" answer—just combine the ideas that seem as if they should go together.

> The woman held a book. It was in her left hand. She was tired. The book was thick. She waited for her ride. She was in the parking lot. Finally a car stopped. It was small and blue. It stopped next to her. She opened the door to the car. A poodle jumped out. It was white. It ran into the parking lot. It ran quickly. It disappeared between the parked cars.

The Embedding Process

One of the most common ways to combine ideas is to use **adjectives** and **adverbs** to modify other words. For instance, in the exercise above, if you described the book the woman was holding as a "thick" book, you used *thick* as an adjective. If you wrote that the poodle ran "quickly" into the parking lot, you used *quickly* as an adverb.

What's the difference? It is that adjectives modify nouns and pronouns while adverbs modify verbs, adjectives, and other adverbs. However, knowing these definitions is not as important here as recognizing when a word in one sentence is related to a word in another sentence.

In sentence combining, the act of placing words or phrases from one sentence into another is called **embedding**. Look at the following examples. Note how the underlined adjective or adverb in the second sentence can be embedded within the first sentence.

EXAMPLES

The movie was about a tomato.
The tomato was <u>enormous</u>.   (adjective)

The movie was about an <u>enormous</u> tomato.

The lamp fell to the floor.
It fell <u>suddenly</u>.   (adverb)

The lamp <u>suddenly</u> fell to the floor.

Prepositional phrases also modify words, so in a sense they are adjectives and adverbs too. You use them all of the time in your speech and in your writing. You use prepositional phrases when you write that you are <u>in the house</u> or <u>on the step</u> or <u>at the store</u> or <u>from Indiana</u>.

Each prepositional phrase starts with a preposition and ends with a noun (or a pronoun), called the *object* of the preposition. Between the preposition and its object you may find modifiers. For example, in the prepositional phrase "from the tired old man," *from* is the preposition, *man* is the object, and the words between the two are modifiers.

preposition	modifiers	object of the preposition
from	the tired old	man

Here is a list of common prepositions:

above	before	for	on	under
across	behind	from	onto	until
after	below	in	over	up
among	beside	into	past	upon
around	between	in spite of	till	with
as	by	like	through	without
at	during	near	to	
because of	except	of	toward	

Prepositional phrases should be embedded in sentences they're related to just as adjectives and adverbs should be. Look at the following examples:

EXAMPLES

The lawnmower was old and rusty.

The lawnmower was <u>in the garage</u>.   (prep. phrase)

The lawnmower <u>in the garage</u> was old and rusty.

Wild Bill Hickok was killed when he was shot.

He was killed <u>during a poker game</u>.   (prep. phrase)

He was shot <u>in the back</u>.   (prep. phrase)

Wild Bill Hickok was killed <u>during a poker game</u> when he was shot <u>in the back</u>.

EXERCISE   Rewrite each of the following groups of sentences into one sentence by embedding the underlined adjective, adverb, or prepositional phrase in the first sentence of the group.

EXAMPLE

We washed the dishes.

We washed them <u>after dinner</u>.

We washed them <u>carefully</u>.

The dishes were <u>expensive</u>.

<u>After dinner</u>, we <u>carefully</u> washed the <u>expensive</u> dishes.

1. The horse stood.
   The horse was <u>in the pasture</u>.
   The horse was <u>old</u>.
   The horse was <u>swaybacked</u>.
   The pasture was <u>deserted</u>.

2. It switched its tail at the flies.
   The flies were <u>on its back</u>.
   The flies were <u>irritating</u>.
   It switched its tail <u>slowly</u>.

3. A boy climbed into the pasture.
   He climbed <u>over the fence</u>.
   He climbed <u>carefully</u>.

4. He approached the horse and called its name.
   He approached it <u>slowly</u>.
   The horse was <u>tired</u>.
   He called it <u>softly</u>.

5. The horse turned and reared up.
It turned <u>toward the boy</u>.
It reared <u>suddenly</u>.
It reared up <u>on its hind legs</u>.

EXERCISE

Combine each of the following sets of sentences into one sentence by embedding adjectives, adverbs, and prepositional phrases.

1. The novel was about a murder.
It was a mystery novel.
It was new.
The murder was violent.
The murder was in St. Patrick's Cathedral.
St. Patrick's Cathedral is in New York City.

2. The newspapers carried the story.
The story was on the front pages.
These newspapers were in almost every city.
They carried the story prominently.
The story was of the murder.

3. The basketball game was held in the gym.
It was for the state championship.
It was in a small town.
The town was on the banks of a river.
The river was wide and muddy.

4. The game was held in the afternoon.
The game was sold out.
It was on a Saturday.
It was held between one team and another team.
One team was from a small town.
The other team was from a large city.

5. When the team won, the town held a parade.
The team from the small town won.
The town was surprised.
The parade was big.
It was held in celebration of the players.

EXERCISE   The exercise below is substantially more difficult than the previous ones. In each case, the original version of the sentence can be found in one of the reading selections in this chapter. Combine each group of sentences into one sentence. Use the first sentence as the base sentence, and embed the underlined adjectives, adverbs, and prepositional phrases into it.

EXAMPLE

Hunting was a sport. Squirrel hunting was a popular one in West Caldwell. This was in the 1940s.

Squirrel hunting was a popular sport in West Caldwell in the 1940s.

1. I loaded my rifle, cocked the spring, and waited. I was waiting <u>on the steps of the porch</u>, and it was my <u>homemade</u> rifle.

2. When I came in my mother told me that she had seen the suffering I had caused. She told me this <u>reproachfully</u>. I came <u>into the house</u>. She said that she had seen me <u>from the kitchen window</u>.

3. Bill Jacobus's father, to help combat the shortage and to supplement rationing, had built a coop. It was the <u>wartime food</u> shortage he was combatting. He built a <u>chicken</u> coop. It was <u>in his backyard</u>.

4. The reason is fear. It is the <u>most common and forgivable</u> reason. It is the main reason <u>for the cautious, obedient life</u>.

5. Cowardice is a condition. It is <u>like alcoholism</u>. It is a <u>lifelong</u> condition.

6. Think again of your self: the lady sitting on the porch. This is your <u>future</u> self. The lady is <u>little</u> and <u>old</u>, and she is sitting on the porch <u>of the old folks' home</u>.

7. Myself, I keep a postcard. It is a <u>dumb</u> one, and I keep it <u>in my desk drawer</u>.

8. Henry left the record. It was the <u>classic</u> record, and it was a story <u>of the unlived life</u>. He left it <u>in "The Beast in the Jungle."</u>

9. One person illustrated the seriousness of his conviction. This was a <u>newly found</u> conviction. He illustrated it <u>with a change</u>. It was a <u>modified name</u> change.

10. Names were a remnant, they said, created to establish ownership. They were talking about <u>last</u> names. They said they were a <u>patriarchal</u> remnant, and it was <u>male</u> ownership they meant.

CHAPTER TWO

Reading for the Central Idea

Hagar the Horrible © 1994 by King Features Syndicate, Inc. World rights reserved. Reprinted with permission.

In Chapter 1, you read that part of the writing process consists of developing a clearly worded statement of your central idea. Such a statement—whether it is a topic sentence or a thesis statement—serves as a guide for your readers, identifying for them the point you are trying to make.

Of course, in the "writing-reading conversation," you are a reader as often as you are a writer—and your ability to identify a central idea as a reader is certainly as important as your ability to express a central idea as a writer. In fact, in many college situations you will find that your ability to write a clear central idea depends first upon your ability to identify central ideas in what you read.

In the cartoon on the facing page, Hagar the Horrible and his companion have apparently not identified the central idea of the signs they have just read. (And the writer of the signs has not yet learned how to use *lay* and *lie*.) Of course, the message that Hagar and his friend have overlooked is a fairly clear one. Unfortunately, however, the central ideas of many paragraphs and essays are not always as clear—not necessarily because the paragraph or essay is written poorly, but because it is complex and demands close attention.

In this chapter, you will practice reading to identify and to summarize central ideas, and you will practice writing in response to those ideas.

Paragraphs and Topic Sentences

In a paragraph, the sentence that states the central idea is called the **topic sentence**. It is often the first sentence (or two) of the paragraph, although a paragraph often has its topic sentence in the middle or at the end. Look at the following paragraphs. Their topic sentences are in italics. Following each paragraph is an example of how you could state its central idea in your own words.

> *Football has replaced baseball as the favorite American spectator sport largely because of television.* A comparison between a telecast of a football game on one channel and a baseball game on another could reveal baseball as a game with people standing around seemingly with little to do but watch two men play catch. Football would appear as twenty-two men engaged in almost constant, frenzied action. To watch baseball requires identification with the home team; to watch football requires only a need for action or a week of few thrills and the need for a touch of vicarious excitement.
> —*Jeffery Schrank, "Sport and the American Dream"*

Summary of Central Idea:

Television has helped football to replace baseball as the favorite American spectator sport.

In the next paragraph, the "topic sentence" actually consists of more than one sentence.

*Some people say the business about the jolly fat person is a myth, that all of us chubbies are neurotic, sick, sad people. I disagree. Fat people may not be chortling all day long, but they're a hell of a lot **nicer** than the wizened and shriveled.* Thin people turn surly, mean, and hard at a young age because they never learn the value of a hot-fudge sundae for easing tension. Thin people don't like gooey soft things because they themselves are neither gooey nor soft. They are crunchy and dull, like carrots. They go straight to the heart of the matter while fat people let things stay all blurry and hazy and vague, the way things actually are. Thin people want to face the truth. Fat people know there is no truth. One of my thin friends is always staring at complex, unsolvable problems and saying, "The key thing is . . . ." Fat people never say that. They know there isn't any such thing as the key thing.

—*Suzanne Britt, "That Lean and Hungry Look"*

Summary of Central Idea:

The writer of this paragraph thinks that fat people are more pleasant to be around than thin people.

Paragraphs Without Topic Sentences

Some paragraphs that you read will not have topic sentences. In these paragraphs, the topic sentence is *implied* (that is, it is not stated), but you can tell what the central idea is without it. Here is an example:

The loose bones of Lincoln were hard to fit with neat clothes; and, once on, they were hard to keep neat; trousers go baggy at the knees of a story-teller who has the habit, at the end of a story, where the main laugh comes in, of putting his arms around his knees, raising his knees to his chin, and rocking to and fro. Those who spoke of his looks often mentioned his trousers creeping to the ankles and higher; his rumpled hair, his wrinkled vest. When he wasn't away making speeches, electioneering or practicing law on the circuit, he cut kindling wood, tended to cordwood for the stoves in the house, milked the cow, gave her a few forks of hay, and changed her straw bedding every day.

—*Carl Sandburg,* Abraham Lincoln: The Prairie Years

Summary of Central Idea:

> Abraham Lincoln was an ordinary man who was not concerned about his appearance and who was willing to do ordinary work.

Many paragraphs in newspapers also do not have topic sentences. The columns in newspapers are so narrow that every third or fourth sentence is indented—not because a new topic idea has started, but because an article is easier to read that way. Look at the following three paragraphs from a newspaper and notice how they all support the same topic sentence in the first paragraph:

> *First, economists are virtually unanimous on the fact that jobs will be lost if the minimum wage is increased.* The Minimum Wage Study Commission concluded in 1981 that every 10 percent increase in the minimum wage could eliminate 70,000 to 200,000 jobs for teenagers alone. Total job loss could be substantially higher.
>
> Given a 40 percent increase, the legislation proposed by Kennedy and Hawkins would jeopardize an additional 400,000 to 800,000 jobs, denying opportunities to thousands more.
>
> Simply put, the minimum wage won't mean a thing—whatever the rate is—if people are forced out of their jobs. A higher wage is little consolation for someone who doesn't have a job.
>
> —*Senator Orrin G. Hatch, "Raising the Minimum Wage Will Put People Out of Work"*

Summary of Central Idea:

> If the minimum wage is increased, fewer jobs will be available.

EXERCISE

Read each of the following paragraphs. For each one, underline the topic sentence. Then, summarize its central idea in your own words. Remember that the topic sentence might be the first sentence, or it might occur later in the paragraph; it might consist of more than one sentence, or it might be implied.

1. Don't meddle with old unloaded firearms, they are the most deadly and unerring things that have ever been created by man. You don't have to take any pains at all with them; you don't have to have a rest, you don't have to have any sights on the gun, you don't have to take aim, even. No, you just pick out a relative and bang away, and you are sure to get him. A youth who can't hit a cathedral at thirty yards with a Gatling gun in three-quarters of an hour, can take up an old empty musket and bag his grandmother every time at a hundred.

    —*Mark Twain, "Advice to Youth"*

2. In the warmth of the inner Solar System a comet releases clouds of vapor and dust that form the glowing head and then leak into the tail, which is the cosmic equivalent of an oil slick. Pieces of the dust later hit the Earth, as meteors. A few survivors among the comets evolve into menacing lumps of dirt in tight orbits around the Sun. For these reasons comets are, in my opinion, best regarded as a conspicuous form of sky pollution.

—*Nigel Calder,* The Comet Is Coming

3. A TV set stood close to a wall in the small living room crowded with an assortment of chairs and tables. An aquarium crowded the mantelpiece of a fake fireplace. A lighted bulb inside the tank showed many colored fish swimming about in a haze of fish food. Some of it lay scattered on the edge of the shelf. The carpet underneath was sodden black. Old magazines and tabloids lay just about everywhere.

—*Bienvenidos Santos,* "Immigration Blues"

Essays and Thesis Statements

The central idea of a complete essay is called its **thesis statement**. Usually, it appears toward the start of the essay (in the introduction), although, like a topic sentence in a paragraph, it can appear in the middle or at the end of an essay, or it might not appear at all because it is implied.

Sometimes a thesis statement is quite straightforward and easy to see. For example, in the following brief essay, the thesis (shown in italics) is clearly stated in the first paragraph:

Three Passions I Have Lived For

BERTRAND RUSSELL

Three passions, simple but overwhelmingly strong, have governed my life: the longing for love, the search for knowledge, and unbearable pity for the suffering of mankind. These passions, like great winds, have blown me hither and thither, in a wayward course over a deep ocean of anguish, reaching to the very verge of despair.

I have sought love, first, because it brings ecstasy—ecstasy so great that I would often have sacrificed all the rest of my life for a few hours of this joy. I have sought it, next, because it relieves loneliness—that terrible loneliness in which one shivering consciousness looks over the rim of the world into the cold unfathomable lifeless abyss. I have sought it, finally, because in the union of love I have seen, in a mystic miniature, the prefiguring vision of the heaven that saints and poets have imagined. This is what I sought, and though it might seem too good for human life, this is what—at last—I have found.

With equal passion I have sought knowledge. I have wished to under-   3
stand the hearts of men. I have wished to know why the stars shine. . . . A little of this, but not much, I have achieved.

Love and knowledge, so far as they were possible, led upward toward   4
the heavens. But always pity brought me back to earth. Echoes of cries of pain reverberate in my heart. Children in famine, victims tortured by oppressors, helpless old people a hated burden to their sons, and the whole world of loneliness, poverty, and pain make a mockery of what human life should be. I long to alleviate the evil, but I cannot, and I too suffer.

This has been my life. I have found it worth living, and would gladly   5
live it again if the chance were offered me.

From The Autobiography of Bertrand Russell. *Reprinted by permission of the Bertrand Russell Peace Foundation c/o Routledge Publishing Co.*

Summary of Central Idea:

Bertrand Russell states that his life has been governed by the search for love and for knowledge and by a sense of pity for those who suffer.

Unfortunately, not everything you read will have a thesis statement as clear as the one above. Sometimes essays, articles, or chapters in texts will have their thesis statements in the second or third paragraph—or even later in the work. Sometimes the thesis statement will be most clearly worded in the conclusion. And sometimes it will not be directly stated at all. The point is that you need to read college material carefully and closely. Certainly one of the most important reading skills you will need to develop in college classes is the ability to recognize the central idea of what you read even when it is not directly stated.

Readings

Read the two articles below. After you have read each one, write a sentence that briefly summarizes its central idea. Underline any sentences that seem to state the thesis idea of the article.

Jailbreak Marriage

GAIL SHEEHY

Although the most commonplace reason women marry young is to "complete" themselves, a good many spirited young women gave another reason: "I did it to get away from my parents." Particularly for girls whose educations and privileges are limited, a *jailbreak marriage* is the usual thing. What might appear to be an act of rebellion usually turns out to be a transfer of dependence. 1

A lifer: that is how it felt to be Simone at 17, how it often feels for girls in authoritarian homes. The last of six children, she was caught in the nest vacated by the others and expected to "keep the family together." Simone was the last domain where her mother could play out the maternal role and where her father could exercise full control. That meant goodbye to the university scholarship. 2

Although the family was not altogether poor, Simone had tried to make a point of her independence by earning her own money since the age of 14. Now she thrust out her bankbook. Would two thousand dollars in savings buy her freedom? 3

"We want you home until you're 21." 4

Work, her father insisted. But the job she got was another closed gate. It was in the knitting machine firm where her father worked, an extension of his control. Simone knuckled under for a year until she met Franz. A zero. An egocentric Hungarian of pointless aristocracy, a man for whom she had total disregard. Except for one attraction. He asked her to marry him. Franz would be the getaway vehicle in her jailbreak marriage scheme: "I decided the best way to get out was to get married and divorce him a year later. That was my whole program." 5

Anatomy, uncontrolled, sabotaged her program. Nine months after the honeymoon, Simone was a mother. Resigning herself, she was pregnant with her second child at 20. 6

One day, her husband called with the news, the marker event to blast her out of the drift. His firm had offered him a job in New York City. 7

"Then and there, I decided that before the month was out I would have the baby, find a lawyer, and start divorce proceedings." The next five years were like twenty. It took every particle of her will and patience to defeat Franz, who wouldn't hear of a separation, and to ignore the ostracism of her family. 8

At the age of 25, on the seventh anniversary of her jailbreak marriage (revealed too late as just another form of entrapment), Simone finally 9 escaped her parents. Describing the day of her decree, the divorcée sounds like so many women whose identity was foreclosed by marriage: "It was like having ten tons of chains removed from my mind, my body—the most exhilarating day of my life."

From Gail Sheehy, Passages, © *1974, 1976 by Gail Sheehy. Used by permission of Dutton Signet, a division of Penguin Books, USA, Inc.*

How to Stay Alive

ART HOPPE

Once upon a time there was a man named Snadley Klabberhorn who was the healthiest man in the whole wide world. 1

Snadley wasn't always the healthiest man in the whole wide world. When he was young, Snadley smoked what he wanted, drank what he wanted, ate what he wanted, and exercised only with young ladies in bed. 2

He thought he was happy. "Life is absolutely peachy," he was fond of saying. "Nothing beats being alive." 3

Then along came the Surgeon General's Report linking smoking to lung cancer, heart disease, emphysema and tertiary coreopsis. 4

Snadley read about The Great Tobacco Scare with a frown. "Life is so peachy," he said, "that there's no sense taking any risks." So he gave up smoking. 5

Like most people who went through the hell of giving up smoking, Snadley became more interested in his own health. In fact, he became fascinated. And when he read a WCTU tract which pointed out that alcohol caused liver damage, brain damage, and acute *weltanschauung,* he gave up alcohol and drank dietary colas instead. 6

At least he did until The Great Cyclamate Scare. 7

"There's no sense in taking any risks," he said. And he switched to sugar-sweetened colas, which made him fat and caused dental caries. On realizing this he renounced colas in favor of milk and took up jogging, which was an awful bore. 8

That was about the time of The Great Cholesterol Scare. 9

Snadley gave up milk. To avoid cholesterol, which caused atherosclerosis, coronary infarcts and chronic chryselephantinism, he also gave up meat, fats and dairy products, subsisting on a diet of raw fish. 10

Then came The Great DDT Scare. 11

"The presence of large amounts of DDT in fish . . ." Snadley read with anguish. But fortunately that's when he met Ernestine. They were made for each other. Ernestine introduced him to homeground wheat germ, macrobiotic yogurt and organic succotash. 12

They were very happy eating this dish twice daily, watching six hours of color television together and spending the rest of their time in bed. 13

They were, that is, until The Great Color Television Scare. 14

"If color tee-vee does give off radiations," said Snadley, "there's no sense taking risks. After all, we still have each other." 15

And that's about all they had. Until The Great Pill Scare. 16

On hearing that The Pill might cause carcinoma, thromboses and lingering stichometry, Ernestine promptly gave up The Pill—and Snadley. "There's no sense taking any risks," she said. 17

Snadley was left with jogging. He was, that is, until he read somewhere that 1.3 percent of joggers are eventually run over by a truck or bitten by rabid dogs. 18

He then retired to a bomb shelter in his back yard (to avoid being hit by a meteor), installed an air purifier (after The Great Smog Scare) and spent the next 63 years doing Royal Canadian Air Force exercises and poring over back issues of The Reader's Digest. 19

"Nothing's more important than being alive," he said proudly on reaching 102. But he never did say anymore that life was absolutely peachy. 20

Participating Actively in the Writer-Reader Dialogue

What would you do if a friend showed up at your door with something important to tell you? Would you tell her to go ahead and talk while you finished watching a television show? Probably not. If you believed what she had to say was important, you'd invite her in, turn off the TV, and sit down to talk to her. If her message was complicated, you might find yourself asking her to repeat parts of it, or you might repeat to her what you thought she had said. Perhaps you would nod your head as she spoke to show that you were listening to her and understood her.

The point is, when you think something is important, you listen to it *actively*. You ask questions; you look for clarification; you offer your own opinions. Above all, you *participate* in the conversation.

As we said earlier, reading and listening are very similar. Sometimes we read very casually, just as sometimes we listen very casually. After all, not everything needs (or deserves) our rapt attention. But some reading, like some listening, *does* demand our attention. The reading that you will do in college classes will, of course, demand active participation from you. So will reading related to your job or to major decisions that you must make in your life. In each of these cases, you must read in a way that is quite different from the casual way you might read a newspaper in the morning.

So what is active reading? How does one go about it? Here are some steps that you should learn to apply to all the reading you do in your college classes.

1. Establish your expectations.

Before you read an article or chapter or book, look at its title. Does it give you an idea of what to expect? Does it sound as if it is announcing its central idea? Read any background information that comes with the reading material. Does it tell you what to expect?

2. First reading: underline or mark main points.

With a pen, pencil, or highlighter in hand, read the material from start to finish, slowly and carefully. During the first reading, you're trying to get an overall sense of the central idea of the selection. Don't try to take notes during this first reading. Instead, just underline or highlight sentences or ideas that seem significant to you as you read. Often these sentences will express the thesis idea of the reading selection or the topic ideas of individual paragraphs. In addition, mark any details or explanations that seem more important than others.

3. Second reading: annotate.

This step is of major importance if you intend to fully understand what you have read. *Reread* what you underlined. As you do, briefly summarize those points in the margin. If you think a point is especially important, make a note of it in the margin. If you have questions or disagree with something, note that in the margin.

4. Summarize the reading.

Briefly write out the central idea of the reading. In your own words, state the thesis idea of the entire essay and the supporting topic ideas of the paragraphs.

5. Respond to the reading.

Write out your own response to what you have read. Do you agree with the writer's idea? Did it remind you of anything that you have experienced? Did it give you a new insight into its topic? You might write this response in a journal or as an assignment to be used for class discussion. Your instructor will guide you here.

Should you go through these five steps every time you read? Absolutely not. Who would want to underline, annotate, and summarize when relaxing with a good novel on a Saturday afternoon? However, you should take these steps when what you are reading demands close attention—when you read material you must analyze for a report or a paper, for example.

Here is an example of an article that has been read by an active reader:

Printed Noise — *see last line*

GEORGE WILL

The flavor list at the local Baskin-Robbins ice cream shop is an anarchy of names like "Peanut Butter 'N Chocolate" and "Strawberry Rhubarb Sherbet." These are not the names of things that reasonable people consider consuming, but the names are admirably businesslike, briskly descriptive.

cuteness in commerce

Unfortunately, my favorite delight (chocolate-coated vanilla flecked with nuts) bears the unutterable name "Hot Fudge Nutty Buddy," an example of the plague of cuteness in commerce. There are some things a gentleman simply will not do, and one is announce in public a desire for a "Nutty Buddy." So I usually settle for a plain vanilla cone.

a gentleman won't say "Nutty Buddy"!

Example of man who wouldn't say "Yumbo"

I am not the only person suffering for immutable standards of propriety. The May issue of *Atlantic* contains an absorbing tale of lonely heroism at a Burger King. A gentleman requested a ham and cheese sandwich that the Burger King calls a Yumbo. The girl taking orders was bewildered.

"Oh," she eventually exclaimed, "you mean a Yumbo."

Gentleman: "The ham and cheese. Yes."

Girl, nettled: "It's called a Yumbo. Now, do you want a Yumbo or not?"

Gentleman, teeth clenched: "Yes, thank you, the ham and cheese."

Girl: "Look, I've got to have an order here. You're holding up the line. You want a Yumbo, don't you? You want a Yumbo!"

Whereupon the gentleman chose the straight and narrow path of virtue. He walked out rather than call a ham and cheese

=outdated, but the author likes him

a Yumbo. His principles are anachronisms but his prejudices are impeccable, and he is on my short list of civilization's friends.

more examples

That list includes the Cambridge don who would not appear outdoors without a top hat, not even when routed by fire at 3 a.m., and who refused to read another line of Tennyson after he saw the poet put water in fine port. The list includes another don who, although devoutly Tory, voted Liberal during Gladstone's day because the duties of prime minister kept Gladstone too busy to declaim on Holy Scripture. And high on the list is the grammarian whose last words were: "I am about to—or I am going to—die: either expression is correct."

Hah! This is funny!

Gentle reader, can you imagine any of these magnificent persons asking a teenage girl for a "Yumbo"? Or uttering "Fishamagig" or "Egg McMuffin" or "Fribble" (that's a milk shake, sort of)?

fun restaurants replaced by fun menus

At one point in the evolution of American taste, restaurants that were relentlessly fun, fun, fun were built to look like lemons or bananas. I am told that in Los Angeles there was the Toed Inn, a strange spelling for a strange place shaped like a giant toad. Customers entered through the mouth, like flies being swallowed.

But the mature nation has put away such childish things in favor of menus that are fun, fun, fun. Seafood is "From Neptune's Pantry" or "Denizens of the Briny Deep." And "Surf 'N Turf," which you might think is fish and horsemeat, actually is lobster and beef.

Hamburger names

To be fair, there are practical considerations behind the asphyxiatingly cute names given hamburgers. Many hamburgers are made from portions of the cow that the cow had no reason to boast about. So sellers invent distracting names to give hamburgers cachet. Hence "Whoppers" and "Heroburgers."

Howard Johnson's menu- no excuse

But there is no excuse for Howard Johnson's menu. In a just society it would be a flogging offense to speak of "steerburgers," clams "fried to order" (which probably means they don't fry clams for you unless you order fried clams), a "natural cut" (what is an "unnatural" cut?) of sirloin, "oven-baked" meat loaf, chicken pot pie with "flaky crust," "golden croquettes," "grilled-in-butter Frankforts [*sic*]," "liver with smothered onions" (smothered by onions?), and a "hearty" Reuben sandwich.

Verbal litter = language becomes printed noise

America is marred by scores of Dew Drop Inns serving "crispy green" salads, "garden fresh" vegetables, "succulent" lamb, "savory" pork, "sizzling" steaks, and "creamy" or "tangy" coleslaw. I've nothing against Homeric adjectives ("wine-dark sea," "wing-footed Achilles") but isn't coleslaw just coleslaw? Americans hear the incessant roar of commerce without listening to it, and read the written roar without really noticing it. Who would notice if a menu proclaimed "creamy" steaks and "sizzling" coleslaw? Such verbal litter is to language as Muzak is to music. As advertising blather becomes the

thesis —→ nation's normal idiom, language becomes printed noise.

Summary of the Reading

George F. Will calls advertising language, especially the kind we see on menus, "printed noise." He gives examples of many silly or unnecessary names given to food (like the "Yumbo"), and he admires people who resist what he calls "verbal litter."

Personal Response to the Reading

I thought this article was really funny. I remember feeling stupid the first time I had to ask for an "Egg McMuffin." The name sounds like something on a kindergarten menu. But I don't really think about those names anymore. I guess I've just gotten used to them. The article reminded me how much they are all around us, even though I don't notice them. How about "Wienerdude"? That's the stupidest name I've ever heard. When I first heard it, I thought I'd never order one of those, just because the name is so insulting to any intelligent person. But maybe it's really a good hot dog—so I guess I really would order one. I suppose I agree with the article's point that after a while you don't even notice these things anymore. They are like "verbal litter."

Readings

Read each of the following essays *actively*. That is, as you read each essay, *underline or highlight* its thesis statement, topic sentences, and any examples or ideas that seem important to you. Then reread the parts you have marked and *annotate* the essay. Finally, write a brief *summary* of the article and a brief *personal response paragraph*.

How We Have Evolved into a Culture of Rudeness

MARTIN J. SMITH

The scene: a popular souvenir shop. The topic: the decline of civility. [1]
"I keep wanting to do a 'remember when' book," says customer [2]
Cecilia de Baca, 41. "Remember when someone sneezed and everyone
would say, 'God bless you'? Remember when people would see an older
person and offer them their seat?"

She is speaking to the manager, behind whom hangs a sign: "Shop- [3]
lifters will be beaten to death." A key-ring display on the counter shrieks
slogans full of hostility and attitude, including "Chill me, thrill me, fulfill
me, then leave me the hell alone." The T-shirt rack behind her bristles
with messages—"It's not a beer belly. It's a fuel tank for a sex machine"—
that suggest crudeness these days can be a profitable commodity.

"There really are a lot of nice people that come in," says Jeff Balaam, [4]
34, manager of the Seal Beach, Calif., souvenir shop, "but there also are
a lot of jerks. I like the ones that come in, go straight to the back and use
the restroom, then just walk out. They don't even pretend to look
around. And they don't say thank you."

Highbrow prudes? Hardly. They are, after all, in a beachside souvenir [5]
shop.

But lamentations about the decline of common courtesy and civility [6]
transcend economic, social and racial lines like the ratings of a particularly juicy "Geraldo" show.

"It has nothing to do with money or social class," insists Letitia [7]
Baldrige, an authority on manners who has written 13 books on the subject. "It has everything to do with character and the way Mama and
Papa brought you up, and that doesn't cost money. Some of the lowest
economic classes have the best brought-up children, and some of the
highest economic classes have the least civility."

So how did we go from a ma'am-ing and sir-ing society where polite- [8]
ness really counted to a society where even a corporate giant such as Del
Taco feels safe distributing children's prizes imprinted with the slogan
"Shut up and eat your beans"?

What social pathology explains the reluctance of so many people to [9]
pull over for passing funeral processions, to make small talk with fellow
bus passengers, to exchange the pleasantries that for generations helped
lubricate social discourse?

What impulse moved an antique-store owner to tape a photocopied   10
cartoon in the store's front window showing two vault-type safes, apparently copulating, above the caption "Safe sex"?

Does the world really need to see unauthorized and explicit honey-   11
moon video outtakes of Tonya Harding and Jeff Gillooly, as presented in
the new *Penthouse* magazine, or the full video available, reportedly, on
pay-per-view TV this fall?

Experts agree on the symptoms but aren't sure how to explain the   12
decline of civility and the rise of crudeness. They cite everything from
the anti-Establishment movement of the 1960s to the unraveling of
close-knit neighborhoods to the rise of feminism. "One reason is the
legitimization of protest movements in North America and the West in
general," said Alexander Moore, a professor of anthropology at the
University of Southern California.

"That legitimized bad behavior, especially among youth, and has influ-   13
enced the problem. Protests have gone from the gentle nonviolence of
Martin Luther King to the antics of ACT-UP and Queer Nation and others that use rudeness as a way of gaining attention."

Psychology Professor Jerald Jellison blames the phenomenon on "a   14
40-year shift away from a social life guided by social customs and personal character."

"We used to have informal rule systems which governed life," says   15
Jellison, author of "I'm Sorry I Didn't Mean To & Other Lies We Love
to Tell."

Now, Jellison says, that informal mandate for public behavior has   16
been replaced by more formal rules and government-based laws. The
question "Is it proper?" has been replaced by the question "Is it legal?"

"If it's not illegal, then a lot of people will go ahead and do it," he   17
says. "They don't worry about upsetting people. It may be offensive, but
they think, 'There's no law against it. And even if there is a law, then I
probably won't get caught. And even if I get caught, I'll get a good attorney and get out of it.' That's a large change in our society, and there are
problems associated with it."

Moore, the JSC anthropologist, says the issue of civility seemed espe-   18
cially relevant during the recent World Cup, during which competing
players frequently helped up one another from the ground and winners
often consoled losers. The behavior was very different than the in-your-
face style of more traditional U.S. sports.

Baldrige says recent events "reminded people of a different era when   19
people behaved nicely to one another"—the death of Jacqueline Kennedy

Onassis, the pomp and ceremony surrounding the death of former President Richard Nixon, the patriotic fervor of the D-Day celebrations. "In the space of a few months," she says wistfully, "there were a lot of tragic but very dignified events that harkened back to a time of graciousness and kindness and caring."

© *1994 by* The Orange County Register. *Reprinted with permission.*

Suggestions for Summarizing

1. The title of this article should help you to determine its thesis idea. With the title in mind, briefly state what Martin Smith seems to be saying about the topic of rudeness.

2. What ideas in the article support Smith's thesis idea? Include them in your brief summary too.

Suggestions for Personal Responses

1. Describe different types of rude behavior that you have encountered in your own life. Try to remember specific examples that you have experienced or observed.

2. Do you think your own behavior is sometimes rude? Describe situations when that might be the case.

3. Try taking the opposite point of view. Describe examples of graciousness and kindness and caring that you have observed in your own life.

4. Discuss this article with other members of your class. Develop ideas of your own about the possible causes of the rudeness in today's society.

Kids Won't Step on Cracks—or Give Up on Superstitions

ROY RIVENBURG

When 11-year-old Beth Huber of Orange finds a rubber band on the sidewalk, she puts it on her wrist and makes five wishes before throwing it back on the ground. 1

Across town, Gary Martinez bounces a toothpaste cap against the sink on the night before exams. If the cap lands on the counter, the 13-year-old considers it a good omen. 2

One of his classmates, Heather Estrada, also 13, holds her breath whenever she passes a graveyard. She regards it as protection against bad luck. 3

In the world of childhood superstitions, even stepping on a crack can break a mother's back, listening to the wrong Beatles record can kill peo- 4 ple and sitting in a certain chair by the TV can influence the outcome of the game on the screen.

Odd as such beliefs might sound, they play an important role in growing up, experts say. Superstitions reflect a child's thought processes, fears and personality. Some appear generation after generation; others come out of nowhere. A few signal psychological disorders.   5

Fueling it is a phenomenon called "magical thinking," says Michael Rothenberg, co-author of *Dr. Spock's Baby and Child Care* and professor emeritus of psychiatry and pediatrics at the University of Washington.   6

Young children, unable to distinguish fantasy from reality, commonly believe that inanimate objects, like stuffed animals, have feelings—and that thoughts have magical powers over events, Rothenberg says.   7

It's a perfect environment for superstitions.   8

Growing up in Brooklyn, Philip Goldberg believed he could help the Dodgers win by wearing his lucky cap and sitting on a certain stool at the local luncheonette as he watched the team on television.   9

"There's a part of us that instinctively feels a connection between things we care about and our own behaviors and thoughts," says Goldberg, whose novel, *This Is Next Year*, revolves around boyhood superstitions and the 1955 World Series.   10

As children get older, however, the nature of superstitions shifts. The intellectual belief in magic gives way to an emotional belief—and superstitions evolve and a "more sophisticated, less embarrassing" version of teddy bears and security blankets, says Nancy Hornstein, a child psychiatrist and assistant clinical professor at UCLA.   11

The rituals offer a feeling of safety and protection as children learn to cope with such uncertainties as dating and tests.   12

Among the superstitions surrounding romance, for example: When crossing railroad tracks in a car or bus, lift your feet and put your hand on the ceiling or you'll lose your boyfriend.   13

For quizzes and exams, try rubbing a troll doll's hair, says Lauren Eyrich, a seventh-grader from Santa Ana. Other classmates suggest putting pennies in your shoes or writing with a lucky pen or pencil.   14

"Sometimes we encourage such superstitions," Hornstein says. If a child is fearful of leaving his house, for instance, "we have him find a magical object to help."   15

Such practices get discarded after a child gains confidence or mastery over the particular situation.   16

In theory.   17

"There's always that flicker of doubt," says Greg Cynaumon, a psychologist in Newport Beach.   18

Superstitions also serve as social rituals.   19

Some mainly function as games: When two people say the same thing at once, for example, one is supposed to shout "jinx" and count to 10 before the other person says "stop." But the bad luck that supposedly befalls the loser is incidental to the competition itself.   20

Other superstitions seem part of some unwritten social code: If, heaven forbid, you should somehow spit on yourself, you absolutely, positively must not wipe it off, cautions Patrick Smith, 13, of Orange. "I don't know why; you just can't."   21

Many such beliefs—passed through generations—are almost institutionalized in childhood.   22

The rest are personal inventions, usually known only to their creators.   23

A San Diego County man wouldn't play the Beatles' "Sgt. Pepper" album for years as a boy because he thought it would cause someone he knew to die. Why? He was listening to the record when his mother informed him that a family friend had been killed in a car crash.   24

The Fab Four became indelibly associated with the traumatic event, psychiatrists say.   25

Magic formulas are another private superstition. One girl made up a rule that she had to eat her Cheerios two O's at a time and that if she finished the bowl with a solo Cheerio, it meant bad luck, Hornstein says. The only escape (pay attention, General Mills marketing department) was to add more Cheerios—a random number, of course—and try again.   26

Grownups also subscribe to magic formulas. The late actor Lorne Greene used to add up the numbers on license plates until he found one that totaled seven, a good omen, he told a magazine writer.   27

Other formulas have more specific meaning. A 14-year-old invented the superstition that if he heard two particular songs back to back on the radio, he would get a girlfriend. The underlying purpose, Hornstein theorizes, was to counter the teen's anxiety about attracting the opposite sex. "He didn't feel like he had the ability to control his fate, so he made up some kind of formula to believe in."   28

Kids who are "timid, unsure of themselves and maybe have low self-esteem tend to put a lot more credence in this type of stuff, Cynaumon says.   29

In contrast, confident youngsters often disregard or even flaunt the rules. Take the perennial "Step on a crack, break your mother's back,"   30 he says. A self-assured child will laugh off the belief, ignore it or stomp his foot on a crack for all to see and proclaim, "See? Nothing happens."

Hornstein agrees—in part. Although it's generally true that insecure people are more superstitious, she says, mystical behaviors turn up "across all sorts of personality types," especially in situations that are inherently uncertain.   31

One such area is sports—where superstition is virtually *de rigueur,* adults included. Former Oakland Raiders coach John Madden, for example, was reported to have refused to let his team leave the locker room until running back Mark van Eeghen had belched.   32

Other professional methods for summoning luck have included wearing a Jetsons T-shirt under the uniform (pitcher Charlie Kerfeld, when he played with the Houston Astros), not washing socks when he was on scoring streaks (former hockey great Bobby Orr) and eating chicken every day before a game (Wade Boggs of the Boston Red Sox).   33

Kids pick up the weird rituals and then manufacture their own, Cynaumon says.   34

An eighth-grade soccer player, for example, ties pretzels in his shoelaces for luck. Members of an Orange County Little League team, meanwhile, rely on the ceremonial rolling down of socks and rolling up of sleeves just before game time.   35

Failure to follow the prescribed practice can reinforce the superstition by creating a self-fulfilling prophecy, Cynaumon says: If Mom washes the "lucky jersey" in the middle of a youngster's winning streak, the kid might subconsciously make himself mess up.   36

As puzzling and exasperating as these beliefs might seem to parents, children's superstitions rarely are cause for worry, experts agree.   37

However, Rothenberg says, "things cross the line when the pattern of behavior begins to interfere with normal, everyday activities."   38

Some children develop painstaking rituals such as having to touch every object in a room—and having to start over again if a certain thought enters their mind, Hornstein says.   39

Even seemingly innocent superstitions can get out of hand. For example, a ritual of having to touch every third picket in a fence is normal unless it starts making a child late for school.   40

Overboard superstitions should be reported to a pediatrician or family doctor for advice, experts say.   41

In other cases—the lucky shirts and magic pretzels and counting of Cheerios—parents should just play along, psychiatrists say.   42

Of course, they might end up playing for a very long time.   43

Childhood superstitions, it seems, aren't only for kids. *Psychology Today* found a lot of lucky pens when it looked into study aids used by college students. 44

And pro baseball's maxim about not walking on foul lines bears suspicious resemblance to "Step on a crack." 45

Novelist Goldberg, too, hasn't exactly abandoned his boyhood rituals. At Dodger games, he still wears a lucky cap. "I don't necessarily believe in it to the degree I did as a kid," he says. Still, he doesn't want to take chances. 46

"The old saying is that there are no atheists in foxholes. Well, there aren't many in the bleachers, either." 47

© *1992 by the* Los Angeles Times. *Reprinted by permission.*

Suggestion for Summarizing

1. Try to state the thesis idea of this article in your own words as clearly as possible. Then briefly state each of the major points that Roy Rivenburg makes about superstitions.

Suggestions for Personal Responses

1. Are you or have you ever been a superstitious person? Describe in what ways you have ever acted in a superstitious manner.

2. Do you know people who are superstitious? Describe things they do or ways they act that could be called superstitious.

3. Rivenburg's article makes a number of different points about superstitions. Choose one or more of those points and give examples of your own to further illustrate what Rivenburg has to say.

4. Talk to other members of the class or to people you know about their superstitions. Make a list of the most unusual ones.

Assignments
Writing a Personal Response

1. Write a paper that responds to *one* of the following questions about "How We Have Evolved into a Culture of Rudeness."

   a. It's easy to criticize the rudeness of others, but perhaps not as easy to identify our own problems in this area. Describe in what way your own actions might contribute to what Martin Smith calls our "culture of rudeness."

    b. Do you encounter any particular types of rude behavior on a regular basis? Explain what types of rude behavior seem most common to you and describe some situations when you have observed them.

    c. In his last paragraph, Smith quotes Letitia Baldrige, who remembers a time "of graciousness and kindness and caring." Do you still find those characteristics in the people you know? Give several examples to illustrate your response.

2. Write a paper that responds to *one* of the following questions about "Kids Won't Step on Cracks—or Give Up on Superstitions."

    a. If you are a superstitious person (or if you used to be superstitious), write a paper that explains and gives examples of your superstitions.

    b. If you know people who have some interesting superstitions, write a paper that explains and gives examples of what they believe. Or if you know one person who is quite superstitious, write a paper that explains and gives examples of that person's superstitions.

    c. Rivenburg discusses several types of superstitions in his article. Write a paper in which you use examples of your own to illustrate some of the superstitious behaviors that Rivenburg explains.

    d. Interview several of your classmates or survey your friends and relatives about their superstitions. Write a paper describing the most unusual ones you find, or write a paper that organizes the superstitions you find into different types.

3. In "Printed Noise," George Will describes some of the ridiculous ways restaurants name or advertise their food. If you think his observations have merit, write a paper that gives examples of your own. If you would like to, use a different type of product, such as cigarettes, liquor, cars, or grocery items. If you think Will is overreacting or has missed the purpose of such advertising, write a paper that explains why you think so, illustrating your points by referring to specific products.

Evaluating Sample Papers

Using the Student Model Checklist on pages 21–22, evaluate the effectiveness of the following student paragraphs and essays.

Student Paragraph 1

    As I read Roy Rivenburg's article "Kids Won't Step on Cracks—or Give Up on Superstitions," I found myself able to identify with several distinct points addressed within the article. One, superstitions are a normal part of childhood. Two, magical thinking offers a feeling of safety and protection as children learn to cope with lifes uncertainties. Third, such beliefs generally disappear after a child becomes more mature, confident, and self-assured. Some common adolescent superstitions are the breaking of a mirror resulting in seven years bad luck, finding a penny face up signifying good luck, and stepping on a crack will break your mothers back. Some personal examples to further illustrate these points are: First, I recall having to take my lucky blue rabbits foot everywhere I went including dates, camping trips and even school. The rabbits foot seemed to provide protection and reassurance that nothing bad would happen. Another example of my magical thinking is the usage of a lucky pen for taking exams, filling out job applications or writing letters. As I become older, more mature, and self confident my belief in these superstitions slowly fades and shifts from an emotional belief to an intellectual one. In conclusion, belief in superstitions, regardless of age, appears to be an accepted norm and very much a part of our lives, upbringing, and culture.

Student Paragraph 2

As you go through your daily business, you can often bet that someone will try to break your stride by deliberately being rude. The rude behaviors I witness most often are played out by people who know exactly what they are doing. For example, I have a friend who longs for the moment someone asks him for directions because he gets a real laugh out of telling that person to go back the way he or she came. I remember one time when my friend did this, and it was funny because the person asking for directions was so excited that he busted a U-turn on a one way street in downtown San Diego. But funny or not, my buddy will commit this offensive behavior with every opportunity. Rudeness can take form anywhere, but I'm sure you all have had a person deliberately cut infront of you in a slow moving line. One encounter I had with a conscious line cutter was in a high school lunch line. After she stepped right infront of me without an excuse, I informed her about how she had basically told the whole line to get lost. She then looked at me like I had no right to claim my spot in line. One last experience I've had with purposely rude people comes in response to a glance. I'll be walking to a class and looking around at the other individuals, and I catch someone watching me. This look is fine, but then he keeps on looking, so not to be rude I'll nod or gesture in some way to acknowledge his presence. When this motion of acknowledgment is given without receiving one in return, I think it purposely offending. Now if people mean to be rude or just happen to be rude it doesn't matter because whoever received the rude act has already taken offense, and the rude dog at hand doesn't care either way, so as you go about your day try not to let those rude dogs trip your stride because if you do your letting them get the best of you.

Student Essay 1

Superstitions are not always fun and games like people perceive them to be. For some people, it can be an embarrassing emotional belief and an uncontrollable nuisance.

For instance, when I was in fifth grade, a lady named Martha lived in the neighborhood with us. Many of the neighbors thought she was strange, but I didn't know why. I finally found out one day on my way to the school bus stop, where I noticed her in the open garage. Martha was wiping the garage floor after every step she made so that she was actually walking backwards. I thought to myself, "That's weird! Why is she doing that?" I didn't mention anything to the lady. I only stared until she closed the garage door. I was later told by my older sister, Liza, that Martha thinks the dust will be bad luck if it isn't wiped up.

Superstitions can even be harmful sometimes. Last year, in my English class, we discussed the bad habits people have. That was when Jennifer, an acquaintance of mine, admitted to the class that she washes her hands constantly. She said, "I wash my hands because I think the dirt on my hands will cause a family illness. What's worse is that I do it about eighty to one hundred times a day." When she said this, I immediately glanced at her hands. They looked sore, red, chapped, and very dry. A superstition such as this annoys that person, but it cannot be controlled.

Both of these people had something in common. They each believed in some form of superstition that affected them in an unusual way. As odd as these beliefs may sound, they are more serious to its believers than they seem to be.

Student Essay 2

After I read "How We Have Evolved into a Culture of Rudeness" I realized that a lot of people around me do not consider the feeling of other people. In fact, I think people can be rude and selfish in many ways.

On the road people do not consider the feeling of the other drivers around them. They can be very rude for the sake of catching the next green light. For example, last Sunday I had to pick up my friend, who lives by the mall, for church. When I was almost by the mall, there was a huge traffic jam because the traffic lights were out of order, so I had to wait in a long traffic line. Finally, it was my turn to go, but suddenly this big truck came from nowhere and cut in front of me. I was really mad, but the thing that I was most mad about was that the guy did not even apologize.

Another example of rude and selfish behavior happened last summer while I was working as a cashier at the Rice King, a Chinese restaurant. One day an old lady came in and said "Give me the damn noodles." I could not believe what she said. I was very angry with her, but knowing how most old people are, I brushed off her statement and promptly filled out her order. When I gave her the food, she opened the box in front of me and said, "There is no meat." She kept picking at the food until I finally ended up giving her more meat.

Finally, last month when I went to Nickelodean Theaters to see a movie called *Legends of the Fall* with my friend. While we were watching the movie, this guy in back of us started burping really loudly. The smell of nachos he had been eating attacked my nose to the point where I was sick to my stomach. What made it so bad was that he continued to do it throughout the movie, as though it was funny, and he did not even say "Excuse me."

In my opinion, people that are rude and selfish usually do not think about other people's feelings and act however they choose, even though it would not be appropriate. The most common rude and selfish behavior comes from people wanting to satisfy themselves and disrespecting others.

Sentence Combining
Coordination

In Chapter 1, you practiced *embedding* simple modifiers (adjectives, adverbs, and prepositional phrases) next to the words they modify in a sentence. Such embedding may have seemed rather easy to you, for it is something we all learned to do quite automatically at an early age. (Almost everyone would automatically change "I wrote a letter. It was long." to "I wrote a long letter.") However, not all combining of related ideas is as easily performed. As writers become more and more proficient, they develop the ability to create quite sophisticated sentence structures as well as very simple ones—but they develop that ability gradually, after much practice.

In this section, you will practice *coordinating* ideas. Like embedding simple modifiers, the process of coordination can be natural and easy. However, effective coordination also has its complexities, which we will take up in this section.

Using Coordinating Conjunctions

Coordination consists of joining ideas that are grammatically alike, usually by using one of the seven **coordinating conjunctions:** *and, but, or, nor, for, so,* and *yet.* You can easily memorize these seven conjunctions by learning the acronym BOYSFAN. (An acronym is a word made up from the first letters of other words.)

But   **O**r   **Y**et   **S**o   **F**or   **A**nd   **N**or

Of course, when we talk, we use each of these seven words all of the time. They are so common to our language, in fact, that we rarely think about them. When we want to join two ideas, it takes practically no thought at all to stick an *and* or a *but* or some other coordinating conjunction into our speech and to go on.

Writing, however, is more precise than speech. When someone else reads what we have written, we are usually not there to clarify things that might be confusing, so a careful choice of words the first time through is much more important in writing than in speech. For instance, is there a difference between these two sentences?

> *Huck Finn was very superstitious, and he knew he was in trouble when he spilled the salt.*
> *Huck Finn was very superstitious, so he knew he was in trouble when he spilled the salt.*

Both sentences suggest a relationship between the ideas of Huck's being superstitious and of his spilling the salt, but only the second sentence is *precise* in stating the relationship clearly. By using the word *so*, the second sentence makes it clear that Huck's belief about spilling salt was a *result* of his being superstitious.

When you use the coordinating conjunctions, keep their *precise* meanings in mind:

And suggests *addition*. It is used to "add" one idea to a similar one.

> *My grass needs to be mowed, <u>and</u> my garden needs to be weeded.*

Nor also suggests *addition*, but it adds two negative ideas.

> *I have not mowed my lawn in the past two weeks, <u>nor</u> have I weeded the garden.*

But suggests a *contrast* or *opposition*.

> *I should mow the lawn today, <u>but</u> I think I'll watch a movie instead.*

Yet also suggests a *contrast* or *opposition*.

> *I feel guilty about not mowing the lawn, <u>yet</u> I really don't want to work today.*

Or suggests *alternatives*.

> *I will mow the lawn tomorrow, <u>or</u> perhaps I'll wait until next weekend.*

For suggests a *result-cause* relationship. The first statement is the *result*; the second statement is the *cause*.

> (result)   (cause)
> *My yard is becoming the neighborhood eyesore, <u>for</u> I hate to do yardwork.*

So suggests a *cause-result* relationship. The first statement is the *cause*; the second statement is the *result*.

> (cause)   (result)
> *My neighbors have stopped talking to me, <u>so</u> maybe I should clean up my yard today.*

EXERCISE   Combine the following sentences using the coordinating conjunctions that most accurately express the relationship between them.

EXAMPLE

The forecast was for rain with strong winds. I decided to cancel our picnic.
The forecast was for rain with strong winds, <u>so</u> I decided to cancel our picnic.

1. Many ideas have been suggested to improve automobiles. Some are much stranger than others.

2. In 1926, Leander Pilton decided to design a car that could be parked almost any-where. He had grown tired of looking for a parking space.

3. He added a platform with rollers to the back of his car. Then he tried to tip the car onto its end.

4. His plan was to roll the car into a parking space that was slightly larger than the size of a refrigerator. His plan had some flaws.

5. He never explained how he would tip the car onto its end. He did not say how he would prevent the gas, oil, and water from draining out of the car while it was stand-ing on end.

6. Charles Ramage was terribly bored with normal driving. He invented a somersaulting automobile.

7. He combined an engine with a simple chassis. Then he placed a semicircular roll bar around the entire vehicle.

8. He could drive down the street like any ordinary driver. He could flip a lever that would turn the car over onto its front end.

9. The vehicle's momentum would keep it rolling forward. It was able to turn a complete somersault in the middle of the street.

10. Ramage's automobile was fun to watch. It was not very welcome on city streets.

EXERCISE   Each of the following sentences uses *and* as a coordinating conjunction. Where needed, change the *and* to a more precise and accurate coordinating conjunction. Some of the sen-tences may not need to be changed.

EXAMPLE

Last year I spent $300 on a membership to a local gym, <u>and</u> I used the gym only two times all year long.

Last year I spent $300 on a membership to a local gym, but I used the gym only two times all year long.

1. The horn of a rhinoceros is one of its unique features, <u>and</u> the commercial value of that feature threatens the survival of the rhinoceros.

2. Rhino horns are sought by many poachers, <u>and</u> they are currently worth more than their weight in gold.

3. In some cultures rhino-horn walking sticks are symbols of prestige, <u>and</u> in other cultures rhino-horn products are used for everything from headaches to labor pains.

4. In North Yemen, daggers carved from rhino horns were so expensive, costing as much as $12,000, that very few people could buy them, <u>and</u> today oil wealth has put that price within reach of many Yemeni.

5. Today, an East African farmer can double his annual income by killing a single rhino, <u>and</u> the temptation to hunt rhinos illegally is hard to resist.

6. Game wardens may try to stop poachers, <u>and</u> they may themselves be lured into this very lucrative activity.

7. Rhinos are not difficult to approach, <u>and</u> they are not hard to kill with today's advanced weapons.

8. Professional poachers today use many sophisticated hunting techniques, <u>and</u> they are able to decimate entire populations of rhinos with very little effort.

9. One can tell that the mature rhino is disappearing, <u>and</u> the average size of the illegal rhino horn has dropped 60% since 1973.

10. The poachers cut off the horns of the dead rhinos, <u>and</u> then they ship the horns out of the country.

In each of the above exercises and examples, a comma has been placed before the coordinating conjunction because the statements being combined could stand alone as separate sentences. However, when a coordinating conjunction joins two sentence parts that can *not* stand alone as separate sentences, do not use a comma before the conjunction. (For a further discussion of this comma rule, see Chapter 17.)

EXAMPLE

(comma)   *Mario worked all night on the new computer program, and his brother worked with him.*

(no comma)   *Mario worked all night on the new computer program and all the next day on his accounting work.*

Using Semicolons

So far, we have seen that using a comma and a coordinating conjunction is one way to combine related sentences. Another way to combine sentences is to use a *semicolon*, usually (but not always) with a conjunctive adverb. Here are some common **conjunctive adverbs:**

accordingly	however	otherwise	for example
also	instead	similarly	for instance
besides	meanwhile	still	in addition
consequently	moreover	then	in fact
finally	namely	therefore	on the other
further	nevertheless	thus	hand
furthermore	next	undoubtedly	
hence	nonetheless	as a result	

EXAMPLES

Henry ate all of the potato chips; however, he was still hungry.

Tuan knew that he should buy a new car; on the other hand, he really wanted a motorcycle.

The movie was too violent for Sabrina; the concert was too dull for Rocky.

If you use a semicolon to combine related sentences, remember these points:

1. Most writers—professional and nonprofessional—use semicolons *much less frequently* than the other methods of combining sentences that are discussed in this and other sections.

2. Conjunctive adverbs *are not* coordinating conjunctions and should *not be used to combine sentences with commas.*

EXAMPLES

(incorrect)   *Sylvia had always wanted to visit the Far East, however she never had enough money to do so.*

(correct)   *Sylvia had always wanted to vist the Far East; however, she never had enough money to do so.*

3. It is the *semicolons* that join sentences, not the conjunctive adverbs. As a result, conjunctive adverbs may appear *anywhere that makes sense* in the sentence.

EXAMPLES

It rained for fifteen straight days. <u>Nevertheless</u>, my father jogged every day.

It rained for fifteen straight days; my father, <u>nevertheless</u>, jogged every day.

It rained for fifteen straight days; my father jogged every day, <u>nevertheless</u>.

EXERCISE   Combine the following sentences, either by using a comma with a coordinating conjunction or by using a semicolon with or without a conjunctive adverb.

EXAMPLE

Hillary wanted to attend college full-time. She needed to work forty hours a week to support her family.

Hillary wanted to attend college full-time, but she needed to work forty hours a week to support her family.

or

Hillary wanted to attend college full-time; however, she needed to work forty hours a week to support her family.

1. For hundreds of years, people have considered the number thirteen to be unlucky. Surveys have shown that the fear of the number thirteen is the most widespread of all bad-luck superstitions.

2. The French, for instance, never issue the house address thirteen. The Italian national lottery omits the number thirteen.

3. Americans also fear the number thirteen. Modern skyscrapers, condominiums, and apartment buildings label the floor that follows twelve as fourteen.

4. When a new luxury apartment building labeled a floor thirteen, it rented units on all other floors. It could rent only a few units on the thirteenth floor.

5. The owners recognized the problem. They changed the floor number to twelve-B and were soon able to rent out the rest of the apartments.

6. Fear of the number thirteen has been attributed to the Last Supper, when Christ with his apostles numbered thirteen. It has an older source in Norse mythology.

7. According to Norse mythology, the evil god Loki grew angry when he was not invited to a banquet with twelve other gods. He decided to attend anyway, bringing the total to thirteen.

8. The other gods battled Loki. Balder, the favorite of the gods, was killed.

9. In the United States, thirteen should be considered a lucky number. The nation started with thirteen colonies.

10. On the Great Seal of the United States, the bald eagle holds in one claw an olive branch with thirteen leaves and thirteen berries. It holds in the other claw thirteen arrows.

Combining Parts of Sentences

So far, we have focused on using coordination to combine *separate sentences*. Another way to improve your writing is to use a coordinating conjunction to join *part* of one sentence to *part* of another sentence. This type of sentence combining is more difficult than the simple joining of entire sentences, but it usually results in more concise and direct writing. For instance, here are two sentences as they might have been written by Gail Sheehy in "Jailbreak Marriage." The parts of each sentence that could be combined are underlined.

Simone was the last domain <u>where her mother could play out the maternal role</u>. She was also the last place <u>where her father could exercise complete control</u>.

Of course, Sheehy recognized that these two ideas could really be expressed as one sentence, so she wrote this:

Simone was the last domain <u>where her mother could play out the maternal role</u> and <u>where her father could exercise complete control</u>.

Here is another example, taken from "Kids Won't Step on Cracks—or Give Up on Superstitions," by Roy Rivenburg. When describing some childhood superstitions, Rivenburg could have written three sentences. The parts of each sentence that could be combined are underlined.

In the world of childhood superstitions, even <u>stepping on a crack can break a mother's back</u>. For that matter, <u>listening to the wrong Beatles record can kill people</u>. Some children even believe that <u>sitting in a certain chair by the TV can influence the outcome of the game on the screen</u>.

Here is how Rivenburg actually wrote the sentence:

In the world of childhood superstitions, even <u>stepping on a crack can break a mother's back</u>, <u>listening to the wrong Beatles record can kill people</u> and <u>sitting in a certain chair by the TV can influence the outcome of the game on the screen</u>.

Note: When joining three or more items, as has been done here, you need to use the coordinating conjunction only before the last item.

Parallel Sentence Structure

When you use coordination to join ideas, you should do your best to word those ideas similarly so they are clear and easy to read. Coordinate ideas that are worded similarly are said to be *parallel* in structure. Notice the difference between the following two examples:

Nonparallel Structure *My favorite sports are <u>swimming</u> and <u>to jog</u>.*

Parallel Structure *My favorite sports are <u>swimming</u> and <u>jogging</u>.*

Do you see how much clearer the parallel sentence is? Now let's look once more at the examples from the articles by Gail Sheehy and Roy Rivenburg. Notice how the coordinate ideas have been written so that they are parallel in structure.

Simone was the last domain

<u>where her mother could play out the maternal role</u>

and <u>where her father could exercise complete control</u>.

In the world of childhood superstitions, even

<u>stepping on a crack can break a mother's back</u>,
<u>listening to the wrong Beatles record can kill people</u>
and <u>sitting in a certain chair by the TV can influence the outcome of the game on the screen</u>.

As you can see, recognizing related ideas and combining them in parallel structure can result in sentences that are more direct and less repetitious than the original sentences.

Note: For a more thorough discussion of parallel sentence structure, see Chapter 6.

EXERCISE   Combine each group of sentences into one sentence by using coordinating conjunctions to join related ideas. Wherever possible, use parallel sentence structure. Parallel ideas that can be combined are underlined in the first five groups.

EXAMPLE

People who stereotype others are often insensitive to the pain they cause. The same is true for people who tell ethnic jokes.

People who stereotype others or who tell ethnic jokes are often insensitive to the pain they cause.

(Note that a comma has not been used before the coordinating conjunction or because it does not start a new sentence.)

1. According to legend, Calamity Jane was a fierce Indian fighter. She also was a brave scout. In addition, legend describes her as a beautiful, vivacious tamer of the Old West.

2. In reality, however, she often brought misfortune into her own life. She brought misfortune into the lives of others, too.

3. Although born in Princeton, Missouri, she spent most of her life in Deadwood, South Dakota, a town notorious for its collection of miners and Civil War veterans. It was also full of gamblers and outlaws, and it was the home of many prostitutes.

4. It is said that she drank as heavily as any mule skinner. In addition, she cursed as coarsely as the roughest of men.

5. Calamity's life was characterized by drunkenness. It was also full of lawlessness. It even included prostitution.

6. Dime-store novels helped to spread her legend by describing her as a natural beauty. She was referred to as the sweetheart of Wild Bill Hickok.

7. Calamity Jane did know Wild Bill Hickok. She was part of his gang for a while, but there is no evidence that he romanced her. There is also no evidence that he even paid much attention to her.

8. Easterners viewed the Westward movement as adventurous. To them, it was romantic. It was exciting, so they preferred stories that idealized the West. They also liked stories that made their heroes seem larger than life.

9. From 1900 through 1903, Calamity Jane was a featured attraction in "Wild West" shows, where she demonstrated her authentic ability as a sharpshooter. In her act, she rode wildly about the ring in a wagon with a six-horse team.

10. While dying of pneumonia in 1903, Calamity Jane asked what the date was. She then uttered her last request: "It's the twenty-seventh anniversary of Bill's death. Bury me next to Bill."

CHAPTER THREE

Supporting the Central Idea

Poor Irving! He wants a nice, fuzzy, somewhat vague relationship, but Cathy wants specifics. She wants Irving to explain *why* he had a great time, to elaborate upon *what* was great about it. We're often the same way, aren't we? If we ask a friend how he or she liked a movie, we're not usually satisfied with answers like "Great!" or "Yuck!" We want to know specifically *why* the person liked or disliked it. Was it the plot or the acting or the special effects or the quality of the popcorn that caused our friend to react in a certain way? The more specific our friend can be, the more he or she will help us to decide whether we want to see the film too.

The same is true of responses to other media, such as novels and television, or to public issues, such as elections or gun control or capital punishment. The more specific information we have on these issues, the better informed our decisions will be.

In the same way, the more you can support your topic sentence or your thesis statement with specific information, the more convincing your writing will be. The most common types of support are brief or extended examples, statistics, and expert opinion or testimony.

Brief Examples

From Personal Experience

One of the most interesting and convincing ways to support your ideas is by relating brief examples drawn from your own personal experience. When we are discussing issues casually with acquaintances, we just naturally share our own experiences. Note how several brief examples are used in the following paragraph to support its central idea.

> People, at least the ones in my town, seem to have become ruder as the population has increased. Twice yesterday drivers came up behind me and gestured rudely even though I was driving ten miles per hour over the speed limit. The other day, as my friend and I were sitting on the seawall watching the sunset and listening to the ocean waves, a rollerblader with a boom box going full blast sat down next to us. When we politely asked him to turn off his radio, he cursed at us and skated off. Everyday I see perfectly healthy people parking in spaces reserved for the handicapped, smokers lighting up in no-smoking areas and refusing to leave when asked, and people shoving their way into lines at movie theaters and grocery stores.

Personal examples are usually not enough to prove a point, but they do help to illustrate your ideas and make your writing more specific and interesting. In fact, good writing is always moving from the general to the specific, with the emphasis on the specific, and the use of brief examples is one of the most effective ways of keeping your writing interesting, convincing, and informative. Notice how the lack of examples in the following paragraph results in uninteresting, lackluster writing.

There are a lot of animals to be found in Carlsbad. They come in all sizes and shapes. There are all kinds of birds and other animals besides dogs and cats.

Now let's see if it can be improved with the addition of brief examples.

The typical yard in Carlsbad is visited by a wide variety of animals. Birds, especially, are present in abundance. House finches and sparrows flit through the trees and search the ground for seeds. Mockingbirds sing day and night, claiming their territory. The feisty and mischievous scrub jays, with their blue plumage, raid the food set out for cats. The homely California towhee, whose call sounds like a squeaky wheel, rustles among the fallen leaves looking for insects. And the exotic and mysterious ruby-throated hummingbirds go from flower to flower, searching for nectar, or visit feeders hung out for them. At night the slow-witted possum rambles about, getting into garbage cans and dog dishes. The elegant and clever raccoons compete with the possums. Occasionally one can sense that a skunk has visited someone's yard. In some places, bands of escaped domestic rabbits can be seen frolicking and raiding gardens. Lizards and snakes ply the underbrush, searching for insects and small rodents. If one is observant and lucky, one can experience a multitude of critters right in the backyard.

As you can see, the many brief, specific examples in this paragraph improve it immensely, giving it texture, color, and interest. They also make the writing believable. Any reader would easily be convinced that this writer knows what he is talking about and has taken the time to observe the animals in Carlsbad carefully and to report them accurately.

From Other Sources

Brief examples from other sources are quite similar to brief personal examples or anecdotes. They may come from places such as books, magazines, television, films, or lectures, or they may come from the experiences of people you know. Like personal examples, they make your abstract ideas and arguments concrete and therefore convincing.

Here are some brief examples from recent news broadcasts that were offered in support of a gun control bill:

Larry and Sharon Ellingsen were driving home from their 29th wedding anniversary party in Oakland, California, when a passing driver on the freeway sent a bullet through their window, killing Mr. Ellingsen instantly.

Mildred Stanfield, a 78-year-old church organist from quiet Broad Ripple, Indiana, was shot twice in the chest at a bus stop when she tried to stop a 15-year-old boy from stealing her purse.

Cesar Sandoval, a 6-year-old kindergartener, was shot in the head while riding home on a country school bus in New Haven, Connecticut. He and six classmates were caught in drug-related crossfire among three teenagers.

Extended Examples

From Personal Experience

Extended examples from personal experience are longer, more detailed narratives of events that have involved you or people you know. Sometimes several brief examples just won't have the emotional impact that an extended example will. Sometimes people need to hear the *full* story of something that happened to a real person to really understand the point you are trying to make. Suppose, for instance, that you are writing about the senseless violence that seems to be occurring more and more frequently in our society today. You could illustrate that violence with several brief examples, or you could emphasize its heartlessness and brutality with an extended example such as the following:

> The senseless, brutal violence that we read about in the newspapers every day seems very distant from the average person, but it is really not far away at all. In fact, it can strike any of us without any warning—just as it struck my uncle Silas last week. After having dinner with his wife and two children, Silas had driven to the Texaco gas station at the corner of Vista Way and San Marcos Drive, where he was working part-time to earn extra money for a down payment on a house. Some time around 11:00 p.m., two young men carrying Smith and Wesson 38's approached him and demanded money. Uncle Silas was a good, brave man, but he was also a realistic person. He knew when to cooperate, and that's just what he did. He opened the cash register and the safe, then handed the intruders the keys to his new truck. They shot him in the head anyway.

Wouldn't you agree that the above extended example carries an emotional impact that brief examples might not carry? This anecdote might be used in a pro–gun control essay or even in an anti–gun control essay (Uncle Silas should have had his own gun). Or it could be part of an essay on capital punishment. In any case, it would add dramatic interest to a piece of writing. As you can see, examples of personal experience can be brief, perhaps only one sentence long, or extended, taking up several paragraphs.

From Other Sources

Extended examples taken from magazines, newspapers, books, or newscasts can also provide dramatic and persuasive support for your papers. Professional writers know the effect that extended examples can have on the reader, so they use such examples frequently. Notice how Ellen Goodman, a nationally known writer, uses the following extended example in an article debating the right of people to commit suicide:

> It is certain that Peter Rosier wouldn't be on trial today if he hadn't been on television two years ago. If he hadn't told all of Fort Myers, Florida, that "I administered something to terminate her life."

His wife Patricia, after all, a woman whose lung cancer had spread to 2
her other organs, had told everyone that she intended to commit suicide.
Indeed she planned her death as a final elaborate production.

Perhaps it was a dramatic attempt to control, or shape, or choose the 3
terms of her death. Perhaps it was an attempt to win some perverse victory over her cancer. Either way, Patricia Rosier, forty-three, picked the
date, the time, even the wine for her last meal. She picked out the pills
and she swallowed them.

Death, however, didn't play the accommodating role that had been 4
scripted for it. While the Rosier children slept in the next room, the deep
coma induced by twenty Seconal pills began to lighten. Her husband,
Peter, a pathologist, went desperately searching for morphine. And then,
as he said a year later, he "administered something."

—*Ellen Goodman,* Making Sense
© 1989 by the Boston Globe Newspaper Co./
Washington Post Writers Group. Reprinted with permission.

The details of Patricia Rosier's death, particularly the descriptions of the cancer that had
spread throughout her body and of her careful plans to take her own life, help the reader
to understand the complexity of the decision that Peter Rosier had to make. Is he guilty of
murder? Should he have ignored his wife's desire to avoid a painful death by cancer? In the
face of detailed, real experience, answering such questions is not easy.

EXERCISE Choose one of the following sentences and support it with several brief examples. Try to
provide at least three examples. Then choose another of the sentences and support it with
one extended example.

1. I like to go to the fair because of all the interesting attractions there.

2. My brother [or sister] is sometimes unfair.

3. My best friend and I have done some pretty crazy things.

4. My weekends are usually full of activities.

5. One day last week nothing seemed to go right.

6. Used imported compact cars are often the best choice for students.

7. Some banks offer a wide variety of services.

8. School cafeterias should meet the nutritional needs of all students.

9. Traveling by motorcycle has its advantages.

10. The computer is a useful tool for college students.

Statistics

Examples are very effective ways to support your ideas, but sometimes examples just aren't enough. Sometimes you need support that is more objective and measurable than an example. Sometimes you need support that covers more situations than one or even several examples could possibly cover. At times like these, statistics are the perfect support. In fact, if statistics are used fairly and correctly and are drawn from reliable sources, they are just about the most credible and effective type of support. We are impressed, perhaps overly impressed, when a writer can cite clear numbers to support an argument. Notice how the editorial writer Joseph Perkins uses statistics in his article about the effect TV violence has on young people:

> In fact, according to a study by the American Psychological Associa-   1
> tion, the average American child will view 8,000 murders and 100,000
> other acts of violence before finishing elementary school. The average
> 27 hours a week kids spend watching TV—much of it violent—makes
> them more prone to aggressive and violent behavior as adolescents and
> adults.
>
> Of course, TV executives have known this for a long time. One of the   2
> most comprehensive studies of the impact of violent TV was commis-
> sioned by CBS back in 1978. It found that teenage boys who watched
> more hours of violent TV than average before adolescence were commit-
> ting such violent crimes as rape and assault at a rate 49 percent higher
> than boys who watched fewer than average hours of violent TV.
>
> —*Joseph Perkins, "It's a Prime-Time Crime"*

As the above paragraphs illustrate, statistics can be quite impressive. It is startling to read that the average child will view over 100,000 acts of violence before he or she leaves elementary school or that children spend an average of 27 hours per week watching television. Be aware, however, that statistics can also be misleading. How many of these acts of violence consist of Wile E. Coyote chasing the Road Runner in Saturday morning cartoons? Is there any difference between that kind of violence and the violence found in police shows or murder mysteries?

EXERCISE   Choose one of the states or some country and compose a paragraph that describes with statistics one of its characteristics. For instance, you might choose to describe its population, agriculture, or industry. This type of information is readily available in world atlases or in other reference works, such as the *Encyclopædia Britannica*.

Expert Opinion or Testimony

Another kind of support that can be quite convincing is information from or statements by authorities on the subject about which you are writing. Let's suppose that you are trying to decide whether to have your child vaccinated against the measles. You have heard other parents say that a measles vaccination can harm a child, but you have never really known any parents who said their own children were harmed. So what do you do? Probably you call your pediatrician and ask for her expert opinion. After all, she is the one who has studied the field and who has vaccinated hundreds, perhaps thousands, of children.

In the same way, if you are writing a paper about a constitutional issue—such as the relationship of the Second Amendment to the need for gun control—you might decide to consult the experts for their opinions. And who are they? Probably legal scholars, political scientists, and even Supreme Court justices. Of course, you won't call these people on the phone; instead, you'll use quotations that you have found in articles and books from your college library. Here is an example of one such use of expert testimony:

> Parents must strive to find alternatives to the physical punishment of children. Almost every effect of corporal punishment is negative. Dr. Bruno Bettelheim, famous psychologist and professor at the University of Chicago, writes, "Punishment is a traumatic experience not only in itself but also because it disappoints the child's wish to believe in the benevolence of the parent, on which his sense of security rests."

If you do use expert opinion or testimony, don't believe everything you read too easily. When choosing authorities, you should consider not only their expertise, but also their reputations for such qualities as integrity, honesty, and credibility. Also, you should determine whether other experts in the same field disagree with the expert whose opinion you have cited. After all, if the experts don't agree, testimony from just one of them won't be very convincing. In fact, since experts often *do* disagree, it is a good idea to use expert testimony only *in combination with* the other types of support discussed in this chapter.

Combining Types of Support

Combining the different types of support is a very effective way to develop your ideas. Rarely will you find professional writers relying only on examples or statistics or expert testimony to support what they have to say. Instead, the more convincing writers provide many different types of support to make their point. Usually, the better and wider the support you use, the better your chance of persuading your reader.

The following excerpt from an article on cheating appeared in the *Los Angeles Times*. Examine it for each type of support discussed in this chapter.

Cheating, studies show, is pervasive. It involves students struggling for A's and admission to prestigious graduate schools as well as those flirting with academic failure.

A landmark survey of 6,000 students in 31 of the country's prestigious colleges and universities two years ago found that nearly 70% had cheated—if all manner of minor infractions were taken into account. The figure approached 80% for non–honor code schools and 60% for those with codes. . . .

The move back to honor codes is symptomatic of a larger change on college campuses, said Gary Pavela, president of the National Center for Academic Integrity, a consortium of 60 colleges and universities collaborating on issues involving honor codes, student ethics and academic integrity.

"All across the country, college administrators are beginning to take back authority that they gave up to students in the 60's and 70's," he said. "But the area of academic integrity is the only one where authority is still moving toward the students. . . ."

In 1976, 152 cadets were kicked out of the U.S. Military Academy for cheating on an exam. After a long investigation, 98 were reinstated the following year. In 1984, 19 Air Force Academy seniors were suspended for cheating on a physics exam, and cadet honor boards' handling of academic cheating was temporarily halted.

The most excruciating cheating affair in the history of the military service schools is still being played out on the stately campus of the U.S. Naval Academy at Annapolis. There, a panel of senior officers appointed by the Secretary of the Navy is hearing the last cases of as many as 133 midshipmen involved in cheating on an electrical engineering examination in December, 1992.

From The Los Angeles Times, *April 3, 1994, E1.*
Reprinted by permission of Rudy Abramson.

Writing Introductions and Conclusions

So far in this chapter, we have been discussing how to support your ideas. In many ways, however, how you introduce and conclude your paper is as important as how you support it. In the next few pages, we will discuss some strategies you can use to write effective introductions and conclusions.

The Introductory Paragraph

As we all know, first impressions can be deceptive, but they can also be of great importance. The opening paragraph of a paper provides the first impressions of the essay and of the writer. Thus, it is one of the most important paragraphs of your essay. Your introductory paragraph, serves a number of important purposes:

- It gains the attention of your reader in the lead-in.
- It informs your reader about such details as the background of your subject and the purpose of your essay.
- It gives the reader some idea of you, the writer, particularly through its tone.
- It presents the thesis statement and often the plan or organization of your essay.

The Lead-in

The lead-in generally consists of the first several sentences of the introduction. It may take any number of forms.

A General Statement

One of the most common ways of developing the introduction is to begin with a general statement and then follow it with ever more particular or specific statements leading to your thesis statement. This introductory strategy is sometimes referred to as a *funnel introduction* because, like a funnel, it is broad at the opening and narrow at the bottom. The following brief introduction from a student essay follows the general-to-particular pattern.

general statement	When disaster strikes, American people respond with their good hearts and numerous organized systems to help families cope with the disaster and its effects. There is beauty in a neighbor's heartfelt response to a disaster. My children and
specific thesis	I discovered just how much caring and assistance Americans will help families with when a disaster strikes.

Here is another general-to-particular introduction. Note that the thesis in this introduction presents two particular points on which the paper will focus.

general statement	Some time around the middle of November, about half the population seems to begin griping about the "secularization" of Christmas. They become nostalgic for some old, ideal, traditional Christmas that may never have existed. They fume about artificial trees and plastic creches. However, P. H. Terzian, in an article entitled "A Commercial Christmas Is Not So Crass," states that these grouches are wrongheaded, and I agree. Terzian and I feel that the Christmas spirit is alive and well for

specific
thesis

> several reasons: Christmas has always been a healthy mixture of the sacred and profane, and it has always been about joyfully getting, giving, and receiving.

A Question

Many writers open their essays with a question that is meant to attract the interest of the reader. Sometimes writers use a *rhetorical question*—that is, a question for which no answer is expected because the intended answer is obvious. Here is a rhetorical question: "Should we allow child abuse to continue?" Obviously, the answer to this question is "No." Even though the answer is obvious, a writer might open an essay with such a question to make the reader wonder why s/he is asking it and to draw the reader into the essay. Other times a writer might open an essay with a question that requires an answer—and the need to hear the answer keeps the reader reading. Here is a student's introductory paragraph that begins with a question:

question

> Is Tipper Gore overreacting? In her article "Curbing the Sexploitation Industry," Gore emphasizes the dangers posed for our children by what she calls the sexploitation industry. She claims that entertainment producers do not take our children into consideration when they present violent material. She says we should be concerned about the mental health of our children and the dignity of women. I do not think she is overreacting at all. Our society is facing a serious threat from the

specific
thesis

> sexploitation industry: TV networks show excessive sex scenes, movie producers make films with excessive graphic violence, and rock recordings contain explicit sexual lyrics.

An Anecdote or Brief Story

We all enjoy stories. For most of us, reading about real people in real situations is far more convincing and interesting than reading about general ideas. For that reason, opening an essay with a short description of a person, place, or event can be an effective way of grabbing your reader's attention. The following introduction opens with a short anecdote:

anecdote

> I found a *Penthouse* magazine in my twelve-year-old's room last week, and I panicked. I recalled that Ted Bundy, who roamed the country mutilating, murdering, and raping, had said right before his execution that he had been influenced by pornography. Was my son on his way to a life of violent crime? Probably not. But a recent article, "Ted Bundy Shows Us the

Crystallizing Effect of Pornography," raises some serious concerns. We need to be more vigilant about what our children (and our fellow citizens of all ages) are experiencing in all of the media, and we need to make our lawmakers aware of our

specific thesis

concern. However, we need to accomplish these missions without weakening the First Amendment to the Constitution and without harming the world of art.

A Quotation

A good quotation from someone connected with your topic, from an article you're writing about, or from an expert on your subject can be a good way of opening your introduction. Or you might look up a famous quotation on your subject in a book such as *Bartlett's Familiar Quotations*. Notice how the following student paragraph moves from a quotation to a specific thesis statement:

question

Martin Luther King, Jr. once said, "I have a dream that my four little children will one day live in a nation where they will not be judged by the color of their skin, but by the content of their character." Dr. King would certainly be disappointed if he could read a recent article by Richard Cohen in the *Washington Post*, entitled "A Generation of Bigots Comes of Age." The author claims that we are seeing an increase in bigotry, especially from the generation just coming of age (those in their twenties). He cites a great deal of information and statistics from the Anti-Defamation League and from a Boston polling

specific thesis

firm. I believe Mr. Cohen because lately I have experienced an increase in prejudice at work, at school, at shopping malls, and at many other places.

A Striking Statement or Fact

"Coming soon to your local cable system: VTV, violent television, 24 hours a day of carnage and mayhem." This quotation was the lead-in for a recent article on the amount of violence children see on television and the effects it may be having on them. Later in the article, the writer pointed out that one hundred acts of violence occur on television each hour. This fact could also be used as a striking lead-in to your essay. Once you have captured the attention of your reader through a strategy like this, s/he will tend to keep reading. Here is an introduction based on the above quotation:

striking statement

"Coming soon to your local cable system: VTV, violent television, 24 hours a day of carnage and mayhem." So writes Joseph Perkins in his article "It's a Prime-Time Crime." Perkins cites the American Psychological Association and the quarterly journal *The Public Interest* to support his idea that the enormous amount of violence viewed by American children may be doing them irreparable harm. I find the overwhelming evidence that violence on TV is making children overly aggressive and

specific thesis

is having a negative effect on their mental health quite convincing, especially because so many of my own observations confirm that evidence.

The Concluding Paragraph

Final impressions are as important as initial ones, especially if you want to leave your reader with a sense of completeness and confidence in you. Although the content of your conclusion will depend on what you have argued or presented in your essay, here are some suggestions as to what you might include:

- A restatement of your thesis, presented in words and phrases different from those used in your introduction
- A restatement of your supporting points, presented in words and phrases different from those used in your body paragraphs
- Predictions or recommendations about your proposals or arguments
- Solutions to the problems you have raised
- A quotation or quotations that support your ideas
- A reference to an anecdote or story that appeared in your introduction

Here are some concluding paragraphs that use some of these strategies:

A restatement of the main points
A prediction or recommendation

The following is a concluding paragraph from an article on the effects of TV violence on children. The author summarizes his main points and also offers a recommendation.

> Given the overwhelming evidence that violent TV has deleterious effects on children, that it increases the level of violence throughout American society, it hardly seems unreasonable that the government ask that [the] TV industry tone down its violent programming. Those who find that request objectionable should forfeit their privileged use of public airwaves.
>
> —*Joseph Perkins, "It's a Prime-Time Crime"*

A solution to a problem that has been raised

Here is a conclusion from a rather unusual essay. Its thesis is that laws allowing men but not women to go topless at the beach are discriminatory and reflect our male-dominated culture. It offers two possible solutions to the problem.

It was not too long ago that the law also attempted to shield children from pregnant teachers. But the Supreme Court held pregnancy no grounds for a forced leave of absence. Another court has ruled that unmarried pregnant students cannot be excluded from public schools—not unless unmarried expectant fathers are also excluded. It is time for the same equality to be applied to bathing attire. Whether that is accomplished by allowing all people to go topless or by requiring men to wear tops, the end result will be the same: discarding one more premise of a male-defined society.

A restatement of the main points
A quotation that supports the ideas
The following conclusion to a student essay sums up the writer's ideas on her subject and then presents an effective quotation from the author of the article that she is responding to.

Diversity, in America, is supposed to be good. This country was formed for freedoms like religion, speech, and sexual preference. America was formed for all ethnic groups and all traditions. When a certain group thinks that they are above all, that is when the problems begin. It is important to educate others on your background and to celebrate your heritage, to a certain extent. It is also important to learn about other cultures so that we feel comfortable and not threatened by others. As Schoenberger says, "I would much prefer them to hate or distrust me because of something I've done, instead of hating me on the basis of prejudice."

A restatement of the main points
A reference to an anecdote or story from the introduction
A solution to a problem that has been raised
This conclusion is drawn from the article "Getting to Know about You and Me," which appears later in this chapter. Its introduction tells the story of the author's being invited to join the Diversity Committee at her high school, an invitation she declined. The conclusion refers again to that invitation.

I'm now back at school, and I plan to apply for the Diversity Committee. I'm going to get up and tell the whole school about my religion and the tradition I'm proud of. I see now how important it is to celebrate your heritage and to educate others about it. I can no longer take for granted that everyone knows about my religion, or that I know about theirs. People who are suspicious when they find out I'm Jewish usually don't know much about Judaism. I would much prefer them to hate or distrust me because of something I've done, instead of them hating me on the basis of prejudice.

EXERCISE   Examine the articles you have read in Chapters 1 and 2 to determine what types of introductions and conclusions you find in them. Identify those that fit into the types discussed above and explain why those that do not fit into those types are nevertheless effective. (Remember that the introductions in many of these articles may consist of several brief paragraphs rather than one longer paragraph.)

Readings

As you read each of the following selections, pay particular attention to the type of support each writer uses and to the introduction and conclusion of each article.

Male Fixations

DAVE BARRY

Before You Read

1. Are you familiar with Dave Barry? If you are not, you may be in for a surprise. Ask some friends or other students who he is.

2. What could the title "Male Fixations" possibly refer to? What is a fixation?

Most guys believe that they're supposed to know how to fix things. This is a responsibility that guys have historically taken upon themselves to compensate for the fact that they never clean the bathroom. A guy can walk into a bathroom containing a colony of commode fungus so advanced that it is registered to vote, but the guy would never dream of cleaning it, because he has to keep himself rested in case a Mechanical Emergency breaks out.   1

For example, let's say that one day his wife informs him that the commode has started making a loud groaning noise, like it's about to have a baby commode. This is when the guy swings into action. He strides in, removes the tank cover, peers down into the area that contains the mystery commode parts, and then, drawing on tens of thousands of years of guy mechanical understanding, announces that *there is nothing wrong with the commode.*   2

At least that's how I handle these things. I never actually fix anything. I blame this on tonsillitis. I had tonsillitis in the ninth grade, and I missed   3 some school, and apparently on one of the days I missed, they herded the guys into the auditorium and explained to them about things like carburetors, valves, splines, gaskets, ratchets, grommets, "dado joints," etc. Because some guys actually seem to understand this stuff. One time in college my roommate, Rob, went into his room all alone with a Volvo transmission, opened his toolbox, disassembled the transmission to the point where he appeared to be working on *individual transmission molecules*, then put it all back together, and it *worked*. Whereas I would still be fumbling with the latch on the toolbox.

So I'm intimidated by mechanical guys. When we got our boat trailer, the salesman told me, one guy to another, that I should "re-pack" the "bearings" every so many miles. He said this as though all guys come out of the womb with this instinctive ability to re-pack a bearing. So I nodded my head knowingly, as if to suggest that, sure, I generally re-pack a couple dozen bearings every morning before breakfast just to keep my testosterone level from raging completely out of control. The truth is that I've never been 100 percent sure what a bearing is. But I wasn't about to admit this, for fear that the salesman would laugh at me and give me a noogie.

The main technique I use for disguising my mechanical tonsillitis is to deny that there's ever anything wrong with anything. We'll be driving somewhere, and my wife, Beth, who does not feel that mechanical problems represent a threat to her manhood, will say, "Do you hear that grinding sound in the engine?" I'll cock my head for a second and make a sincere-looking frowny face, then say no, I don't hear any grinding sound. I'll say this even if I have to shout so Beth can hear me over the grinding sound; even if a hole has appeared in the hood and a large, important-looking engine part is sticking out and waving a sign that says HELP.

"That's the grommet bearing," I'll say. "It's supposed to do that."

Or, at home, Beth will say, "I think there's something wrong with the hall light switch." So I'll stride manfully into the hall, where volley-ball sized sparks are caroming off the bodies of recently electrocuted houseguests, and I'll say, "It seems to be working fine now!"

Actually, I think this goes beyond mechanics. I think guys have a natural tendency to act as though they're in control of the situation even when they're not. I bet that, seconds before the *Titanic* slipped beneath the waves, there was some guy still in his cabin, patiently explaining to his wife that it was *perfectly normal* for all the furniture to be sliding up the walls. And I bet there was a guy on the *Hindenburg* telling his wife that, oh, sure, you're going to get a certain amount of flames in a dirigible. Our federal leadership is basically a group of guys telling us, hey, *no problem* with this budget deficit thing, because what's happening is the fixed-based long-term sliding-scale differential appropriation forecast has this projected revenue growth equalization sprocket, see, which is connected via this Gramm-Rudman grommet oscillation module to . . .

From Dave Barry, Dave Barry Talks Back. © *1991 by Dave Barry.*
Reprinted by permission of Crown Publishers, Inc.

After You Read

Work with other students to develop responses to these questions or to compare responses that you have already prepared.

1. Now that you've read the article, explain the male fixation referred to in the title.

2. What is Barry's point about this male fixation?

3. What does Barry mean when he says that he has "mechanical tonsillitis"?

4. What is Dave Barry's thesis idea? Identify any sentences that seem to express it.

5. What types of support does Dave Barry use? Identify any brief or extended examples. Does he use any statistics or expert opinions?

6. Examine the introduction and conclusion to this article. How does each accomplish its purpose?

Go Ahead, Try to Define Your "Self" in One Descriptive Word

JAMES BARRON

Before You Read

1. Look at the title. What does it suggest that the essay will discuss?

2. Take a moment to decide what single word best sums up who you are.

Is it possible to define oneself in just a single word? Can one sort out all   1
the complicated, complicating factors of public and private life, measure all the facets of one's personality, cast off what's extraneous and then name an essential, identifying characteristic?

Without a lot of soul-searching, without reading social philosophers   2
like Martin Buber (whose writings included the book "I and Thou") or paying homage to bubble-gum bands like the Monkees ("I'm a

Believer"), some answers come to mind quickly: the Rev. Jesse Jackson's trademark, "I am somebody." Or Cicero's "I am a Roman citizen." Or Descartes' "I think, therefore I am." Or the poet Robert Lowell's "I myself am hell."

But even in the fast-forward '90s, when everything from cooking times in the kitchen to sound bites on television have been compressed to a minimum, narrowing one's identity to a single word is still a difficult order. Perhaps that is why the results are so thought-provoking. 3

When asked what word best defined her, Karen Finley, the performance artist whose work takes sexual and political issues to raw and graphic extremes, chose "normal." 4

"I'm your average American," she declared. "I believe in freedom of expression, I work for a living, I've got credit cards, I watch 'Jeopardy,' I screen my phone calls and I can't stand slow drivers." 5

If she seems to be casting herself against type, she is hardly alone. Gov. Mario Cuomo of New York, elected as a leader, settled on "participant." 6

"I am a part of the whole," he said, "evolving with the rest of us." 7

Martina Navratilova chose none of the labels by which she could be identified—tennis star, celebrity, lesbian. Instead she chose a word that might surprise some of her opponents: "kind." 8

"Because I am," she said. "I'm always very aware of people around me and always try to make them feel better." 9

And if you ask 1,136 adults to describe themselves in only one word as a New York Times/CBS News poll did last year, you'll get about 200 different answers. 10

While this open-ended question posed during telephone interviews may not yield the kind of hard-and-fast data that a pre-election survey or poll about economic confidence does, it provides a compelling sociological snapshot. 11

Generally, the respondents seemed to resist labeling themselves as members of a "special interest group" or easily identifiable minority group, avoiding stereotyping and choosing either a broader affiliation or a narrower, more personal response. 12

For example, none of the 97 black respondents said "black," and none of the 967 whites said that being white was the defining fact of their lives. Instead, the word given most often in the survey was "American." Fully 10 percent of the people questioned, by far the largest single group, came up with that one word. 13

They were evenly distributed across the country, in large- and medium-sized cities, suburbs and rural towns, indicating, perhaps, that "the 14 cultural glue is stronger and thicker than is often thought," said Michael Marsden, a dean and popular culture expert at Northern Michigan University. And discussing national identity and patriotism is, he said, "déclassé."

Yet, he said: "Maybe when you scratch the surface—what are you at the core?—'American' is what it is." 15

That is what some people in the survey who chose "American" said when they were re-interviewed later. Constance Ploss, an unemployed real-estate broker from Manchester, N.H., said the first thing that came to mind when she heard the question was her state's slogan, "Live free or die." 16

But later she had second thoughts. "Maybe," she said, "I should have said something more about being a woman." 17

Maybe fame changes the parameters of self-image. In a score of interviews with well-known people, the word "American" didn't come up. Sen. Bob Dole, the Senate minority leader, came the closest, with "Kansan." "Like Dorothy in 'The Wizard of Oz,'" he said, "I've never forgotten where I came from." 18

But not everyone was impressed with this kind of patriotism. "I'm always stunned when people describe themselves as 'American,'" said Peter Jennings, the ABC News anchor, who is a Canadian (and who said his word was "impassioned"). "It seems not to say an awful lot. 'American' is where you begin." 19

Marsden agreed. "The fact that we can identify as Americans takes away the threat of diversity," he said. "The existence of a unifying concept allows us to be different in greater measure. I may be different than you, but I'm not threatened by that because I know that at the heart of it, we share the same values." 20

After "American," no one word was mentioned by more than 4 percent of those in the poll. "Average," which may have been a sort of non-answer for people who couldn't think of a more descriptive off-the-cuff answer or felt pressed for time in the telephone interviews, was next overall, with 4 percent of the total (but only 2 percent of the women). "Me" or "myself" also drew 4 percent. Three percent—including 9 percent of the blacks, but only 2 percent of the whites—said they were "concerned." 21

Women were more likely to say they were a "parent" first and foremost: 4 percent, vs. 1 percent of the men. Women were also more likely to describe themselves as "caring," or say they were "survivors." Men were more likely to mention where they stood on the economic ladder 22 ("rich," "poor," or "middle class"), and to name a political philosophy ("liberal" or "conservative"). No one mentioned marital status as the defining characteristic.

Religion or faith was cited by a greater percentage of women than of men; over all, 2 percent of the respondents fell into this category. For the most part, they identified themselves as Christians or "born again."   23

Some may be looking at the world through rose-colored glasses. Beyond those most frequently chosen words, positive responses tended to outweigh negative ones. Seven said "optimist" or "optimistic," one person was "joyous" and a third was "radiant." Jackie Vienticinque of Providence, R.I., gave "helpful" as her answer.   24

About 20 others defined themselves by their work or by its effects on them. One person's word was "workaholic" (17 others said "hard-working"). There was one "truck driver" and four "taxpayers."   25

About 200 in the poll could not come up with a word. And Michael Kinsley, who writes several hundred words for the *New Republic* maga-zine every week and utters several hundred more on CNN five nights a week, would not choose one, declaring, "I just think that's a stupid question."   26

For those who did answer, it was certainly a challenge. "You cannot reduce yourself to one, it's too complicated," said Suzanne Keller, a soci-ologist at Princeton University. "People really feel multiple. They have multiple poses and attitudes and roles, and one is no more important than the next. If they're forced to choose between family and work and leisure roles, which are not even roles but personas, they can't, really, because they live a multifaceted, multitudinous life, not single track."   27

Author Margaret Atwood seemed to feel the same way when asked to define herself in one word. She picked "indescribable," warning that: "One must always resist the tyranny of adjectives."   28

After You Read

Work with other students to develop responses to these questions or to compare respons-es that you have already prepared.

1. Would you define yourself the same way as any of the people in the survey defined themselves?

2. Did you find yourself changing your idea of how you would define yourself as you read the article?

3. Use your own words to express the thesis idea of this essay. Then examine the essay to see if any sentence(s) express that thesis.

4. Identify the types of support used in this article.

5. Examine the introduction and conclusion, explaining how each contributes to the article.

Getting to Know about You and Me

CHANA SCHOENBERGER

Before You Read

1. What do you know about religions or denominations other than your own?

2. Do you feel uncomfortable around people who are different from you? Have you ever felt uncomfortable around any *particular* group of people?

3. What does the title suggest will be the focus of this article?

As a religious holiday approaches, students at my high school who will be celebrating the holiday prepare a presentation on it for an assembly. The Diversity Committee, which sponsors the assemblies to increase religious awareness, asked me last spring if I would help with the presentation on Passover, the Jewish holiday that commemorates the Exodus from Egypt. I was too busy with other things, and I never got around to helping. I didn't realize then how important those presentations really are, or I definitely would have done something.

This summer I was one of 20 teens who spent five weeks at the University of Wisconsin at Superior studying acid rain with a National Science Foundation Young Scholars program. With such a small group in such a small town, we soon became close friends and had a good deal of fun together. We learned about the science of acid rain, went on field trips, found the best and cheapest restaurants in Superior and ate in them frequently to escape the lousy cafeteria food. We were a happy, bonded group.

Represented among us were eight religions: Jewish, Roman Catholic, Muslim, Hindu, Methodist, Mormon, Jehovah's Witness and Lutheran. It was amazing, given the variety of backgrounds, to see the ignorance of some of the smartest young scholars on the subject of other religions.

On the first day, one girl mentioned that she had nine brothers and sisters. "Oh, are you Mormon?" asked another girl, who I knew was a

Mormon herself. The first girl, shocked, replied, "No, I dress normal!" She thought Mormon was the same as Mennonite, and the only thing she knew about either religion was the Mennonites don't, in her opinion, "dress normal."

My friends, ever curious about Judaism, asked me about everything from our basic theology to food preferences. "How come, if Jesus was a Jew, Jews aren't Christian?" my Catholic roommate asked me in all seriousness. Brought up in a small Wisconsin town, she had never met a Jew before, nor had she met people from most of the other "strange" religions (anything but Catholic or mainstream Protestant). Many of the other kids were the same way.

"Do you all still practice animal sacrifices?" a girl from a small town in Minnesota asked me once. I said no, laughed, and pointed out that this was the 20th century, but she had been absolutely serious. The only Jews she knew were the ones from the Bible.

Nobody was deliberately rude or anti-Semitic, but I got the feeling that I was representing the entire Jewish people through my actions. I realized that many of my friends would go back to their small towns thinking that all Jews liked Dairy Queen Blizzards and grilled cheese sandwiches. After all, that was true of all the Jews they knew (in most cases, me and the only other Jewish young scholar, period).

The most awful thing for me, however, was not the benign ignorance of my friends. Our biology professor had taken us on a field trip to the EPA field site where he worked, and he was telling us about the project he was working on. He said that they had to make sure the EPA got its money's worth from the study—he "wouldn't want them to get Jewed."

I was astounded. The professor had a doctorate, various other degrees and seemed to be a very intelligent man. He apparently had no idea that he had just made an anti-Semitic remark. The other Jewish girl in the group and I debated whether or not to say something to him about it, and although we agreed we would, neither of us ever did. Personally, it made me feel uncomfortable. For a high-school student to tell a professor who taught her class that he was a bigot seemed out of place to me, even if he was one.

What scares me about that experience, in fact about my whole visit to Wisconsin, was that I never met a really vicious anti-Semite or a malignantly prejudiced person. Many of the people I met had been brought up to think that Jews (or Mormons or any other religion that's not mainstream Christian) were different and that difference was not good.

Difference, in America, is supposed to be good. We are expected—at least, I always thought we were expected—to respect each other's traditions. Respect requires some knowledge about people's backgrounds. Singing Christmas carols as a kid in school did not make me Christian, but it taught me to appreciate beautiful music and someone else's holiday. It's not necessary or desirable for all ethnic groups in America to assimilate into one traditionless mass. Rather, we all need to learn about other cultures so that we can understand one another and not feel threatened by others. 11

In the little multicultural universe that I live in, it's safe not to worry about explaining the story of Passover because if people don't hear it from me, they'll hear it some other way. Now I realize that's not true everywhere. 12

Ignorance was the problem I faced this summer. By itself, ignorance is not always a problem, but it leads to misunderstandings, prejudice and hatred. Many of today's problems involve hatred. If there weren't so much ignorance about other people's backgrounds, would people still hate each other as badly as they do now? Maybe so, but at least that hatred would be based on facts and not flawed beliefs. 13

I'm now back at school, and I plan to apply for the Diversity Committee. I'm going to get up and tell the whole school about my religion and the tradition I'm proud of. I see now how important it is to celebrate your heritage and to educate others about it. I can no longer take for granted that everyone knows about my religion, or that I know about theirs. People who are suspicious when they find out I'm Jewish usually don't know much about Judaism. I would much prefer them to hate or distrust me because of something I've done, instead of them hating me on the basis of prejudice. 14

After You Read

Work with other students to develop responses to these questions or to compare responses that you have already prepared.

1. What point is Schoenberger making in her references to the girl who responded that she "dressed normal" when she was asked if she was a Mormon?

2. What is her point about the professor who said he "wouldn't want [the EPA] to get Jewed"?

3. How would you express the thesis idea of this article? Use your own words. Then find any sentence(s) in the article that express that thesis.

4. Where does the introduction end? In what way does it introduce the article? Which paragraph(s) make up the conclusion? Why is it an effective conclusion?

5. What kind of support does Schoenberger use? Identify the different types of support that you see.

Writing Assignments

1. Dave Barry's article "Male Fixations" takes a humorous look at the behavior of some males who act as if they can fix everything. Can you think of any other group of people who have a particular fixation? For example, do mothers have fixations of their own? Do fathers? How about boyfriends, girlfriends, teachers, or some other group of people? Use appropriate support to develop an essay on the fixation(s) of one particular group. Introduce and conclude your essay with one of the types of introductions and conclusions discussed in this chapter.

2. In "Go Ahead, Try to Define Your 'Self' in One Descriptive Word," James Barron points out how difficult and thought-provoking it is to identify yourself with only one word. Write an essay in which you attempt to define yourself using one word. Your individual paragraphs should present different reasons that the word you have chosen defines you, and those reasons should be developed with appropriate support. Introduce and conclude your essay with one of the types of introductions and conclusions discussed in this chapter.

3. Another approach to "Go Ahead, Try to Define Your 'Self' in One Descriptive Word" would be to admit that one word is not enough. Write an essay in which you use two, three, or four terms to define yourself, devoting one paragraph to each term and developing each paragraph with appropriate support. Introduce and conclude your essay with one of the types of introductions and conclusions discussed in this chapter.

4. In her essay "Getting to Know about You and Me," Chana Schoenberger argues that widespread, often unintentional, religious intolerance exists in the United States. On a broader scale, diversity in various forms—religion, race, gender, sexual preference, and so forth—is often not very well tolerated in America. Compose an essay in which you explain the ways you and/or other people have experienced intolerance, whether as victim(s) or perpetrator(s). Use appropriate support to develop each paragraph of your essay, and introduce and conclude your essay with one of the types of introductions and conclusions discussed in this chapter.

Evaluating Sample Papers

Use the following checklist to determine which of the student essays on the next few pages is most effective.

1. Thesis Statement

Underline the thesis statement of the essay. Does it express a clear and specific central idea?

1   2   3   4   5   6

2. Introduction

Does the introduction clearly introduce the central idea of the writer's paper? Does it end with a thesis statement?

1   2   3   4   5   6

3. Topic Sentences

Underline the topic sentence of each paragraph. Does each one clearly state the central idea of its paragraph?

1   2   3   4   5   6

4. Support

Examine the supporting details in each paragraph. Are they specific and clear? Should they be more detailed, or should more support be included?

1   2   3   4   5   6

5. Conclusion

Does the conclusion adequately bring the essay to a close?

1   2   3   4   5   6

6. Sentence Structure

Do the sentences combine ideas that are related, using coordination and subordination when appropriate? Are there too many brief, choppy main clauses? (See the Sentence Combining section of this chapter for a discussion of subordination.)

1   2   3   4   5   6

7. Mechanics, Grammar, and Spelling

Does the paper contain a distracting number of these kinds of errors?

1   2   3   4   5   6

8. Overall Ranking of the Essay

1   2   3   4   5   6

The following essays were written in response to the assignments on page 86.

Student Essay 1

Getting me to describe myself in a few words is exceedingly hard to do. It reminds me of coloring a rainbow when I was a little child. The rainbow was to be colored with only three colors, but looking at a box of sixty-four crayons it was hard to choose which crayons to use. Well, I'm looking into my box of sixty-four crayons and chose the colors: loud-mouth, goofy, and mature. These colorful traits are an important part of my rainbow and describe who I am.

As a matter of fact, it is very simple to have the word "loud-mouth" describe me, because of all the predicaments it got me into. For example, a few of my friends and I decided to stay at a hotel for a few days and have some fun. On the last night, all of us were getting really loud, especially me. Suddenly we heard a knock at the door. I graciously answered it and saw the manager, who was warning us to keep the noise down. I completely agreed with her and apologized for us being rude. However, we forgot the fact to keep quiet and began to get extremely loud. Of course, I was the loudest of them all. Just then the manager came up with a security guard, asking us "to please leave the building." I really never thought that my mouth was that loud.

Sometimes, to make people laugh by acting goofy, is one of those things I'm good at. Just the other day, I was at my friend's house playing pool and suddenly I started to imitate Mel Brooks in the film *Life Stinks!* My friends were doubled over with laughter and almost to the point of crying. Actually, I'm well known to my friends and family for making them laugh at my interpretations of how some people dance. Now, I don't mean to offend anyone, but some people just can't dance. As I was saying, my imitation is so absurd that one time my mother was on the ground laughing, and then called her friends about what her talented daughter can do.

On the other hand, I can be mature and lady-like for when the situation calls for it. For instance, on Christmas Day, I dined with my grandparents at a "high class" restaurant. The problem was, was that there was no problem. I don't mean to brag, but I knew which fork was for the salad, not to keep your spoon in your bowl, etc. . . . I did not have one dilemma through the entire meal. Most people my age don't know the language of having manners or being mature, so that's why I believe it is an important trait.

Just like having to pick out a few colors in a box of sixty-four, similarly it's just as difficult to pick out a few describing traits about myself. Although, the ones I did pick made me feel really good about myself.

Student Essay 2

"Getting to Know about You and Me" by Chana Schoenberger shows how unaware people are about the differences in religions. Schoenberger says that because of this unawareness/ignorance, people tend to hate or distrust someone because of their background or religion. Schoenberger, a teen, was amazed at the ignorance of even the most intelligent of her fellow students.

Too many people try to force their religion on others. Ever had strange men in suits come to your front door selling their religion? Those men and going to church on a regular basis has made me aware of other religions. According to Schoenberger, "If there weren't so much ignorance about other people's backgrounds, people wouldn't hate each other as badly as they do now." This ignorance leads to prejudice and hatred. Many of society's problems are based on prejudice and hatred. As for those men who go door to door, I believe it is intolerable for people to try to force their religion on you. I understand that they want you to learn about their religion, but I do not like to be pushed or harassed into something I do not agree with. "If people were educated in other backgrounds, then hatred would be based on facts and not flawed beliefs," says Schoenberger.

I became a victim of religious intolerance in my own church. Some members of the church and I went on a weekend trip up north to "spread the word." Although I willingly went, I felt I was pressured into going. I felt as if I was one of those men selling my religion, which I disagree with very much. This incident has made me hesitant to go to church. Do not get me wrong, I know what I believe in I just do not like being pressured into things I do not want to do. My friend took a religious studies course at school, and she said the teacher tried to force his religion on the class. It is good to be proud of your background, but thinking it is best for all is intolerable.

Diversity, in America, is supposed to be good. This country was formed for freedoms like religion, speech, and sexual preference. America was formed for all ethnic groups and all traditions. When a certain group thinks that they are above all, that is when the problems begin. It is important to educate others on your background and to celebrate your heritage, to a certain extent. It is also important to learn about other cultures so that we feel comfortable and not threatened by others. As Schoenberger says, "I would much prefer them to hate or distrust me because of something I've done, instead of hating me on the basis of prejudice."

Student Essay 3

While reading Dave Barry's article "Male Fixations," I couldn't help but to think of my neighbor's who have different types of fixations. The fixations that I see in some of my neighbors are similar to Barry's because they seem to be know-it-alls who refuse to admit that they really don't know as much as they claim, they will be embarrassed at their mistakes, and go into a state of denial when proven wrong.

Many of my neighbors seems to have a know-it-all attitude when it comes to certain things, only later to learn that they really don't know much about what they were talking about. For example, my neighbor Gabe seems to know everything about the O.J. Simpson trial because he is always telling me what the defense team is going to do everyday in court with the prosecution's witnesses, only later to find that he was only guessing and didn't really know that much about it to begin with. Another example of a know-it-all neighbor is Bob. I remember the time that I had bought my computer, and Bob came over to my house to help get it set up because he believed that he was a computer expert. He said that to set up a computer was a basic thing and that anyone with half a brain should be able to set it up without having to use the enclosed instructions. After an hour of watching him getting frustrated and calling the machine a few choice words, I told him that we could finish it the next day. When he left I referred to the instructions and got the job done in a timely manner, and the next day I just thanked him for his help and gave him lots of credit.

Some of my neighbors seem to get embarrassed when they are wrong about something simple. One morning I went outside to move my car off the street so I wouldn't get fined by the street sweeper. My neighbor Peg was outside, and she told me that the steet sweeper wasn't coming by that day and that it would be crazy for me to move my car. I believed her and later found a ticket on my windshield from the street sweeper for not moving my car. Even though I told her that it was a simple mistake, she was extremely embarrassed about it for weeks to follow.

Finally, the best example of a neighbor going into a state of denial is a situation with Bob in which he just wouldn't accept his wrong verdict of a problem and wouldn't let himself be proved wrong. Even though my washer broke down really late one night, Bob was quick to be on the scene to give his opinion on the mechanics of my washer that wasn't draining. He quickly came to the conclusion that something was in the pipe blocking the drain hose. I took his advice to try to unplug it, but it had then occurred to me that there is a filter on the washer to prevent such a thing from happening. I suggested to him that the problem could be an electrical failure, but he thought that I was kidding around with him. After we unsuccessfully tried looking for the blockage, I broke down and called a repairman the next day. Although it turned out that there was a problem with a switch, Bob just does not accept the fact that he was wrong and goes on by saying that whatever was blocking the pipe had been cleared.

My neighbors are good hearted persons that are eager to please. I believe that they do have practical ideas on how to fix things, but sometimes they are not always correct. It seems that whenever something goes wrong at my house with anything mechanical, a neighbor is there to assist because it is the neighborly thing to do. I guess I just have to accept the fact that they may have an opinion about everything, be embarrassed at their mistakess, and not accept their wrong solutions to certain problems.

Sentence Combining
Using Subordination

In Chapter 2, you practiced using appropriate coordinating conjunctions in your sentences. When you use coordination, you are suggesting that the ideas in your sentences are all of equal importance. On the other hand, when you employ subordination, you indicate to your reader which ideas are more important than others. The subordinate ideas in a sentence are usually the ones of lesser importance. Look at the following pairs of simple statements.

I awoke from my nap.
A burglar was smashing the window in my back door.

The snow was falling lightly on the mountain road.
A huge truck barreled straight at us.

The professor stomped towards me and began to yell.
I would not stop talking.

A very dear friend recently sent me a baby alligator.
She lives in Pittsburgh.

As you can see, in each pair of sentences, one sentence contains much more important information than the other. In the first two pairs, the second sentences convey the more important ideas. In the last two pairs, the first sentences seem to be more important.

(Admittedly, deciding which sentences are more "important" can be rather subjective, yet you must attempt to make such distinctions when you combine related ideas.)

Subordinating Conjunctions and Relative Pronouns

One way to combine ideas is to write the less important information as a **subordinate clause**. Doing so will emphasize the relative importance of the ideas as well as clarify *how* the words are related. To write a subordinate clause, begin the clause with a **subordinator** (either a **subordinating conjunction** or a **relative pronoun**). Here is a list of subordinating conjunctions and relative pronouns that you can use to start subordinate clauses.

Subordinating Conjunctions			Relative Pronouns	
after	even though	until	that	who(ever)
although	if	when	which	whom(ever)
as	since	whenever		whose
as if	so that	where		
as long as	than	wherever		
because	though	while		
before	unless			

You can combine the above four pairs of sentences by using subordinators. Here is how the sentences look when the less important sentences are written as subordinate clauses. Each subordinate clause is underlined.

> ***When*** *I awoke from my nap, a burglar was smashing the window in my back door.*
> ***As*** *the snow was falling lightly on the mountain road, a huge truck barreled straight at us.*
> *The professor stomped toward me and began to yell **because** I would not stop talking.*
> *A very dear friend **who** lives in Pittsburgh recently sent me a baby alligator.*

As you can see, each subordinate clause begins with a subordinator that expresses the relationship between the main clause and the subordinate clause. Notice also that the subordinate clause can appear at the start, at the end, or in the middle of the sentence.

EXERCISE

Each of the following sentences is drawn from one of the reading selections in this chapter. Underline each subordinate clause and circle its subordinator.

Example: *(If) she seems to be casting herself against type, she is hardly alone.*

1. I'm always stunned when people describe themselves as American.

2. The fact that we can identify as Americans takes away the threat of diversity.

3. But even in the fast-forward '90s, when everything from cooking times in the kitchen to sound bites on television has been compressed to a minimum, narrowing one's identity to a single word is still a difficult order.

4. As a religious holiday approaches, students at my high school who will be celebrating the holiday prepare a presentation on it for an assembly.

5. This summer I was one of 20 teens who spent five weeks at the University of Wisconsin at Superior studying acid rain with a National Foundation Young Scholars program.

6. He apparently had no idea that he had just made an anti-Semitic remark.

7. Rather, we all need to learn about other cultures so that we can understand one another and not feel threatened by others.

8. If there weren't so much ignorance about other people's backgrounds, would people still hate each other as badly as they do now?

9. He said this as though all guys come out of the womb with this instinctive ability to re-pack a bearing.

10. So I'll stride manfully into the hall, where volley-ball sized sparks are caroming off the bodies of recently electrocuted houseguests, and I'll say, "It seems to be working fine now!"

Punctuating Subordinate Clauses

There are a few rules you need to know in order to punctuate sentences with subordinate clauses correctly.

1. Use a comma after a subordinate clause that precedes a main clause.

   Because I have a meeting in the morning, I will meet you in the afternoon.

2. In general, do not use a comma when the subordinate clause follows a main clause.

   I will meet you in the afternoon because I have a meeting in the morning.

3. Use commas to set off a subordinate clause beginning with *which, who, whom,* or *whose* if the information in the subordinate clause is not necessary to identify the word the clause refers to.

   Dave Barry, who is a very funny man, writes for the Miami Herald.
   (Because the information contained in the subordinate clause is not necessary to identify Dave Barry, it is set off with commas.)

4. On the other hand, do not use commas to set off a subordinate clause beginning with *which, who, whom,* or *whose* if the information in the subordinate clause is necessary to identify the word it refers to.

The woman <u>who stepped on my toes in the theater</u> apologized profusely.

(The clause "who stepped on my toes in the theater" identifies the woman you are referring to.)

5. No commas are used with subordinate clauses that begin with *that*.

Subordinate clauses *that begin with that* are never enclosed in commas.

EXERCISE

Combine each of the following pairs of sentences by changing one of the sentences in each pair into a subordinate clause. Use commas where they are needed.

EXAMPLE

I was anxious. I prepared my tax return.

I was anxious after I prepared my tax return.

or

Because I was anxious, I prepared my tax return.

1. I always thought that my friends and I weren't prejudiced. I now know that we have our share of biases.

2. My cousin came over to my house. She didn't feel comfortable talking to her parents.

3. One night I was extremely happy and in good spirits. I felt I could not contain my energy.

4. I would describe myself as an energetic person. I don't like to sit around doing nothing.

5. *Neurotic* is another word I would use to describe myself. I am embarrassed to admit it.

6. My neighbor Gabe thinks he knows everything about the judicial system. He tells me what he thinks the verdict will be whenever there is a major trial.

7. Last week I bought a new computer. Bob came over to my house to help me set it up. He thinks he is a computer expert.

8. A friend of mine works as a mechanic at a local garage. He told me that my battery was weak and needed to be recharged.

9. One of my neighbors can no longer drive. She gave me a list and some money and asked me to pick up some groceries for her.

10. He told me that he was going to do the dishes. I became upset with him. We were late for the party.

11. Josefina had always lived along the coast. She moved to Nevada. Her company offered her a better position there.

12. Snowboarding is a popular sport in our local mountains. It makes a person feel as if she were surfing on snow.

13. I attended a trade school after high school. I met a student named Jack. He owned a black 1975 Corvette.

14. A couple of weeks ago a close friend and I were talking on the phone. He asked me a question. Would I consider dating someone of a different race?

15. Edna was driving home in the pouring rain. She decided to stop at Home Depot. She picked up fifteen pounds of lawn seed.

REVIEW EXERCISE Combine each of the following groups of sentences into one sentence. Use subordination and coordination where appropriate. Embed adjectives, adverbs, and prepositional phrases. Use commas where they are needed.

1. Capital punishment today is reserved for "serious" crimes.
   They may be crimes such as murder, treason, espionage, or rape.
   In ancient and medieval times, people were executed for many crimes.
   We would consider these crimes trivial.

2. In India, people could be executed for killing a cow.
   They also could be executed for stealing a royal elephant.
   In Egypt, death was once the punishment for injuring a cat.

3. In ancient Babylon, you could be sentenced to death for selling bad beer.
   In Assyria, a good haircut was a sign of nobility.
   In Assyria, you might be executed for giving a bad haircut.

4. For many centuries the early Christian Church burned heretics alive.
   It kept the definition of heresy broad.
   Anyone with a new idea might find himself going up in flames.

5. For a while in colonial America, women were branded as witches.
   They were executed.
   This occurred if they possessed a demonic gaze.
   This occurred if they kept a black cat.
   This occurred if they were sexually attractive.
   This occurred if they raised the suspicions of almost anyone who wanted to accuse them of witchcraft.

6. Throughout history, executions have been held in public view.
   The executions were cruel and painful.
   They were a way to deter other crimes.

7. Public executions were meant to terrify the average citizen.
   In England they turned into weekly festivals.
   They also became family outings.
   They were full of merrymaking, drunkenness, and more crime.

8. In Babylon, a poorly built house collapsed on its owner and killed him.
   The architect of the house would be executed.
   The owner's wife was killed.
   The architect's wife would be executed too.

9. Noble men or women were sentenced to death.
   They were often allowed to select their own means of execution.
   Socrates did.
   He drank poison in the presence of his family and friends.

10. For thousands of years, hanging was considered a lowly way to die.
    It involved humiliating kicking, gasping, and flailing.
    Beheading was considered an honorable way to be executed.
    The death came swiftly and cleanly.

CHAPTER FOUR

Unity and Coherence

From "Peanuts." Reprinted by permission of UFS, Inc.

Unity

As you can see from the "Peanuts" cartoon on the facing page, Sally is having trouble staying focused on her topic. Her tendency to drift from the subject of her report ("this stupid leaf") to why Christmas is the saddest time of year is called a break in **unity**.

Think about the word *unity* for a moment. It means *oneness* or *singleness of purpose*. A *unified* paragraph or essay is one that stays focused on its central idea. It does not wander into areas that are unrelated to that central idea. To put it another way, all the details, facts, examples, explanations, and references to authorities with which you develop a unified paper should clearly relate to and develop the central idea of that paper. If they do not do so the paper lacks **unity.**

A good time to check the unity of your writing is after you have written the first draft. Until that time, you are still prewriting, and during the prewriting stage you really should not worry too much about unrelated material that creeps into your writing. Remember, when you prewrite, you concentrate on getting as many ideas on paper as you can. When you write, you produce your draft. And when you revise, you improve that draft. Checking your paper for unity will usually occur as you revise—before you submit your paper to your instructor but after you have produced a first draft.

EXERCISE

Read the following paragraphs and identify the topic sentence of each one. Then identify any sentences that break the unity of the paragraph.

A. 1 The names of the seven days of the week have some rather interesting origins. 2 The names *Sunday* and *Monday*, for example, come from Old English words that refer to the sun (*sunne*) and moon (*mona*), respectively. 3 *Tuesday, Wednesday, Thursday,* and *Friday* all refer to gods in Germanic mythology. 4 Tiu (for Tuesday) was a god of war. 5 Most cultures have some kind of name for a war god. 6 The Roman name was Mars; the Greek name was Ares. 7 Woden (for Wednesday) was the chief Germanic god. 8 He is known to many people as Odin. 9 The corresponding chief god in Roman mythology would be Jupiter, and in Greek mythology it would be Zeus. 10 Thor (for Thursday) was the Germanic god of thunder; Freya (for Friday) was the goddess of love and beauty. 11 Interestingly, *Saturday* comes from the name of a Roman god, not a Germanic one. 12 Saturn was the Roman god of agriculture. 13 How agriculture is related to the huge planet we know as Saturn may be confusing to some people, but it obviously did not worry the Romans very much.

B. 1 Folk remedies, which are passed on from one generation to another, are sometimes quite effective and at other times absolutely worthless. 2 One example of effective folk wisdom is the advice to eat chicken soup when you have the flu. 3 Many people love the taste of chicken soup, especially during cold weather. 4 Several scientific studies have shown that chicken soup improves the functioning of the fibers in the upper respiratory tract that help people get rid of congestion. 5 Usually, people buy over-the-counter drugs to alleviate the symptoms of the flu, and today generic brands are much more popular than name brands. 6 Unfortunately, not all folk remedies are as effective as chicken soup. 7 Scientists say, for example, that slices of raw potato placed on the forehead will do nothing for a fever, although many people believe otherwise. 8 In fact, many people believe almost anything they are told. 9 A friend of mine once told some children that the world used to have only two colors—black and white—and that was why old movies looked that way. 10 And the children believed him! 11 Another bit of folk advice that scientists say is untrue is that taping a child's ears back at night will change the positions of ears that stick out too much. 12 Finally, scientists say that boiling skim milk for children with diarrhea is dangerous as well as ineffective.

C.   1 For many years, ice cream was a treat enjoyed only by the nobility. 2 When Marco Polo returned to Italy from China in 1271 with a recipe for a new dessert made of fruit mixed with ice and milk, the dish quickly became a favorite of the Italian nobility. 3 However, the nobility did not share the recipe with the common people. 4 Marco Polo went on to become one of the most famous travelers in history. 5 His book, *The Travels of Marco Polo*, describes China as a country far superior to his own in culture and technology. 6 Several hundred years later, in 1533, Catherine de Medici of Italy introduced the recipe to the French nobility when she married a son of the King of France. 7 A creative French chef experimented with the recipe, beating a mixture of fruit and cream in a bowl surrounded by ice. 8 Of course, French chefs are known for their creativity and imagination, which is why French restaurants are regarded as special, expensive places by most Americans. 9 The result was a dessert much like our ice cream of today, but the recipe was still kept a closely guarded secret. 10 When King Charles I of England brought the dessert to his country in 1625, he was so determined to keep the recipe secret that he even refused to tell his own nobility how to make it. 11 That is just like the English, though. 12 They are known for keeping things to themselves. 13 Finally, in 1670, ice cream appeared for the first time on the menu of a Paris restaurant, and soon people throughout the world were sharing this "new" taste treat.

Coherence

Another way to improve the clarity of your writing is to work on its **coherence,** which involves clarifying the *relationships* between ideas. When ideas (or sentences) are *coherent,* they are understandable. And when they are understandable, one sentence makes sense in relation to the sentence before it. When ideas (or sentences) are *incoherent,* they do not make much sense because they are not clearly related to each other or to the central idea of the paper.

For example, imagine someone passing you a note that read "Snow! Last winter! Trees! Gone!" What in the world could such a person possibly be trying to tell you? That the snow that fell on the trees last winter is gone? That the trees that were snowed on last winter are gone? That last winter's snow killed the trees? What is missing here is **coherence,** the connections between the ideas.

Of course, a person's writing is rarely as incoherent as the above example, but all writers—from students who are taking their first writing classes to professionals who make their living by writing—must consistently work on the clarity of what they have written. Here is an example of a paragraph that needs more work in coherence.

> 1 Some television viewers claim that Donald Duck cartoons are immoral. 2 For fifty years, Donald has kept company with Daisy. 3 Donald's nephews—Huey, Dewey, and Louie—are apparently the children of a "Miss Duck," who was last seen in a comic book in 1937. 4 Donald is drawn without pants. 5 The opinions of these persons have been largely ignored by the general public.

The above paragraph lacks coherence because each sentence seems to jump from one unrelated detail to the next. A careful reader will probably be able to figure out that each sentence is meant to be an example of the "immorality" of Donald Duck cartoons, but the relationship of each sentence to that central idea and to the idea in the sentence before it needs to be made much clearer. Clarifying such relationships involves working on the coherence of the paper.

There are a number of techniques that will help you improve the coherence of your writing.

1. **Refer to the central idea.** One of the most effective ways to improve coherence is to use words that refer to the central idea of your paper as you write your support. In the above paragraph about Donald Duck cartoons, the central idea is that some people think they are "immoral," but none of the supporting sentences clearly refer to that idea. The relationship between the supporting sentences and the central idea will be clearer—and the coherence improved—if the writer uses words that connect her support to the central idea of immorality.

> 1 Some television viewers claim that Donald Duck cartoons are immoral. 2 For fifty years, Donald has kept company with Daisy, a relationship that to some seems **suspicious and dishonorable.** 3 Donald's nephews—Huey, Dewey, and Louie—are apparently the **illegitimate** children of a "Miss Duck," who was last seen in a comic book in 1937. 4 It seems **improper and indecent** to these critics that Donald is drawn without pants. 5 Donald's dressing habits **clearly upset** these particular television viewers. 6 The opinions of these persons have been largely ignored by the general public.

Now the relationship of each supporting idea to the central idea of the paragraph has become much clearer. Notice how the boldfaced words keep the emphasis of the paragraph on the "immorality" of Donald Duck cartoons.

2. **Use common transitional words and phrases.** Transitions tell you what direction a sentence is about to take. When a sentence starts with *However*, you know that it is about to present a contrast; when it starts with *For example*, you know that it is about to move from a general statement to a specific illustration of that statement. Clear transitions will improve the coherence of your paper because they will signal to your readers how the sentence that they are about to read is related to the sentence that they have just finished reading.

Many transitions are so common that they are worded the same way no matter who is doing the writing. They are like road signs (*Stop, Yield, School Zone*) that all drivers are expected to recognize and respond to. These common transitions can improve your paper, but do not overuse them. Too many of them will make your writing sound artificial and awkward.

To show a movement in time: *first, second, next, finally, then, soon, later, in the beginning, at first, meanwhile*

To move to an example: *for example, to illustrate, for instance, as a case in point*

To add another idea, example, or point: *in addition, furthermore, and, also, second, third, next, moreover, finally, similarly*

To show a contrast: *on the other hand, however, but, yet, instead, on the contrary, nevertheless*

To show a result: *so, therefore, as a result, consequently, hence, thus*

To conclude: *finally, in conclusion, as a result, hence, therefore, clearly, obviously*

Notice how the addition of three transitions helps to improve the paragraph about Donald Duck cartoons.

> 1 Some television viewers claim that Donald Duck cartoons are immoral. 2 **For example,** for fifty years, Donald has kept company with Daisy, a relationship that to some seems suspicious and dishonorable. 3 **In addition,** Donald's nephews—Huey, Dewey, and Louie—are apparently the illegitimate children of a "Miss Duck," who was last seen in a comic book in 1937. 4 **Finally,** it seems improper and indecent to these critics that Donald is drawn without pants. 5 Donald's dressing habits clearly upset these particular television viewers. 6 **However** the opinions of these persons have been largely ignored by the general public.

3. **Write your own transitional phrases, clauses, or full sentences.** The most effective transitions are those written in your own words as phrases, clauses, or complete sentences. Transitions such as these often **repeat a word or idea** from the previous sentence. They also often **refer to the central idea** of a paper in order to introduce a new element of support.

Note the transitional phrases, clauses, and full sentences in the paragraph below.

---

1 Some television viewers claim that Donald Duck cartoons are immoral. 2 **According to these viewers, Donald's relationship with Daisy is an example of his immorality.** 3 For fifty years, Donald has kept company with Daisy, a relationship that to some seems suspicious and dishonorable. 4 In addition, **some people question the morality of a cartoon that features three children of unknown parentage.** 5 Donald's nephews—Huey, Dewey, and Louie—are apparently the illegitimate children of a "Miss Duck," who was last seen in a comic book in 1937. 6 Finally, it seems improper and indecent to these critics that Donald is drawn without pants. 7 **Although few people ever expect to see *any* animal in pants,** Donald's dressing habits clearly upset these particular television viewers. 8 **Luckily for the famous duck,** the opinions of these persons have been largely ignored by the general public.

In the above paragraph, sentence 2 is a full *transitional sentence*. It replaces the phrase *for example*, and it emphasizes the central idea of the paragraph by using the word *immorality*. Sentence 3 is another *transitional sentence*. Again, this sentence improves the coherence of the paragraph by emphasizing the central idea of *morality*. Sentence 7 now includes a *transitional clause*. Notice that the clause refers to the idea of animals "in pants," which was mentioned at the very end of sentence 6. Sentence 8 contains a *transitional phrase* that allows the reader to move easily into the concluding idea of the paragraph.

5. **Write transitions between paragraphs as well as within paragraphs.** So far we have discussed coherence *within* paragraphs, but coherence is required *between* paragraphs as well. Remember, coherence involves clarifying *relationships* between ideas. When you move from one paragraph to another within an academic essay, you can clarify the relationships between paragraphs by paying particular attention to the opening of each paragraph. Consider the following questions when you write an essay:

   a. **Does each paragraph open with a transition to move away from the topic in the paragraph before it?** Such a transition might be a brief reference to the central idea of the previous paragraph, a common transitional phrase, or a transitional phrase or sentence of your own.

   b. **Does each paragraph open with a reference to the central idea of the thesis statement of the essay?** Since each paragraph should be developing the thesis of the essay, its opening sentence(s) should naturally refer to the central idea of the thesis.

   c. **Does each paragraph identify the new central idea of this particular paragraph?** Since paragraphs in most academic writing start with topic sentences, the opening sentence(s) of each paragraph should identify its central idea.

Examine the following essay and note how the coherence between paragraphs is handled. Each paragraph opens with a transition (underlined once), with a reference to the central idea of the thesis statement (underlined twice), and with an identification of its own particular central idea (in boldface).

In the article "School Sports—Latest New Age Target," John Leo tells us that many gym teachers across America are opposed to competition in school sports because they think such competition harms the children who aren't outstanding players. He refers to an article from *The New York Times*, which he says "carries the implicit message that win-lose games are dangerous." Leo, however, disagrees with the *Times* article. He believes that one can "lose without humiliation and win without feeling superior." I agree with him. In fact, after the experiences I have had with school sports in my own life, **I believe that the competition in school sports benefits students in many ways.**   1

One of the benefits of competition in school sports is that it **motivates**   2
students to do their best. For example, when I was taking a swim class last semester, I could not swim one hundred yards without stopping. When the teacher said that he was going to time every one of us to see who could finish one hundred yards in the least amount of time, I was worried because I was sure I could not swim that far. During the competition, the only thought that came into my mind was that I did not want to be the last one to finish, and that thought motivated me to continue swimming even though I was very tired. When I reached the finish line, I was astounded to find that I was in fourth place. From this experience and from many others like it, I can say the competition did indeed bring out the best in me.

In addition to motivating students, competition in school sports   3
prepares young people for the competition they will face in real life. My younger brother has benefited from school sports this way. Since he is the youngest member of our family, we always used to let him win when we played games with him because that was the only way we could keep him happy. Then one day he came home from school depressed. When I asked him what had happened, he said that he had lost to a friend in a school race. After I heard his story, I realized that my brothers and I had spoiled him and that school sports were giving him a dose of reality. I decided that the next time he wanted to beat me at checkers, he would have to really compete with me because that is the only way to teach him what life is really like.

Not only does competition benefit people by motivating them and teaching them about life, but it also benefits them by **revealing their own inner strengths and weaknesses.** My friends Minh and Hoa are good illustrations of this point. Minh is a quiet person who never seems very secure about his tennis talent. On the other hand, Hoa, a talkative person, always brags about how well he plays tennis. Hoa was sure that he was a better tennis player than Minh, but one day he had to face Minh in a school tennis tournament. When Hoa lost the game, he realized that he really could not play tennis as well as he thought. This competition pointed out Hoa's weakness, but it also revealed to Minh his own hidden strength. If they had not competed, neither would have discovered the truth about himself.

Clearly, competition in school sports can benefit people in many ways. It motivates students to do their very best, it teaches them about real life, and it reveals to them their own strengths and weaknesses. Like John Leo, I believe that school sports are a valuable part of school life.

EXERCISE   Work with several other students in a small group to identify the topic sentence and central idea in each of the following paragraphs. Write "C.I." above all references to the central idea. Circle all words or ideas that are repeated from one sentence to the next. Finally, underline all common transitional words and phrases.

EXAMPLE

1 Folk remedies, which are passed on from one generation to another, are sometimes quite effective and sometimes absolutely worthless. 2 One example of effective folk wisdom is the advice to eat chicken soup when you have the flu. 3 Several scientific studies have shown that chicken soup improves the functioning of the fibers in the upper respiratory tract that help people get rid of congestion caused by the flu. 4 Unfortunately, not all folk remedies are as effective as chicken soup. 5 Scientists say, for example, that slices of raw potato placed on the forehead will do nothing for a fever, although many people believe otherwise. 6 Another bit of folk advice that scientists say is untrue is that taping a child's ears back at night will change the position of ears that stick out too much. 7 Finally, scientists say that boiling skim milk for children with diarrhea is dangerous as well as ineffective.

A.   1 If you think dainty butterflies are lily-livered weaklings, think again. 2 Most male butterflies are gutsy and aggressive within their own habitat and will pick a fight at the slightest provocation. 3 This trait is often seen when a male is on the prowl for a mate. 4 The European grayling butterfly, for example, will perch on a twig or leaf to wait for Ms. Right. 5 When he scents a female of his own species, he will begin an elaborate courtship dance and emit his own identifying scent. 6 But he will rough up almost anyone else who ventures into his territory, whether it's another butterfly twice his size, a dragonfly or a small bird. 7 He'll even lunge at his own shadow. 8 Black swallowtail butterflies, an especially aggressive species, have been known to chase after terrified birds for as long as half a minute. 9 When vying for the favors of the same female, two male butterflies will repeatedly ram each other in midair until one surrenders and flees.

—Irving Wallace et al., Significa

B.   1 In competition, losing should not necessarily be seen as failing. 2 If a runner finishes behind Bill Rogers in the marathon but runs the race twenty minutes faster than he has ever before, one cannot say that he has failed. 3 If a person enters a city tennis tournament and is eliminated in the third round, he cannot be said to have failed if neither he nor anyone else expected him to survive the first round. 4 The point is simple: failure in competition is not to be identified with losing *per se* but rather with performing below reasonable expectations. 5 Only when one could reasonably have expected to win does losing mean failing. 6 In most competition, someone wins and someone or many lose, but this does not mean that many (or even *any*) have performed below reasonable expectations and have, therefore, failed.

—Richard Eggerman, "Competition as a Mixed Good"

C.   1 When a man and a woman walk together, convention says the man takes the curb side. 2 A common historical explanation of this custom is that in the days when garbage was hurled into the street from upper-story windows, it was the man's duty to bear the majority of the refuse. 3 More reasonable is the explanation that a man on the outside is in a better position to protect his female companion from the hazards of the street itself, which until fairly recently included runaway horses and street brawlers. 4 Though Emily Post dutifully approved the custom, she denied its usefulness in the days of automobiles. 5 Apparently she had never negotiated a New York City sidewalk just after a downpour.

—Tad Tuleja, Curious Customs

EXERCISE   Revise the following paragraphs to improve their coherence by referring more clearly to the central idea, by repeating words and ideas from one sentence to the next, and by adding appropriate transitional words and phrases. You may also need to add complete sentences to emphasize how the details are related to the central idea of the paragraph. Consider working with other students as you revise two of these paragraphs. Then revise one on your own.

A. 1 Driving on freeways today has become a frightening experience. 2 I glanced into my rear-view mirror to find a blue Ford pickup driving sixty-five miles per hour only two feet from my rear bumper. 3 When I changed lanes, he changed lanes too. 4 He pulled off the freeway at the next exit. 5 The local "freeway skiers" weave in and out of traffic as if they were in an Olympic slalom event. 6 Some small red sportscar will swing onto the freeway, race up the lane next to mine, change lanes, and then repeat the same maneuver as it weaves up the freeway. 7 There are the people who are much too busy to be driving. 8 They are reading reports, checking makeup, combing mustaches, drinking soft drinks, or talking on the telephone. 9 People have changed the nature of freeway driving.

B. 1 Most fathers that I know seem to be much more awkward and nervous than mothers when it comes to caring for their babies. 2 My brother's baby, Kaori, had a slight cold. 3 My brother insisted that she should be taken to the hospital. 4 His wife said that Kaori would be fine in a day or so. 5 The child recovered completely. 6 My brother became sick because he hadn't slept all night. 7 My father would always avoid holding my little brother when we were younger. 8 At Disneyland, my mother asked him to hold my brother while she used the restroom. 9 The entire time, my dad paced back and forth. 10 Whenever my mother held the child she seemed completely at ease. 11 I suppose it is natural for mothers to feel comfortable with their young children. 12 I don't see any reason for fathers to be as awkward as they are.

C. 1 After reading G. Gordon Liddy's "Without Emotion," I was reminded of times in my own life when I felt that I had to act without emotion just to make it through an unpleasant experience. 2 I had to go through a divorce. 3 I had no financial support, and I had an eleven-month-old son to take care of. 4 I had to think about handling the pressing issues of finding food, clothing, shelter, and a job. 5 Another time, I was laid off from a typesetting position with a local newspaper. 6 I immediately busied myself with the task of finding another job. 7 I think Liddy was trying to get to the point where he could act without emotion if he ever really had to. 8 For me, it was either act without letting my emotions get to me or allow myself to be defeated by my circumstances.

Readings

Rambos of the Road

MARTIN GOTTFRIED

Before You Read

1. The title refers to "Rambos." Who was Rambo? What does the reference to him tell you about the article?

2. What kind of driver are you? Considerate? Defensive? Aggressive?

The car pulled up and its driver glared at us with such sullen intensity, such hatred, that I was truly afraid for our lives. Except for the Mohawk haircut he didn't have, he looked like Robert DeNiro in *Taxi Driver*, the sort of young man who, delirious for notoriety, might kill a president. 1

He was glaring because we had passed him and for that affront he pursued us to the next stoplight so as to express his indignation and affirm his masculinity. I was with two women and, believe it, was afraid for all three of us. It was nearly midnight and we were in a small, sleeping town with no other cars on the road. 2

When the light turned green, I raced ahead, knowing it was foolish and that I was not in a movie. He didn't merely follow, he chased, and with his headlights turned off. No matter what sudden turn I took, he followed. My passengers were silent. I knew they were alarmed, and I prayed that I wouldn't be called upon to protect them. In that cheerful frame of mind, I turned off my own lights so I couldn't be followed. It was lunacy. I was responding to a crazy *as* a crazy. 3

"I'll just drive to the police station," I finally said, and as if those were the magic words, he disappeared. 4

Elbowing fenders: It seems to me that there has recently been an epidemic of auto macho—a competition perceived and expressed in driving. People fight it out over parking spaces. They bully into line at the gas pump. A toll booth becomes a signal for elbowing fenders. And beetle-eyed drivers hunch over their steering wheels, squeezing the rims, glowering, preparing the excuse of not having seen you as they muscle you off the road. Approaching a highway on an entrance ramp recently, I was strong-armed by a trailer truck so immense that its driver all 5 but blew me away by blasting his horn. The behemoth was just inches from my hopelessly mismatched coupe when I fled for the safety of the shoulder.

And this is happening on city streets, too. A New York taxi driver told me that "intimidation is the name of the game. Drive as if you're deaf and blind. You don't hear the other guy's horn and you sure as hell don't see him."   6

The odd thing is that long before I was even able to drive, it seemed to me that people were at their finest and most civilized when in their cars. They seemed so orderly and considerate, so reasonable, staying in the right-hand lane unless passing, signaling all intentions. In those days you really eased into highway traffic, and the long, neat rows of cars seemed mobile testimony to the sanity of most people. Perhaps memory fails, perhaps there were always testy drivers, perhaps—but everyone didn't give you the finger.   7

A most amazing example of driver rage occurred recently at the Manhattan end of the Lincoln Tunnel. We were four cars abreast, stopped at a traffic light. And there was no moving even when the light had changed. A bus had stopped in the cross traffic, blocking our paths: it was normal-for-New-York-City gridlock. Perhaps impatient, perhaps late for important appointments, three of us nonetheless accepted what, after all, we could not alter. One, however, would not. He would not be helpless. He would go where he was going even if he couldn't get there. A Wall Street type in suit and tie, he got out of his car and strode toward the bus, rapping smartly on its doors. When they opened, he exchanged words with the driver. The doors folded shut. He then stepped in front of the bus, took hold of one of its large windshield wipers and broke it.   8

The bus doors reopened and the driver appeared, apparently giving the fellow a good piece of his mind. If so, the lecture was wasted, for the man started his car and proceeded to drive directly *into the bus*. He rammed it. Even though the point at which he struck the bus, the folding doors, was its most vulnerable point, ramming the side of a bus with your car has to rank very high on a futility index. My first thought was that it had to be a rented car.   9

Lane merger: To tell the truth, I could not believe my eyes. The bus driver opened his doors as much as they could be opened and he stepped directly onto the hood of the attacking car, jumping up and down with both his feet. He then retreated into the bus, closing the doors behind him. Obviously a man of action, the car driver backed up and rammed the bus again. How this exercise in absurdity would have been resolved   10 none of us will ever know for at that point the traffic unclogged and the bus moved on. And the rest of us, we passives of the world, proceeded, our cars crossing a field of battle as if nothing untoward had happened.

It is tempting to blame such belligerent, uncivil and even neurotic behavior on the nuts of the world, but in our cars we all become a little crazy. How many of us speed up when a driver signals his intention of pulling in front of us? Are we resentful and anxious to pass him? How many of us try to squeeze in, or race along the shoulder at a lane merger? We may not jump on hoods, but driving the gauntlet, we seethe, cursing not so silently in the safety of our steel bodies on wheels—fortresses for cowards.   11

What is it within us that gives birth to such antisocial behavior and why, all of a sudden, have so many drivers gone around the bend? My friend Joel Katz, a Manhattan psychiatrist, calls it "a Rambo pattern. People are running around thinking the American way is to take the law into your own hands when anyone does anything wrong. And what constitutes 'wrong'? Anything that cramps your style."   12

It seems to me that it is a new America we see on the road now. It has the mentality of a hoodlum and the backbone of a coward. The car is its weapon and hiding place, and it is still a symbol even in this. Road Rambos no longer bespeak a self-reliant, civil people tooling around in family cruisers. In fact, there aren't families in these machines that charge headlong with their brights on in broad daylight, demanding we get out of their way. Bullies are loners, and they have perverted our liberty of the open road into drivers' license. They represent an America that derides the values of decency and good manners, then roam the highways riding shotgun and shrieking freedom. By allowing this to happen, the rest of us approve.   13

From Newsweek, *Sept. 8, 1986. Reprinted by permission of the author.*

After You Read

Work with other students to develop responses to these questions or to compare responses that you have already prepared.

1. Use your own words to state the thesis idea of the article. Then identify any sentence or sentences in the article that seem to express the thesis.

2. Divide the article into sections according to each major point that Gottfried makes.

3. In three or four sentences, briefly summarize the thesis of the article and its major supporting points.

4. Identify the types of support that Gottfried uses. Where does he use brief or extended examples? Where does he use a reference to authority?

5. Choose one paragraph from the article and explain how its coherence is maintained from sentence to sentence.

How Fathers Talk to Babies

BARRY MCLAUGHLIN

Before You Read

1. Look at the title. How do you think fathers talk to babies? What ideas do you expect to find in this article?

2. This article compares the ways fathers and mothers talk to babies. Watch for transitions that allow the writer to move back and forth between the ways fathers and mothers talk to their children.

Much of what we know about the way children learn language comes from studies in which researchers observe mothers with their babies. . . . When mothers speak to their young children, their speech becomes slower, shorter, less complex, more repetitious, uses fewer pronouns. In fact, this way of talking is often called motherese. 1

Little is known about how fathers talk to babies, but one study indicates they do not say much. Every two weeks during the first three months of 10 babies' lives, Freda Rebelsky and Cheryl Hanks recorded everything fathers said to their infants in a 24-hour period. The fathers spoke to them an average of merely 38 seconds. 2

One of the few studies concerned with fathers' speech to young children was conducted by William Corsaro of Indiana University, who found that fathers asked more questions than did mothers during interactions with their two-year-olds. Nearly half of the fathers' utterances were leading questions: What is this? (no response). Is this a camel? (no response). Can you say that, camel? (no response). Camel? 3

Placed in the same situation, the children's mothers devoted only 18 percent of their utterances to questions of this sort. Such questions are one of the safest routes adults can take in conversation with small children. By asking leading questions, the adult feels comfortable with the child and controls the conversation. 4

The father's tendency to use a controlling language style with young children has been borne out of recent research I conducted with Caleb 5

Schutz and David White. We found that fathers used significantly more imperatives with their five-year-old children than mothers did in the same situation.

In our experiment we recorded the conversations of 24 parents and their children while they were playing a table game called Capture the Hat. The game was new to the children, and the parents had to teach them the rules. What struck us immediately was the difference in teaching styles between the mothers and fathers. Mothers were involved with the children, they were careful about making rules clear, and they corrected mistakes and rule infractions. Fathers, on the other hand, were less involved; they often failed to cover the rules and tended to gloss over the children's mistakes or infractions. Although there were exceptions, fathers seemed uncomfortable and intent on getting the game over with. In fact, we found it difficult to find fathers who would participate in the study. 6

When playing the game, fathers appeared uncertain as to how to talk to their children. They often talked down to them, saying, "All right, say you roll five. How would you move? Show me how many you would move. You would like this: One, two, three, four, five." In contrast, mothers tended to say the same thing more succinctly and less condescendingly: "Now, whatever number comes on the die, you get to move one of your hats that many places." Mothers did not count aloud because they knew the children could count spaces on a game board. 7

Although some fathers used speech that was too simple, underestimating what their children understood, others used language that was too advanced. In such cases the children did not understand the game, but their fathers' concern was not to explain it; they wanted to get it over with. These fathers glanced around uncomfortably, allowed rules to be broken, and seemed generally uninterested in the task. 8

Indirect information on the way fathers talk to young children comes from a study by Elaine Andersen at Stanford University, who had children aged between three and six play the role of parents. When the children pretended to be the father, their speech became shorter, their intonation changed (it became deeper, with less range in pitch), and they used more imperatives and fewer terms of endearment than when they played the mother. 9

Experimenter (taking the child's role): Tell me a story. 10
Child (in father's role): Mommy will.
Experimenter: No, I want you to.
Child: I'm going to sleep.
Experimenter: Please tell me a story.
Child: Ask your mother.

Experimenter: Please, please.
Child: All right. Sit down. Once upon a time. The end.

Other research suggests that the language of fathers to their children   11
is less attuned to the child's needs than is the speech of mothers. Fathers
neither repeat nor expand the speech of young children who are learning
to talk to the same extent that mothers do. Fathers are generally less
skilled in motherese, although there has been so little research on fathers'
speech to young children that we do not know, for example, whether this
is true of fathers who are equally involved with the mothers in the child's
upbringing. It appears that as long as most fathers leave the business of
bringing up children to the mother, the language to which infants are
exposed will continue to be principally the "mother tongue."

From Barry McLaughlin, "Second Look, The Mother Tongue," from Human Nature,
©1978 by Human Nature, Inc., reprinted by permission of the publisher.

After You Read

Work with other students to develop responses to these questions or to compare responses
that you have already prepared.

1. Use your own words to state the thesis idea of the article. Then identify any sentence or
   sentences in the article that seem to express the thesis.

2. Divide the article into sections according to each major point that McLaughlin makes.

3. In three or four sentences, briefly summarize the thesis of the article and its major supporting points.

4. Identify the types of support that McLaughlin uses. Where does he use references to
   authority? Where does he use brief examples? Are his examples specific or general? Are
   they convincing?

5. Compare McLaughlin's examples to Gottfried's. In what way are they different? Does
   one seem more convincing than the other to you?

6. Look at paragraph 6 and explain how its coherence is maintained from sentence to
   sentence.

School Sports—Latest New Age Target

JOHN LEO

Before You Read

1. Consider the title of the following article. What does it lead you to expect? Will the article criticize or defend school sports?

2. What is your opinion of school sports? Are they overly competitive?

If you read *The New York Times*, always look first at the bottom of Page One. That's where the editors sometimes insert a warm and fuzzy article to get your mind off the real front-page news about Bosnia, famine, Sen. Bob Dole and other unsolvable problems.

One day last week, the fuzziness and warmth radiated smartly out of an article headlined "New Gym Class: No More Choosing Up Sides." The story was that basketball and other games are disappearing from gym classes across America, mostly because gym teachers think the games damage the feelings of children who aren't outstanding players.

Even games like dodgeball "have fallen into disrepute," wrote reporter Melinda Henneberger, who perhaps had a harrowing time in traditional gym class. She described P.E. in the past, with "all but the best athletes hoping the bell would rescue them from some fresh humiliation," and says that "now competition is out and cooperation is in."

Sure enough, right above the article was a photo of six children in a gym, each up on one leg doing an interpretive dance. Nearby a grim phys-ed teacher looks on, perhaps to make sure that none of the kids made a break for it and tried to start an illicit basketball game.

Kids can still shoot some hoops on their own, the *Times* said, but "even then, the goal is not so much to learn to score a basket as to develop body awareness, hand and motion skills and the confidence to try new activities."

This is a New Age approach to sports, drained of fun and skill. "Body awareness," "space awareness" and various concepts and feelings are excruciatingly important to this form of basketball. Actually putting the ball in the basket is not.

The *Times* article carries the implicit message that win-lose games are dangerous. Losing inevitably means humiliation. Kids have such fragile egos that it's better to avoid any challenge or competition that might send them into a tailspin. (Chalk up much of this attitude to the self-esteem movement.) There's also the hint that these games are vaguely undemocratic because the kids who play them are suddenly separated into winners and losers.

A lot of the anti-competition theory made the rounds in the late '60s, when giant balls were pushed around by whole classes so everybody could be on the same team. Later, books of non-competitive games started to appear, with titles like *Everybody Wins*, the first sign that losing at kickball was about to be defined as traumatic.

In fairness, the game theorists who stressed group fun and de-empha-   9
sized competition had a point. This is a very competitive, hyperindividu-
alistic culture that undervalues cooperation. School sports shouldn't be
used to turn out little predators or the screaming Little League parents of
tomorrow.

The trouble is that the anti-competition people couldn't seem to hold   10
up the ideal of cooperation without going berserk over team games. Alfie
Kohn, author of the 1986 book *No Contest*, argues that competition in
the classroom and in the gym inevitably has destructive effects.

Even a choose-up game of hoops? Yes, he told me. "There are still   11
destructive effects—anxiety, a sense of failure, and lack of interest in
exercise. Fun doesn't require adversarial activities. The way we feel
about people is affected by the structure of the game."

But kids in a pickup game are not learning the dangerous lesson that   12
"other people are obstacles to my success" (Alfie Kohn's phrase). They
are simply playing, and perhaps learning about cooperation, discipline
and excellence along the way.

The attack on competitive sports in schools comes in two new forms   13
these days. One has to do with gender. Since boys tend to grow up
throwing a ball against a wall or a stoop, and most girls may not, there's
a feeling that girls reach school age with an athletic disadvantage. The
schools are addressing this problem, but some people want to avoid the
whole issue by downgrading or eliminating team games.

Rita Kramer, author of *Ed School Follies*, a book on theories at   14
schools of education, thinks a feminist argument against competitive
sports is emerging. "This is one of those hidden-agenda items for femi-
nists," she says. "Some of them don't want masculine skills to be valued
too highly in the schools."

The other, more serious argument comes from the cooperative learning   15
movement and other school movements that promote "equity issues,"
and are less concerned with excellence than with equality. The basic
teaching, that nobody is better than anybody else, leads believers to
oppose any activity that produces winning individuals.

From an "equity" point of view, it's better to have everybody hopping   16
up and down on one leg than to risk the inequality of having winners.

There are many obvious things to say here. The anti-achievement ethic   17
buried in the "equity" argument is a deadly one. People can lose without
humiliation and win without feeling superior. Through sports, children

learn how to handle defeat as well as victory—no sulking, gloating or rubbing it in. Aerobics and interpretive dancing have their place, but so do team sports. And it's always best to keep ideologues out of the gym.

Come on. Let's play ball.   18

From U.S. News & World Report. *Reprinted by permission of John Leo.*

After You Read

Work with other students to develop responses to these questions or to compare responses that you have already prepared.

1. Use your own words to state the thesis idea of the article. Then identify any sentence or sentences in the article that seem to express the thesis.

2. Divide the article into sections according to each major point that Leo makes.

3. In three or four sentences, briefly summarize the thesis of the article and its major supporting points.

4. Examine the types of support that Leo uses. How is his support different from that found in McLaughlin's and Gottfried's articles?

5. Read the first five paragraphs of the article and identify the techniques used to maintain coherence from sentence to sentence and from paragraph to paragraph.

Writing Assignments

1. In "Rambos of the Road," Martin Gottfried suggests that none of us are exempt from the type of behavior he describes. He says that "in our cars we all become a little crazy." Are you, perhaps, a "Rambo" driver? Describe some driving situations which have caused you to react in a "belligerent, uncivil and even neurotic" manner.

2. Discuss "Rambos of the Road" with members of your class. Have they seen the type of driver Gottfried describes? Use both your own experiences and the experiences of others to describe different kinds of "Rambo" drivers that you and your classmates have encountered.

3. Many groups of people (joggers, police officers, teachers, surfers, musicians) include one particular type of person whose behavior makes him or her stand out from the other members of the group. Consider different groups that you might be a part of. Is there a type of person in one such group whose behavior makes him or her stand out? Interview members of your class or talk to people you know for more ideas on this topic. Then use examples to describe the behavior of the type of person you have chosen.

4. In "How Fathers Talk to Babies," Barry McLaughlin suggests that fathers and mothers talk to babies in very different ways. Do your own personal experiences support this idea at all? Have you seen behavior like this in your own family or in other families? Consider your own knowledge and then discuss this article with other members of your class and with people you know. Write a paper in which you describe some of your observations.

5. "How Fathers Talk to Babies" focuses on one particular area in which fathers treat their children differently than mothers do. Explain other ways in which fathers act differently from mothers. Use examples of incidents you have observed or examples that you develop from discussions with other people to support your explanations.

6. Discuss the kinds of experiences you or members of your class have had with competition in school sports. Was such competition enjoyable? Was it beneficial or detrimental in any way? Was competition overemphasized? Write a paper in which you briefly respond to John Leo's article "School Sports—Latest New Age Target." Describe your reaction to competitive school sports, using examples drawn from your own experience or from the experiences of people you have talked to.

7. Competition does not have to be restricted to sporting events. Work with members of your class to identify other areas of life in which you find yourself competing. Write a paper explaining whether or not you find that competition beneficial. Use specific examples to illustrate your ideas.

Evaluating Sample Papers

As you read and evaluate the quality of the essays on the following pages, consider these areas:

1. Thesis Statement

Underline the thesis statement of the essay. Does it express a clear and specific central idea?

1   2   3   4   5   6

2. Topic Sentences

Underline the topic sentence of each paragraph. Does it clearly state the central idea of the paragraph?

1   2   3   4   5   6

3. Support

Examine the supporting details in each paragraph. Are they specific and clear? Should they be more detailed, or should more support be included?

1   2   3   4   5   6

4. Unity

Does each paragraph clearly relate to and develop the *central idea* expressed in the thesis statement? Do the supporting details *within* each paragraph clearly relate to and develop the *central idea* expressed in the topic sentence of that paragraph?

1   2   3   4   5   6

5. Coherence

Does each paragraph open with a transition, a reference to the central idea of the thesis statement, and an identification of its own central idea? Are the sentences within each paragraph clearly related to each other by the use of transitions or by references to the central idea of the paragraph?

1   2   3   4   5   6

6. Sentence Structure

Do the sentences combine ideas that are related, using coordination and subordination when appropriate? Are there too many brief, choppy main clauses?

1   2   3   4   5   6

7. Mechanics, Grammar, and Spelling

Does the paper contain a distracting number of errors of these kinds?

1   2   3   4   5   6

8. Overall Ranking of the Essay

1   2   3   4   5   6

Student Essay 1

According to John Leo, who wrote "School Sports—Latest New Age Target," competitive games such as basketball and dodgeball are becoming scarce among gym classes across America. He reports that a *New York Times* article suggests that win-lose games are dangerous because losing means humiliation and the breaking of children's fragile egos. Although he believes that competition can be stressed too much, Leo thinks that competition doesn't have to be destructive. My own experiences make me agree with him.

In my experience, the competition in team sports teaches kids cooperation and discipline, life skills which every child should learn.

Kids' egos might be fragile, but they are mended just as quickly as they are broken. Two children on my block, each around nine years of age, play little league baseball and are on opposing teams. Their teams both made it to the championship game, which I had the pleasure of watching. The game was close when one of the boys made the mistake of not running all the way to home plate; instead, he stopped half way there and then ran back to third while his teammate was on base. The terrible mistake caused him to get into a pickle and eventually be tagged out. His ego was broken that night on the field, but when I saw him the next day out on our street playing games with the other neighbors, he seemed fine. It seemed as if his ego had mended and he had regained his pride overnight. Later on in life, I'm sure this boy will be able to hold his composure during bad times. Holding one's pride after bad times is a quality I wish many people had.

In the twentieth century, women are having to compete with men all the time. Competition starts at the elementary level in the classroom and team sports. Girls can be just as good athletes as boys or even better. Many a time I have swum with faster girls, lost a game of volleyball against a team of girls, and been beaten by a girl in a game of tennis. Last year, my senior year in high school, my view of students was that girls were better students than boys. Healthy competition of the opposite sex at a young age is an indirect way for these girls to have the confidence they need when they get older and have to compete against men for jobs.

My feelings on competition in school are the same as John Leo's. Kids want to have fun playing games. I think it's the adults who have the problem, not the kids. Competition is present in everyday life in many different forms, and kids need to learn how to deal with competition at a young age so they are ready when they enter the real world. Cooperation and discipline are good features which I hope my kids learn at an early age.

Student Essay 2

In "Rambos of the Road," Martin Gottfried explains that "recently there has been an epidemic of auto macho—a competition perceived and expressed in driving." He gives examples of people fighting it out for parking spaces and pushing their way into line at the gas pump, and he points out that in our cars we all become a little crazy. As I driver, I too have witnessed the craziness of the Rambos of the road. They seem to be everywhere, but some situations cause them to appear more frequently than others. Since I began to drive, I have witnessed many incidents of the typical crazy Rambo driver on a rampage.

I have seen instances when a driver goes on a rampage after being cut off by another driver. This type of driver will often speed up, honk his or her horn, and yell nasty names out the window to the driver who cut him or her off. Just the other day I witnessed this type of situation. I was driving down Vista Way when a Mazda 626 next to me was cut off by a small Porsche. The driver of the Mazda, a gray-haired old man, suddenly went crazy. He sped up, almost hitting the Porsche, honked his horn, and practically hung out the window cursing at the other driver. I couldn't believe what I was seeing. I have seen similar incidents on the freeway. Have you ever seen the typical "Rambo" driver who is cut off on the freeway? He proceeds to tailgate the person who cut him off for the next two miles. I have seen this happen many times, especially at the end of an on ramp to the freeway. Many of the drivers who are merging seem to cut off the drivers who already are on the freeway. This is when "Rambos" come alive and start tailgating cars.

I have witnessed the craziness of "Rambo" driving not only in cutting off other cars but also in fighting over parking spaces. The other day when I was at Lucky's, I saw two drivers almost hit each other over a parking space. The driver of a big blue truck was waiting to pull into a parking space when another driver coming from the opposite direction pulled into the space that the driver of the truck was waiting for. The driver of the blue truck was so angry that he was actually going to hit the other car. He was even yelling nasty names out his window. I have also seen this type of situation occur at self-serve car washes. Many times when a person arrives at the car wash, there is a line to get a stall. A lot of times two drivers will actually race to get the same stall when it opens. They act as if they are on a race track and drive like maniacs just so they don't have to wait another five minutes.

Another type of "Rambo" driver I have seen is one who will follow a person for a few minutes to make the person mad. I have seen my brother drive like this many times. When some other car cuts him off or almost hits him, he will follow the person, flipping him off and cursing at him or her. It is so ridiculous. He often acts like the driver on a rampage but not quite as bad.

I have witnessed many drivers with the "Rambo" attitude and style since I began to drive. I have seen the crazy things they do. Sometimes I even find myself acting in a "Rambo" kind of way, like almost all drivers do. Everyone who drives witnesses or experiences the "Rambo" type of driving. Like Martin Gottfried says, we all become a little crazy in our cars.

Student Essay 3

In the article "How Fathers Talk to Babies," Barry McLaughlin discusses how little is known of how fathers talk to babies and about different studies about fathers asking more questions than mothers. He says that fathers use controlling language and have impatient teaching styles and are less involved than mothers. In addition, I have seen fathers discipline babies different from mothers in my family.

For instance, my brother-in-law Steve disciplines his two-year-old son, Christopher, much more strictly than my sister Ruby. Steve is somewhat rough and talks to his son as if Christopher was ten years old. "Children should be disciplined rough at a young age, for when they get older they can deal with life," says Steve. At times when the baby cries, Steve grabs him and puts him in the crib in the nursery until the baby stops crying. If the baby cries for one hour, he will leave him there for that long. Steve feels that if he doesn't do that, the baby will not learn to behave at other people's houses. Ruby, on the other hand, feels that a baby that age should be treated with lots of tender, loving care. She baby talks him and feels that she should not have to put him in his room for crying because he is still too young and doesn't know any better.

Another example is how Steve finds the baby's diet somewhat more unimportant than Ruby. When feeding time comes, Steve is not all that concerned about giving his son healthy dishes. At one time Steve gave his son a raw weanie, even though Ruby felt it should have been cooked. Although my sister feels soft drinks are totally unhealthy and that babies should never drink them, Steve allows the baby to have soft drinks—not only one but all he can drink. Steve is never sure about what he should feed the baby. If he has to choose between a hamburger and a dish with chicken and vegetables, he will choose the hamburger. Because he does not find it all that important, he feeds him just about anything without thinking whether it's healthy or not. He says that as long as the baby eats something it's okay. Ruby, on the other hand, always tries to choose the most nutritious dishes and is always concerned about what Christopher eats.

Another thing I see is that Steve is always trying to teach the baby something, but Ruby feels he is much too young to want to learn. Steve buys many different learning books for him and expects Ruby to read them to the baby. Ruby finds it somewhat frustrating because Christopher would rather run around and play with his toys. She feels he is too young to have to sit down and listen to her reading, but Steve insists that the baby should listen to all these different learning cassettes so he can get smart. Ruby, feeling that the baby is much too young to sit there and listen to these cassettes as well as having to sit in his crib with a cassette player, thinks he instead should be running around exploring and discovering new things around the house.

There are many ways that fathers discipline their babies differently from mothers, and I feel most fathers do not have that special touch that mothers have.

Sentence Combining: Verbal Phrases

The verbal phrase is an easy and effective way to add more information to your sentences without using a full clause to do so. In fact, you already use verbal phrases every day, both in your speech and in your writing. When you write "The man crossing the street waved at the irate motorists," you use a verbal phrase ("crossing the street"). The sentence "The plan to rob the bank was nearly flawless" also contains a verbal phrase ("to rob the bank").

Although people use verbal phrases unconsciously in their speech and writing, learning how to use them in a planned, conscious manner can improve your writing two ways. First, using verbal phrases will allow you to add more action and description to your writing without using additional sentences. As a result, your writing will have a sense of depth and detail that will distinguish it from the prose of the average writer. Second, using these phrases will allow you to vary the structure of the sentences that you write, and a varied sentence structure makes for more interesting reading than sentence after sentence written exactly the same way.

A **verbal** is simply a verb form that is not used as a verb. For example, in the following sentences, the underlined verb forms are used as adjectives, not as verbs.

The <u>singing</u> cowboy made everybody angry.
The police officer assisted the <u>confused</u> motorist.

Each type of verbal has its own specific name. In the above examples, *singing* is a **present participle** and *confused* is a **past participle**.

Present and Past Participles

The **present participle** is the "-ing" form of a verb used as an adjective.

A <u>traveling</u> sales representative decided that he needed a new pair of shoes.
Mr. Ingham did not know what to do about the <u>barking</u> dogs.

The **past participle** is also used as an adjective. Some past participles end in "-d" or "-ed" (*picked, fired, tossed*); others end in "-n" or "-en" (*eaten, thrown, spoken*); still others have their own unique forms (*sung, brought, gone*). To determine the past participle form of any verb, ask yourself how you would spell the word if "have" preceded it.

The <u>exhausted</u> jogger decided to rest for an hour.
The patient with the <u>broken</u> leg was ready to leave the hospital.

Present and Past Participial Phrases

Present and past participial phrases consist of present and past participles with other words added to them to give more details. The following examples are drawn from "Rambos of the Road," "How Fathers Talk to Babies," and "School Sports—Latest New Age Target."

Approaching a highway on an entrance ramp recently, I was strongarmed by a trailer truck. . . .

A bus had stopped in the cross traffic, blocking our paths: it was normal-for-New-York-City gridlock.

Placed in the same situation, the children's mothers devoted only 18 percent of their utterances to questions of this sort.

The anti-achievement ethic buried in the "equity" argument is a deadly one.

Infinitive Phrases

The **infinitive** is another type of verbal. It consists of the base form of a verb preceded by "to" (*to throw, to breathe, to eat*). The **infinitive phrase** consists of the infinitive with other words added to it to give more details. Here are some examples from "How Fathers Talk to Babies":

The father's tendency to use a controlling language style with young children has been borne out of recent research. . . .

In fact, we found it difficult to find fathers who would participate in the study.

Using Verbal Phrases

Participial and infinitive phrases can be used to improve your writing in several ways:

1. **Use verbal phrases to develop sentences by adding details and ideas.**

   Participial phrases are particularly effective for adding details to your sentences. Since participles are verbals, they work especially well when you are describing actions. Notice how the writers of the articles in this chapter used verbal phrases to expand their sentences.

   And beetle-eyed drivers hunch over their steering wheels.

   And beetle-eyed drivers hunch over their steering wheels, squeezing the rims, glowering, preparing the excuse of not having seen you as they muscle you off the road.

   Through sports, children learn how to handle defeat as well as victory.

   Through sports, children learn how to handle defeat as well as victory—no sulking, gloating or rubbing it in.

2. **Use verbal phrases to combine related sentences.**

   Verbal phrases often can be used to create one sentence from two or more related sentences. Note how the following sentences can be combined using verbal phrases.

   Two sentences: *Seymour stared at his lottery ticket in amazement. He could not believe that he had just won ten million dollars.*

   One sentence using a present participial phrase: *Staring at his lottery ticket in amazement, Seymour could not believe that he had just won ten million dollars.*

Two sentences: A body was found in the Alps last year. <u>It had been frozen for over three thousand years.</u>

One sentence using a past participial phrase: A body <u>frozen for over three thousand years</u> was found in the Alps last year.

Two sentences: <u>Michelle wanted to pass the midterm on Monday.</u> She knew that she should study all weekend.

One sentence using an infinitive phrase: Michelle knew that she should study all weekend <u>to pass the midterm on Monday</u>.

3. **Use verbal phrases to be concise.**

Many subordinate clauses can easily and more concisely be written as verbal phrases.

The sycamore tree <u>that is growing next to our driveway</u> has started to drop its leaves.
The sycamore tree <u>growing next to our driveway</u> has started to drop its leaves.

<u>Because he thought that he had seen a ghost,</u> Herman began to scream.
<u>Thinking that he had seen a ghost,</u> Herman began to scream.

The person <u>who was accused of shoplifting</u> insisted that she had paid for all her items.
The person <u>accused of shoplifting</u> insisted that she had paid for all her items.

EXERCISE

Develop the following sentences by adding verbal phrases to them where indicated. Use verbals derived from the verbs in parentheses.

EXAMPLE

^ *Lyle stared at the paper in front of him. (confuse, determine)*
Confused by the unclear directions but determined to pass the test, Lyle stared at the paper in front of him.

1. ^ Calvin jogged fifteen miles every day. (prepare)

2. ^ The mangy alley cat slowly licked its lips. (stare)

3. The driver in the blue Isuzu was driving erratically ^ . (honk, cut, weave)

4. ^ George was not in the mood to shop for Christmas trees. (irritate, bother)

5 My six-year-old daughter ^ walked out of the rain and into our living room. (wear, hold)

6. Narcissus stood before the mirror ^ . (gaze, wonder)

7. Frankie looked at Annette and told her about his plans ^ . (quit, buy, move)

8. The UFO ^ flew into space and never returned. (observe, photograph)

9. ^ The seven dwarves headed for the mine. (whistle, sing)

10. Last summer we drove over three thousand miles. ^ (visit, tour, relax)

EXERCISE   Combine each of the following groups of sentences* into one sentence. Change each underlined sentence into the type of verbal phrase suggested in parentheses.

EXAMPLE

The macaw emitted an earsplitting shriek.
It flew from the tree.
(present participial phrase)

Emitting an earsplitting shriek, the macaw flew from the tree.

1. A rogue elephant separates itself from the herd and roams alone.
It is often quite dangerous.
(present participial phrase)

2. A solitary rogue elephant can be savage.
It attacks and kills everyone it can.
(present participial phrase)

3. A. A. Kinlock, a British authority, wrote that a rogue will often haunt a particular road.
It will stop traffic for as long as it remains.
(present participial phrase)

4. One particular rogue in India seemed determined.
It killed many people and even destroyed their homes.
(infinitive phrase)

5. Carl Ackley was seized and mutilated by a rogue elephant.
Carl Ackley, the father of modern taxidermy, became convinced that the elephant was the most dangerous of all animals.
(past participial phrase)

6. The Asian elephant is considered less temperamental than the African elephant.
It nevertheless more commonly turns rogue.
It accounts for the deaths of more than fifty persons per year.
(past participial phrase and present participial phrase)

7. A rogue elephant wants to destroy its victim.
It will catch him and dismember him.
It will smash him against the ground or a tree.
It will toss him into the air.
(infinitive phrase and two present participial phrases)

*Adapted from Lawrence D. Gadd, *The Second Book of the Strange*, Prometheus Books. © 1981 by Newspaper Enterprise Association. Reprinted by permission of the publisher.

8. An elephant may turn rogue because it is suffering from a wound.
<u>The wound may have been inflicted by another elephant or by hunters.</u>
(past participial phrase)

9. In many instances, elephants were found to have been suffering from painful sores and old wounds.
<u>These elephants had been identified as rogues and killed.</u>
(past participial phrase)

10. <u>One Indian rogue suffered from a huge sore at the end of its tail.</u>
It caused great damage.
<u>It chased travelers.</u>
<u>It killed several natives.</u>
(present participial phrases)

Avoiding Dangling Modifiers

Since verbal phrases are not verbs, they do not have subjects. However, they do express an action, and the "doer" of that action is usually the subject of the sentence. Whenever you open a sentence with a verbal phrase, be sure that the subject of the sentence is also the "doer." If the subject cannot logically perform the action in the verbal phrase, you have a dangling modifier that needs to be rewritten. (See Chapter 16 for a more thorough discussion of dangling modifiers.)

(dangling modifier)   *<u>Sighing with relief,</u> the golf ball rolled into the cup.*
(A golf ball cannot sigh with relief.)

(possible correction)   *<u>Sighing with relief,</u> the golfer watched as his golf ball rolled into the cup.*
(A logical subject has now been supplied. A golfer can sigh with relief.)

(possible correction)   *<u>As the golfer sighed with relief,</u> the golf ball rolled into the cup.*
(The verbal phrase has been rewritten into a subordinate clause with its own subject and verb.)

EXERCISE   Revise any dangling modifiers in the following sentences, either by supplying a logical subject or by rewriting the verbal phrase as a subordinate clause. Some sentences may be correct.

EXAMPLE

(incorrect)   *Surprised by the unexpected rainstorm, our clothing was soon soaked.*

(correct)   *Surprised by the unexpected rainstorm, we were all soon soaked.*

(correct)   *Because we were all surprised by the unexpected rainstorm, our clothing was soon soaked.*

1. Staring at the boiling noodles, the pasta was almost ready.

2. Damaged by the intense heat, Cheryl threw the videocassette into the trash.

3. Turning green with slime and algae, parts of Lake Elsinore soon became a local eyesore.

4. Breaking in through the kitchen window, the stereo equipment and television set were stolen.

5. Frightened by the low moaning sounds coming from the cellar, Herman's hand reached for the phone.

EXERCISE

Combine the following sentences using verbal phrases. In each case, the first sentence is the main sentence. Each following sentence should be revised as a verbal phrase and added to the beginning or to the end of the main sentence or, occasionally, within the main sentence. Be careful not to write a dangling modifier when you start a sentence with a verbal phrase.

1. A zombie is the body of a dead person.
   The dead person has been reanimated by a voodoo sorcerer.
   The sorcerer is called a *boko.*

2. Haitian folklore is filled with stories of zombies.
   It cites many cases of people who have reappeared after they were already buried.

3. According to folklore, a *boko* reanimates the corpse.
   He will use it as his slave.

4. The *boko* causes people to think a person has really died.
   He uses certain drugs that induce a state of lethargy similar to death.

5. After the person's burial, the body is recovered by the *boko.*
   The body has been deprived of its soul.
   The body has been reduced to a zombie.

6. The zombie can return to its grave only after the time decreed for its natural death has arrived.
   The zombie serves the *boko* who has reanimated it.

7. Believers in zombies will poison or stab a corpse.
   They want to prevent their relatives from becoming zombies.
   They want to be sure the corpse is really dead.

8. Supposedly, feeding a zombie salt will free it from its condition.
   It will allow the zombie to seek out its grave and die.

9. Some people say that zombies are actually victims of a potent drug that incapacitates them.
   The drug inhibits speech and will power.
   It allows motion.

10. A *boko* may use hypnosis and suggestion.
    Hypnosis and suggestion may increase the power of the drug.
    Hypnosis and suggestion may further incapacitate the person.

PART TWO

Writing About Reading

In the first four chapters of this text, you have written papers on topics similar to those in the reading selections. In a sense, you have used the topics in the reading selections as springboards for your own ideas, and then you have supported those ideas with examples drawn from real life experiences.

In the next four chapters, you will move from writing on topics that are similar to those in the reading selections to writing about the reading selections themselves. Often called *academic* papers because they are required in many college-level courses, the writing assignments in the next four chapters will introduce you to accurately summarizing what you have read, to evaluating and responding to the ideas in a reading selection, to synthesizing ideas from several articles, and to arguing a point based on information drawn from a number of sources. In other words, you will be asked to write *about* what you have read.

Of course, *academic writing* does not mean that you will no longer use personal experiences to support your points. As a means of supporting your ideas, the real experiences of real people are just as important as ever. You will find, however, that much of your support will also be drawn from the articles you read. For that reason, the clear and accurate reading you have been practicing in Chapters 1 through 4 will be of critical importance. Obviously, you cannot write thoughtfully about an article if you have not first read it in a thoughtful manner.

CHAPTER FIVE

Summarizing and Responding to Reading

Clear and accurate summarizing is one of the most important skills you can learn in college. Your ability to summarize effectively will help you to study for and take tests, to write reports and papers (particularly papers involving research), and to give thorough, convincing oral presentations. Summarizing is also a skill in demand in the business world, especially when you must report information to other people. The person who can read and *accurately* report what he or she has read will always have an advantage over the person who cannot.

It seems as if summarizing should be such a simple task. After all, when you summarize, you merely explain what you have read to somebody else. And in many ways summarizing *is* simple. Yet it also can be quite a challenging assignment. A good summary demands that you read carefully, that you accurately identify the main points of what you have read, and that you then successfully communicate those ideas to another person. The following explanations should help you to write successful summaries.

Characteristics of a Successful Summary

- A summary accurately communicates the author's ideas.
- It includes all of the author's main points.
- It usually does *not* include supporting details.
- It does *not* include your opinions or reactions.
- It does *not* alter the author's meaning in any way.
- It uses your own words and writing style.

Writing a Brief Summary

Because most summaries present only the central idea and main points of a reading selection, they are usually quite brief, often no more than one or two paragraphs long. To write a summary, follow these steps:

1. As you read the material that you intend to summarize, underline or highlight whatever seems significant to you. Mark statements that seem to express the central idea and the main points of the reading selection. Even particularly vivid facts or other supporting details may be marked.

2. Reread the material, annotating it and dividing it into major sections so that each section reflects one main point.

3. Write the opening sentence of your summary. It should identify the name of the reading selection, the author, and the central idea, purpose, thesis, or topic of the reading.

4. After the opening sentence, briefly summarize each of the author's main ideas. Often you will need no more than one sentence to summarize each main idea.

5. Revise what you have written so that your summary is expressed in your own words and in your own style of writing. Where needed, add transitions that refer to the author between main points.

Reading

Read the following article. As you do, identify its central idea and main points. Then reread the article, annotating it and dividing it into major sections. A sample brief summary follows the article. Note how the central idea and main points of the article are incorporated into the summary.

The Decline of Neatness

NORMAN COUSINS

Anyone with a passion for hanging labels on people or things should have little difficulty in recognizing that an apt tag for our time is the Unkempt Generation. I am not referring solely to college kids. The sloppiness virus has spread to all sectors of society. People go to all sorts of trouble and expense to look uncombed, unshaved, unpressed.

The symbol of the times is blue jeans—not just blue jeans in good condition but jeans that are frayed, torn, discolored. They don't get that way naturally. No one wants blue jeans that are crisply clean or spanking new. Manufacturers recognize a big market when they see it, and they compete with one another to offer jeans that are made to look as though they've just been discarded by clumsy house painters after ten years of wear. The more faded and seemingly ancient the garment, the higher the cost. Disheveled is in fashion; neatness is obsolete.

Nothing is wrong with comfortable clothing. It's just that current usage is more reflective of a slavish conformity than a desire for ease. No generation has strained harder than ours to affect a casual, relaxed, cool look; none has succeeded more spectacularly in looking as though it had been stamped out by cookie cutters. The attempt to avoid any appearance of being well groomed or even neat has a quality of desperation about it and suggests a calculated and phony deprivation. We shun conventionality, but we put on a uniform to do it. An appearance of alienation is the triumphant goal, to be pursued in oversize sweaters and muddy sneakers.

Slovenly speech comes off the same spool. Vocabulary, like blue jeans, is being drained of color and distinction. A complete sentence in everyday speech is as rare as a man's tie in the swank Polo Lounge of the Beverly Hills Hotel. People communicate in chopped-up phrases, relying on grunts and chants of "you know" or "I mean" to cover up a damnable incoherence. Neatness should be no less important in language than it is in dress. But spew and sprawl are taking over. The English language is one of the greatest source of wealth in the world. In the midst of accessible riches, we are linguistic paupers.

Violence in language has become almost as casual as the possession of handguns. The curious notion has taken hold that emphasis in communicating is impossible without the incessant use of four-letter words. Some screenwriters openly admit that they are careful not to turn in scripts that are devoid of foul language lest the classification office impose the curse of a G (general) rating. Motion-picture exhibitors have a strong preference for the R (restricted) rating, probably on the theory of forbidden fruit. Hence writers and producers have every incentive to employ tasteless language and gory scenes.

The effect is to foster attitudes of casualness toward violence and brutality not just in entertainment but in everyday life. People are not as uncomfortable as they ought to be about the glamorization of human hurt. The ability to react instinctively to suffering seems to be atrophying. Youngsters sit transfixed in front of television or motion-picture screens, munching popcorn while human beings are battered or mutilated. Nothing is more essential in education than respect for the frailty of human beings; nothing is more characteristic of the age than mindless violence.

Everything I have learned about the educational process convinces me that the notion that children can outgrow casual attitudes toward brutality is wrong. Count on it: if you saturate young minds with materials showing that human beings are fit subjects for debasement or dismembering, the result will be desensitization to everything that should produce revulsion or resistance. The first aim of education is to develop respect for life, just as the highest expression of civilization is the supreme tenderness that people are strong enough to feel and manifest toward one another. If society is breaking down, as it too often appears to be, it is not because we lack the brainpower to meet its demands but because our feelings are so dulled that we don't recognize we have a problem.

Untidiness in dress, speech and emotions is readily connected to human relationships. The problem with the casual sex so fashionable in films is not that it arouses lust but that it deadens feelings and annihilates privacy. The danger is not that sexual exploitation will create sex fiends but that it may spawn eunuchs. People who have the habit of seeing everything and doing anything run the risk of feeling nothing.

My purpose here is not to make a case for a Victorian decorum or for namby-pambyism. The argument is directed to bad dress, bad manners, bad speech, bad human relationships. The hope has to be that calculated sloppiness will run its course. Who knows, perhaps some of the hip designers may discover they can make a fortune by creating fashions that are unfrayed and that grace the human form. Similarly, motion-picture and television producers and exhibitors may realize that a substantial audience exists for something more appealing to the human eye and spirit than the sight of a human being hurled through a store-front window or tossed off a penthouse terrace. There might even be a salutary response to films that dare to show people expressing genuine love and respect for one another in more convincing ways than anonymous clutching and thrashing about. 9

Finally, our schools might encourage the notion that few things are more rewarding than genuine creativity, whether in the clothes we wear, the way we communicate, the nurturing of human relationships, or how we locate the best in ourselves and put it to work. 10

A Sample Brief Summary

In "The Decline of Neatness," Norman Cousins argues that a "sloppiness virus" is affecting all areas of our society. According to Cousins, the sloppy clothing that is so fashionable today reflects our desperate need to conform, making us look as if we had been "stamped out by cookie cutters." Our sloppy speech reflects the same need, but it goes beyond the slovenly to the violent. And this sloppily violent speech results in casual attitudes toward all violence and brutality. Cousins claims that we seem to be losing the ability to react to suffering. He says that the violence and brutality in movies and television are "desensitizing" our children and that such casual attitudes toward violence will not be outgrown. Finally, he suggests that our sloppy clothing, speech, and emotions affect human relationships, as is evident in the casual attitude toward sex in films, an attitude that is deadening our feelings and destroying our privacy. Cousins concludes by stating that he does not want to return to Victorian attitudes, although he does hope that our "calculated sloppiness" will soon disappear and that we will all begin to "locate the best in ourselves and put it to work."

EXERCISE   Identify the paragraph or paragraphs from "The Decline of Neatness" that are covered in each sentence of the above summary. Are all of the main points of "The Decline of Neatness" clearly and accurately summarized?

Writing Paraphrases and Quotations

Paraphrasing

As you can see from the above sample summary, most of what you write in a summary consists of the author's ideas put into your own words. Each time you reword what an author has written so that the *author's idea* is now expressed in *your writing style*, you have **paraphrased** the author. Here are some points to consider when you paraphrase:

1. Paraphrases must reflect your own writing style, not the author's.

2. Paraphrases must not change or distort the author's ideas in any way.

3. Paraphrases must be clearly identified as presenting the author's ideas, not your own.

4. Paraphrases use the present tense when referring to the author.

Here are some paraphrases that appeared in the sample summary of "The Decline of Neatness," along with the original passages.

(original)   *The ability to react instinctively to suffering seems to be atrophying.*

(paraphrase)   *Cousins claims that we seem to be losing the ability to react to suffering.*

(original)   *Untidiness in dress, speech, and emotions is readily connected to human relationships. The problem with the casual sex so fashionable in films is not that it arouses lust but that it deadens feelings and annihilates privacy.*

(paraphrase)   *Finally, he suggests that our sloppy clothing, speech, and emotions affect human relationships, as is evident in the casual attitude toward sex in films, an attitude that is deadening our feelings and destroying our privacy.*

Note that both of the above paraphrases accurately state the ideas in the original, yet they do so in a writing style quite different from that of the original. Both paraphrases clearly refer to the author of the article, and the words that refer to the author are written in the present tense.

Quoting

A quotation is an exact reproduction of an author's words. To let the reader know that the words are not your own, you must use quotation marks. However, you should be careful to use quotations sparingly in your writing. For the most part, *your* writing should be in *your* style, not in someone else's, so most references to what you have read should appear as paraphrases, not as quotations. In general, quote only those words, phrases, or sentences that you really want to emphasize or that would not be as emphatic if they were paraphrased. In fact, notice how *few* quotations appear in the brief summary of "The Decline of Neatness" above. With that said, let's discuss the points you should keep in mind when you use quotations in your writing.

1. Quotations must be accurate.

(original)　　*People go to all sorts of trouble and expense to look uncombed, unshaved, unpressed.*

(inaccurate)　*As Cousins says, "People go to <u>a lot</u> of trouble and expense to look uncombed, unshaven, <u>and</u> unpressed."*

2. *Every* quotation should be integrated into your text with a transition that refers to its source.

Cousins says, "Slovenly speech comes off the same spool."
Next, Cousins discusses sloppy speech, saying it "comes off the same spool" as sloppy dress.

3. Use correct punctuation to separate transitions from quotations.

　　a. Use commas to set off transitional phrases that introduce a complete-sentence quotation.

　　　According to Cousins, "The sloppiness virus has spread to all sectors of society."
　　　"The sloppiness virus," according to Cousins, "has spread to all sectors of society."
　　　"The sloppiness virus has spread to all sectors of society," according to Cousins.

　　b. Use a colon to separate a complete-sentence quotation from a complete-sentence transition.

　　　Cousins is emphatic in his assertion that sloppiness affects us all: "The sloppiness virus has spread to all sectors of society."

　　c. Do not use any punctuation to set off partial quotations unless you would have used punctuation even if the quotation marks were not there.

　　　Cousins insists that sloppiness affects "all sectors of society."

4. Use brackets if you need to add one or more of your own words for clarity and an ellipsis (three spaced dots) if you leave out material.

(original)   *People go to all sorts of trouble and expense to look uncombed, unshaved, unpressed.*

(quotation)   *Cousins claims that many people today go to great lengths to appear "uncombed, unshaved, [and] unpressed."*

(original)   *If society is breaking down, as it too often appears to be, it is not because we lack the brainpower to meet its demands but because our feelings are so dulled that we don't recognize we have a problem.*

(quotation)   *According to Cousins, "If society is breaking down . . . it is not because we lack the brainpower to meet its demands. . . ."*

Note: Words added in brackets must *not* alter the author's idea, and words omitted need *not* be replaced with an ellipsis if it is obvious that they have been omitted. Notice that none of the partial quotations in any of the above examples need ellipses. Also notice that the last example has *four* spaced dots. The fourth dot is a period.

5. Use single quotation marks to indicate a quotation that appears within another quotation.

Cousins states that people today speak in "chopped-up phrases, relying on grunts and chants of 'you know' or 'I mean' to cover up a damnable incoherence."

6. Punctuate the end of a quotation correctly.

a. Place periods and commas within quotation marks.

Cousins also states, "Nothing is wrong with comfortable clothing."

"Nothing is wrong with comfortable clothing," Cousins states.

b. Place semicolons and colons outside quotation marks.

Cousin also states, "Nothing is wrong with comfortable clothing"; however, he does object to our "slavish conformity."

c. Place question marks and exclamation points within quotation marks if the quotation is a question or exclamation. In all other situations, place them outside.

Do you agree when Cousins writes, "Violence in language has become almost as casual as the possession of handguns"?

In "Rambos of the Road," Martin Gottfried asks, "How many of us speed up when a driver signals his intention of pulling in front of us?"

EXERCISE   Write a brief summary of Barry McLaughlin's "How Fathers Talk to Babies," which appears on pages 111–113. Your summary should identify the central point and main ideas of the article. Follow the above suggestions for writing paraphrases and quotations in your summary.

Writing an Extended Summary

Although brief summaries are handy for expressing the main ideas of something you have read, many papers, reports, or presentations will require a more detailed summary of your source, one that explains the main ideas more thoroughly, pointing out which ideas the author has emphasized and how the author has supported those ideas. Writing an extended summary is excellent practice for such assignments. To write a successful extended summary, you need to read carefully and accurately and to communicate what you have read clearly and completely to someone else.

The steps in the writing of an extended summary are essentially the same as those in the writing of a brief summary. However, the extended summary is written as a brief essay, with individual paragraphs explaining the author's points in more detail than in a brief summary. Below is an extended summary of "The Decline of Neatness." Notice how each paragraph focuses on one of the article's main points.

A Sample Extended Summary

In his article "The Decline of Neatness," Norman Cousins claims that a "sloppiness virus" has infected all areas of our society. His evidence focuses specifically on our style of dress, our casual speaking habits, our apathetic attitude toward violence and brutality, and our ineffective human relationships.

Cousins first examines the way we dress. He points out that the torn, sloppy jeans worn by so many people today can stand as a symbol of our times. According to Cousins, today it is fashionable to look disheveled, but such sloppiness is really not much more than a "slavish conformity." In fact, he says that today's sloppy dress makes people look as if they had been "stamped out by cookie cutters." It suggests, he says, a phoniness, as if the mere "appearance of alienation" were our goal.

In addition to the sloppiness in our dress, Cousins discusses the sloppy speech so common today. He says that people today speak in "chopped-up phrases," rarely use complete sentences, and lack the ability to use the English language effectively. Our speech, he says, is violent and foul, so foul in fact that screenwriters today resist turning in scripts that are too tame in order to avoid receiving any rating lower than an R (restricted).

Our foul and violent speech, according to Cousins, results in casual attitudes towards all violence and brutality. Cousins claims that we seem to be losing the ability to react to suffering, that "mindless violence" is the characteristic of our age. He says that the violence and brutality in movies and television are "desensitizing" our children and that such casual attitudes toward violence will not be outgrown.

Cousins' final point concerns human relationships. He suggests that our sloppy clothing, speech, and emotions affect human relationships, as is evident in the casual attitude toward sex in films. Our willingness to accept such casual sex, he says, deadens our feelings and destroys our privacy. It turns us not into lustful people, but into people who are incapable of feeling anything. Norman Cousins closes his article by stating that he does not want to return to Victorian attitudes, although he does hope that our "calculated sloppiness" will eventually disappear. He suggests that fashion designers and movie or television producers might someday discover that people would respond to clothes and movies that show respect for the human form and spirit, and he hopes that schools will find ways to encourage students to pursue "genuine creativity" in all areas of their lives.

EXERCISE   Work with other students to develop responses to these questions or to compare responses that you have already prepared.

1. Examine the introductory paragraph of the sample extended summary above. Where does it state the central idea of "The Decline of Neatness"? What other information does it include?

2. Identify the topic sentence of each body paragraph. Which paragraph or paragraphs from "The Decline of Neatness" does that topic sentence introduce?

3. Identify the transitions between paragraphs.

4. Examine the support within each paragraph. Have any points been left out of it that you think should have been included?

Writing a Summary-Response Essay

Many college writing assignments will ask you both to summarize what you have read and to respond to it. After all, your ability to express your own reaction to a topic is certainly as important as your ability to summarize that topic. Although the structure of such an essay will vary, depending on the topic and the expectations of your instructor, one common format consists of a brief summary in your introductory paragraph, followed by a clear thesis statement of your own in the same introductory paragraph, followed by several body paragraphs that support and develop your thesis statement. When you write a summary-response essay, keep the following points in mind:

1. The introduction should include a brief summary of the article and its main points.

2. The introduction should include a thesis statement that expresses your response to the topic.

3. Each body paragraph should open with a topic sentence that clearly refers to and develops the thesis statement.

4. Each body paragraph should support its topic sentence with explanations, facts, examples, statistics, or references to authority.

5. Each sentence should reflect a sense of coherence by exhibiting a clear relationship to the sentence before it or to the topic sentence of the paragraph.

Sample Summary-Response Essay

In "The Decline of Neatness," Norman Cousins argues that a "sloppiness virus" is affecting all areas of our society. According to Cousins, the sloppy clothing that is so in fashion today reflects our desperate need to conform, making us look as if we had been "stamped out by cookie cutters." Our sloppy speech reflects the same need, but it is more than just sloppy: it is foul and violent. He says that our sloppy language results in casual attitudes toward all violence and brutality and that, as a result, our children are losing the ability to react to suffering. Finally, he suggests that our sloppy clothing, speech, and attitudes affect human relationships, resulting in a sexual exploitation that "deadens feelings and annihilates privacy." I believe that Cousins's points are well worth considering. In fact, I have found that his "sloppiness virus" has affected my life and the lives of people I know in a number of significant areas.

A quick jaunt down the freeway will reveal the sloppiness virus at work in the way we drive our cars. Many drivers today either do not care about other people on the road or do not realize how dangerous their sloppy driving habits really are. Cars switch from one lane to the other and back again without signaling; they weave in and out of traffic; they race up to the rear bumper of the car in front of them—even if both cars are in the right lane—and tailgate for miles. Not too many months ago I was nearly killed by a sloppy driver in a white Celica. Traffic was heavy, moving at only about forty-five miles per hour, when he raced up behind me and began to flash his brights—as if there were anywhere I could go. As soon as he had the chance, he changed lanes to the left, raced past, me, changed lanes again so that he was now in front of me, and then plowed into the rear of a bus. I had just enough time to brace myself before I smashed into him. I awoke in the hospital with a broken hip and a smashed ankle—all because of one person's sloppy driving habits.

As well as turning drivers into life-threatening idiots, the sloppiness virus affects our attitudes toward relationships. Many people today (myself included) act as if relationships should be easy, as if "love" should smooth out all the rough spots and keep us comfortable. I know of couple after couple who have separated or divorced or broken up after their relationship became more work than romance. But I also know a few couples who have managed to drop the sloppy expectation that relationships should be easy. One person in particular, a friend named Bob, nearly walked out of a sixteen-year marriage last year, but today he and his wife are closer than I have ever seen them. When I asked him what made the difference, he said that he decided to act *as if* he still loved his wife until he really did feel love for her again. He said, "I faked it until I made it." Don't misunderstand me. I'm not saying that we should never have the courage to end unhealthy relationships, but something is wrong when more than 50% of all marriages end in divorce.

Finally, I see the sloppiness virus at work every day in my own thinking and in the thinking of people I know. When a person is faced with a situation that is uncomfortable or that challenges his or her beliefs, it is easier *not* to think. It is easier to grab hold of the nearest, safest stereotype and believe in that. When the issue of gays in the military recently arose, for example, I had to laugh at how many people refused to consider the issues and took refuge in their stereotypical fears that gays are some sort of moral deformity that will invade the barracks and seduce all of our helpless young boys, destroying the "morale" of our troops. I see the same sort of thing happen when people from different races marry. When our new neighbors moved in—a young white woman and her black husband—many people around us were appalled (and yet these same people would never consider themselves racists). Unfortunately, it is just too easy for many of us to retreat into our sloppy thinking and hasty moral judgments.

Norman Cousins has raised an issue that touches us all, for all of us, in our sloppiness, want things to go *our* way. We do not want to have to change ourselves. The driver on the freeway wishes cars would part before him so he can be as reckless as he wants to be; the lover in a relationship wishes the other person would change so that he or she does not have to; and all people wish life itself would stop challenging them with situations that force them to think for themselves. We are, indeed, all victims of the sloppiness virus. Perhaps that virus is part of being a human being.

EXERCISE   Work with other students to develop responses to these questions or to compare responses that you have already prepared.

1. The introduction to the summary-response essay is much more developed than the introduction to the extended summary essay. Why? What is it doing that is different?

2. Identify the thesis statement of the essay.

3. Identify the topic sentence of each body paragraph. Does it clearly introduce the topic of the paragraph?

4. Identify the transitions between paragraphs. Also, explain how each topic sentence is clearly connected to the thesis statement.

5. Examine the support in each paragraph. Point out which sentences are generalized explanations and which are specific examples.

6. Examine the concluding paragraph and explain what it does to bring the essay to a satisfactory close.

Readings

It Is Time to Stop Playing Indians

ARLENE B. HIRSCHFELDER

Before You Read

1. What might Hirschfelder mean by "playing Indians"? What sort of attitude toward Native Americans does "playing Indians" suggest?

2. Where have you seen references to Native Americans in our culture? Would you describe those references as respectful? Playful? Harmful?

It is predictable. At Halloween, thousands of children trick-or-treat in Indian costumes. At Thanksgiving, thousands of children parade in school pageants wearing plastic headdresses and pseudo-buckskin clothing. Thousands of card shops stock Thanksgiving greeting cards with images of cartoon animals wearing feathered headbands. Thousands of teachers and librarians trim bulletin boards with Anglo-featured, feathered Indian boys and girls. Thousands of gift shops load their shelves with Indian figurines and jewelry.

Fall and winter are also the seasons when hundreds of thousands of sports fans root for professional, college and public school teams with names that summon up Indians—"Braves," "Redskins," "Chiefs." (In New York State, one out of eight junior and senior high school teams call themselves "Indians," "Tomahawks" and the like.) War-whooping team mascots are imprinted on school uniforms, postcards, notebooks, tote bags and car floor mats.

All of this seems innocuous; why make a fuss about it? Because these   3
trappings and holiday symbols offend tens of thousands of other
Americans—the native American people. Because these invented images
prevent millions of us from understanding the authentic Indian America,
both long ago and today. Because this image-making prevents Indians
from being a relevant part of the nation's social fabric.

Halloween costumes mask the reality of high mortality rates, high   4
diabetes rates, high unemployment rates. They hide low average life
spans, low per capita incomes and low educational levels. Plastic war
bonnets and ersatz buckskin deprive people from knowing the complexity of Native American heritage—that Indians belong to hundreds of
nations that have intricate social organizations, governments, languages,
religions and sacred rituals, ancient stories, unique arts and music forms.

Thanksgiving school units and plays mask history. They do not tell   5
how Europeans mistreated Wampanoags and other East Coast Indian
peoples during the 17th century. Social studies units don't mention that,
to many Indians, Thanksgiving is a day of mourning, the beginning of
broken promises, land theft, near extinction of their religions and languages at the hands of invading Europeans.

Athletic team nicknames and mascots disguise real people. Warpainted,   6
buckskin-clad, feathered characters keep the fictitious Indian circulating
on decals, pennants and team clothing. Toy companies mask Indian identity and trivialize sacred beliefs by manufacturing Indian costumes and
headdresses, peace pipes and trick-arrow-through-the-head gags that
equate Indianness with playtime. Indian figures equipped with arrows,
guns and tomahawks give youngsters the harmful message that Indians
favor mayhem. Many Indian people can tell about children screaming in
fear after being introduced to them.

It is time to consider how these images impede the efforts of Indian   7
parents and communities to raise their children with positive information about their heritage. It is time to get rid of stereotypes that, whether
deliberately or inadvertently, denigrate Indian cultures and people.

It is time to bury the Halloween costumes, trick arrows, bulletin-board   8
pin-ups, headdresses and mascots. It is has been done before. In the
1970s, after student protests, Marquette University dropped its "Willie
Wampum," Stanford University retired its mascot, "Prince Lightfoot,"
and Eastern Michigan University and Florida State modified their savage-
looking mascots to reduce criticism.

It is time to stop playing Indians. It is time to abolish Indian images   9
that sell merchandise. It is time to stop offending Indian people whose

lives are all too often filled with economic deprivation, powerlessness, discrimination and gross injustice. This time next year, let's find more appropriate symbols for the holiday and sports seasons.

Reprinted by permission of the author.

After You Read

Work with other students to develop responses to these questions or to compare responses that you have already prepared.

1. State the thesis of the article in your own words. What sentences in the article, if any, best express the thesis idea?

2. Divide the article into sections according to each major point that Hirschfelder makes.

3. Briefly summarize the thesis of the article and its major supporting points.

4. Hirschfelder believes that the images of Native Americans in our society stereotype them. Do you agree? Why or why not?

5. What other groups of people do we stereotype, and in what way?

What Your Body Language Says about You

GERALD ASTOR

Before You Read

1. Do you already know what *body language* is? Define it as best you can before you read the article.

2. What parts of your body reveal how you feel or what you think to other people?

"Your lips say, 'No, no, no,' but your eyes say, 'Yes, yes, yes'" is a line from an old popular song. It may sound somewhat phony, but the author was hinting at that kind of nonverbal communication known as body language. It can reflect a person's views more accurately than any words coming from his or her mouth. 1

Body language covers the infinite range of facial and body movements, including the myriad ways to smile, to walk, to manipulate your eyes, to move your hands and arms. We draw messages from body language, whether it's the "no" that a shake of the head conveys, the "I'm not interested" that a turning away of the head can suggest, or the "Hey, I'm bad" statement Richard Pryor and Gene Wilder expected their swaggers 2 to make in *Stir Crazy*. Sometimes, the messages are conveyed through deliberate, conscious gestures; other times, our bodies talk without our even knowing. But conscious or not, our body language helps us portray a wide range of feelings, including boredom, amusement, impatience, fatigue, concentration, interest, puzzlement, and embarrassment.

Some of our body-language expressions are common idioms. To most people, for example, the thumb and forefinger forming a circle means "Everything's okay." A fist with the thumb pointing up is "Good luck" or "All systems go." Desmond Morris, a behavioral scientist and the author of *The Naked Ape* (McGraw-Hill), was among those who studied the interpretations of twenty specific gestures by people in Europe, North Africa, and the Middle East. He found similarities in understanding despite the geographic and cultural differences. (The most universally recognized signal was the thumb at the tip of the nose with the fingers spread!)

Body language becomes more complicated when we try to translate the movements, postures, and facial expressions that a person has little or no control over—the actions that spring from the dark well within us, our unconscious. These bits of body language are often subtle, may contradict our words, and frequently involve a series of actions.

The eyes are one of the most revealing instruments of body language. Keith, seventeen, from Montclair, New Jersey, learned the hard way about one message the eyes can convey. "I had a teacher who graded heavily on classroom discussion," Keith says. "He seemed to have a weird ability to know just when I didn't have the answers. I couldn't figure out how he could be so sharp. Then it dawned on me. Whenever I didn't know the answer, I would avoid looking at him. When I did know what to say, I always stared straight back at him. From that moment on, I taught myself to look him in the eye, whether I knew the work or not. That trick has saved me a lot of grief."

Many people, including some policemen, believe eye contact is a good test of honesty. If someone can't look you dead in the eye, then he or she is not playing straight, they insist. After many experiments, however, a number of experts have concluded that good liars can fake eye contact. (If you still believe that a chap staring straight into your baby blues will never lie to you, then someday, I'd like to interest you in a share of the Grand Canyon.)

Eye contact, though not a sure sign of honesty, is a clear way to show interest in another person. When a person looks at you and continues to do so, you know his attention is focused on you. When he turns his head away, his mind is probably elsewhere: you are no longer "numero uno." But there are exceptions. A shy person may have trouble making and maintaining eye contact, no matter how interested he is in the other person. And certain nationalities, such as the British and the Germans, are much less oriented to eyeball-to-eyeball encounters than, say, the French and the Arabs.

When the eyes act in concert with other parts of the face, communication becomes increasingly explicit. In a study in which psychologists A. Thayer and W. Schiff showed a series of facial diagrams to a panel of people, there was a very strong agreement on the messages (the results of their study were published in the *American Journal of Psychology* in 1969). Pleasure widens the eyes and is usually accompanied by a smile. Thus, poker players who are dealt a good hand must learn to control their body language and develop a "poker face." The "drop dead" or "if looks could kill" expression is produced by wrinkling the eyebrows, narrowing the eyes, and turning down the corners of the mouth. Surprise sends the eyebrows skyward and widens the gaze. Despair hoods the eyes, makes the mouth droop, and often causes the entire body to slump. 8

Like the eyes, the smile is remarkably varied. The genuinely happy smile flashes both upper and lower teeth and is accompanied by open eyes and relaxed brows. In the sheepish smile—you've spilled your soda pop and that nice fellow offers his help—the corners of the mouth are turned up, the eyebrows lifted. The fiendish smile consists of a wide grin and a scrunching of the eyebrows. 9

Hand movements are another area where there is common understanding of the action. Shake your fist, and everyone realizes that you're angry. Rub your palms together, and you're probably anticipating something good. Rub your palms and the backs of your hands, and you're probably just cold. Point and you are signaling a direction. Point a finger at someone, and you're making an accusation. 10

Sometimes a person brings a hand up to his mouth while talking. That gesture could be an effort to stop others from hearing or an unconscious admission of doubt or that there's something being concealed. A hand at the throat may indicate some uncertainty about the words being spoken. 11

Politicians frequently use hand movements to hold the attention of an audience. Former President Gerald Ford, regarded as a less than spellbinding orator, was once counseled by advisers to add a number of gestures to punctuate a speech. He did so—but apparently unsuccessfully. A poll of those who listened revealed that one third agreed with Ford, one third disagreed, and one third were so distracted by his gesticula- 12 tions that they didn't know what he had said. Artificial movements are the bad grammar of body language and confuse listeners (which is why some politicians and actors rely on experts to coach them in effective nonverbal communication).

One of the most clearly recognized expressions of body language is the handshake. (It is believed that originally a handshake was a way of showing a person that one came unarmed.) We draw information from the quality of the squeeze. A flabby grip suggests weakness or a lack of interest. Too much pressure signals a desire to dominate. 13

The position of the entire body is also important when interpreting nonverbal communication. "When I meet someone sitting with his legs or ankles crossed tightly and his arms folded over his chest, I feel that he's closed off from me and uninterested," says sixteen-year-old Julie, a Brooklyn high school senior. She has correctly interpreted a posture that translators of body language classify as "closed." If an individual feels relaxed, giving, and receptive, he's usually in an "open position": His arms are unclasped, and his legs apart. 14

Closed positions tend to discourage intruders. And as Marianne La France and Clara Mayo, the authors of *Moving Bodies* (Wadsworth) note, anyone in this posture is also far less likely to be convincing in a discussion; listeners may feel he's not revealing as much as he should. It's important, though, to keep in mind that whether or not a person assumes a closed or open position may have a lot to do with upbringing. Women, for example, because of the female tradition of wearing skirts, have customarily been taught to assume a "ladylike" position and keep their legs together (though that may be changing with the growing acceptance of women wearing pants). 15

Of course, there are other communicative postures besides the closed and open positions. For example, resting the chin upon the hand—the posture of Rodin's sculpture "The Thinker"—is an accepted sign of cogitation. But, says Ellen, an eighteen-year-old from New York, "When a person rests his cheek on his hand, it can mean, 'I'm uninterested.'" 16

Posture—indeed, all of body language—is wrapped up in a person's self image. People uncomfortable with their bodies may adopt a round-shouldered slouch and wear baggy clothes. People who are content with their self-image are more likely to stand straight and wear form-fitting apparel. 17

Body language can also serve as a kind of dialogue between two people. For example, if two people sit on a couch with their arms and legs in similar positions, it usually means they're in agreement. A man 18 and a woman on the same couch who have adopted widely different ways of sitting and who are not looking at one another are probably out of touch with each other. A male and female sitting on a couch, facing each other, are announcing closeness. If one leans forward, that one is trying to get even closer. If the other is not interested in more involvement, he or she may lean back.

But once again, cultural differences play a role. Wendy, a high school   19
junior from Scarsdale whose parents are Korean and who spent her first years of life in Korea, says, "I don't like showing signs of closeness in public. I feel uncomfortable greeting people at a party with a hug or kiss. I wasn't brought up that way." Those unaware of the cultural differences might mistakenly read her body language as a sign of aloofness or coldness.

Other mistakes are common when trying to translate body language.   20
Says Kathy, a seventeen-year-old from New York, "When someone just spreads himself out, I can't tell whether he's terribly relaxed or just a slob." When an adolescent slouches in front of an adult, it may be a rebellious statement (parents are always demanding that one stand up straight), or it may be that the person is very much at ease.

But although you can never fully understand another's body   21
language—or fully control your own—you can be aware that nonverbal cues are as important to communication as words. Increase your knowledge of body language, and you'll be a little less confused in a world of many different messages.

From Seventeen *magazine. ©1981. Reprinted by permission of the author.*

After You Read

Work with other students to develop responses to these questions or to compare responses that you have already prepared.

1. State the thesis of the article in your own words. What sentences in the article, if any, best express the thesis idea?

2. Divide the article into sections according to each major point that Astor makes.

3. Briefly summarize the thesis of the article and its major supporting points.

4. Do you use the body language described by Astor? Describe actual situations that further illustrate the points he makes.

5. What other types of body language do you use? Give specific examples of how body language reveals who you are.

College Lectures: Is Anybody Listening?

DAVID DANIELS

Before You Read

1. What do you think are the major drawbacks of lecture classes as opposed to discussion classes?

2. What are the benefits of lecture classes?

A former teacher of mine, Robert A. Fowkes of New York University, likes to tell the story of a class he took in Old Welsh while studying in Germany during the 1930s. On the first day the professor strode up to the podium, shuffled his notes, coughed, and began, *"Guten Tag, Meine Damen und Herren"* ("Good day, ladies and gentlemen"). Fowkes glanced around uneasily. He was the only student in the course.

Toward the middle of the semester, Fowkes fell ill and missed a class. When he returned, the professor nodded vaguely and, to Fowkes's astonishment, began to deliver not the next lecture in the sequence but the one after. Had he, in fact, lectured to an empty hall in the absence of his solitary student? Fowkes though it perfectly possible.

Today, American colleges and universities (originally modeled on German ones) are under strong attack from many quarters. Teachers, it is charged, are not doing a good job of teaching, and students are not doing a good job of learning. American businesses and industries suffer from unenterprising, uncreative executives educated not to think for themselves but to mouth outdated truisms the rest of the world has long discarded. College graduates lack both basic skills and general culture. Studies are conducted and reports are issued on the status of higher education, but any changes that result either are largely cosmetic or make a bad situation worse.

One aspect of American education too seldom challenged is the lecture system. Professors continue to lecture and students to take notes much as they did in the thirteenth century, when books were so scarce and expensive that few students could own them. The time is long overdue for us to abandon the lecture system and turn to methods that really work.

To understand the inadequacy of the present system, it is enough to follow a single imaginary first-year student—let's call her Mary—through a term of lectures on, say, introductory psychology (although any other subject would do as well). She arrives on the first day and looks around the huge lecture hall, taken a little aback to see how large the class is. Once the hundred or more students enrolled in the course discover that the professor never takes attendance (how can he?—calling the role would take far too much time), the class shrinks to a less imposing size.

Some days Mary sits in the front row, from where she can watch the professor read from a stack of yellowed notes that seem nearly as old as he is. She is bored by the lectures, and so are most of the other students, to judge by the way they are nodding off or doodling in their notebooks. Gradually she realizes the professor is as bored as his audience. At the end of each lecture he asks, "Are there any questions?" in a tone of voice that makes it plain he would much rather there weren't. He needn't worry—the students are as relieved as he is that the class is over.

Mary knows very well she should read an assignment before every lecture. However, as the professor gives no quizzes and asks no questions, she soon realizes she needn't prepare. At the end of the term she catches up by skimming her notes and memorizing a list of facts and dates. After the final exam, she promptly forgets much of what she has memorized. Some of her fellow students, disappointed at the impersonality of it all, drop out of college altogether. Others, like Mary, stick it out, grow resigned to the system and await better days when, as juniors and seniors, they will attend smaller classes and at last get the kind of personal attention real learning requires.

I admit this pictures is overdrawn—most universities supplement lecture courses with discussion groups, usually led by graduate students, and some classes, such as first-year English, are always relatively small. Nevertheless, far too many courses rely principally or entirely on lectures, an arrangement much loved by faculty and administrators but scarcely designed to benefit the students.

One problem with lectures is that listening intelligently is hard work. Reading the same material in a textbook is a more efficient way to learn because students can proceed as slowly as they need to until the subject matter becomes clear to them. Even simply paying attention is very difficult: people can listen at a rate of four hundred to six hundred words a minute, while the most impassioned professor talks at scarcely a third of that speed. This time lag between speech and comprehension leads to daydreaming. Many students believe years of watching television have sabotaged their attention span, but their real problem is that listening attentively is much harder than they think.

Worse still, attending lectures is passive learning, at least for inexperi-   10
enced listeners. Active learning, in which students write essays or perform experiments and then have their work evaluated by an instructor, is
far more beneficial for those who have not yet fully learned how to
learn. While it's true that techniques of active listening, such as trying to
anticipate the speaker's next point or taking notes selectively, can
enhance the value of a lecture, few students possess such skills at the
beginning of their college careers. More commonly, students try to write
everything down and even bring tape recorders to class in a clumsy effort
to capture every word.

Students need to question their professors and to have their ideas   11
taken seriously. Only then will they develop the analytical skills required
to think intelligently and creatively. Most students learn best by engaging
in frequent and even heated debate, not by scribbling down a professor's
often unsatisfactory summary of complicated issues. They need small
discussion classes that demand the common labors of teacher and students rather than classes in which one person, however learned, pro-
pounds his or her own ideas.

The lecture system ultimately harms professors as well. It reduces   12
feedback to a minimum, so that the lecturer can neither judge how well
students understand the material nor benefit from their questions or
comments. Questions that require the speaker to clarify obscure points
and comments that challenge sloppily constructed arguments are indis-
pensable to scholarship. Without them, the liveliest mind can atrophy.
Undergraduates may not be able to make telling contributions very
often, but lecturing insulates a professor even from the beginner's naive
question that could have triggered fruitful line of thought.

If lectures make so little sense, why have they been allowed to con-   13
tinue? Administrators love them, of course. They can cram far more students into a lecture hall than into a discussion class, and for many
administrators that is almost the end of the story. But the truth is that
faculty members, and even students, conspire with them to keep the lecture system alive and well. Lectures are easier on everyone than debates.
Professors can pretend to teach by lecturing just as students can pretend
to learn by attending lectures, with no one the wiser, including the participants. Moreover, if lectures afford some students an opportunity to
sit back and let the professor run the show, they offer some professors
an irresistible forum for showing off. In a classroom where everyone
contributes, students are less able to hide and professors less tempted to
engage in intellectual exhibitionism.

Smaller classes in which students are required to involve themselves 14
in discussion put an end to students' passivity. Students become actively
involved when forced to question their own ideas as well as their instructor's. Their listening skills improve dramatically in the excitement of
intellectual give and take with their instructors and fellow students. Such
interchanges help professors do their job better because they allow them
to discover who knows what—before final exams, not after. When
exams are given in this type of course, they can require analysis and synthesis from the students, not empty memorization. Classes like this
require energy, imagination, and commitment from professors, all of
which can be exhausting. But they compel students to share responsibility for their own intellectual growth.

Lectures will never entirely disappear from the university scene both 15
because they seem to be economically necessary and because they spring
from a long tradition in a setting that rightly values tradition for its own
sake. But the lectures too frequently come at the wrong end of the students' educational careers—during the first two years, when they most
need close, even individual, instruction. If lecture classes were restricted
to junior and senior undergraduates and to graduate students, who are
less in need of scholarly nurturing and more able to prepare work on
their own, they would be far less destructive of students' interests and
enthusiasm than the present system. After all, students must learn to listen before they can listen to learn.

©1987 by Trend *magazine. Reprinted by permission of the publisher.*

After You Read

Work with other students to develop responses to these questions or to compare responses
that you have already prepared.

1. State the thesis of the article in your own words. What sentences in the article, if any,
   best express the thesis idea?

2. Divide the article into sections according to each major point that Daniels makes.

3. Briefly summarize the thesis of the article and its major supporting points.

4. Describe your own experiences in lecture classes. Are they similar to the experiences of
   other members of your class?

5. Explain what you think the student's responsibility is in the learning process. Does this
   article address that responsibility?

Writing Assignments

1. Write a brief summary of one of the four reading assignments in this chapter or of a reading assignment from Part Four of this text.

2. Write an extended summary of one of the four reading assignments in this chapter or of a reading assignment from Part Four of this text.

3. Write a summary-response essay on Arlene Hirschfelder's "It Is Time to Stop Playing Indians." After briefly summarizing her article, your introduction should include a thesis of your own that responds to one of the following topics or to a topic assigned by your instructor:

   a. What do you think of the ways Native Americans are portrayed in our society? Following Hirschfelder's example, examine several different areas that reflect our attitudes toward Native Americans and explain your reaction to those attitudes. You may use the same areas discussed by Hirschfelder, but the support you use and the points you make should be your own.

   b. Stereotyping groups of people is, unfortunately, a common human activity. Respond to Hirschfelder's essay by explaining in what ways another group of people is stereotyped and why that stereotyping is unfair or inaccurate. Remember to support your points with clear explanations and specific details.

4. Write a summary-response essay on Gerald Astor's "What Your Body Language Says about You." After briefly summarizing his article, your introduction should include a thesis of your own that responds to one of the following topics or to a topic assigned by your instructor:

   a. Using the points discussed by Astor, analyze your own body language. What do you do that reveals who you are or what you are thinking or feeling? Cover several different types of body language in your response, and remember to support your points with clear explanations and specific details of your own.

   b. Astor suggests that a person's body language unconsciously reveals a wealth of information to other people. Spend some time watching the people you encounter, then write an essay in which you explain what their body language communicated to you.

5. Write a summary-response essay on David Daniels's "College Lectures: Is Anybody Listening?" After briefly summarizing his article, your introduction should include a thesis of your own that responds to one of the following topics or to a topic assigned by your instructor.

   a. Daniels clearly believes that larger lecture classes are less effective than smaller discussion classes. Have you experienced any exceptions to his argument? Write an essay in which you explain a few of the strengths of lecture classes and the weak-nesses of discussion classes. Or, if you prefer, write an essay in which you further illustrate the weaknesses of lecture classes with examples of your own.

    b. Daniels suggests that smaller class sizes would benefit both students and professors. Of course, the argument that "smaller is better" can be applied to many areas of life. Write an essay in which you discuss several areas of life where smaller is better. Remember to support your points with clear explanations and specific details of your own.

6. Write a summary-response essay on one of the reading assignments in Part Four of this text. After briefly summarizing the article, your introduction should include a thesis of your own that responds to a topic assigned by your instructor.

Evaluating Sample Papers

Extended Summaries

As you read and evaluate the following extended summaries, consider these areas:

1. Introduction

Underline the sentence(s) that states the central idea of the article. Is it accurate and clear? Does the introduction prepare the reader for an extended summary and not for a summary-response?

    1   2   3   4   5   6

2. Unity

Does each paragraph have a clear and specific topic sentence that accurately introduces one of the major sections of the article? Does the material in each paragraph clearly relate to its topic sentence?

    1   2   3   4   5   6

3. Support

Are all of the major points in the article summarized? Is each point accurately and fully explained?

    1   2   3   4   5   6

4. Coherence

Are transitions used between paragraphs? Where needed, are transitions used between sentences within each paragraph?

    1   2   3   4   5   6

5. References to the Text

Are direct quotations and paraphrases correctly introduced and smoothly incorporated into the text? Do they reflect the author's points accurately?

1   2   3   4   5   6

6. Sentence Structure

Do the sentences combine ideas that are related, using coordination, subordination, or verbal phrases when appropriate? Are there too many brief, choppy main clauses?

1   2   3   4   5   6

7. Mechanics, Grammar, and Spelling

Does the paper contain a distracting number of errors of these kinds?

1   2   3   4   5   6

8. Overall Ranking of the Essay

1   2   3   4   5   6

Student Summary 1

In his article, "The Decline of Neatness," Norman Cousins explains that a "sloppiness virus" has spread to all categories of life. His evidence of this virus is directed towards the way we dress, the way we speak, the way we treat one another, and the way we act in relationships.

In his first point, Norman Cousins speaks of our clothing. According to Cousins, "The symbol of the times is blue jeans." He describes our blue jeans as frayed, torn, and discolored, and he shows that the more worn and "ancient" the jeans look, the higher the price on the tag will be. Cousins writes, "Disheveled is in fashion; neatness is obsolete." He implies that this generation tries desperately to appear as individuals, but we come out looking like we stepped off an assembly line. He shows that in order to be different, we must be well groomed and even neat.

In the next section of his article, Cousins shows that our vocabulary has been "drained of color as well," and communication has progressed into grunts, chants, chopped up phrases, and "the incessant use of four letter words." He demonstrates this point by mentioning that screenwriters will not turn in a script without at least a handful of obscene words because they do not want to receive a "'G' rating." These screenwriters "employ tasteless language and gory scenes" so that they receive the strongly preferred "'R' rating."

Next, Cousins moves into the idea that our sloppiness in attitudes is directly related to our casualness toward violence. He states," People are not as uncomfortable as they ought to be about the glamorization of human hurt." He suggests that we take "debasement and dismembering" of human beings for granted and that if we continue to let this happen, the younger generation will be desensitized "to everything that should produce revulsion or resistance." He says our aim should be to educate the younger people to respect and cherish life.

Cousins' final point helps summarize the article by showing that our short-comings in other aspects in life, such as clothing and vocabulary, have a direct impact on how we view our relationships. Cousins states, "Untidiness in dress, speech, and emotions is readily connected to human relationships." He implies that we have become apathetic because we have seen too much and have become immune to our feelings. He reminds us that because we are so casual with our feelings and our privacy, casual sex is as "fashionable" as our clothing.

In conclusion, Cousins points out that the outlook may be positive. Maybe a fashion designer will create a fashion that is not frayed and "grace[s] the human form." Maybe a screen writer will write a movie "to show people expressing genuine love and respect for one another." Maybe our schools could "encourage the notion that fewer things are more rewarding than gen-uine creativity." Cousins implies that the choice is ours: do we want to be "cookie cutters" or do we want to be unique?

Student Summary 2

According to Norman Cousins in his article, "The Decline of Neatness," the sloppiness virus has spread to all sectors of society. He thinks people go to great lengths and expense to look uncombed, unshaved, and unpressed. Anyone who is passionate about labels, he says, can tag us the Unkempt gen-eration. He certainly makes us think about our appearance.

One factor he uses as a basis for that opinion is the fashion in blue jeans today. They are torn, discolored and look as though they have been discarded by a house painter. The fashion of today is disheveled. The author is not opposed to comfortable clothing. He thinks the desire for nonconformity has created people like cookie cutters. They are desperate not to be well groomed, their appearance takes on an uncaring quality.

Mr. Cousins attacks the modern day slovenly speech. He compares it to the blue jeans, and it is drained of color, with chopped up phrases, grunts, and chants. The violence in our language and the four letter words are a sign of decline. Some screen writers use four letter words so they don't get rated G. Violence is also affecting people. Battering and mutilations on TV and in movies leave us desensitized to the dismembering of humans. It also fosters attitudes of casualness, and children cannot outgrow the casualness.

Human relationships are connected to the lack of tidiness in dress, speech, and emotions. Sexual exploitation, which is fashionable is films today, does not create sex fiends, on the contrary, it deadens feelings. "People who have the habit of seeing everything and doing anything run the risk of feeling nothing.'

He goes on to say that his purpose is not to make a case for the return to Victorian decorum, but rather to examine bad dress, manners, speech, and human relationships. He hopes fashion designers and motion picture producers will realize that there are people who want something better. Films that show genuine love and respect.

In conclusion, Norman Cousins says that schools may begin to encourage genuine creativity in clothes fashion, communication and human relationships. Perhaps, he says, we can locate the best in ourselves and put it to work.

Summary-Response Essays

As you read and evaluate the following summary-response essays, consider these areas:

1. Introduction

Does the introduction contain a clear and accurate brief summary of the central idea and major supporting points of the article? Does it prepare the reader for a summary-response essay by moving to a thesis of the writer's own?

1   2   3   4   5   6

2. Thesis Statement

Underline the thesis statement of the essay. Does it express a clear and specific central idea?

1   2   3   4   5   6

3. Topic Sentences

Underline the topic sentence of each paragraph. Does it clearly state the central idea of the paragraph?

1   2   3   4   5   6

4. Support

Examine the supporting details in each paragraph. Are they specific and clear? Should they be more detailed, or should more support be included?

1   2   3   4   5   6

5. Unity

Does each paragraph clearly relate to and develop the *central idea* expressed in the thesis statement? Do the supporting details *within* each paragraph clearly relate to and develop the *central idea* expressed in the topic sentence of that paragraph?

1   2   3   4   5   6

6. Coherence

Does each paragraph open with a transition, a reference to the central idea of the thesis statement, and an identification of its own central idea? Are the sentences within each paragraph clearly related to each other by the use of transitions or by reference to the central idea of the paragraph?

1   2   3   4   5   6

7. Sentence Structure

Do the sentences combine ideas that are related, using coordination, subordination, and verbal phrases when appropriate? Are there too many brief, choppy main clauses?

1   2   3   4   5   6

8. Mechanics, Grammar, and Spelling

Does the paper contain a distracting number of errors of these kinds?

1   2   3   4   5   6

9. Overall Ranking of the Essay

1   2 ·   3   4   5   6

Student Summary-Response 1

In the article "It Is Time to Stop Playing Indians" Arlene B. Hirschfelder argues that our society has been stereotyping and offending Indian people for hundreds of years. According to her, Halloween customs mislead our society by hiding the reality and the problems that Indian people are facing every day. For Native Americans, Thanksgiving is a day of "mourning" and not a day of celebration. She also says that athletic team nicknames and toy companies denigrate their culture. Finally, she concludes by making a plea. She hopes that we soon stop playing Indians, that we stop discriminating against them and be more careful with costumes we buy for Halloween and nicknames we use for sports teams. I believe that Hirschfelder's point of view is quite effective and that discrimination and stereotyping reflect the reality of our society. In fact, I have seen that discrimination and stereotyping have hit the Mexican community living in the United States harder than ever in many different ways.

One of the hottest topics of politicians all over the United States is illegal immigration. Every night I turn on my TV to watch the news. The first thing I hear is "Our top story tonight is that the U.S. Department of Defense is planning on sending more troops to patrol the U.S.-Mexican border. . . . Pete Wilson, the Governor of California, has proposed a new legislation to ban education for illegal immigrants. . . . Senator Diane Feinstein is planning on visiting the border next week." Those types of comments are a part of our life here in the State of California. However, the problem starts when we (Mexicans) are walking on the streets or working. Many Anglo-Americans think that all of us are here illegally. For instance, when I was working for K-mart, a man approached me and asked me for a medium size bag of popcorn. I was so busy at that time that I gave him a small bag. When he saw the small bag, he told me that he had asked me for a medium one. I told him that I was sorry, but he got angry and told me, "No, you should go back to where you came from. We are sick and tired of you Mexicans." At that point I got very angry. However, the only thing I told him was that I have been here longer than he has. Misunderstandings like the one I just mentioned have been increasing due to the racist comments that politicians have been making in the last couple years.

Mexicans in the U.S. are not only stereotyped as illegals but also as troublemakers. The perception that people have towards Mexicans is that we are either thieves or drug dealers. For example, my friends and I like to wear baggy clothes, so every time we enter a store, we have one or two employees behind us. Because of the way we are dressed, they have the impression that we are going to steal something. That really upsets me. I do not know if they chase me for the way I dress or for the color of my skin. Whatever the reason is, I believe that they should pay more attention to the needs of the customers than to the appearance of people. I know that there are some bad guys, but it is also unfair to stereotype people for the way they dress or for the color of their skin.

In addition to the stereotype of illegals and thieves that Mexicans have, we are blamed for the economic problems that the state of California is facing. The image that American people have is that Mexicans come to the United States and go straight to the welfare system. Weeks ago, I was listening to KUSI 640, John and Keen. The topic was "Should We Continue to Pay for the Medical Care of Illegals?" The number of people calling was amusing. They were arguing that 99% of Mexicans come to this country to take advantage of the welfare system. I think that is an accusation they are making without looking at the facts. In reality, the facts are that only 12% of the welfare recipients are Hispanics, which include Mexicans, Salvadorans, Guatemalans, and Colombians. 36% of them are whites and 52% are blacks. By looking at those statistics, we can clearly see that radio talk shows stereotype the whole Mexican community, even those who have never received a penny from the government.

In summary, stereotypes and racism will never go away from our lives. I believe that they are a common human activity that sooner or later we have to face. On the other hand, Mexicans living in this country must learn how to cope with stereotypes and racism and work hard to improve themselves and become more productive members of this society.

Student Summary-Response 2

In the article "What Your Body Language Says about You," Gerald Astor categorizes and explains the various form of nonverbal communication and to identify the body parts along with their communicative functions. According to Gerald Astor, a behavioral scientist by the name of Desmond Morris did a study on common idioms and found them to be universal regardless of the culture or geographical location. Many people believe the eyes along with other facial expressions are a good test of honesty or a show of intrigue in someone. Astor suggests that hand gestures indicate many different meanings ranging from boredom to domination, or using it to hold the attention of a group of people whether it's large or small. As explained by Astor, the positioning of the body can translate various forms of non-verbal communications. He mentions cultural differences once again are misconstrued when trying to understand body language. Without any doubt, I have witness a number of times where peoples body language expressed a nonverbal communication of some sort.

A lot of people don't realize what they are communicating to homeless people using body language when walking past them. Some people today don't realize the extent of the problems with the homeless or they just don't care. Last week my wife and I were shopping at Horton Plaza in San Diego, and after a while we decided to get something to eat at one of the sidewalk cafes, and I noticed a couple of homeless people across the street. I began to notice how people walked around them, giving them strange looks as if they had a disease or would pretend they didn't exist.

The average persons body language communication changes from time to time whether it's over a very short or long time span. It's typical for someone to go to work in a good mood and having their body language reflecting the mood they're in. For instance, last week my boss Andre was in a good mood until later that evening when the big bosses came in I could tell by his body language things were not going as Andre had expected.

At times it's easy to understand ones body language when your on a personal level with someone. It is most common to understand friends, family, and loved ones body languages regardless of the mood they're in. For example, my wife I can tell when she has had a bad day without even asking. She sits on the couch, crosses her arms, and has an expression on her face that says to leave me alone!

As you can see, a persons body language along with their facial expressions and body posture indicates their emotional condition whether they're experiencing joy or sorrow, pain or pleasure, not to mention stress.

Student Summary-Response 3

In "College Lectures: Is Anybody Listening?" David Daniels suggests that colleges should abandon the lecture system they now have and introduce an alternative style of teaching. He states that it is hard to listen effectively when a student is just starting out and he defines lecturing as "passive learning." He says that we still have college lectures today because that is what the administration wants. I feel that in life smaller is better because it seems that a person gets more out of a smaller situation, and smaller is more economical and efficient.

Working for a small business is an example of smaller being better. In the small business the employers seem to care more for the employees, and the employees have a better opportunity for pay raises and promotions then they do working for a large company. I have been able to experience both types of jobs and when I worked for NAPA Auto Parts, a small business, I was able to talk to my manager on a personal as well as professional basis. At least every sixty days we would have store meetings just to make sure that everything and everyone was running smooth. As often as possible, maybe every 3-4 months, I would receive a raise, and within six months I was an assistant manager of the delivery system. The atmosphere was more of a family then of a team, which to me is more of a personal enjoyment.

As well as the small business, a simple vacation is more economical and enjoyable to me. Many people enjoy an extravagant vacation to Europe or Hawaii, and they spend thousands of dollars just to enjoy themselves. However, I have enjoyed countless trips to the desert as well as to the river for the same price as one trip to Europe or Hawaii. Robert and I can enjoy a peaceful weekend at the desert spending money on food, gas, and drinks for only two hundred dollars, yet for the two of us to fly to Hawaii it would cost about two thousand dollars. Although trips to the desert aren't extravagant, but it is a lot less expensive then a trip to Hawaii.

Another example of small being better is having a small house. Having a small house seems more efficient because it is easier to take care of. I lived in a small-to-average size house almost all of my life and it was a lot easier to maintain outside as well as inside. Just about three years ago we moved to an average-to-larger size house with a lot more land and the maintenance inside and outside has doubled in time and money spent.

Smaller is better because it is more efficient and easier to deal with. Small business, small vacations, and a small house are all the most economical because there is less to deal with.

Sentence Combining: Appositives

As you know from the earlier sentence-combining sections of this text, in English there are many ways to add information to the basic sentence. So far, you have practiced using adjectives, prepositional phrases, main clauses, subordinate clauses, and verbal phrases in your sentences. The **appositive** is yet another way to add interest and depth to your writing. Like most of the other sentence-combining methods you have studied, the appositive allows you to consolidate ideas into one sentence that otherwise might be expressed in two or more separate sentences.

At its simplest level, an **appositive** is simply a noun or a pronoun renaming or identifying another noun or pronoun. Usually the appositive is set off by commas, and it normally follows the noun or pronoun it is renaming. Here are some examples from the articles you have read in this chapter:

> *A former teacher of mine, **Robert A. Fowkes of New York University,** likes to tell the story of a class he took in Old Welsh while studying in Germany during the 1930s.*
>
> *Because these trappings and holiday symbols offend tens of thousands of other Americans—**the Native American people**.*

Notice that in each of the above examples a noun renames a noun. The noun *Robert A. Fowkes* renames *teacher* in the first sentence, and *Native American people* renames *Americans* in the second. As is usually the case, each appositive follows and is set off from the noun it renames—by commas in the first example and by a dash in the second.

Another characteristic of the appositive is that it usually includes modifiers of its own—adjectives, adverbs, or other modifiers that add information to the appositive word. Notice the modifiers of the appositive word in the following examples from "College Lectures: Is Anybody Listening?" and "What Your Body Language Says about You":

*Nevertheless, far too many courses rely principally or entirely on lectures, **an arrangement much loved by faculty and administrators but scarcely designed to benefit the students.***

*Wendy, **a high school junior from Scarsdale whose parents are Korean and who spent her first years of life in Korea,** says, "I don't like showing signs of closeness in public."*

Punctuating Appositives

As in the above examples, most appositives are set off with commas. However, occasionally they are set off with dashes or with a colon. In general, follow these guidelines:

1. Use commas to set off most appositives.

   *Two dogs, **an Irish setter and a German shepherd,** ran into the lobby of the hotel.*

2. Use dashes to set off an appositive that consists of a series or that already uses internal commas.

   *Only three people—**a real estate agent, the manager of the local grocery store, and the town's only banker**—attended the Chamber of Commerce mixer.*

3. Use a colon to set off an appositive at the end of a sentence if you want to establish a formal tone.

   *Last Christmas, Jason visited only one person: **his father.***

   (Note that the above appositive could also have been set off with a comma or with a dash.)

Recognizing When to Use Appositives

You have the opportunity to use an appositive almost any time you have a sentence consisting of a form of the verb *be* followed by a noun or pronoun. If you omit the verb, set off the resulting phrase with commas, and then continue with your sentence, you have created an appositive.

Original sentence with form of *be*:	*Alex Haley was the author of* Roots.
Omit the verb and set off the resulting phrase with commas:	*Alex Haley, the author of* Roots,
Complete the sentence:	*Alex Haley, the author of* Roots, *died in 1992.*

If you watch for them, you will find many opportunities to create appositives when you have written sentences using a form of the verb *be* followed by a noun or pronoun. Notice, for example, how two of the following three sentences use *was* and *is* to introduce a noun.

*Mr. Erickson **was** the winner of the Florida lottery. He gave all of his money to Helping Hands. Helping Hands **is** a small orphanage in New York.*

Now notice how those same three sentences can be written as one sentence with two appositives.

Mr. Erickson, **the winner of the Florida lottery,** gave all of his money to Helping Hands, **a small orphanage in New York.**

EXERCISE   Use appositives and appropriate punctuation to combine the following sentences. In each case, the words to be made into an appositive are underlined.

EXAMPLES

Robert Louis Stevenson was <u>a British novelist.</u> He wrote Treasure Island.

Robert Louis Stevenson, a British novelist, wrote Treasure Island.

Johann von Goethe lived from 1749 to 1832. He was a <u>poet, dramatist, and novelist.</u>

Johann von Goethe—a poet, dramatist, and novelist—lived from 1749 to 1832.

1. Jean-Baptiste Sanson was <u>the official executioner of France in the early 1700s.</u> He was only seven years old when he was appointed to the post.

2. He inherited the position from his father, who had inherited it from Jean-Baptiste's grandfather. Jean-Baptiste's grandfather was <u>the first member of the Sanson family to be the nation's executioner.</u>

3. At first Jean-Baptiste was too young to behead anybody, so his deputy performed the task. His deputy was <u>François Prud'homme</u>.

4. Two kinds of weapons were used. They were <u>an ax (for commoners) and a sword (for aristocrats)</u>.

5. Jean-Baptiste's eldest son, who was executioner during the French Revolution, beheaded over 2,700 persons. His eldest son was <u>Charles-Henri Sanson</u>, and beheading over 2,700 persons was <u>a family record</u>.

Changing Adjective Clauses to Appositives

Another opportunity to use an appositive arises whenever you write an adjective clause containing a form of the verb *be* followed by a noun or pronoun. In such cases, you can omit the relative pronoun that starts the adjective clause and the verb. The result will be an appositive.

EXAMPLE:

(using an adjective clause)   Amoxil, **which was** the most frequently prescribed drug in 1991, is an antibiotic.

(using an appositive)   *Amoxil, the most frequently prescribed drug in 1991, is an antibiotic.*

EXERCISE   Use appositives and appropriate punctuation to combine the following sentences or to change adjective clauses to appositives. In each case, the words to be made into an appositive are underlined.

1. In the United States, legal help for battered children came originally from an unexpected source, which was the Society for the Prevention of Cruelty to Animals.

2. In 1874, Etta Wheeler, who was a church worker, heard about Mary Ellen. She was a nine-year-old child who was being whipped daily, stabbed with scissors, and tied to a bed by her guardians.

3. There was no legal way to rescue Mary Ellen, so Wheeler called Henry Bergh. Bergh was a member of the SPCA.

4. Bergh had the child removed from her home by arguing that she was a member of the animal kingdom, and that was the area over which the SPCA had jurisdiction.

5. A picture of Mary Ellen still hangs at the New York SPCA. She was a pathetic waif when she was rescued.

EXERCISE   Use appositives and appropriate punctuation to combine the following sentences or to change adjective clauses to appositives.

1. The Great Pyramid of Khufu contains 2.3 million blocks of limestone averaging 2½ tons each. It is the largest of all the pyramids.

2. Both Hansel and Gretel looked politely at the little old lady's new appliance, which was an extra-large General Electric oven.

3. More than 75% of the world's 850 active volcanoes lie within the "Ring of Fire." It is a zone running along the west coast of the Americas and down the east coast of Asia.

4. Medusa could not do a thing with her hair, but Perseus, who was the son of Zeus, soon solved that problem.

5. The first toothbrush was the "chew stick." It was a twig with one end frayed to a soft, fibrous condition.

6. Achilles stared in irritation at his heel, which was the only sore spot on his body.

7. Mercury is the nearest planet to the sun. It is the second smallest of the nine planets known to be orbiting the sun.

8. Henry watched the battle between two armies of tiny combatants while he ate his favorite food. The combatants were red ants and black ants, and the food he ate was freshly baked bread.

9. Paul was uncomfortable around his father, who was a rough, drunken coal miner, but not around his mother. She was a woman who now regretted her marriage.

10. Amanda recalled the high point of her life while Laura stared at her favorite possession, which was a small glass unicorn. Amanda's high point was the time she had seventeen gentlemen callers.

REVIEW EXERCISE Combine the following sentences, using coordination, subordination, verbal phrases, or appositives.

1. The "Trail of Tears" refers to one of the many forced "removals" of Native Americans from their native lands.

   These "removals" resulted in the deaths of thousands of men, women, and children.

2. In the 1830s, these so-called removals focused on what are generally referred to as the Five Civilized Tribes of the Southeast.

   These were the Choctaw, Chickasaw, Creek, Cherokee, and Seminole nations.

3. Each of these Native American societies had developed a culture.

   The culture was compatible with white society.

   It even emulated European styles in many respects.

4. There was a problem, however.

   It was that these tribes resided in valuable territory.

   The territory was cotton-growing land.

5. The Indian Removal Act was passed in 1830.

   Thousands of Choctaws, Chickasaws, and Creeks were forced to move.

   They moved from the Southeast to territory west of Arkansas.

6. The forced move caused many hardships.

   Hundreds and eventually thousands of Native Americans died.

   They suffered from pneumonia, cholera, and other diseases.

7. Gold was discovered in Cherokee country in Georgia.

   The state of Georgia tried to force the Cherokee to leave.

   The Cherokee took their case to the United States Supreme Court.

8. At this time, the Cherokee were not nomads.

   They were a nation of Native Americans.

   They had built roads, schools, and churches.

   They even had a system of representative government.

9. The Supreme Court ruled against them.

   Seventeen thousand Cherokee were forced to travel the "Trail of Tears" to Oklahoma.

10. Along the way, 4,000 of the 17,000 died.

    Another 1,000 escaped.

    They hid in the Great Smoky Mountains.

11. In the following years, the Cherokee eventually won back 56,000 acres.

    Seven million acres of land had been taken from them.

Evaluating Reading Selections

The students in the Trudeau cartoon seem to be doing an excellent job of recording what their instructor has to say. Since they are listening carefully, their notes will probably be accurate summaries of the lecture. However, wouldn't you agree that something is missing from the students' activities in this cartoon? Shouldn't they have some reaction to the statements "Jefferson was the Antichrist! Democracy is Fascism! Black is white! Night is Day!"? The problem, of course, is that taking careful notes is just not enough. These students need to **evaluate** as well as record.

Evaluating what you read (or hear) is a valuable skill. We have all heard the old saying "Don't believe everything that you read," and certainly most people follow that advice. Unfortunately, what we do or do not believe is often not based on careful evaluation. Instead, many people merely accept material that confirms what they *already* believe and reject material that does not confirm their previously held beliefs.

Evaluation demands that you approach an idea with an open mind, that you be willing to consider its validity on the basis of the evidence presented, not on the basis of any preconceptions you might have. It demands that you be willing to change your ideas if the evidence suggests that you should. And it demands that you make an effort to understand the purpose of what you are reading so that you not criticize something for failing to do what it was not intended to do in the first place.

Audience and Purpose

Perhaps the first step in evaluating anything that you read is to determine the audience and the purpose of the article. The **audience** of an article is its intended readers. Obviously, an article in *Ms.* magazine on the sexual exploitation of women will have a different audience from an article on the same subject published in *Playboy*, and those different audiences may influence the authors' choices of ideas to be covered. Of course, no matter who the audience is, a writer must still provide reasonable support for his or her points.

An evaluation should also consider the **purpose** of any article that you read. Clearly it would be unfair to criticize a writer for failing to discuss the responsibilities of parenthood if that writer's purpose was to entertain you with humorous stories about the frustrations of living with a teenager. Here are four common purposes that you should consider whenever you read:

- **To inform.**
  This type of writing is often called *expository.* It generally consists of facts rather than opinions or arguments. Most newspaper reporting has *informing* as its purpose, as does most of the material that you read in textbooks.
- **To entertain.**
  Generally, nonfiction *entertainment* writing tends to be humorous and often focuses on situations that are common to the average person. Dave Berry and Erma Bombeck are two nationally syndicated entertainment columnists.

■ **To persuade**

Persuasive writing tends to focus on controversial issues, presenting opinions and arguments that are supported (effectively or ineffectively) with facts, examples, explanations, statistics, and/or references to authority. Editorials in newspapers and magazines are common examples of persuasive writing.

■ **To raise an issue or provoke thought.**

This type of writing is similar to persuasive writing in that it examines controversial issues, but its purpose is not necessarily to persuade the reader that the writer's particular argument is the correct one. Instead, its intent is often to unsettle the reader, to raise questions that need to be answered but that are not fully answered in the article itself. Such articles are often found in newspaper and magazine editorials.

In this chapter, you will write evaluations of articles designed to persuade, to raise an issue, or to provoke thought. As you read each article in this chapter, you must ask yourself if the article's purpose is to convince you of a particular argument or if it is merely to get you to think about the issue at hand. Of course, at times, the purpose may be a little of both, so you should consider that possibility too.

Evaluating Support

In addition to considering the audience and the purpose of what you read, you need to examine the evidence or support that is presented to you. For example, if a writer claims that we should do away with the minimum wage, you should look to see not only what reasons he gives but also what facts, statistics, examples, or references to authority he offers to explain his reasons.

When you do look closely at a written argument—especially an editorial in a newspaper or magazine—you will often find that the support is quite sketchy. Much of the argument may consist of opinions or explanations rather than facts or other specific types of support. In such cases, you must decide if more support is needed or if the argument is reasonably convincing as it stands. However, an argument without sufficient support should be looked at skeptically, no matter how well it is written.

Facts

Facts are tricky things. Most people consider a fact to be something "true" or "correct" or "accurate." But not everyone agrees about what is or is not true. For example, is it a fact that drinking coffee is bad for your health? Some people might *claim* that such a statement is accurate, but as many others would say it is not. And science itself has provided few answers about the long-term effects of coffee drinking. So is it or is it not true that coffee is bad for your health? Surely such a statement cannot be treated as a fact if there is so much disagreement about it.

The best way to define a fact is to move away from the idea of "truth" or "correctness" and toward the idea of objective, physical verification. Treat as a fact any statement that has been objectively verified through direct experience, measurement, or observation. Statistics, then, are facts, as are historical or current events, scientific observations, and even personal experience. If it has been verified that caffeine increases a person's blood pressure, then such a statement is a fact. If you visited a Toyota dealership yesterday and felt uncomfortable talking to the salesperson, your statement that such an event occurred and that you reacted the way you did are facts. If the distance between the sun and the earth has been measured as 92,900,000 miles, such a statement is a fact.

Of course, even using objective verification, you cannot assume all facts are always accurate. For many years, people believed it was a fact that the sun circled the earth, not vice versa. After all, anyone could see that each day the sun rose in the east and set in the west. In this case, objective verification was not accurate enough to lead us to the fact that the earth circled the sun. So how do you know which facts have been accurately verified and which have not? Often you must consider the source. If the writer of an article says that 24,700 murders were committed in the United States in 1991, you will probably accept that statement as a fact if the writer is a professional reporter or columnist whose career is riding on his or her accuracy. Of course, that does not mean that you should accept the writer's *conclusions*, especially if the writer is trying to persuade you to accept his or her particular point of view.

EXERCISE

Discuss which of the following statements can be objectively verified as facts and which can not.

1. In California, bicycle riders under the age of eighteen are required by law to wear a bicycle helmet.

2. If I had not eaten any sugar at the fair yesterday, I would have had a better time.

3. No loyal American would ever burn the American flag.

4. I saw a Plymouth Voyager hit a Nissan Sentra on the freeway today.

5. Former President Gerald Ford's middle name is Rudolph.

6. Betsy Ross sewed the first American flag.

7. The 1994 earthquake in Northridge, California, registered 6.6 on the Richter scale.

8. "Dear Abby" is the most widely published advice column in the world.

9. Most homeless people won't work even if you offer them jobs.

10. Cashews taste better than peanuts.

As you can see from the above sentences, some statements are more clearly facts than others. That the Northridge earthquake measured 6.6 on the Richter scale could easily be verified if you had to do so, but how would you verify the statement that most homeless people won't work even if they are offered jobs? You would need to find a study of all homeless people in America; they would all have to have been offered jobs, and most would have to have refused. How likely is it that you will find such a study?

For that matter, how would you verify that cashews taste better than peanuts? Such a statement would be a fact only if it were worded this way: "I like cashews better than peanuts." Do you see the difference? The second statement refers only to the speaker's personal preference, which the speaker verifies merely by making the statement. By the way, one of the ten sentences above has long been accepted as a fact by most people even though scholars know that it has never been verified and is probably not a fact at all. Which sentence is it?

Opinions

When people say something like "That's just my opinion," they usually mean that they don't want to argue about the point. In fact, "That's just my opinion" is often a way of saying that you don't have any facts to support your idea. Of course, at one time or another we all hold opinions without having examined the facts behind them. Perhaps we hold them because people we respect—our parents, friends, or teachers—hold them or because they reinforce what we already believe to be true about the world or the society in which we live.

Clear, responsible thinking, however, demands that we examine our opinions and discard those that are not well supported. Although it is true that we are all entitled to our own opinions, certainly the unexamined, unsupported opinion is not as valuable as the opinion formed after one has carefully considered the facts. When you think about opinions, consider these three distinctions:

- **Personal opinion.**

   The term *personal opinion* is often used when the speaker really means *unsupported* or *unexamined opinion*. If you hear someone say (or if you yourself say) "Well, that's just my personal opinion," be aware that such a statement probably means the opinion has not been very thoroughly examined. In addition to referring to an unexamined opinion, a personal opinion may also refer to matters of personal taste, such as "Suspense novels are more fun to read than science fiction novels."

- **Considered opinion.**

   A *considered opinion* is one reached after you have considered the relevant facts and other types of support. If, for example, you have read various articles on the pros and cons of handgun control, you can be said to have developed a considered opinion of your own. Remember, however, that any considered opinion should be open to change if new evidence or support demands it.

■ **Expert opinion.**

As you learned in Chapter 3, one type of support is *reference to authority*. For the most part, you should be able to accept an opinion held by experts in a particular field as long as their opinion is related to their field of expertise. For example, you would probably accept an orthopedic surgeon's opinion about the usefulness of a particular knee brace, but there would be no reason to accept that surgeon's opinion about a particular political issue. In addition, even an expert's opinion about an issue in his or her own field must be questioned if other experts in the same field disagree.

EXERCISE

Indicate which of the following opinions you would take more seriously than others. Which of these opinions are more likely to be personal opinions, considered opinions, or expert opinions?

1. Your neighbor says that the Los Angeles Lakers are more fun to watch than the New York Knicks.

2. A person at a party says that capital punishment discriminates against those who cannot afford expensive attorneys.

3. A palm reader advises you not to take that trip to Hawaii.

4. One vagrant tells another that a particular police officer will not care if he sleeps on the park bench.

5. A Marine Corps colonel says that only a coward would refuse to fight for his country.

6. A local business owner says that the state lottery takes money from the people who can least afford to spend it.

7. A state senator says that restricting handgun sales will not help to reduce crime.

8. A member of the city council says that crime will not be reduced until we start locking up criminals and throwing away the key.

9. Your girlfriend (or boyfriend, or wife, or husband) says that you are no longer as romantic as you used to be.

10. A Honda salesperson says that Hondas have better maintenance records than Buick Skylarks.

Generalizations Versus Specific Statements

Much of your ability to evaluate what you read will depend on how well you can distinguish between a generalization and a specific statement. A specific statement will refer to specific people, places, events, or ideas, usually giving names and dates as it does, while a generalization will refer to groups of people, places, events, or ideas. For example, here is a specific statement:

Yesterday, John McIntyre, a homeless man in San Diego, California, went the entire day without eating a thing.

Here, on the other hand, is a generalization:

Many homeless people often go an entire day without eating a thing.

Both specific statements and generalizations can be facts or opinions, depending on what they say. For example, one of the following specific statements is clearly a fact, and one is clearly an opinion.

This morning Samantha spilled a cup of coffee on Angelo.
This morning Samantha's carelessness caused her to spill a cup of coffee on Angelo.

As you can see, both of the above statements are specific, but only one can be called a fact.

Like specific statements, generalizations may be either facts or opinions. Generalizations that are based on obviously verified facts rarely require support and are usually treated as facts, while generalizations requiring further support are treated as opinions. Of the following generalizations, which should be treated as a fact and which should not?

People who smoke face a higher risk of developing lung cancer than people who don't smoke.
Students' sloppy style of dress today reflects a general "I don't care" attitude toward all of society.

As you can see, both specific statements and generalizations can express facts, so both can be used to support a writer's ideas. However, most writing instructors will ask you to provide specific statements as often as possible, primarily because specific statements are more interesting to read and are more persuasive than generalizations. It is simply more compelling to hear that someone's best friend, who smoked two packs of cigarettes a day, died two days ago after a painful battle with lung cancer than it is to hear the generalization that people who smoke die of lung cancer more often than people who don't.

EXERCISE

First, explain whether each of the following statements is a generalization or a specific statement. Then explain whether each statement should be considered a fact or an opinion. If it is an opinion, discuss whether or not it could be reasonably supported with facts.

1. Throughout most of civilized history, people have relied on animals or on their own feet for transportation.

2. The Honda Accord was the best-selling car in the United States in 1990 and 1991.

3. The cartoon characters Beavis and Butthead caused my sister's son to set fire to the First Interstate Bank.

4. Today's social problems are indicators of our immoral society.

5. Many people today do not discipline their children very effectively.

6. Jerry has AIDS because God is punishing him for being a homosexual.

7. Rioting swept South Central Los Angeles when the police officers accused of assault and the use of excessive force in the arrest of Rodney King were acquitted.

8. The gang problem has become a serious concern in high schools throughout the United States.

9. Uneducated people are crass and insensitive.

10. Lee Harvey Oswald was not the only person who fired shots when John F. Kennedy was assassinated.

Considering Your Own Knowledge and Experience

Evaluating the support in a text demands that you also think about what *you* know to be true and compare it to what you are reading. For example, if you are a single mother who is successfully raising a happy, well-adjusted child, your experience will certainly contradict an article that asserts that single mothers cannot provide a healthy home environment for their children. You must then consider whether the argument in the article is flawed or overgeneralized or if your own experience is an unusual exception. Whatever you decide, remember that your own knowledge and experience are important sources of information that you should consult before accepting the support offered by any writer.

Considering Unstated Objections

A final point to think about as you evaluate an argument is whether or not the writer has considered points that might contradict or otherwise weaken his or her position. For instance, if you are reading a newspaper editorial arguing that competition in school sports damages our children, consider what objections may not have been addressed by the writer. Do school sports benefit children in any ways that the writer has ignored? Is competition a valuable quality in any way?

Of course, a writer does not have to cover every—or any—objection to write an interesting, thought-provoking paper. If the purpose of the article is to raise issues that the reader should think about, you may not find any objections considered at all. However, the more a paper is intended to convince or persuade the reader, the more thoroughly the writer must consider and respond to major objections.

Steps in Evaluating a Text

1. Read the text actively.
   - Determine its purpose and intended audience.
   - Identify its thesis.
   - Identify its main points.

2. Determine how well the main points are supported.
   - Distinguish between facts and opinions.
   - Distinguish between specific support and generalizations.
   - Identify statistics, examples, and references to authority.

3. Test the article's points against your own knowledge and experience.

4. Consider any obvious objections that have been ignored.

Readings

I Wish They'd Do It Right

JANE DOE

Before You Read

1. What is your opinion about people who live together without being married? Upon what is your opinion based?

2. Should people who live together without marrying consider how their actions affect other members of their families?

My son and his wife are not married. They have lived together for seven years without benefit of license. Though occasionally marriage has been a subject of conjecture, it did not seem important until the day they announced, jubilantly, that they were going to have a child. It was happy news. I was ready and eager to become a grandmother. Now, I thought, they will take the final step and make their relationship legal. 1

I was apprised of the Lamaze method of natural childbirth. I was prepared by Leboyer for birth without violence. I admired the expectant mother's discipline. She ate only organic foods, abstained from alcohol, avoided insecticides, smog and trauma. Every precaution was taken to insure the arrival of a healthy, happy infant. No royal birth had been prepared for more auspiciously. All that was lacking was legitimacy. 2

Finally, when my grandson was two weeks old, I dared to question their intentions. 3

"We don't believe in marriage," was all that was volunteered. 4

"Not even for your son's sake?" I asked. "Maybe he will." 5

Their eyes were impenetrable, their faces stiffened to masks. "You wouldn't understand," I was told. 6

And I don't. Surely they cannot believe they are pioneering, making revolutionary changes in society. That frontier has long been tamed. 7

Today marriage offers all the options. Books and talk shows have surfeited us with the freedom offered in open marriage. Lawyers, psychologists and marriage counselors are growing rich executing marriage contracts. And divorce, should it come to that, is in most states easy and inexpensive.

On the other hand, living together out of wedlock can be economically impractical as well as socially awkward. How do I present her—as my son's roommate? his spouse? his spice, as one facetious friend suggested? Even my son flounders in these waters. Recently, I heard him refer to her as his girl friend. I cannot believe that that description will be endearing to their son when he is able to understand.   8

I have resolved that problem for myself, bypassing their omission, introducing her as she is, as my daughter-in-law. But my son, in militant support of his ideology, refutes any assumption, however casual, that they have taken vows.   9

There are economic benefits which they are denying themselves. When they applied for housing in the married-students dormitory of the university where he is seeking his doctorate, they were asked for their marriage certificate. Not having one, they were forced to find other, more expensive quarters off campus. Her medical insurance, provided by the company where she was employed, was denied him. He is not her husband. There have been and will be other inconveniences they have elected to endure.   10

Their son will not enjoy the luxury of choice about the inconveniences and scurrility to which he will be subject from those of his peers and elders who dislike and fear society's nonconformists.   11

And if in the future, his parents should decide to separate, will he not suffer greater damage than the child of divorce, who may find comfort in the knowledge that his parents once believed they could live happily ever after, and committed themselves to that idea? The child of unwed parents has no sanctuary. His mother and father have assiduously avoided a pledge of permanency, leaving him drifting and insecure.   12

I know my son is motivated by idealism and honesty in his reluctance to concede to what he considers mere ceremony. But is he wise enough to know that no one individual can fight all of society's foibles and frauds? Why does he persist in this, a battle already lost? Because though he rejects marriage, California, his residence, has declared that while couples living together in imitation of marriage are no longer under the jurisdiction of the family court, their relationship is viewed by the state as an implicit contract somewhat like a business agreement. This position was mandated when equal property rights were granted a woman who had been abandoned by the man she had lived with for a number of years.   13

Finally, the couple's adamancy has been depriving to all the rest of the   14
family. There has been no celebration of wedding or anniversaries. There
has been concealment from certain family elders who could not cope
with the situation. Its irregularity has put constraint on the grandparents, who are stifled by one another's possible embarrassment or hurt.

I hope that one day very soon my son and his wife will acknowledge   15
their cohabitation with a license. The rest of us will not love them any
more for it. We love and support them as much as possible now. But it
will be easier and happier for us knowing that our grandson will be
spared the continued explanation and harassment, the doubts and anxieties of being a child of unmarried parents.

After You Read

Work with other students to develop responses to these questions or to compare responses
that you have already prepared.

1. State the thesis of the article in your own words. What sentences in the article, if any,
   best express the thesis idea?

2. This article was originally published in *The New York Times*. Who would you say is Doe's
   audience? What is the purpose of her essay?

3. Divide the article into sections according to each major point that Doe makes.

4. Consider the support that Doe provides for each of her points. Does she use generalizations or specific statements? Facts or opinions? Are her opinions reasonably supported?

5. Consider your own experience or the experiences of people you know. Do they confirm
   or contradict Doe's points?

6. Do any of Doe's points seem particularly weak or particularly strong? Why?

7. Are there any objections to Doe's arguments that you should consider?

The Thin Grey Line

MARYA MANNES

Before You Read

1. In what ways are normally honest, law-abiding citizens sometimes dishonest? In what
   ways do they sometimes break the law?

2. Do you consider these lapses serious? Why or why not?

"Aw, they all do it," growled the cabdriver. He was talking about cops who took payoffs for winking at double parking, but his cynicism could as well have been directed any of a dozen other instances of corruption, big-time and small-time. Moreover, the disgust in his voice was overlaid by an unspoken "So what?": the implication that since this was the way things were, there was nothing anybody could do.

Like millions of his fellow Americans, the cabdriver was probably a decent human being who had never stolen anything, broken any law or willfully injured another; somewhere, a knowledge of what was probably right had kept him from committing what was clearly wrong. But that knowledge had not kept a thin grey line that separates the two conditions from being daily greyer and thinner—to the point that it was hardly noticeable.

On the one side of this line are They: the bribers, the cheaters, the chiselers, the swindlers, the extortioners. On the other side are We—both partners and victims. They and We are now so perilously close that the only mark distinguishing us is that They get caught and We don't.

The same citizen who voices outrage at police corruption will slip the traffic copy on his block a handsome Christmas present in the belief that his car, nestled under a "No Parking" sign, will not be ticketed. The son of that nice woman next door has a habit of stealing cash from her purse because his allowance is smaller than his buddies'. Your son's friend admitted cheating at exams because "everybody does it."

Bit by bit, the resistance to and immunity against wrong that a healthy social body builds up by law and ethics and the dictation of conscience have broken down. And instead of the fighting indignation of a people outraged by those who prey on them, we have the admission of impotence: "They all do it."

Now, failure to uphold the law is no less corrupt than violation of the law. And the continuing shame of this country now is the growing number of Americans who fail to uphold and assist enforcement of the law, simply—and ignominiously—out of fear. Fear of "involvement," fear of reprisal, fear of "trouble." A man is beaten by hoodlums in plain daylight and in view of bystanders. These people not only fail to help the victim, but, like the hoodlums, flee before the police can question them. A city official knows of a colleague's bribe but does not report it. A pedestrian watches a car hit a woman but leaves the scene, to avoid giving testimony. It happens every day. And if the police get cynical at this irresponsibility, they are hardly to blame. Morale is a matter of giving support and having faith in one another; where both are lacking, "law" has become a worthless word.

How did we get this way? What started this blurring of what was once a thick black line between the lawful and the lawless? What makes a "regular guy," a decent fellow, accept a bribe? What makes a nice kid from a middle-class family take money for doing something he must know is not only illegal but wrong? 7

When you look into the background of an erring "kid" you will often find a comfortable home and a mother who will tell you, with tears in her eyes, that she "gave him everything." She probably did, to his ever-lasting damage. Fearing her son's disapproval, the indulgent mother denies him nothing except responsibility. Instead of growing up, he grows to believe that the world owes him everything. 8

The nice kid's father crosses the thin grey line himself in a dozen ways, day in and day out. He pads his expenses on his income-tax returns as a matter of course. As a landlord, he pays the local inspectors of the city housing authority to overlook violations in the houses he rents. When his son flunked his driving test, he gave him ten dollars to slip the inspector on his second test. "They all do it," he said. 9

The nice kid is brought up with boys and girls who have no heroes except people not much older than themselves who have made the Big Time, usually in show business or in sports. Publicity and money are the halos of their stars, who range from pop singers who can't sing to ballplayers who can't read; from teen-age starlets who can't act to television performers who can't think. They may be excited by the exploits of spacemen, but the work's too tough and dangerous. 10

The nice kids have no heroes because they don't believe in heroes. Heroes are suckers and squares. To be a hero you have to stand out, to excel, to take risks, and above all, not only choose between right and wrong, but defend the right and fight the wrong. This means responsibility—and who needs it? 11

Today, no one has to take any responsibility. The psychiatrists, the sociologists, the novelists, the playwrights have gone a long way to help promote irresponsibility. Nobody really is to blame for what he does. It's Society. It's Environment. It's a Broken Home. It's an Underprivileged Area. But it's hardly ever You. 12

Now we find a truckload of excuses to absolve the individual from responsibility for his actions. A fellow commits a crime because he's basically insecure, because he hated his stepmother at nine, or because his sister needs an operation. A policeman loots a store because his salary is 13 too low. A city official accepts a payoff because it's offered to him. Members of minority groups, racial or otherwise, commit crimes because they can't get a job, or are unacceptable to the people living around them. The words "right" and "wrong" are foreign to these people.

But honesty is the best policy. Says who? Anyone willing to get laughed 14 at. But the laugh is no laughing matter. It concerns the health and future of a nation. It involves the two-dollar illegal bettor as well as the corporation price-fixer, the college-examination cheater and the payroll-padding congressman, the expense-account chiseler, the seller of pornography and his schoolboy reader, the bribed judge and the stealing delinquent. All these people may represent a minority. But when, as it appears now, the majority excuse themselves from responsibility by accepting corruption as natural to society ("They all do it"), this society is bordering on total confusion. If the line between right and wrong is finally erased, there is no defense against the power of evil.

Before this happens—and it is by no means far away—it might be well 15 for the schools of the nation to substitute for the much-argued issue of prayer a daily lesson in ethics, law, and responsibility to society that would strengthen the conscience as exercise strengthens muscles. And it would be even better if parents were forced to attend it. For corruption is not something you read about in the papers and leave to courts. We are all involved.

As appeared in McCall's *magazine, Jan. 1964.*

After You Read

Work with other students to develop responses to these questions or to compare responses that you have already prepared.

1. State the thesis of the article in your own words. What sentences in the article, if any, best express the thesis idea?

2. Divide the article into sections according to each major point that Mannes makes.

3. This article was originally published in *McCall's*. Who would you say is Mannes's audience? What is the purpose of her essay?

4. Notice how much of Mannes's support consists of generalizations. Choose one of her points and explain why you do or do not find her generalizations convincing.

5. Consider your own experience or the experiences of people you know. Do they confirm or contradict Mannes's points?

6. Are there any objections to Mannes's points that you should consider?

Why Competition?

ALFIE KOHN

Before You Read

1. What do you consider to be the benefits and the drawbacks of competition? List as many benefits and drawbacks as you can think of.

2. Which list seems stronger—benefits or drawbacks?

3. Explain how your attitude toward competition might be a result of the culture in which you live.

W-H-I-T-E! White Team is the team for me!" The cheer is repeated, becoming increasingly frenzied as scores of campers, bedecked in the appropriate color, try to outshout their Blue opponents. The rope stretched over the lake is taut now, as determined tuggers give it their all. It looks as if a few will be yanked into the cold water, but a whistle pierces the air. "All right, we'll call this a draw." Sighs of disappointment follow, but children are soon scrambling off to the Marathon. Here, competitors will try to win for their side by completing such tasks as standing upside-down in a bucket of shampoo or forcing down great quantities of food in a few seconds before tagging a teammate.

As a counselor in this camp over a period of several years, I witnessed a number of Color Wars, and what constantly amazed me was the abrupt and total transformation that took place each time one began. As campers are read their assignments, children who not ten minutes before were known as "David" or "Margie" suddenly have a new identity; they have been arbitrarily designated as members of a team. The unspoken command is understood by even the youngest among them: Do everything possible to win for your side. Strain every muscle to prove how superior *we* are to the hostile Blues.

And so they will. Children who had wandered aimlessly about the camp are suddenly driven with a Purpose. Children who had tired of the regular routine are instantly provided with Adventure. Children who had trouble making friends are unexpectedly part of a new Crowd. In the dining hall, every camper sits with his or her team. Strategy is planned for the next battle; troops are taught the next cheer. There is a coldness bordering on suspicion when passing someone with a blue T-shirt—irrespective of any friendship B.C. (Before Colors). If anyone has reservations about participating in an activity, he needs only to be reminded that the other team is just a few points behind.

"Why Sport?" asks Ed Cowan (*The Humanist*, November/December 1979). When the sports are competitive ones, I cannot find a single reason to answer his rhetorical query. Mr. Cowan's discussion of the pure—almost mystical—aesthetic pleasure that is derived from athletics only directs attention way from what is, in actuality, the primary impetus of any competitive activity: winning. 4

I would not make such a fuss over Color War, or even complain about the absurd spectacle of grown men shrieking and cursing on Sunday afternoons, were it not for the significance of the role played by competition in our culture. It is bad enough that Americans actually regard fighting as a sport: it is worse that the outcome of even the gentlest of competitions—baseball—can induce fans to hysteria and outright violence. But sports is only the tip of the proverbial iceberg. Our entire society is affected by—even structured upon—the need to be "better than." 5

My thesis is admittedly extreme; it is, simply put, that *competition by its very nature is always unhealthy*. This is true, to begin with, because competition and cooperation are mutually exclusive orientations. I say this fully aware of the famed camaraderie that is supposed to develop among players—or soldiers—on the same side. First, I have doubts, based on personal experience, concerning the depth and fullness of relationships that result from the need to become more effective against a common enemy. 6

Second, the "realm of the interhuman," to use Martin Buber's phrase, is severely curtailed when those on the other side are excluded from any possible community. Worse, they are generally regarded with suspicion and contempt in any competitive enterprise. (This is not to say that we cannot remain on good terms with, say, tennis opponents, but that whatever cooperation and meaningful relationship is in evidence exists in spite of the competitiveness.) Finally, the sweaty fellowship of the locker room (or, to draw the inescapable parallel again, the trenches) simply does not compensate for the inherent evils of competition. 7

The desire to win has a not very surprising (but too rarely remarked upon) characteristic: it tends to edge out other goals and values in the context of any given competitive activity. When I was in high school, I was a very successful debater for a school that boasted one of the country's better teams. After hundreds and hundreds of rounds of competition over three years, I can assert in no uncertain terms that the purpose of debate is not to seek the truth or resolve an issue. No argument, however compelling, is ever conceded; veracity is never attributed to the 8 other side. The only reason debaters sacrifice their free time collecting thousands of pieces of evidence, analyzing arguments, and practicing speeches, is to win. Truth thereby suffers in at least two ways.

In any debate, neither team is concerned with arriving at a fuller under- 9
standing of the topic. The debaters concentrate on "covering" arguments, tying logical knots, and, above all, sounding convincing. Beyond
this, though, there exists a tremendous temptation to fabricate and distort evidence. Words are left out, phrases added, sources modified in
order to lend credibility to the position. One extremely successful
debater on my team used to invent names of magazines which ostensibly
printed substantiation for crucial arguments he wanted to use.

With respect to this last phenomenon, it is fruitless—and a kind of 10
self-deception, ultimately—to shake our heads and deplore this sort of
thing. Similarly, we have no business condemning "overly rough" football players or the excesses of "overzealous" campaign aides or even,
perhaps, violations of the Geneva Convention in time of war (which is
essentially a treatise on How to Kill Human Beings Without Doing
Anything *Really* Unethical). We are engaging in a massive (albeit implicit) exercise of hypocrisy to decry these activities while continuing to condone, and even encourage, the competitive orientation of which they are
only the logical conclusion.

The cost of any kind of competition in human terms is incalculable. 11
When my success depends on other people's failure, the prospects for a
real human community are considerably diminished. This consequence
speaks to the profoundly antihumanistic quality of competitive activity,
and it is abundantly evident in American society. Moreover, when my
success depends on my being *better than*, I am caught on a treadmill,
destined never to enjoy real satisfaction. Someone is always one step
higher, and even the summit is a precarious position in light of the
hordes waiting to occupy it in my stead. I am thus perpetually insecure
and, as psychologist Rollo May points out, perpetually anxious.

> . . . individual competitive success is both the dominant goal in our 12
> culture and the most pervasive occasion for anxiety. . . . [This] anxiety
> arises out of the interpersonal isolation and alienation from others
> that inheres in a pattern in which self-validation depends on triumph-
> ing over others (*The Meaning of Anxiety*, rev. ed.)

I begin to see my self-worth as conditional—that is to say, my good- 13
ness or value become contingent on how much better I am than so many
others in so many activities. If you believe, as I do, that unconditional

self-esteem is a singularly important requirement for (and indicator of) mental health, then the destructiveness of competition will clearly outweigh any putative benefit, whether it be a greater effort at tug-of-war or a higher gross national product.

From the time we are quite small, the ethic of competitiveness is drummed into us. The goal in school is not to grow as a human being or even, in practice, to reach a satisfactory level of intellectual competence. We are pushed instead to become brighter than, quicker than, better achievers than our classmates, and the endless array of scores and grades lets us know at any given instant how we stand on that ladder of academic success.

If our schools are failing at their explicit tasks, we may rest assured of their overwhelming success regarding this hidden agenda. We are well trained to enter the marketplace and compete frantically for more money, more prestige, more of all the "good things" in life. An economy such as ours, understand, does not merely permit competition: *it demands it*. Ever greater profits becomes the watchword of private enterprise, and an inequitable distribution of wealth (a polite codeword for human suffering) follows naturally from such an arrangement.

Moreover, one must be constantly vigilant lest one's competitors attract more customers or conceive some innovation that gives them the edge. To become outraged at deceptive and unethical business practices is folly; it is the competitiveness of the system that promotes these phenomena. Whenever people are defined as opponents, doing everything possible to triumph must be seen not as an aberration from the structure but as its very consummation. (I recognize, of course, that I have raised a plethora of difficult issues across many disciplines that cry out for a more detailed consideration. I hope, however, to at least have opened up some provocative, and largely neglected, lines of inquiry.)

This orientation finds its way into our personal relationships as well. We bring our yardstick along to judge potential candidates for lover, trying to determine who is most attractive, most intelligent, and . . . the best lover. At the same time, of course, *we* are being similarly reduced to the status of competitor. The human costs are immense.

"Why Sport?", then, is a good question to begin with. It leads us to inquire, "Why Miss Universe contests?" "Why the arms race?" and—dare we say it?—"Why capitalism?" Whether a competition-free society can actually be constructed is another issue altogether, and I readily concede that this mentality has so permeated our lives that we find it difficult even to imagine alternatives in many settings. The first step, though,

14

15

16

17

18

consists in understanding that rivalry of any kind is both psychologically disastrous and philosophically unjustifiable, that the phrase "healthy competition" is a contradiction in terms. Only then can we begin to develop saner, richer lifestyles for ourselves as individuals, and explore more humanistic possibilities for our society.

From the Jan./Feb. issue of The Humanist. *Reprinted by permission of the American Humanist Association, ©1980.*

After You Read

Work with other students to develop responses to these questions or to compare responses that you have already prepared.

1. State the thesis of the article in your own words. What sentences in the article, if any, best express the thesis idea?

2. Divide the article into sections according to each major point that Kohn makes.

3. This article was originally published in *The Humanist.* Who would you say is Kohn's audience? What is the purpose of his essay?

4. Consider the support that Kohn provides for each of his points. Does he use generalizations or specific statements? Facts or opinions? Are his opinions reasonably supported?

5. Consider your own experience or the experiences of people you know. Do they confirm or contradict Kohn's points?

6. Are there any objections to Kohn's points that you should consider?

Writing Assignments

1. Write a paper that uses *one* of the following suggestions to evaluate "I Wish They'd Do It Right":

   a. After a discussion with other members of your class, determine which of Jane Doe's points in "I Wish They'd Do It Right" seem particularly weak or particularly strong. Choose the points that you find most or least effective and explain your reaction. (You do not need to cover every point in the article.) Use the "Steps in Evaluating a Text" on pages 175–176 to help you with your evaluation.

   b. One way to evaluate an article is to determine whether your own experiences or the experiences of people you talk to confirm or refute its points. Explain in what ways your own experiences or the experiences of others cause you to accept or reject the different points Jane Doe presents in "I Wish They'd Do It Right."

2. Write a paper that uses to *one* of the following suggestions to evaluate "The Thin Grey Line":

    a. Much of Mannes's article consists of generalizations that she assumes will be accepted by the reader. After discussing the article with other students, decide whether or not you find her generalizations convincing. Write a paper explaining why you do or do not find them convincing. (You do not need to cover every generalization in the article.) Use the "Steps in Evaluating a Text" on pages 175–176 to help you with your evaluation.

    b. One way to evaluate an article is to determine whether your own experiences or the experiences of people you talk to confirm or refute its points. Explain in what ways your own experiences or the experiences of others cause you to accept or reject the different points Mannes presents in "The Thin Grey Line."

3. Write a paper that uses *one* of the following suggestions to evaluate "Why Competition?"

    a. After a discussion with other members of your class, determine which of Alfie Kohn's points in "Why Competition?" seem particularly weak or particularly strong. Choose the points that you find most or least effective and explain your reaction. (You do not need to cover every point in the article.) Use the "Steps in Evaluating a Text" on pages 175–176 to help you with your evaluation.

    b. One way to evaluate an article is to determine whether your own experiences or the experiences of people you talk to confirm or refute its points. Explain in what ways your own experiences or the experiences of others cause you to accept or reject the different points Alfie Kohn presents in "Why Competition?"

4. Choose an article from Section Four and evaluate it according to the guidelines on pages 175–176.

Evaluating Sample Papers

Evaluation Essay

1. Introduction

Does the introduction accurately and clearly state the central idea and purpose of the article? Does it smoothly and easily move the reader into the paper?

    1   2   3   4   5   6

2. Thesis

Does the introduction end in a clear statement of evaluation of the effectiveness of the article?

    1   2   3   4   5   6

3. Unity

Does each paragraph have a clear and specific topic sentence that accurately introduces and states an evaluation of one of the main points of the article? Is the material in each paragraph clearly related to its topic sentence?

1   2   3   4   5   6

4. Development

Is each topic sentence supported with clear references to the article as well as to details and examples from the writer's own knowledge and experience? Are references to ideas from the article accurately explained?

1   2   3   4   5   6

5. Coherence

Are transitions used between paragraphs? Where needed, are transitions used between sentences within each paragraph?

1   2   3   4   5   6

6. References to the Text

Are direct quotations and paraphrases correctly introduced and smoothly incorporated into the text? Do they reflect the writer's point accurately?

1   2   3   4   5   6

7. Subordination and Sentence Variety

Do the sentences combine ideas that are related, using coordination, subordination, or verbal or appositive phrases when appropriate? Are there too many brief, choppy main clauses?

1   2   3   4   5   6

8. Grammar and Mechanics

Does the paper contain fragments, comma splices, fused sentences, errors in subject-verb agreement, pronoun use, modifiers, punctuation, or spelling?

1   2   3   4   5   6

9. Overall Ranking of the Essay

1   2   3   4   5   6

Evaluate the following student essays. Explain which one you find to be the most effective and which the least.

Student Essay 1

In his essay "Why Competition?" Alfie Kohn attacks a trait embedded in the very fabric of American society, competition. By concluding that relationships between both teammates and rivals are undesireable and illustrating the pitfalls competition holds for both individuals and American society, Kohn tries to prove that "competition by its very nature is always unhealthy." Although Kohn uses several strong personal examples to support his claims, the essay contains little substantiated support. However, since Kohn's purpose was "to at least have opened up some provocative, and largely neglected, lines of inquiry," he was successful.

I disagree in part with Kohn's first point which concerns relationships between both teammates and rivals. Kohn believes that the relationships between teammates lack depth and fullness and also observes that rivalry causes the teammates to not only exclude their rivals from "any possible community," but often to regard them with "suspicion and contempt." Kohn supports this two pronged attack with his personal experiences as a camp counselor and also compares teammates to soldiers. After attending scores of high school football games, I cannot disagree with Kohn's observations about rivals, but, as an athlete, I always played on teams with people who were my true friends and not just "comrades."

Kohn's second point is that "the desire to win . . . tends to edge out other goals and values in the context of any given competitive activity." He claims that when people are competing, winning becomes all important, and values fly out the window. His support is another personal experience which consists of his participation on a debate team. Perhaps these "debaters" are just overzealous, or they just take themselves too seriously. When I compete recreationally, whether I'm arguing a point or dribbling a basketball, I'm concerned with having fun first and winning second.

After making it clear that none among us is above behaving competitively, Kohn states his third and most convincing argument, that the cost of competition in human terms is immeasurable. With individual success, says Kohn, comes anxiety. A person's self worth starts becoming conditional. Kohn says, "my . . . values become contingent on how much better I am than so many others in so many activities." With this kind of pressure on us, Kohn continues, we can never be satisfied. Kohn doesn't rely solely on personal experiences to support this argument, but also includes a quote from a psychologist. I agree with this final argument because during my eight years of ballet school, I often felt the envy competition breeds and also found myself measuring my own accomplishments in terms of other, more experienced, dancers.

Although Kohn does bring up some interesting points, his support is mainly from personal experience. The basis of the argument is strong and, with further development, could be pretty convincing. Despite its weaknesses, this essay definitely made me rethink the term "healthy competition."

Student Essay 2

In the article "I Wish They'd Do It Right," Jane Doe points out various reasons that her son and "his wife" should get married. Throughout the article, Doe tries to point out the social and economic reasons why her sons marriage should occur. From the announcement of her grandson, to the simple awkwardness of the "daughter-in law's" introductions to friends, to her grandson dealing with his peers at school. Doe tries to convince her readers that socially "It just isn't right." From housing at the student dormitory, to medical insurance coverage, to California state laws. Doe argues that not being married just isn't "right." I, as a reader, however, am not entirely convinced by this article.

Doe asks, "How do I present her—as my son's roommate? his spouse? his spice? my daugher-in-law?" I'll respond with, "Why don't you ask her?" In the 90's, American's will come across many varieties of "marriages," and the socially correct thing to do should be to ask the couple what they prefer.

Another of Doe's points is that her grandson will have many obstacles in his future in school because his parents are not married. Doe's grandson is growing up in a country that has a fifty percent divorce rate, so when he starts school, all he will know is that his mom and dad live in the same house and show affection for each other.

From an economic standpoint, Doe shows her readers that this couple was denied student dormitory housing and endured "other inconviences." I am somewhat convinced on this point because when I married my husband, we had to show our marriage license to apply for base housing at Camp Pendleton, and also to apply for my military identification card. Without proof of a written document, it would have been impossible to take advantage of these benefits, however, there are many situations that do not require a marriage license.

Doe goes on to say, "the couple's adamancy has been depriving to all the rest of the family. There have been no celebration of wedding or anniversaries." I have been married for three years and have not experienced a "celebration" of my anniversary with my parents or my husband's parents. I do not think Doe was very persuasive on this point.

Overall, Doe states that she "love[s] and support[s]" the couple as much as possible now. The preceding issues in her article do not convince me that Doe supports the couple and their choices. My idea of support would be to show the couple that they make their own decisions and she will wait for them to ask her opinion on raising their child. Doe says her grandson needs to be "spared the continued explanation and harrassment . . . of being a child of unmarried parents." The only "doubts and anxieties" being shown in this article are Doe's.

Student Essay 3

The difference between honesty and dishonesty varies so drastically depending on who you are and what you believe. Marya Mannes shows us this in many important ways throughout her essay "The Thin Grey Line." Including the two sides of this thin grey line, common people who cross the line and how society got this way in the first place. Mannes feels that most people fall somewhere in the middle of this area or on the grey line, I think she is correct in this assumption.

The thin grey line has two sides to it. On one side are the bribers, cheaters, extortioners and on the other side are we the partners and victims. This was stated by Mannes as she tries to show us that there is only one thing that separates us from them. This is that they get caught and we don't. I think this is a true statement. In that I consider myself to be an honest person even though I have flirted with several cops just to get out of getting tickets.

In this next point we show that common people cross this line all the time. Some people do it willingly and others don't realize they have crossed the line of dishonesty at all. My brother crosses this line willingly on many occasions. Including last Christmas when he worked at a Christmas tree lot and carried trees out to people's cars after they had paid the cashier, or that was what he was supposed to do. Instead, he had them pay him cash at their car and never paid for the tree he kept the money for himself. On the other hand when I was flirting with the cop trying to get out of the ticket I did not realize how dishonest that was until my friend pointed it out after we left.

Now that we know how dishonest people can be let's see how we got to be so dishonest. Mannes says that kids that get everything from their parents have missed out on one main thing. They have not learned to be responsible for there actions. Mannes also points out that kids have no real heroes except ballplayers who can't read and singers who can't sing. To be a hero you must stand up and defend the right and fight the wrong. This means responsibility and if they have not learned it then they won't respect a hero who does. I think this is very true because my parents gave my brother everything he wanted and he never had to earn anything, now he lacks any sort of responsibility.

As we now see that the two sides of this line are becoming much too close and that common people tend to cross them more often than not. We must now try to stop this and put more emphasis on honesty and telling right from wrong. "Once the line between right and wrong is finally erased, there is no defense against the powers of evil" was stated by Mannes. We must pay more attention to what we do around kids because they see it and if we are dishonest our kids will follow.

Sentence Combining: Parallelism

You were introduced to the concept of parallelism in Chapter 2 when you used coordination to combine sentences. At that time, you learned that ideas joined with coordinating conjunctions should be worded similarly. For example, two words joined with a coordinating conjunction, such as *and*, should both be nouns, or both adjectives, or both adverbs—the point is that they should both be the same type of word.

The same is true of two phrases or clauses joined with a coordinating conjunction. You can join two prepositional phrases or two participial phrases with a coordinating conjunction, but you should not join a prepositional phrase to a participial phrase with one.

Items in a Series

When you write three or more ideas in a series, you should word them similarly, just as you do when you join two ideas with a coordinating conjunction. The key is to use similar types of words, phrases, or clauses as you write the series. *The principle of parallelism requires that you use similar grammatical constructions when you join two ideas with coordinating conjunctions or when you join several ideas in a series.*

The following sentences are drawn from the reading selections in this chapter. Note that each sentence uses parallel sentence structure.

Parallel Words

nouns   *On the one side of this line are They:* <u>the bribers</u>, <u>the cheaters</u>, <u>the chiselers</u>, <u>the swindlers</u>, <u>the extortioners</u>.

adjectives, nouns	*But it will be easier and happier for us knowing that our grandson will be spared the continued explanation and harassment, the doubts and anxieties of being a child of unmarried parents.*

Parallel Phrases

infinitives	*To be a hero you have to stand out, to excel, to take risks. . . .*
verb phrases	*Like millions of Americans, the cabdriver was probably a decent human being who had never stolen anything, broken any law or will- fully injured another. . . .*
participal phrases	*The only reason debaters sacrifice their free time collecting thousands of pieces of evidence, analyzing arguments, and practicing speeches, is to win.*

Parallel Clauses

subordinate clauses	*A fellow commits a crime because he's basically insecure, because he hated his stepmother at nine, or because his sister needs an operation.*
main causes	*Strategy is planned for the next battle; troops are taught the next cheer.*

As you can see from the above examples, you can use parallelism to join all kinds of sentence parts, as long as they are the same type of sentence part. You can join nouns to nouns, infinitives to infinitives, and subordinate clauses to subordinate clauses.

Items Joined by Correlative Conjunctions

Correlative conjunctions are pairs of words that combine related ideas. The most common correlative conjunctions are *either . . . or*, *neither . . . nor*, *not only . . . but also*, and *both . . . and*. Follow the principles of parallel sentence structure when you use these correlatives. Each word, phrase, or clause joined to another by a correlative conjunction should be worded similarly to the other. The following examples illustrate both correct and incorrect usage.

Incorrect:	*The timber wolf will **either** adapt to its new environment **or** it will die a slow death* (verb phrase combined with main clause)
Correct:	*The timber wolf will either adapt to its new environment **or** die a slow death*. (verb phrase combined with verb phrase)
Correct:	***Either** the timber wolf will adapt to its new environment **or** it will die a slow death*. (main clause combined with main clause)

EXERCISE   Use parallel sentence structure to combine each group of sentences into one sentence.

> **EXAMPLE**
>
> *Chelsea was startled by the sudden applause. She was also confused by the bright lights. She stuttered a few words. Then she ran from the stage.*
>
> *Startled by the sudden applause and confused by the bright lights, Chelsea stuttered a few words and then ran from the stage.*

1. The swan was waddling out of the lake. It was heading toward Leda. It had a strange look in its eye.

2. Last week's storm caused mudslides in the foothills. The storm also caused traffic jams on the freeways. Power outages throughout the city were another result.

3. The winning skier slipped. She broke her ankle. It happened after the race had ended. It was before the medal was awarded.

4. The horse was wandering down the freeway. It was stopping all the traffic. It was soon captured by the police officer.

5. Spiderman climbed out of the window. He scaled the side of the building. He fired his spiderweb at the thief.

6. Carmen could not decide if she wanted to risk the earthquakes on the west coast. Another possibility was that she could risk the hurricanes on the east coast.

7. The produce manager knew it. The price of the oranges was too high. The quality of the oranges was too low.

8. Senator Milkwood proposed his new legislation. He was determined to preserve the disappearing forests. He was also determined to promote the lumber industry.

9. The Sphinx looked at Oedipus and asked, "What creature goes on four feet in the morning? The same creature goes on two feet at midday. It also goes on three feet in the evening."

10. By the time the play was over, Hugo was thoroughly disgusted. The play had made him completely depressed. He decided to buy a gallon of vanilla ice cream. He planned to cover it with chocolate sauce. Then he was going to eat it all by himself.

EXERCISE   Revise the following sentences to correct any errors in parallelism.

> **EXAMPLE**
>
> *The farmer knew that for the rest of his life he would be planting seeds, his crops needed tending, and prayers for a good harvest.*

The farmer knew that for the rest of his life he would be planting seeds, tending his crops, and praying for a good harvest.

1. In the early 1800s, John Palmer, a farmer with a long white beard, stood by his principles and refusing to be intimidated.

2. When the people in his town told him that he should be not only ashamed of his beard but also that he should cut it off, he refused.

3. Children jeered at him, stones were heaved through his windows by grown men, and women crossing to the opposite side of the street.

4. Saying that he was a vain man and with the insistence that he cut his beard, the local pastor denounced him.

5. When several men tried to grab him, hold him down, and shave him, he fought back.

6. As a result, he was arrested, a trial was held, and jailed for "unprovoked assault."

7. He was told either that he could cut his beard or stay in jail.

8. When Henry David Thoreau and Ralph Waldo Emerson heard of his plight, they persuaded people to support his cause and his release was arranged with their help.

9. Joseph Palmer refused to leave his jail cell, saying that his jailers must admit that they were not only wrong but also must publicly state that he had a right to wear a beard.

EXERCISE   Use parallel sentence structure to combine each group of sentences into one sentence.

1. The unicorn is a legendary animal. It resembles a horse. It also is said to resemble a deer. Or it could be described as looking like a kid. It has a single horn on its forehead.

2. It has also been described as having other characteristics. It has been described as having the hind legs of an antelope. In addition, some have said it has the tail of a lion. It has also been said to have the beard of a goat.

3. The unicorn is represented in the art of Asian cultures. It is also in the art of European cultures. It is in art that is ancient. In addition, it is in medieval art.

4. In 400 B.C. a Greek physician described the unicorn. He said it has a white body. Its head is purple. It has a horn that is straight.

5. He said that the horn has a white base. The horn's middle is black. It has a red tip.

6. The unicorn was said to be a fleet animal. It was also supposed to be fierce. It was a solitary animal too. It would fight savagely when cornered. However, it was gentle at mating time.

7. Many people believed that the powdered horn of a unicorn would protect them. They thought it would give them protection from poison. It was also supposed to prevent stomach trouble. Epilepsy was supposed to be prevented by it too.

8. True powder from unicorn horns was supposed to do certain things. It was supposed to generate bubbles in water. It emitted a sweet odor when burned. Poisonous plants and animals were killed by it.

9. In medieval times the unicorn represented chastity. It also stood for purity. It could only be tamed by the touch of a virgin.

10. In some medieval paintings the unicorn is associated with the Virgin Mary. Jesus is represented by it in other medieval paintings.

REVIEW EXERCISE Combine the following sentences, using coordination, subordination, verbal phrases, appositives, and parallel sentence structure where appropriate.

1. Of the five senses, many animals possess at least one that is special.

   That one is much more highly developed than it is in other animals.

   The five senses are sight, hearing, touch, smell, and taste.

2. A buzzard will be flying hundreds of feet in the air.

   It can see a beetle on the ground.

   An owl can hear the slight rustle of a mouse.

   It can home in on the rustle.

   That sound is inaudible to the human ear.

3. Most animals that hunt have many rod cells in their eyes.

   Rod cells are sensitive to movement.

   Animals that gather stationary food have many cone cells.

   Cone cells are sensitive to colors.

4. Dogs have over 200 million olfactory cells.

   Humans have 5 million olfactory cells.

   Dogs are literally millions of times better at detecting odors than are humans.

5. A female butterfly carries only 1/10,000 of a milligram of perfume.

   She releases that perfume into the air.

   A male butterfly can detect her scent up to seven miles away.

6. The sense of hearing is spectacularly developed in bats.

   Bats emit high-frequency squeaks.

   They use the echoes to find their way in the dark.

   They also use them to hunt fast-flying insects.

7. Bats often fly in groups of thousands.

   They are always able to recognize the echoes of their own squeaks.

   They never confuse them with those of another bat.

8. Scientists have tried to "jam" the bats' signals.

   They have broadcast on the same wavelength.

   They have broadcast at 2,000 times the volume of a bat's squeak.

   The bats were still able to recognize their own echoes.

9. Bees seem to have a sixth sense.

   It is a sensitivity to the earth's magnetic field.

   It enables them to navigate at great distances from their hive.

10. There are two dimples on each side of a rattlesnake's head.

    They serve as heat-sensing organs.

    They allow the snake to locate its prey.

    They also allow it to determine the size of its prey.

    And they help the snake determine the shape of its prey.

CHAPTER SEVEN

Synthesizing Ideas from Reading Selections

The Small Society. Reprinted by permission of King Features Syndicate.

One of the goals of a college education is to learn to search out new ideas and to consider those that are different from our own. After all, we really can't claim to be educated about an issue if we know only one side of it. Many college assignments will ask you to discuss or explain the various issues involved in a particular topic. A philosophy instructor, for example, might ask you to explain the concept of love as it is developed by a number of different philosophers; a health instructor might ask you to discuss different theories about the best way to prevent high cholesterol; and a political science instructor might ask you to write about the arguments involved in the debate over the balanced-budget amendment.

People who are able to consider ideas from a number of different sources, to see the relationships among those ideas, and to pull those ideas together into one coherent whole possess a valuable skill. They are the people who will be able to consider all sides of an issue and then reach reasonable, considered judgments about how they should vote, where they should work, or why they should accept one idea rather than another. They are also the people who will not oversimplify a complex issue, who will recognize that sometimes there is no one "correct" answer but rather merely one alternative that is only slightly better than other possible alternatives.

A **synthesis** is a paper or report that pulls together related ideas. In one sense, a synthesis is similar to a summary in that both papers require careful reading and accurate reporting. However, writing a synthesis is often more difficult than writing a summary because a synthesis requires that you read a number of sources, identify the related ideas, and then explain how those ideas are related. Sometimes several sources on the same topic will discuss very different points yet reach the same conclusion, and your synthesis will need to reflect that. Sometimes related sources will discuss the same points but reach quite different conclusions. And sometimes sources will simply repeat ideas you have already read in other sources.

Preparing the Synthesis

1. The first step in writing a good synthesis is to identify the ideas discussed by each writer. On a sheet of paper, identify the thesis idea of each writer. Then make a list of the supporting ideas discussed by that writer. If any examples, statistics, or other types of support seem particularly important, make a note of them too.

2. Once you have listed the ideas that each writer discusses, you need to look for the relationships among those ideas. Sometimes the relationships are easy to see. For instance, let's say you have read several articles on gun control and have noticed that most of them referred in one way or another to the Second Amendment to the Constitution. Part of your synthesis paper, then, would report how the writers used the Second

Amendment in their arguments. Unfortunately, sometimes the relationships between ideas are not easy to see. If you do not see any clear relationships among the points you have listed, consider these questions:

a. Do one writer's ideas support another writer's ideas? If so, how?

b. Do the writers who reach the same conclusion use the same ideas in their writing? Or do they use very different ideas to reach the same conclusion?

c. Do the writers who disagree discuss similar points, or do they discuss completely different points?

d. Are any of the ideas you have listed actually the same idea in different words?

Organizing the Synthesis

How you organize your synthesis will depend upon the sources that you have read. Let's consider the following example: Suppose you have read several articles about protecting an endangered species in America's northwestern forests. One of the articles was written by a spokesperson for the logging industry, one by a member of the Sierra Club, one by a homeowner in Seattle, Washington, and one by a biologist at Washington State University. Perhaps each article reached a different conclusion about protecting the endangered species, yet you were able to find three or four points that some of the articles had in common—even if they disagreed about those points. You could organize such a paper this way:

Point-by-Point Organization
I.   Introduction
II. One point discussed by two or more of the articles
III. Another point discussed by two or more of the articles
IV. Another point discussed by two or more of the articles
V.   An optional paragraph mentioning one or more major points discussed in only one article each
VI. Conclusion

The above organization will work if you can identify similar points discussed by different sources. (Remember, the sources do not need to agree about the points.) However, sometimes you will read several articles that do not discuss *any* similar points, even though they are about the same topic. In such a case, you can briefly summarize what each source has to say. If each source focuses on one major issue, you can summarize the major issue in each paragraph.

Source-by-Source Organization
I.   Introduction
II. Summary of one source
III. Summary of another source
IV. Summary of another source
V.   Conclusion

Alternate Source-by-Source Organization

I.   Introduction
II. One major point discussed by only one source
III. Another major point discussed by only one source
IV. Another major point discussed by only one source
V.   Conclusion

Of course, as often as not, you will find some points that overlap from article to article and some that do not. In such cases, you can use an organization that is a blend of the ones shown above.

A Blended Organization

I.   Introduction
II. One point discussed by two or more articles
III. Another point discussed by two or more articles
IV. One major point discussed by only one source
V.   Another major point discussed by only one source
VI. Conclusion

Documenting Your Sources

Whenever you use someone else's words or ideas in your writing, you must let the reader know the source of those words or ideas. It really doesn't matter whether you have paraphrased, summarized, or quoted—in each case, you must let the reader know whose material you are using.

Up to this point, your writing assignments have focused on one reading selection at a time. In them you have used simple transitions to tell the reader when you were using material from the reading selection. (See Chapter 5 for a discussion of transitions with paraphrases, summaries, and quotations.) There are, however, more formal methods of documentation that you will need to learn to use as you write in college classes.

The two most common methods of documentation are the MLA (Modern Language Association) method, used primarily in the humanities, and the APA (American Psychological Association) method, used mostly in the social sciences. Both methods use parentheses within the paper to identify the author and page number of a particular passage that is paraphrased, summarized, or quoted. They also both use a separate page at the end of the paper to give more detailed and complete identification of the sources used. In most classes, your instructor will tell you which method to use and will suggest a documentation guide that you should purchase.

Because this text includes its own reading selections, you do not need to write a separate page that gives detailed identification about the sources you use. However, the papers you write for Chapters 7 and 8 will be clearer if you learn to use parentheses to identify the particular article you are referring to at any given time. Use these guidelines to help you:

■ Each paraphrase, summary, and quotation should be identified by author and page number in parentheses. Do not use the author's first name within the parentheses.

According to one writer, "Educational TV corrupts the very notion of education and renders its victims uneducable" (Robinson 212).

In defense of television, another writer claims that many schoolchildren learn the alphabet from Sesame Street *and that high school students learn about the problems that our planet faces (Henry 208).*

■ If the author's name is already included in the transition, it does not need to be repeated in the parentheses.

According to Paul Robinson, "Educational TV corrupts the very notion of education and renders its victims uneducable" (212).

In defense of television, William Henry III claims that many schoolchildren learn the alphabet from Sesame Street *and that high school students learn about the problems that our planet faces (208).*

■ When your source quotes or paraphrases someone else and you want to use that material, indicate it by using "qtd. in" as is done in the following example. (Here the quotation of Daniel Anderson comes from the article by Madeline Drexler that is included in this chapter.)

According to Daniel Anderson, a psychologist at the University of Massachusetts at Amherst, children watching TV "muse upon the meaning of what they see, its plausibility and its implications for the future—whether they've tuned in to a news report of a natural disaster or an action show" (qtd. in Drexler 216).

■ No punctuation is placed between the author's last name and the page number (see above examples).

■ The parenthetical citation is placed at the end of the borrowed material but before the period at the end of the sentence (see above examples).

Readings

THE TOY WEAPON DEBATE

Before You Read

1. The following articles were written by fathers who reached different conclusions about whether or not they should buy toy guns for their children. What issues would you expect to see discussed in such a debate?

2. Do you think parents should buy toy guns for their children? Why or why not?

Why I Bought My Son a Toy Gun

MICHAEL GOLDEN

During my college years, you could have called me a peacenik. In my pantheon of heroes, Mahatma Gandhi and Dr. Martin Luther King, Jr., rank only behind Mickey Mantle. My wife, Joan, considers it an act of violence to step on any multi-legged creature that crawls (with the possible exception of large, hairy spiders). The only guns either of us ever touch are the caulking and staple guns that I use solely under extreme duress. And after our son, Andrew, was born, we raised him on a steady diet of Dr. Seuss, *Sesame Street*, and *Reading Rainbow*.

Now, in a world saturated with violence, I find myself in a rather ironic position: defending my decision to buy my son a toy gun. I think, however, that I can justify this apparent contradiction.

When we bought Andrew his first toy gun, he was all of six years old—an age so advanced that most of his friends had already acquired arsenals that would be the envy of several Third World countries.

We were in a gift shop in Disney World, having just viewed the "Pirates of the Caribbean" exhibit. Andrew was fascinated by pirates and was eagerly eyeing the authentic-looking replica of a pirate's pistol. Joan and I looked at each other, waiting.

"Please, please, can I get this gun?" Andrew asked.

Joan tried plea bargaining first. "You know how Mommy feels about guns, Andrew. Why, just look at this wonderful book about pirates. Or this model of a pirate ship. Wouldn't you rather have one of those?"

Andrew wouldn't bite. He turned to me.

"But Dad, you said I could get something in the gift shop. Can't I please get this gun?"

Looking at my eager, questioning child, I said what I presume any father would under the circumstances:

"You know how your mother feels about guns, Andrew."

"But, Dad, it's only a toy. It's not like a real gun."

Six-year-old logic won out over parental reservations.

As I look back on this incident three years later, questions surface: Did Joan and I "give in," abandoning our parental authority? Did we, by buying him that first gun, somehow sanction what guns represent: violence, bloodshed, death, and mayhem?

I don't think so. As parents, we have to pick and choose our battles, to   14
know when to stand firm and when to compromise. This was just not an
issue on which we were prepared to dig in our heels.

Why? For one thing, we felt that it was not realistic to think that for-   15
bidding Andrew to play with toy guns would keep him from doing so.
He would play with them anyway at his friends' houses or fashion them
out of any available material, from sticks to blocks. Or he might, as boys
so often do, simply use his pointing finger and some sound effects for a
rousing shoot-out. And besides, we wondered, wouldn't denying him his
own guns only make them that much more attractive (the "forbidden
fruit" theory)?

But the practical arguments, admittedly, don't make it right to buy a   16
toy gun; the everybody's-doing-it and forbidden fruit theories are not
morally compelling. We had to consider what message we were giving
Andrew by purchasing the gun.

The message *wasn't* that real guns are acceptable or that real violence   17
is. Andrew had already shown us that he understood that the gun we
bought him is a toy and that toys don't kill. And he knows our attitude
toward guns and violence; he understands that allowing the use of a toy
gun does not give him license to commit acts of destruction.

I also believe that it is healthy for Andrew to act out his fantasies and   18
actively engage his imagination. I would rather see him play cops and
robbers with his toy gun than see him sit in front of a mindless television
program.

Finally, as a father, I retain some of the little boy in me, vestiges of my   19
childhood that enable me to relate to Andrew in an intimate way. As a
small boy, my heroes were often symbols of authority and order: the
policeman, the soldier, the gun-toting cowboy. I emulated them by acting
out bold adventures, secure in the knowledge that the sharp-shooting
good guys would win. I recall lining up my "enemy" soldiers and mow-
ing them down with my cork rifle, not from any bloodthirsty impulse
but out of desire to destroy the "bad guys" that threatened my world.

In the end, it came down to this: If I enjoyed playing with toy guns in   20
my youth and managed to grow up and become a reasonably responsible, nonviolent adult, how could I justify denying my son the same
opportunity?

Now, three years later, Joan and I are convinced that the purchase of   21
that gun did not signify a lapse in our moral judgment. We are proud of
Andrew; he occasionally plays with his toy guns, but he also plays the
piano and violin, and tennis and chess and baseball. He is, we feel, devel-

oping a healthy and balanced set of values. Most important, he is sensitive and caring—even, remarkably, to the five-year-old sister who loves to torment him.

And so Andrew has his toy guns, and Joan and I are at peace with our   22
decision. Despite the dilemma it posed, we don't feel we had to "bite the bullet" on this one.

Why I Won't Buy My Sons Toy Guns

ROBERT SHAFFER

I've often seen a child go up to another child or an adult, pull a trigger   1
on a toy gun (or a pretend trigger on a pretend gun), and exclaim
"You're dead." Just yesterday, my seven-year-old son was "attacked" by
a total stranger, a boy of eight or nine carrying a two-foot-long plastic
gun. Usually, I just move on after such an incident, although living in
New York City, where death by stray bullets regularly makes headlines, I
shudder whenever I witness these make-believe murders.

I cannot shrug off, however, the mother I know who apologized for her   2
son's similar behavior by saying, 'I can't understand where Steven gets
these ideas. It's not like his father and I sit around talking about killing
people, or going 'bang-bang' to everything we see." In fact, Steven's
parents did sanction his behavior by providing him with a roomful of
toy weapons, whose only function is to attack people, and by allowing
him to sit in front of television shows filled with fights, shootings, and
mutilations.

Any toy is a teacher. A toy hammer helps children act out repair or   3
construction activities they see around them. A toy typewriter helps our
sons model my work as a teacher. Bakers' caps, play food, and sample
menus put children in charge of the restaurant experience.

Toy weapons, too, develop children's skills and coping mechanisms.   4
But the lesson toy guns teach is that solving problems with violence is
acceptable. These are not skills my wife and I want to encourage in our
two sons, so we won't be buying any toy weapons for them this holiday
season, just as we haven't in past years.

Does our stance mean that we never expect our children—Alan, seven,   5
and Ross, five—to act out their emotions with pretend or real violence?
Of course not. Last night Ross was uneasy about sitting in the car next

to an adult friend of ours. He demonstrated his discomfort by punching our friend and pretending to shoot him. A little attention and a familiar toy to hold on to calmed his fears.

Allowing anger and aggressive play to surface is not the same as encouraging play with toy weapons, however—and buying a toy gun or missile is encouragement. I have, of course, often seen a block, a stick, a finger, a doll, or even a half-eaten cookie become, in the hands and minds of my sons, a gun or a club. But the same process of imagination that made weapons of these objects can make them into constructive and peaceful objects. The blocks on the living room floor right now were a fort yesterday, but over the last three days they have also been a garage, a kitchen, and a "safe place" to put little people and animal figures. A toy weapon, however, stays a toy weapon.

Furthermore, so many of the toy weapons for sale are hopelessly inter-twined with violent television shows which determine how children will play with the toys. Nancy Carlsson-Paige and Diane Levin, in their excellent recent book about war toys, *Who's Calling the Shots?* (New Society Publishers), bemoan the increasingly imitative nature of war play, as opposed to creative and dramatic play. Aggressive play and war play, they say, *could* have a value in allowing children to develop ideas of right and wrong, good and bad, teamwork, and organizational skills. Increasingly, however, the toys rather than the children write the script.

In addition, Carlsson-Paige and Levin point out that the Reagan admin-istration in the 1980s deregulated commercial children's television to allow more product tie-ins, more ads, and more violence at the same time that military spending skyrocketed. Not surprisingly, sales of war toys soared in the late 1980s, to become a billion-dollar-a-year industry.

Many parents I know do not like to buy war toys but do so upon insis-tent and incessant demands from their children. We've found, however, that laying down certain ground rules has limited Alan's and Ross's demands for war toys.

We discourage our children from watching commercial television, avoid television news shows, and tell relatives and close friends that war toys are not welcome as presents.

We've also checked our sons' day-care centers and schools to make sure they do not allow toy weapons. Friends' houses are more difficult, but we don't encourage play dates at other children's homes if we know that they will mainly watch TV or play with war toys.

Can the elimination of toy weapons eliminate war? Modern wars are caused by many factors more complex than the legacies of childhood war play, but toy weapons certainly serve to make war appear more acceptable to future voters and future soldiers. In a season ostensibly devoted to peace and good will, we certainly will not participate in purchasing toy weapons.

After You Read

Work with other students to develop responses to these questions or to compare responses that you have already prepared.

1. Is Robert Shaffer's idea that any toy is a teacher related to any point that Michael Golden makes?

2. What does each writer have to say about the role of the imagination in his argument?

3. What other ideas do the writers consider?

HOW DOES TELEVISION AFFECT US?

Before You Read

1. Has television had both positive and negative influences on your life? Discuss what those influences are.

2. Has television affected the lives of people you know? Explain how.

The Meaning of TV

WILLIAM HENRY III

We tend to talk about television as though it has always been there, as though it provides the same experience for everyone, as though it were a single, living organism. In conversation almost everyone speaks of "television" doing this or that, intending this or that. A moment's thought is enough to recall that "television" is made up of a score and more broadcast and cable networks, some 1,300 local stations and countless production companies. The medium is collaborative; there are few if any *auteurs*. Yet TV is so potent a presence that it seems to have a mind, and personality, of its own.

If TV has changed over time, we take it mostly as a reflection of how we who view it have changed, and in a sense that is right. While TV may not sense our moods and respond to them like a friend or family member, the people who administer, advertise on and program television all devote themselves to research that tracks each zig and zag of national mood. Their goal is to keep television exactly in step with mainstream taste, so that in most homes it will resemble a family member or a congenial neighbor. If television really were a personality, it would qualify as almost everyone's closest friend.

The average American watches TV about four hours a day; the average   3
household has the set on for seven hours in all. Even people who say they "don't watch much television" turn out to be forgetting to count news, or sports, or Mister Rogers with the toddlers, or old movies, or vintage reruns, or something or other that they somehow consider to be not mere TV. Just why do people in all walks of life feel such guilt about watching TV, or assert such superiority in pretending that they do not? Because, despite their affection for TV, they think watching it is too passive, an inert substitute for exercise or reading, or conversation—or study.

The reality is that TV can provide plenty of learning, and not merely   4
on Sunrise Semester. For every schoolchild whose reading problems might be blamed on an excess of TV, there is probably another who learned the alphabet from Sesame Street and began see-and-say reading with the on-screen words of commercials. High school students may have trouble spotting South America on a map, but through TV they have grasped some basic truths about the planet. Wherever they live, they were shaken last summer by images of beaches closed to bathers because the sands were strewn with toxic hospital waste. Among television's diehard critics, the print journalists, it is an open secret that the most important source of news flow during any election night or political crisis is the television set, around which editors and reporters cluster to stay abreast and to test their news judgment. And the same scholars and opinion-makers who profess to view television with disdain are nearly always avid to appear on it—fully expecting that their friends will see them. Most of the nation's elite seem to live by at least the latter half of Gore Vidal's reported dictum, "There are two things in life one must never refuse. One is sex, and the other is television."

Perhaps TV's deepest power is not the change it works on sports or   5
commerce or any other branch of reality, but the way its innocuous-looking entertainment reaches deep into the national mind. TV has the ability to generate, or regenerate, national mythology. The great characters of television embody human truths as profound as the great characters in Moliere or Ibsen, and for vastly bigger audiences. The viewership

for even one modestly successful airing of a prime-time series would fill every theater on Broadway, eight performances a week, for a couple of years. These characters linger in memory because they epitomize what the nation feels about itself. They teach behavior and values. They enter the language. Say the name Falstaff, and some minority of the population will know that you mean a vainglorious coward; say Ralph Kramden, and everyone will know what you mean. The Mary Richards character created by Mary Tyler Moore summed up their own lives for a whole generation of thirtysomething single women who could have any careers they wanted, but often at the expense of satisfaction at home. This is not new with television. The great civilizing effect of all literature is that it takes people's vision beyond the immediate, the clan and the tribe. It enables them to make the philosophical leap that Jean-Paul Sartre described as "seeing the other as another self." Television simply does this more effectively, more touchingly, than any kind of art that went before. Unlike the stage and movies, the episodic TV series does not end in catharsis. The characters come back week after week, evolving at the slow pace of ordinary life, exposing themselves more fully than most relatives or friends. Other literature provides occasional experiences. Television becomes an ongoing part of life and for some susceptible people is only barely distinguishable from real life itself.

It is hard to imagine a world without television, harder still to imagine   6
what the world of the last half century would have been without those first flickering images from NBC and all that followed. We might have fewer terrorists, because there would be no worldwide pulpit for their propaganda. We might have a less violent society, because the typical child would not have been exposed to tens of thousands of actual and simulated violent crimes on news and entertainment by the time he or she reached adulthood. We might have a society in which people still felt respect for established institutions and their leaders, instead of one in which TV-bred skepticism had lowered the approval rating for Congress, business executives and even judges to between 20 and 40 percent. We might have a healthier society, one in which children played outside instead of watching the box hour after hour, one in which meals cooked from scratch at home had not been outdistanced by snacks and fast food loaded with sugar, salt and fat, all enticingly advertised. We might have a more restrained, less libertine world, one in which virginity and marriage were still revered while premarital pregnancy and divorce were still treated with distaste rather than sympathy. All of these effects have been attributed, sometimes convincingly, to TV. But we might also

have a less alert world, one in which citizens were not so widely
informed about the economy, about medical matters, about foreign military adventures that run the risk of war. We might have a less concerned
world, one in which starvation in Ethiopia could never inspire Live Aid,
one in which the homeless of Manhattan or Chicago might remain
unseen by the rest of the nation. We might have a lonelier, more isolated
world in which the old lived without much entertainment, without much
company, without the sense of involvement in life that can be conferred
even by watching Donahue.

Only one thing can be said for certain. Whatever world we would   7
have, it would be different in many and unimaginable ways from this
one. Like fire and the wheel and the alphabet, television has changed the
world that humans live in. And more, perhaps, than any invention or
discovery before it, television has changed the definition of what it
means to be human.

From William Henry III in Life *magazine. Reprinted with permission of Time, Inc.*

TV Can't Educate

PAUL ROBINSON

On July 20 [1978] NBC aired a documentary on life in Marin County,   1
a bedroom community just across the Golden Gate Bridge from
San Francisco. The program was called "I Want It All Now" and its single theme was the predominance of narcissism in Marin. The program's
host, Edwin Newman, introduced viewers, in his studied casual manner,
to a variety of "consciousness-raising" groups ensconced in Marin and
insinuated that this new narcissistic manner was leading to a breakdown
not only of the family (a divorce rate of 75 percent was mentioned three
times) but also of traditional civic virtue. The following day the *San
Francisco Chronicle* carried a long front-page article on the outraged
reaction of Marin's respectable citizenry to what it considered a grossly
distorted portrait of itself. Several residents argued, persuasively, that
Marin was in fact a highly political suburb—that it had been a hot spot
of the anti-Vietnam war movement, and that only last year it had
responded dramatically to the water crisis in California, cutting back on
water use much more than was required by law. Television journalism
appeared to be up to its old tricks: producers saw what they wanted to
see, and they were not about to pass up the chance to show a woman

being massaged by two nude men and chirping about how delightful it was to "receive" without having to "give."

I was reminded, however, improbably, of an experience in Berlin, where I had spent the previous six months teaching. The Germans are all exercised over a recent movie about Adolf Hitler (*Hitler: Eine Karriere*), which is based on a biography by the journalist Joachim Fest. The charge leveled against the film is that it glorifies Hitler (though it uses nothing but documentary footage; there are no actors), and it has been linked with a supposed resurgence of Nazism in Germany, particularly among the young. I saw only parts of the film and therefore can't speak to the justice of the charge. What I wish to report on—and what the Marin program brought to mind—is a lecture I attended by a young German historian from the Free University of Berlin, in which he took issue with the film because it had failed to treat Hitler's relations with the German industrialists, who were crucial in supporting the Nazi Party before it came to power and apparently benefited from its success.

The critics of the Newman program and my young scholar friend in Berlin were guilty of the same error. They both bought the assumption that television and movies can be a source of knowledge, that one can "learn" from them. By knowledge and learning I obviously don't mean an assortment of facts. Rather I have in mind the analytic process that locates pieces of information within a larger context of argument and meaning. Movies and TV are structurally unsuited to that process.

There is no great mystery here. It's a simple matter of time. Learning requires one kind of time, visual media are bound to another. In learning one must be able to freeze the absorption of fact or proposition at any moment in order to make mental comparisons, to test the fact or proposition against known facts and propositions, to measure it against the formal rules of logic and evidence—in short, to carry on a mental debate. Television is a matter of seconds, minutes and hours, it moves inexorably forward, and thus even with the best will in the world (a utopian assumption), it can never teach. In the last analysis there is only one way to learn: by reading. That's how you'll find out about Hitler's relations with the German industrialists, if you can find out about them at all. Such a complex, many-layered phenomenon simply cannot be reduced to a scene (which would presumably meet my scholar-friend's objection) in which Hitler has dinner with Baron Krupp. Similarly, you will not find out about life in Marin county from an hour-long TV program or, for that matter, from a 24-hour-long one. What are the control populations? What statistical methods are being used? Is there more consciousness raising going on in Marin than in Cambridge? What is the correlation between narcissism and income level, educational background, employment, religious affiliation, marital status, sexual inclination and so forth? If these questions have answers, they are to be found in the books and articles of sociologists, not on TV.

I am prepared, indeed eager, to follow my argument to its logical conclusion: the worst thing on TV is educational TV (and not just on educational stations). By comparison the gratuitous violence of most commercial shows is a mere peccadillo. Educational TV corrupts the very notion of education and renders its victims uneducable. I hear grown-ups launching conversations with, "Mike Wallace says that . . . " as if Mike Wallace actually knew something. Viewers hold forth authoritatively about South Africa, or DNA, or black holes, or whatever because they have watched a segment about them on *60 Minutes* or some such program. Complete ignorance really would be preferable, because ignorance at least preserves a mental space that might someday be filled with real knowledge, or some approximation of it.

There is a new form of slumming popular among intellectuals: watching "bad" (i.e. a commercial) TV and even writing books about it (as Dan Wakefield has about the afternoon soap opera *All My Children*). I would like to think that the motive behind this development is revulsion against the intellectual pretensions of "good" TV. But, as often happens with academics, the reaction has been dressed up in phony theoretical garb. *All My Children*, we're supposed to believe, is the great American novel, heir to the tradition of Dickens and Trollope. Of course it's nothing of the sort. But it *is* very good entertainment. And that is precisely what TV is prepared to do: to entertain, to divert, above all to amuse. It is superbly amusing, ironically, for the same reason that it can't educate: it is tied to the clock, which has enormous comic potential. It is not accidental that one speaks of a comedian's "timing." Jack Benny would not be funny in print. He must wait just the right length of time after the robber threatens, "Your money or your life," before responding. (Imagine the situation in a novel: "The robber said, 'Your money or your life.' Jack took ten seconds trying to make up his mind.") Nor can you do a double-take in print, only on the screen. The brilliant manipulation of time made *The Honeymooners* so funny: Art Carney squandered it while Jackie Gleason, whose clock ran at double-time, burned. Audrey Meadows stood immobile, producing a magnificently sustained and silent obbligato to Gleason's frantic buffo patter.

Television, then, is superbly fit to amuse. And amusement is not to be despised. At the very least it provides an escape from the world and from

5
6
7

ourselves. It is pleasurable (by definition, one might say), and it gives us a sense of union with humanity, if only in its foibles. Herbert Marcuse might even contend that it keeps alive the image of an unrepressed existence. Television can provide all this. But it can't educate.

Movies are faced with the same dilemma. The desire to educate accounts, I believe, for the increasingly deliberate pace of movies. It is as if the director were trying to provide room within his time-bound narrative for the kind of reflection associated with analysis. This was brought home to me recently when, during the same week, I saw the movie *Julia* in the theater and *Jezebel* on TV. The later, made in 1938, portrays the tragedy of a strong-willed southern girl who refuses to conform to the rules of antebellum New Orleans society. The most striking difference between the two movies is their pace. *Jezebel* moves along swiftly (there is probably more dialogue in the first 15 minutes than in all of *Julia*), treats its theme with appropriate superficiality and entertains effortlessly. *Julia*, on the other hand, is lugubrious and obviously beyond its depth. It succeeds only with the character of Julia herself, who, like Jezebel, is powerful, beautiful, virtuous and unburdened by intellectual or psychological complexity. By way of contrast, the narrative figure, Lilli, tries vainly to deal with issues that movies can't manage: the difficulty of writing, a relationship with an older man who is at once lover, mentor, and patient-to-be, the tension between literary success and political commitment. All of these are wonderfully captured in Lillian Hellman's memoir, but not even two fine actors like Jane Fonda and Jason Robards can bring such uncinematic matters to life on the screen. The "issue" of the memoir—despite all those meaningful silences—inevitably eluded the movie.

Let us, then, not ask more of movies and TV than they can deliver. In fact, let us discourage them from trying to "educate" us.

8

9

From The New Republic. ©*1978. Reprinted by permission of the publisher.*

Shadows on the Wall

DONNA WOOLFOLK CROSS

I see no virtue in having a public that cannot distinguish fact from fantasy. When you start thinking fantasy is reality you have a serious problem. People can be stampeded into all kinds of fanaticism, folly and warfare.

—ISAAC ASIMOV

Why, sometimes I've believed as many as six impossible things before breakfast.

—QUEEN TO ALICE IN LEWIS CARROLL'S *THROUGH THE LOOKING GLASS*

In Book Four of *The Republic*, Plato tells a story about four prisoners who since birth have been chained inside a cave, totally isolated from the world outside. They face a wall on which shadows flicker, cast by the light of the fire. The flickering shadows are the only reality they know. Finally, one of the prisoners is released and permitted to leave the cave. Once outside, he realizes that the shadows he has watched for so long are only pale, distorted reflections of a much brighter, better world. He returns to tell the others about the world outside the cave. They listen in disbelief, then in anger, for what he says contradicts all they have known. Unable to accept the truth, they cast him out as a heretic. 1

Today, our picture of the world is formed in great part from television's flickering shadows. Sometimes that picture is a fairly accurate reflection of the real world; sometimes it is not. But either way, we accept it as real and we act upon it as if it were reality itself. "And that's the way it is," Walter Cronkite assured us every evening for over nineteen years, and most of us did not doubt it. 2

A generation of Americans has grown up so dependent on television that its images appear as real to them as life itself. On a recent trip to a widely advertised amusement park, my husband, daughter, and I rode a "white-water" raft through manufactured "rapids." As we spun and screamed and got thoroughly soaked, I noticed that the two young boys who shared our raft appeared rather glum. When the ride ended, I heard one remark to the other, "It's more fun on television." 3

As an experiment, Jerzy Kosinski gathered a group of children, aged seven to ten years, into a room to show them some televised film. Before the show began, he announced, "Those who want to stay inside and watch the films are free to remain in the classroom, but there's something fascinating happening in the corridor, and those who want to see it are free to leave the room." Kosinski describes what happened next: 4

> No more than 10 percent of the children left. I repeated, "You know, what's outside is really fantastic. You have never seen it before. Why don't you just step out and take a look?" 5
>
> And they always said, "No, no, no, we prefer to stay here and watch the film." I'd say, "But you don't know what's outside." "Well, what is it?" they'd ask. "You have to go find out." And they'd say, "Why don't we just sit here and see the film first?" . . . They were already too corrupted to take a chance on the outside. 6

In another experiment, Kosinski brought a group of children into a room with two giant video screens mounted on the side walls. He stood in the front of the room and began to tell them a story. Suddenly, as part of a prearranged plan, a man entered and pretended to attack Kosinski, yelling at him and hitting him. The entire episode was shown on the two video screens as it happened. The children did not respond, but merely watched the episode unfold on the video screens. They rarely glanced at the two men struggling in the front of the room. Later, in an interview with Kosinski, they explained that the video screens captured the event much more satisfactorily, providing close-ups of the participants, their expressions, and such details as the attacker's hand on Kosinski's face.

Some children can become so preoccupied with television that they are oblivious to the real world around them. UPI filed a report on a burglar who broke into a home and killed the father of three children, aged nine, eleven, and twelve. The crime went unnoticed until ten hours later, when police entered the apartment after being called by neighbors and found the three children watching television just a few feet away from the bloody corpse of their father.

Shortly after this report was released, the University of Nebraska conducted a national survey in which children were asked which they would keep if they had to choose—their fathers or their television sets. *Over half* chose the television sets!

Evidence of this confusion between reality and illusion grows daily. Trial lawyers, for example, complain that juries have become conditioned to the formulas of televised courtroom dramas.

Former Bronx District Attorney Mario Merola says, "All they want is drama, suspense—a confession. Never in all my years as a prosecutor have I seen someone cry from the witness stand, 'I did it! I did it—I confess!' But that's what happens on prime-time TV—and that's what the jurors think the court system is all about." He adds, "Such misconceptions make the work of a district attorney's office much harder than it needs to be." Robert Daley describes one actual courtroom scene in which the defendant was subjected to harsh and unrelenting cross-examination: "I watched the jury," he says. "It seemed to me that I had seen this scene before, and indeed I had dozens of times—on television. On television the murderer always cracks eventually and says something like 'I can't take it any more.' He suddenly breaks down blubbering and admits his guilt. But this defendant did not break down, he did not admit his guilt. He did not blubber. It seemed to me I could see the jury conclude before my eyes: ergo, he cannot be guilty—and indeed the trial ended in a hung jury. . . . Later I lay in bed in the dark and brooded

7

8

9

10

11

about the trial. . . . If [television courtroom dramas] had never existed, would the jury have found the defendant guilty even though he did not crack?". . .

Don't Touch That Dial

MADELINE DREXLER

Television acts as a narcotic on children—mesmerizing them, stunting their ability to think, and displacing such wholesome activities as book reading and family discussions. Right? 1

Wrong, says researcher Daniel Anderson, a psychologist at the University of Massachusetts at Amherst. Anderson doesn't have any particular affection for *Garfield and Friends*, MTV clips, or *Gilligan's Island* reruns. But he does believe it's important to distinguish television's impact on children from influences of the family and the wider culture. We tend to blame TV, he says, for problems it doesn't really cause. In the process, we overlook our own roles in shaping children's minds. 2

One conventional belief about television is that it impairs a child's ability to think and to interpret the world. But Anderson's own research and reviews of the scientific literature discredit this assumption. While watching TV, children do not merely absorb words and images. Instead, they muse upon the meaning of what they see, its plausibility, and its implications for the future—whether they've tuned in to a news report of a natural disaster or an action show. Because television relies on such cinematic techniques as montage and crosscutting, children learn early how to draw inferences about the passage of time, character psychology, and implied events. Even preschoolers comprehend more than just the information supplied on the tube. 3

Another contention about television is that it displaces reading as a form of entertainment. But according to Anderson, the amount of time spent watching television is not related to reading ability. For one thing, TV doesn't take the place of reading for most children; it takes the place of similar sorts of recreation, such as going to the movies, reading comic books, listening to the radio, and playing sports. Variables such as socioeconomic status and parents' educational background exert a far 4 stronger influence on a child's reading. "Far and away," Anderson says, "the best predictor of reading ability, and of how much a child reads, is how much a parent reads."

Conventional wisdom has it that heavy television-watching lowers IQ scores and hinders school performance. Since the 1960s, SAT scores have dropped, along with state and national assessments of educational achievement. But here, too, Anderson notes that no studies have linked prolonged television exposure in childhood to lower IQ later on. In fact, research suggests that it's the other way around. Early IQ predicts how much TV an older child will watch. "If you're smart young, you'll watch less TV when you're older," Anderson says. Conversely, in the same self-selecting process, people of lower IQ tend to be lifelong television devotees.

When parents watch TV with their young children, explaining new words and ideas to them, the children comprehend far more than they would if they were watching alone. This is due partly to the fact that when kids expect that TV will require thought, they spend more time thinking. What's ironic is that most parents use an educational program as an opportunity to park their kids in front of the set and do something in another room. "Even for parents who are generally wary of television," Anderson says, "*Sesame Street* is considered a show where it's perfectly okay to leave a child alone." The program was actually intended to be viewed by parents and children together, he says.

Because our attitudes inform TV viewing, Anderson applauds the nascent trend of offering high school courses that teach students how to "decode" television. In these classes, students learn to analyze the persuasive techniques of commercials, compare the reality of crime to its dramatic portrayal, inquire into the economics of broadcasting, and understand the mechanics of TV production. Such courses, Anderson contends, teach the kind of critical thinking central to the purpose of education. "Kids can be taught as much about television as about text or computers," he says.

If anything, Anderson's views underscore the fact that television cannot be disparaged in isolation from larger forces. For years researchers have attempted to show that television is inherently dangerous to children, hypnotizing them with its movement and color, cutting their attention span with its fast-paced, disconnected images, curbing intellectual development, and taking the place of loftier pastimes.

By showing that television promotes none of these effects, Anderson intends to shift the discussion to the real issue: content. That, of course,

is a thornier discussion. How should our society judge the violence of
primetime shows? The sexism of MTV? The materialism of commercials? "I feel television is almost surely having a major social impact on
the kids, as opposed to a cognitive impact," Anderson says.

In this context, he offers some advice to parents: First, "Parents should   10
think of their kids as actively absorbing everything on television. They
are not just passively mesmerized—in one eye and out the other. Some
things on TV are probably good for children to watch, like educational
TV, and some things are bad."

Second, "If you think your kid is spending lots of time watching tele-   11
vision, think about what alternatives there are, from the child's point of
view." Does a youngster have too much free time? Are there books, toys,
games, or playmates around? "A lot of the time, kids watch TV as a
default activity: There's nothing else to do."

Finally, "If a child persists in watching too much television, the ques-   12
tion is why. It's rare that TV shows are themselves so entertaining."
More often than not, the motive is escapism. A teen-ager may be uncomfortable with his or her peers; a child may want to retreat from a home
torn by marital strife; there may be problems at school.

For children, as for adults, television can be a source of enlightenment   13
or a descent into mindlessness—depending mostly on the choices of
lucre-driven executives. But as viewers, we can't ignore what we ourselves bring to the medium.

From The Boston Globe, *July 28, 1991. Reprinted by permission of the author.*

After You Read

Work with other students to develop responses to these questions or to compare responses
that you have already prepared.

1. Make a list of the major points discussed in each article. Do any of the articles discuss
   similar points?

2. What points are discussed in one article but not in any of the others?

SCHOOL, TEENAGERS, AND PART-TIME JOBS

Before You Read

1. Consider whether or not you think it is a good idea for teenagers to work part-time
   while they are going to school. What are the advantages and/or disadvantages involved?

2. Did you work as a teenager? If you did, explain in what ways your experience benefited
   you. Did your experience have any negative results?

The Dead-End Kids

Michele Manges

If just showing up accounts for 90 percent of success in life, as Woody Allen claims, then today's teenagers ought to make great recruits for tomorrow's permanent work force.   1

Well over half of them are already showing up in the part-time work force doing after-school and summer jobs. In times past, this kind of youthful zeal was universally applauded; the kids, we thought, were getting invaluable preliminary training for the world of work. But now a lot of people are *worried* about the surge in youth employment. Why?   2

Because a lot of today's eight million working teens—55 percent of all 16- to 19-year-olds—aren't learning anything much more useful than just showing up.   3

Taste of Adulthood

Not that long ago many youngsters could get part-time or summer jobs that taught them the rudiments of a trade they could pursue later. If this wasn't the case, they at least got a taste of the adult world, working closely with adults and being supervised by them. Also, in whatever they did they usually had to apply in a practical way at least some of the skills they'd learned in school, thus reinforcing them.   4

Today, however, a growing majority of working youngsters hustle at monotonous, dead-end jobs that prepare them for nothing. They certainly make up one of the largest groups of underemployed people in the country.   5

Many work in adolescent ghettos overseen by "supervisors" barely older than they are, and they don't need to apply much of anything they've learned in school, not even the simplest math; technology has turned them into near-automatons. Checkout scanners and sophisticated cash registers tot up bills and figure the change for them. At fast-food joints, automatic cooking timers remove the last possibility that a teen might pick up a smidgen of culinary skill.   6

Laurence Steinberg, a Temple University professor and co-author of a book on teenage employment, estimates that at least three out of every four working teenagers are in jobs that don't give them any meaningful training. "Why we think that wrapping burgers all day prepares kids for the future is beyond me," he says.   7

In a study of 550 teens, Prof. Steinberg and his colleagues found that those working long hours at unchallenging jobs tended to grow cynical   8 about work in general. They did only their own defined tasks and weren't inclined to help out others, their sense of self-respect declined, and they began to feel that companies don't care about their employees. In effect, they were burning out before they even joined the permanent work force.

A lot of teenaged workers are just bone-tired, too. Shelley Wurst, a   9
cook at an Ohio franchise steakhouse, got so worn out she stopped working on school nights. "I kept sleeping through my first-period class," she says. "If it wasn't for the crew I'm working with, I wouldn't want to work there at all."

This sort of thing is all too common. "Some kids are working past   10
2 A.M. and have trouble waking up for morning classes," says Larry Morrison, principal of Sylvania (Ohio) Northview High School. Educators like him are beginning to wonder whether teenage work today is not only irrelevant to future careers but even damaging to them; the schoolwork of students who pour so much time and energy into dead-end jobs often suffers—thus dimming their eventual prospects in a permanent job market that now stresses education.

As for the teens themselves, a great number would much rather be   11
working elsewhere, in more challenging or relevant jobs. Some, like Tanya Paris, have sacrificed to do so.

A senior at Saratoga (Calif.) High School, she works six hours a week   12
with a scientist at the National Aeronautics and Space Administration, studying marine algae, for no pay and no school credit. The future biologist hopes that her NASA work will help her decide which area of biology to pursue.

But most others either are lured by the money they can make or can't   13
find what they're looking for. Jay Jackson, a senior at Northview High, says he'd take a pay cut from his $3.40-an-hour job as a stock boy if he could find something allied to psychology, his prospective career field. He hasn't been able to. Schoolmate Bridget Ellenwood, a junior, yearned for a job that had something to do with dentistry but had to settle for slicing up chickens at a local Chick-fil-A franchise—a job, she says, "where you don't learn much at all."

And More to Come

Expect more teen jobs where you don't learn much at all. The sweeping   14
change in the economy from making things to service, together with the

growth of computerized service-industry technology that leaves almost nothing to individual skill and initiative, is expected to accelerate.

So the mindless and irrelevant part-time jobs open to teens in the near future will probably increase, while the better jobs continue to decline. On top of that, a growing labor shortage, which would drive up pay, figures to draw more kids into those jobs—against their interests. "Teenagers would be much better off doing a clerical-type job or studying," says Prof. John Bishop of Cornell University's Industrial and Labor Relations Center.

Efforts have been under way to cut back the number of hours teens can work, but the worsening labor shortage is undercutting them. Many educators are instead urging the states to start or expand more high-school cooperative education programs. These plans tie school and outside work to future career goals and provide more structure and adult supervision than ordinary outside work.

Employers also prefer students with this kind of experience. A recent study by the Cooperative Work Experience Education Association found that 136 of 141 businesses in Arkansas would hire a young applicant who had been in such a program over one who had worked independently. "The goal is not to get kids to stop working," says Prof. Bishop of Cornell. "It's to get them to learn more."

Part-Time Work Ethic: Should Teens Go for It?

DENNIS MCLELLAN

John Fovos landed his first part-time job—as a box boy at Alpha Beta on West Olympic—the summer after his sophomore year at Fairfax High School in Los Angeles. "I wanted to be independent," he said, "and I felt it was time for me to see what the world was really like."

Now an 18-year-old senior, Fovos works the late shift at the supermarket stocking shelves four nights a week. He saves about $50 a week, but most of his paycheck goes to his car payment and membership at a health spa. "The rest is for food—what I don't eat at home—and clothes."

Shelley Staats went to work part-time as a secretary for a Century 21 office when she was 15. Since then, she has worked as a cashier for a marine products company, scooped ice cream at a Baskin-Robbins, cashiered at a Video Depot and worked as a "floater" at May Co.   3

The Newport Harbor High School senior currently works about 25 hours a week in the lingerie department at the new Broadway in Costa Mesa. Although she saves about $200 a month for college, she said she works "to support myself: my car and clothes and just stuff I do, like going out."   4

Working also has helped her to learn to manage both her time and money, Staats said, and her work in the department store is providing experience for a future career in fashion merchandising.   5

But, she acknowledged, there are times when working while going to school has taken its toll.   6

"Last year I was sleeping in my first-period class half the time," admitted Staats, who occasionally has forgone football games and school dances because of work. "After a while, it just wears you out."   7

Nathan Keethe, a Newport Harbor High School senior who works more than 20 hours a week for an exterminating service, admits to sometimes feeling like the odd man out when he sees that fellow students "are out having a good time after school and I'm working. But then I think there's a lot of other kids out there working, too, and it doesn't seem so unusual."   8

Indeed, what clearly was the exception 40 years ago is now the rule.   9

Fovos, Staats and Keethe are riding the crest of a wave of part-time student employees that began building at the end of World War II and has steadily increased to the present. In 1981, according to a study by the National Center for Education Statistics, 80% of high school students have held part-time jobs by the time they graduate.   10

Part-time work during the school years traditionally has been viewed as an invaluable experience for adolescents, one that builds character, teaches responsibility and prepares them for entering the adult world.   11

But the authors of a provocative new book challenge conventional wisdom, contending that an over-commitment to work during the school years "may make teenagers economically wealthy but psychologically poor. . . ."   12

The book, *When Teenagers Work: The Psychological and Social Costs of Adolescent Employment*, is by Ellen Greenberger, a developmental psychologist and professor of social ecology at the University of California, Irvine, and Laurence Steinberg, a professor of child and family studies at the University of Wisconsin.   13

Based on national research data and on the authors' own study of more than 500 working and non-working students at four Orange County [California] high schools, the book reports that: 14

■ Extensive part-time employment during the school year may undermine youngsters' education. Students who work long hours are more likely to cut back on courses at school, taking easier classes and avoiding tougher ones. And, say the authors, long hours of work begun early in the school years increase the likelihood of dropping out. 15

■ Working leads less often to the accumulation of savings of financial contributions to the family than to a higher level of spending on cars, clothes, stereos, concerts and other luxury items. 16

■ Working appears to promote, rather than deter, some forms of delinquent behavior. About 30% of the youngsters in their first part-time job have given away goods or services; 18% have taken things other than money from work; 5½% have taken money from work; and 17% have worked under the influence of drugs or alcohol, according to the Orange County study. 17

■ Working long hours under stressful conditions leads to increased alcohol and marijuana use. 18

■ Teen-age employment—typically in dull or monotonous jobs for which the sole motivation is the paycheck—often leads to increased cynicism about working. 19

Moreover, the authors contend that adolescents who work long hours may develop the superficial social skills of an adult, but by devoting too much time to a job they severely curtail the time needed for reflection, introspection and identity experimentation that is required to develop true maturity. 20

Such findings lead Greenberger and Steinberg to conclude "that the benefits of working to the development of adolescents have been overestimated, while the costs have been underestimated." 21

"We don't want to be read as saying that kids shouldn't work during the school year," Greenberger said in an interview. "Our argument is with over-commitment to work: That working long hours may interfere with other very important goals of the growing years." 22

The authors place the blame partly on the types of jobs available to young people today. By working in unchallenging, monotonous jobs in fast-food restaurants or retail shops, they contend, teen-agers learn few new skills, have little opportunity for meaningful contact with adults and seldom gain work experience that will lead to future careers. 23

"Parents and schools," Greenberger said, "should wake up from the dream that having a kid who works 30 hours a week is promoting his or her transition to adulthood." 24

Greenberger and Steinberg's findings, not surprisingly, do not sit well with the fast-food industry. 25

"The fast-food industry is probably the largest employer of young people in the United States," said Paul Mitchell, spokesperson for Carl Karcher Enterprises, which employs thousands of teen-agers in its Carl's Jr. restaurants. 26

"For most of those young people," Mitchell said, "it's their first job, the first time they are told that you make a product a certain way, the first time they work with money, the first time they are made aware to be there on time and do it right . . . and it's just a tremendous working experience." 27

Terry Capatosto, a spokeswoman for McDonald's, calls Greenberger and Steinberg's findings "absurd, to say the least." 28

"Working at McDonald's contributes tremendously to [young people's] personal development and work ethic," said Capatosto, noting that countless McDonald's alumnae have gone on to professional careers and that about half of the people at all levels of McDonald's management, including the company's president and chairman of the board, started out as crew people. 29

"The whole idea of getting students out in the community during the time they're also a student is a very productive thing to do," said Jackie Oakes, college and career guidance specialist at Santa Ana High School. 30

Although she feels most students work "for the extras kids want," Oakes said they worked for a variety of reasons, including earning money to go on a trip with the school band and saving for college. 31

As for work taking time away from studying, Oakes said, "I think if a kid isn't interested in studying, having a job doesn't impact that." 32

Newport Harbor High School's Nathan Keethe, who usually earns Bs, doesn't think he'd devote more time to schoolwork if he weren't working. "Not really, because even when I wasn't working I wasn't too devoted to school," he said, adding that "for somebody who is, I wouldn't recommend working too much. I do think it would interfere." 33

Fairfax High's John Fovos, who works about 27 hours a week, however, said his grade-point average actually has risen since he began working part time. The motivation? "My parents told me if my job hindered my grades, they'd ask me to quit," he said. 34

Although she acknowledges that some teen-age workers may experience growth in such areas as self-reliance and improved work habits, 35

Greenberger said, "It's not evident that those things couldn't be realized in other settings as well. There's no evidence that you have to be a teen-age drone in order to grow in those areas."

As for the notion that "it would be great to get kids out into the work-place because they'll learn," Greenberger said that "the news is not so good. On the one hand we find that relatively little time on the job is spent using anything resembling higher-order cognitive skills," she said. "Computation nowadays is often done automatically by the cash register; so much for practicing arithmetic. Kids do extremely little writing and reading [on the job]. There's also very little job training. In fact, most of the youngsters in our survey reported their job could be done by somebody with a grade-school education or less." 36

©1986, The Los Angeles Times. *Reprinted by permission.*

Balancing Act: High School Students Making the Grade at Part-Time Jobs

Maureen Brown

First jobs have a way of permanently etching themselves in our memo-ries. Often, more than a paycheck was gained from that initial work-ing experience. 1

Many of today's teens, like teens a generation ago, cut their working teeth at fast-food restaurants. I always find it of interest to learn that a successful executive, attorney, physician or teacher was once a member of this business sector—and in a position well below management. 2

A teen-ager's first job is one of many rites of passage children and parents must go through. A dialogue of limits is appropriate when the subject of taking a job arises. 3

It's important to determine what are acceptable hours of employment and how many hours a week are permitted so that the student can main-tain studies and other school-related activities. What about transporta-tion? Job safety? How will the earnings be spent? 4

For some families, the discussion of employment is frequently not initiated by the child but rather by the parent. "I think it's time we dis-cuss the possibility of a job," has been uttered in numerous households after a weekend of distributing funds to teen-agers for entertainment and clothing. 5

While not feigning to have the answers to the question of employment and teen-agers, a recent discussion with a group of Mira Mesa teen-agers proved that more than money is gained from a job.

6

Charlotte Iradjpanah, 17, a senior at Mira Mesa High, has been working 10 to 20 hours a week at a Mira Mesa Burger King since September.

7

"The job is close to my house and I needed the money for senior activities," says Charlotte. "I'm also saving for college and working keeps me out of trouble. A job is an opportunity to know what it's like to hold responsibility. Sometimes I have to face the fact that I have to go to work today and put aside my personal preferences."

8

Working at Burger King does not exclude Charlotte from participating in extracurricular activities at school. She is a member of the speech and debate team and president of the photography club.

9

"The job has actually strengthened my GPA since I've taken on additional responsibilities," said Charlotte.

10

Jenni Hada, 18, a senior at Mira Mesa Summit High has been at Burger King for 3 months. "I owe my parents some money and want to buy a car, but working actually gives me something constructive to do with my free time," she says.

11

Mike Vo, 17, a junior at Mira Mesa High, who has been at Burger King for the past month, has held a part-time job since he turned 16. "I didn't like living off of my parents," he says.

12

Mike's parents were skeptical when their son first brought up the subject of having a part-time job in addition to school. "Once they saw that I could still bring home good grades and have a job, they felt differently," says Mike.

13

As well as school and a part-time job, Mike is a participant in the junior tennis circuit.

14

Charlotte, Jenni and Mike work with a manager who perceives the commitment and organization it demands to have a part-time job while in high school. Manager Wade Palmer, 28, started work at Burger King at age 17 while in high school and senses the importance of allowing for flexibility in scheduling.

15

"We can work around your schedule," Palmer assures the students.

16

Palmer views "listening to these teen-agers" as an important facet of his role as a manager. Believing that "there are many valuable qualities one can develop on the job," Palmer delights in seeing former student-workers from his decade of work in North County who have gone on into other fields.

17

"One is a banker in Mira Mesa, another is a paralegal, and another is an assistant manager with Dixieline," proudly claims Palmer. 18

Before In-N-Out Burger in Mira Mesa opened its doors in August last year, the company sent out employment flyers and solicited workers in the local high schools and colleges. 19

"We had over 800 applications for employment," says Bill Mayes, 31, the manager of the store on Mira Mesa Boulevard. "Of those 800 applicants, we selected 50." 20

Like Wade Palmer, Mayes started working with In-N-Out Burger at age 17 while still in high school. He continued part-time in college, and eventually went into management. 21

"I think students, with their great amount of energy, work out very well in our restaurant," Mayes says. "At In-N-Out, we're looking for bright, friendly, outgoing people to meet our customers." 22

Ba Hog, 17, a Mira Mesa High student, is one of the 50 applicants who met Mayes' criteria. 23

"At first, my parents doubted I could get a job here—lots of people were applying," recalls Ba. "After I passed the first interview, they cautioned me to not get my hopes up. When I passed the second interview, I could not wait to go home and tell them!" 24

"Since I've had this job, my parents have been giving me a little more freedom—like staying out later," says Ba, who is trilingual—speaking Chinese, Vietnamese and English. "Now they feel I can better decide between what is right and wrong. Plus, my grades have not been affected since I started this job." 25

One other advantage of working, according to Ba, is that he has been able to delegate some of his previous home responsibilities to his older brother, Nghia, 18, who now carries out the trash and rakes leaves for the employed Ba. 26

Michelle Gust, 17, a senior at Mt. Carmel High, has been working 10 to 15 hours a week at In-N-Out since its opening. Balancing school and a part-time job with senior class council, peer counseling groups, cross-country running and the Girl Scouts, which recently awarded her the "Silver Award," has made Michelle aware of meticulous time scheduling. In addition to these activities, Michelle also spent her fall learning about deadlines as she filled out college applications. 27

"Working has taught me the importance of communicating with people," says Michelle. "The management wants you to communicate well with them and the customer. I've learned to be flexible." 28

When the lead part of Corie in the school play "Barefoot in the Park" was won by Kimberley Belnap, 17, of Mt. Carmel High, her work schedule at In-N-Out required adjustment. 29

"My mom also talked to Bill, the manager, and we were able to work out a schedule where I could still continue to work, be in the play and maintain my grades," she said. 30

"I've learned to budget my time. I'm the type of person who, when I have more to do, I find more time," she said. 31

In addition to organizing her schedule, Kimberley notes that since starting work at In-N-Out, she is painfully conscious of the service she receives in other restaurants. "I take a critical look at how others serve the public." 32

After You Read

Work with other students to develop responses to these questions or to compare responses that you have already prepared.

1. As you can see, there are conflicting ideas about whether or not part-time work benefits teenagers who are attending school. To come to terms with the issues involved, list the advantages or disadvantages that are discussed in each article.

2. Look for different ways in which these writers say part-time work affects school performance. Do they discuss positive as well as negative points?

3. Not all of the ideas in these articles are related to school performance. Make a list of the ideas that are not necessarily related to school but that are important to the thesis of each article.

Writing Assignments

Note: Working with several sources can be substantially more difficult than working with only one source. As you respond to one of these assignments, consider working with other students to help you clarify and organize your ideas.

1. The articles about buying toy guns for children were published together in the parents' guide to a children's magazine. As a result, they cover many of the same points from differing points of view. Synthesize the issues discussed. Obviously the writers disagree, but watch for areas where they might be said to agree too. A point-by-point organization would work well here.

2. Write a synthesis of the ideas covered in the articles about the effects of television. Some of the points in these articles overlap, but others do not. Watch for overlapping points that are not immediately obvious because the writers have used different words to express similar ideas. You might need to use a blended organization for this essay.

3. The articles on teenagers who work while attending school reach directly opposing opinions in a number of areas. Write a synthesis that explains the issues discussed in these articles. Use whichever organization seems to work best.

4. Write a synthesis of several related articles from Part Four.

Evaluating Sample Papers

Synthesis Essay

Use the following criteria to evaluate the student essays below:

1. Introduction

Does the first paragraph introduce the topic and establish its complexity? Does the thesis make it clear that the point of the paper is to explain the issues discussed by a number of writers?

1   2   3   4   5   6

2. Unity

Does each paragraph have a clear and specific topic sentence that accurately introduces an idea discussed by one or more of the articles? Is the material in each paragraph clearly related to its topic sentence?

1   2   3   4   5   6

3. Support

Are all of the major points discussed? Is each point accurately and fully explained?

1   2   3   4   5   6

4. Coherence

Are transitions used between paragraphs? Are they used within paragraphs, especially when the writer is moving from what one article says to what is said in another?

1   2   3   4   5   6

5. References to the Text

Are direct quotations and paraphrases correctly introduced and smoothly incorporated into the text? Do they reflect the articles' points accurately?

1   2   3   4   5   6

6. Sentence Structure

Do the sentences combine ideas that are related, using coordination, subordination, verbal phrases, or parallelism when appropriate? Are there too many brief, choppy main clauses?

1   2   3   4   5   6

7. Mechanics, Grammar, and Spelling

Does the paper contain a distracting number of errors of these kinds?

1   2   3   4   5   6

8. Overall Ranking of the Essay

1   2   3   4   5   6

Evaluate the following student essays. Use the criteria above to determine which essay is most effective.

Student Essay 1

When I was young, I owned a toy rifle that I used in many games of "cops and robbers" with other children in my neighborhood. I don't think that my parents gave a moment's thought to whether or not my gun was an appropriate toy. However, today children carry real guns into elementary schools, and gang members shoot innocent bystanders in drive-by shootings, so people worry more about whether they should buy toy guns for their children. Michael Golden in "Why I Bought My Son a Toy Gun" and Robert Shaffer in "Why I Won't Buy My Sons Toy Guns" examine this issue and reach different conclusions.

One area of concern is that toy guns might teach children that violence is no problem. Robert Shaffer says that "the lesson toy guns teach is that solving problems with violence is acceptable" (205). He goes on to say that the kinds of skills taught by toy weapons are not the kind he and his wife want to encourage (205).

Both writers agree that toy weapons can help children learn the difference between right and wrong. Golden says that when he owned a toy gun as a boy, he emulated his heroes who "were often symbols of authority and order . . . " (204). Shaffer says that toy weapons "*could* have a value in allowing children to develop ideas of right and wrong, good and bad . . . " (206). However, he also says that children today do not use toy weapons creatively. Instead, they imitate violent television shows, so they don't develop any worthwhile values in their play with toy weapons (206).

Clearly, it's not easy to decide whether or not to buy toy weapons for children There are many issues involved, and Shaffer and Gordon have covered only a few of them. However, parents today need to consider these issues so that they can make intelligent decisions.

Student Essay 2

Have you ever been in a heated discussion over whether television is good or bad? Often people have strong opinions of whether or not tv is educational, has any values, or confuses reality and illusion. Paul Robinson's "TV Can't Educate," William Henry III's "The Meaning of TV," and Donna Woolfolk Cross's "Shadows on the Wall" are three articles which discuss these issues.

First, Robinson and Henry disagree on whether tv is or is not educational. Robinson claims that tv is not at all educational. In fact, he says "Educational TV corrupts the very notion of education and renders its victims uneducable" (212). Robinson explains that tv programs are not enough to rely on for real knowledge, and that even ignorance is better "because ignorance at least preserves a mental space that might someday be filled with real knowledge . . . " (212). Henry, on the other hand, says that tv can provide useful learning. For instance, he mentions that there are probably children who learn the alphabet from *Sesame Street*, and some older students who "through TV have grasped some basic truths about the planet" (208). Henry also points out that tv makes us aware of occurrences such as beaches being closed to bathers because of toxic wastes on shore. Furthermore, he recognizes the importance of tv as a source of news for editors and reporters during elections (208).

As for the next topic, Robinson and Henry have different ideas of whether tv is significant or valuable. According to Robinson, tv, such as soap operas like *All My Children*, attempts to be similar to the great American novel and therefore of literary value. He doesn't think tv has any literary value, but he says it *does* have entertainment value and is "superbly fit to amuse" (212). Henry points out that tv is strongly influential on our behavioral values, and says its deepest power is "the way its innocuous-looking entertainment reaches deep into the national mind" (208). Henry goes on to say that the characters on tv portray how the nation feels about itself and that "they teach behavior and values" (209). Henry contradicts Robinson by noting a relationship of power between tv and literature, and even sees tv as going one step further that literature's ability to be philosophical. He says, "Television simply does this more effectively, more touchingly, than any kind of art that went before" (209).

The third issue that is discussed is the tendency for tv to cause people to confuse reality and illusion. This topic includes a similar recognition from Robinson, Henry, and Cross, although all three authors have different opinions of whether this is good or bad. Robinson, as he explains that tv is entertaining, yet not educational, implies negativity when he states that tv "at the very least provides an escape from the world and from ourselves" (212). Henry says that unlike stage and movies, "the episodic TV series does not end in catharsis" (209). The characters return, and therefore tv is more representative of ordinary life, and for some, he claims, this is barely distinguishable from reality. Cross has more of an emphasis on this issue throughout her article than Robinson and Henry. She uses two reports to prove her point that people's confusion of reality and illusion caused by tv is bad. The first example is of behavior in the courtroom. She says that juries often expect real-life courtroom activities to be identical to tv's version of courtroom activities. She adds a contributor's story of watching a jury that was confused because the defendant didn't follow the expected role of a defendant (as seen on tv), and the result was a hung jury (215). The second example she used was a crime report that UPI filed explaining that a father was killed. His dead body was found within feet of his children who were watching tv and were clearly oblivious to the killing (215).

As you can see through these comparisons and contrasts, there are unique personal opinions of whether tv is good or bad. Robinson, Henry, and Cross have covered a few issues that they feel are significant.

Sentence Combining: Sentence Variety

Have you ever listened to someone talk who never varies the pitch or tone of his or her voice? Have you ever had to listen to a speaker (perhaps an instructor?) who drones on and on with no changes in the sound of her voice to help emphasize the important points or just to make what she is saying more interesting? If you have heard such a person, you know—as we do—how *boring* such a voice can be. Even if you aren't sleepy to begin with, you are ready to nod off within five minutes, right?

Writers have the same problems as speakers. They need to express their ideas in ways that will prevent their readers from taking a big yawn, closing their eyes, and starting to snore. **Sentence variety** is one technique that writers use to add interest to what they write. As the term implies, *sentence variety* means that the sentences in your paragraph or essay are somehow different from each other—they are *varied*—just as a good speaker's voice is frequently varied to keep the attention of the audience.

Actually, you have been practicing sentence variety throughout the sentence-combining sections of this text. When you embedded adjectives, adverbs, and prepositional phrases in Chapter 1, when you practiced using main and subordinate clauses in Chapters 2 and 3, when you used verbal phrases in Chapter 4 and appositives in Chapter 5, and when you practiced parallelism in Chapter 6—in each case, you were learning ways to vary the kinds of sentences that you write. In this section, you will work on writing sentences that are varied both in length and in structure.

Sentence Length

One of the chief causes of monotonous writing is a series of relatively brief sentences, one after the other. Take a look at the following paragraph.

> It was a warm, miserable morning last week. We went up to the Bronx Zoo. We wanted to see the moose calf. We also needed to break in a new pair of black shoes. We encountered better luck than we had bargained for. The cow moose and her young one were standing near the wall of the deer park. The wall was below the monkey house. We wanted a better view. We strolled down to the lower end of the park. We were by the brook. The path there is not much traveled. We approached the corner where the brook trickles under the wire fence. We noticed a red deer getting to her feet. Beside her was a spotted fawn. Its legs were just learning their business. The fawn was small and perfect. It was like a trinket seen through a reducing glass.

Wouldn't you agree that this writing is rather lackluster? The constant repetition of separate, short sentences makes the writing seem childlike and overly simple. However, with just a little work, many of the ideas in the excessively short sentences can be combined into longer sentences. Here is how the passage was actually written by the well-known essayist E. B. White.

> On a warm, miserable morning last week we went up to the Bronx Zoo to see the moose calf and to break in a new pair of black shoes. We encountered better luck than we had bargained for. The cow moose and her young one were standing near the wall of the deer park below the monkey house, and in order to get a better view we strolled down to the lower end of the park, by the brook. The path there is not much traveled. As we approached the corner where the brook trickles under the wire fence, we noticed a red deer getting

to her feet. Beside her, on legs that were just learning their business, was a spotted fawn as small and perfect as a trinket seen through a reducing glass.

—*E. B. White, "Twins"*

What do you think? Isn't the difference dramatic? E. B. White's paragraph is so effective not just because he is a master of descriptive detail (both paragraphs contain the same details) but because his sentences have a rhythm and flow that result from his ability to vary the lengths of his sentences.

EXERCISE

1. Count the number of sentences in E. B. White's paragraph and compare that to the number of sentences in the choppy paragraph.

2. Now look at the lengths of the sentences in E. B. White's paragraph and point out where the lengths vary. Try to explain the effect of the shorter and longer sentences.

3. Point out where details from the choppy paragraph are embedded in the E. B. White paragraph as prepositional phrases.

4. Point out where E. B. White's paragraph uses coordination and subordination to combine ideas that were separate sentences in the choppy paragraph.

Sentence Structure

Although a series of short, choppy sentences can be quite distracting, a more common cause of lifeless writing is a repetitive sentence structure. Perhaps the most commonly repeated sentence structure—and the easiest to vary—is the sentence that opens with the subject and verb of its main clause. Here are some examples of this common sentence pattern.

> S   V
> *Television has been blamed for a number of problems in our society.*

> S   V
> *The house slid into the ravine after the rain weakened the cliffs below it.*

> S   V
> *The committee voted to reduce the homeowners' fees.*

As you can see, each of the above sentences opens with a main clause, and the subject and verb of each main clause are quite close to the start of the sentence. To add some variety to your writing, try opening many of your sentences with something other than the main clause. Here are some possibilities.

1. Open your sentence with a subordinate clause.

After the rain weakened the cliffs below it, the house slid into the ravine.

2. **Open your sentence with a prepositional phrase.**

   Over the past forty years, television has been blamed for a number of problems in our society.

3. **Open your sentence with a verbal phrase.**

   Responding to the complaints from a majority of the owners, the committee voted to reduce the homeowners' fees.   (present participial phrase)

   Concerned about the rising cost of living, the committee voted to reduce the home-owners' fees.   (past participial phrase)

   To prevent people from having to sell their homes, the committee voted to reduce the homeowners' fees.   (infinitive phrase)

Of course, another way to vary your sentence structures is to use subordinate clauses, prepositional phrases, verbal phrases, and appositives within as well as at the ends of sentences. The trick is to avoid using the same sentence pattern from one sentence to another to another.

EXERCISE   Rewrite the following paragraphs to improve their sentence variety. In both the original and revised versions, compute the average number of words in each sentence by counting all the words and dividing by the number of sentences. In each revised copy, underline any words, phrases, or subordinate clauses that open sentences before the appearance of the main clause.

1.   Silly Putty was one of the most popular toy items of the '50s and '60s. It was originally developed as a possible substitute for rubber. In the 1940s, the U.S. War Production Board was looking for an inexpensive replacement for synthetic rubber. It wanted to use the replacement in jeep and airplane tires. It also wanted to use it in gas masks and other military gear. It asked General Electric to try to develop such a product. James Wright was the engineer who worked on the project. He eventually developed a rubbery goo. It stretched farther than rubber. It rebounded 25 percent more than the best rubber ball. It was impervious to molds and decay. It withstood a wide range of temperatures without decomposing. It delighted children everywhere. It was pressed against the color print of newspaper comic pages. It lifted the image right onto itself. The new product really had no special advantages over synthetic rubber. It was never used commercially. It was not long before a man operating a toy store realized its possibilities. He began to market it inside colored plastic eggs. In its first year, Silly Putty outsold every item in the toy store. For the next two decades it was one of the most popular small toys in the country.

Average number of words per sentence: _____

Average number of words per sentence in your revision: _____

2.   It was in the early years of our country. It was common for both soldiers and officers to wear long hair. They tied the hair back in a ponytail. In 1803 a Tennessee commander ordered all his officers to cut off their ponytails. Colonel Thomas Butler refused. He was a career officer with a distinguished record dating back to the Revolution. Butler was not about to cut his hair so easily. He was arrested and charged with insubordination. Friends of Butler rallied to his defense. Those friends included Andrew Jackson. They petitioned even President Jefferson to intervene on Butler's behalf. The President would not do so. On July 10, 1805, Butler was found guilty of mutinous conduct. He was sentenced to a year's suspension without pay. He died shortly after his conviction. He left a will requesting that a hole be drilled in his coffin. It requested that his ponytail be allowed to hang through it. He wanted everyone to see that, even when dead, he had not obeyed the order to cut it.

Average number of words per sentence: _____

Average number of words per sentence in your revision: _____

CHAPTER EIGHT

Arguing from Several Reading Selections

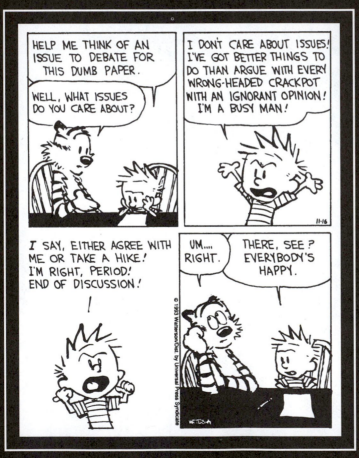

What Is an Argument?

Well, an argument is probably *not* what Calvin proposes in the above cartoon (*"I* say, either agree with me or take a hike!"). Attitudes like Calvin's usually lead to quarrels and angry confrontations, which are, unfortunately, what many people think of when they hear the word *argument.*

The "argument" that you will write in this chapter will not be a quarrel in which you beat your reader into submission. Instead, it will be exactly the kind of writing you have been practicing all semester—a reasonable presentation of facts, statistics, examples, and other support in an attempt to convince your reader that your thesis makes sense. To a degree, you have been arguing every time you have written a paper this semester, for in each assignment you have attempted to support a thesis statement with reasonable and convincing evidence.

The difference between the earlier assignments and what is normally called an "argumentative" paper is that an argumentative thesis takes a stand on a *debatable* subject. As a result, your readers may already have opinions about your subject. Your job is to convince them that the opinion you have expressed in your thesis is reasonable and worthy of their serious consideration. That's easier said than done.

To write a convincing argument, you will need to draw upon the writing skills you have been practicing so far:

- You will need to choose an appropriate topic, one that you can support with facts, examples, statistics, and statements from authority.
- You will need to organize your support into unified paragraphs that are introduced by clear and accurate topic sentences.
- You will need to summarize, paraphrase, and quote accurately when you draw material from reading selections.
- You will need to distinguish between facts and opinions as well as between specific and general statements.

The Attitude of the Effective Arguer

When you argue a position, no matter what the situation, your *attitude* can make all the difference in the world. Obviously, if your attitude, like Calvin's, is "I'm right, period! End of discussion!" you will not have much success. But even if you present evidence to support your ideas, you probably will not have much success if you are close-minded and show no understanding of your opposition's point of view. In fact, on many debatable issues, you should not expect to write a completely convincing argument; after all, an issue is debatable precisely *because* there are convincing arguments on both sides of it. As you approach any complicated, debatable issue, keep in mind the following points:

1. Keep an open mind until you have looked closely at the issue.

Perhaps the biggest mistake that many people make is to *first* decide what they think and *then* set out to prove that they are right. This is probably a natural thing to do—after all, nobody likes to be wrong—but will not lead to clear thinking and well-written arguments.

Whatever your beliefs are, set them aside until you have completed your study of the issue. As you read articles, talk to people, and consider your own experience, *be willing to change your mind* if the evidence suggests that you should—that willingness is one of the characteristics of a clear thinker.

2. Don't write as if your evidence completely resolved the issue.

Debatable topics exist because the "one, true" answer is not at all clear, so don't take the attitude that your support proves your opinion is right and all others are wrong. It probably doesn't. What it *may* prove, if your support is effective enough, is that your opinion is *reasonable* and should be considered by reasonable people. Too often people approach arguments as battles in which the other side must be thoroughly destroyed and discredited. But the "other side" is usually a figment of our imagination. There may be two or three or four or more ways of approaching a debatable issue—not one right way (yours) and one wrong way (theirs).

Don't misunderstand us. You *should* support your argument as well as you can, and you *should* be willing to take a stand. But you should also be willing to recognize points that might weaken your argument and to qualify your position if you need to.

Preparing the Argument

Collecting Information

As you have already read, the first step is *not* to take a stand or write a thesis statement. Even though you may already have an opinion on your topic, remember that the sign of a good thinker is the willingness to modify, qualify, or change an opinion once the information has been collected and examined. For example, suppose you think that watching too much television can cause serious problems, especially for children, so you decide to make television viewing the subject of your essay. Your *first* step is to try your best to set aside your personal opinion, keep an open mind, and start collecting information related to *both sides* of your topic. Your goal should be to come to an understanding of the opposing arguments related to television viewing and *only then* to draw a conclusion of your own. For the most part, the information you collect will come from material you read, from people you talk to, and from your own experiences.

Listing and Evaluating Information

As you collect information, organize it into lists that reflect opposing attitudes toward the subject. For instance, a writer investigating the benefits and drawbacks of television viewing might develop the lists presented below after examining the articles in Chapter 7 by William Henry III, Paul Robinson, Donna Woolfolk Cross, and Madeline Drexler and after considering her personal experiences and the experiences of people she knows. (When you list an item, identify the source it came from so you can look back at the article for more information when you evaluate the arguments.)

I.

TV can provide learning.

- Children learn the alphabet from "Sesame Street."
- High school students learn about toxic waste on beaches.

(Henry)

A study by psychologist Daniel Anderson says children learn to think and draw inferences as they watch TV.

(Drexler)

Same study—TV does not replace reading; it replaces other recreational activities.

(Drexler)

Same study—TV watching does not lower IQs, although people with lower IQs do tend to watch more TV.

(Drexler)

Personal experience—I have used movies such as *Gone with the Wind* to discuss history with my kids. *The Cosby Show* has led to questions about typical lifestyle of African Americans.

I.

TV cannot provide the time needed to *learn*.

- Learning requires time to absorb facts. It requires reading.
- A documentary about Marin County cannot really be accurate because it does not have the time to cover the complexities of life there.
- Educational TV is the worst kind—it makes people think they know something when they really don't.

(Robinson)

II.

TV's characters embody human truths.

- They epitomize what we feel about ourselves.
- They teach behavior and values.
- Character of Mary Richards summed up the lives of a whole generation of women.

(Henry)

Without TV we might be less violent, have more respect for institutions, be healthier, but we also might be less alert, less informed, less concerned about world matters, lonelier.

(Henry)

III.

TV is very good at entertaining.

- Jack Benny and Art Carney would not be nearly as funny in print. You need to see them and watch their timing.

(Robinson)

My personal experience—I use TV to relax and entertain myself.

A study by psychologist Daniel Anderson says when parents and kids watch together, kids tend to think about what they see.

(Drexler)

Personal experience—My children have never confused TV with reality as far as I know, but we watch TV together and talk about what we see.

II.

Opinion of psychologist Daniel Anderson—The violence, sexism, and materialism on TV are having a major social impact on our children.

(Drexler)

Personal knowledge—I have seen news reports about children imitating violent acts they saw on TV.

III.

Images on TV appear as real as life itself to a generation of Americans.

- Boys on a raft ride were disappointed because it was more fun on TV.
- Experiment by Jerzy Kozinski—kids would not leave TV to see something fascinating outside room.
- Also from Kozinski—kids watched a video of a fight rather than the real thing happening in front of them.
- UPI report—children watching TV next to the corpse of their dead father.
- Univ. of Nebraska study—Over half of children chose TV over their fathers.
- Former DA Mario Merola says a jury wants the drama of TV and is less likely to convict if it doesn't get it.

(Woolfolk Cross)

As you can see, there is quite a bit of material to consider before you decide exactly where you stand, and not all of the material can be neatly divided into pro/con arguments. This writer, however, has attempted to divide the points she has found into three general groupings. The first focuses primarily on the educational value of television; the second seems to concern itself with television's impact on our social values; and the third discusses both television's entertainment ability and the fear that television blurs the distinction between what is real and what is not.

At this point, you are in a position to evaluate the evidence. You have before you several major arguments about the benefits and drawbacks of television, some of which seem to directly contradict each other. Which seem more convincing? Consider which arguments use facts, examples, and expert testimony and which seem to rely more on unsupported opinions. Compare your own personal experiences to the arguments presented to see if they support or refute them.

As you evaluate the arguments, do not fall into the trap of thinking that one side must be right and the other must be wrong. Often that is just not the case. Do you see, for example, that it is possible that television has some benefits *and* some drawbacks, that the question is not necessarily a black-or-white, right-or-wrong issue? Such complexity is exactly why debatable, controversial issues *are* debatable and controversial. Both sides usually have points that need to be taken seriously. If you recognize the valid points on both sides of an issue and are willing to admit it when your opposition makes a good argument, you will have a better chance of convincing your reader that your own stand is a reasonable one that you have carefully thought out.

Taking a Stand

Perhaps the most important point to note here is that taking a stand is the *final* step in preparing an argument, not the first step. Once you have collected, listed, and evaluated the various arguments related to your topic, you need to decide exactly what your opinion is. Remember that you do not have to prove that everything your opposition says is wrong for you to hold a differing opinion. Nor do you have to pretend that the reasons you give for your opinion should convince a reasonable person that you are right. What you *will* have to do is take a stand that you can reasonably support with the evidence available and that does not require you to simply ignore evidence that refutes your opinion.

Outlining and Organizing the Argument

There are several ways to organize the material in an effective argument, but they all involve presenting points in support of your position and responding to points that seem to refute your position. *Before* you write the first draft of your paper, you should outline the points you intend to cover and the organizational pattern that will best serve your argument.

Below are some possible organizational patterns you can use. For shorter essays, each Roman numeral indicates a separate paragraph, but for longer essays, each numeral might indicate two or more paragraphs. In either case, you must remember to support each point with facts, examples, statistics, and references to authority, drawn either from your reading or from your own experiences or the experiences of people you know.

I. Introduction and thesis

II. First point in support of your thesis

III. Second point in support of your thesis

IV. Third point in support of your thesis
     (more points as needed)

V. Major objection to your thesis and your response to it

VI. Concluding paragraph

As you can see, this organization focuses primarily on presenting points that support your thesis, saving your discussion of any major objection until the end of the essay. Some topics, however, work better if the major objection is covered first, as in an organization like this:

I. Introduction and thesis

II. Major objection to your thesis and your response to it

III. First point in support of your thesis

IV. Second point in support of your thesis

V. Third point in support of your thesis
     (more points as needed)

VI. Concluding paragraph

Sometimes you may be taking a particularly unpopular stand, to which there are many obvious objections. In such a situation, consider this kind of organization:

I. Introduction and thesis

II. First objection and your response to it

III. Second objection and your response to it

IV. Third objection and your response to it
     (more objections and responses as needed)

V. First point in support of your thesis

VI. Second point in support of your thesis
     (more points as needed)

VII. Concluding paragraph

Obviously, the organization and length of your argument can vary greatly, depending on how many objections you need to respond to and how many points you intend to cover. Here is an outline for a possible paper on the benefits of television.

I. Introduction
- Open with example of when I came home and kids were watching *Wings*.
- Tentative thesis: TV has more benefits than drawbacks.

II. One benefit: It's entertaining and relaxing.
- Support with personal experience of how it helps me after a long day as a student, employee, and mom.
- Use Robinson's point about importance of entertainment.

III. Another benefit: It can educate us and make us better thinkers.
- Use examples from Henry article.
- Use personal examples of *Gone with the Wind* and *Cosby*.

IV. Another benefit: It makes people more aware of the world they live in.
- Use personal examples of my kids asking questions about *I Love Lucy* and *Roseanne*.
- Use Drexler's article about psychologist who says children think when helped by parents.

V. Major objections: Woolfolk Cross says TV blurs reality and fantasy.
- If TV is used incorrectly, she is right.
- Refer to Drexler article again about parents guiding their children.
  Another objection: TV hinders education because it replaces reading.
- Use personal experience of my kids to show this isn't so.

VI. Conclusion

Writing the Argument

If you have outlined and organized your points, writing the first draft of your paper should be no more difficult than writing the first drafts of every other paper you have written so far. Consider these points as you write:

1. Opening your paper with an interesting lead-in. See Chapter 3 for a discussion of the many possibilities available to you.

2. Write a thesis statement that takes a clear position, but do not hesitate to qualify it if you need to. For example, the thesis statement of one of the student essays included later in this chapter is preceded by an important qualification that helps the writer to sound like a reasonable person: "*I know that the television can be abused and misused, but so can any good thing. On the whole, it seems to me that television watching has far more benefits than drawbacks.*"

3. Write clear topic sentences that refer to the central idea expressed in your thesis.

4. Support your topic sentences with facts, examples, statistics, and references to authority drawn either from your reading or from your own experiences or the experiences of people you know.

5. When you use material from the reading selections, identify the sources of all paraphrases, summaries, and quotations. Use clear transitions to introduce borrowed material (as discussed in Chapter 5) and parentheses to identify the author and page number (as discussed in Chapter 7).

6. Respond to major objections in a reasonable manner. If the objection is simply inaccurate, explain why, giving support of your own. If the objection is reasonable yet does not change your point of view, explain why the reader should find your overall argument more persuasive.

7. See Chapter 3 for effective ways to conclude your essay.

Readings

SHOULD DRUGS BE LEGALIZED?

Before You Read

1. What is your initial reaction to the suggestion that drugs be legalized? Would you call your reaction a personal opinion or a considered opinion?

2. What arguments do you expect to find in favor of and opposed to legalizing drugs?

3. As you read the following articles, set aside any personal opinions you may hold. Try to keep an open mind as you collect information about the issue.

Police and Jails Have Failed

LIONEL VAN DEERLIN

Legalize narcotics? It was deemed unthinkable as recently as five years ago. But no longer.   1

We're being told that America's drug laws and their enforcement are a   2
disaster . . . that they have failed to curb our worst social problem, tend-

ing instead to make it worse . . . that the answer is to "decriminalize" drug use, or to legalize all but the most debilitating substances, like crack cocaine.

It is not the druggies or their looney friends telling us this. The talk   3
about overhauling drug laws comes lately from a broad sweep of national leadership—from the ranks of law enforcement, from judges, from professional people and from the clergy. Try this array of advocates:

■ The new attorney general, Janet Reno.

■ George Shultz, who held three cabinet posts in the Nixon years and was Ronald Reagan's secretary of state.

■ Milton Friedman, the dean of conservative economists, a Nobel laureate.

■ Judicial figures ranging from New York's federal judges Robert W. Sweet and Whitman Knapp to Superior Judge James P. Gray of hidebound Orange County.

■ William F. Buckley, the rightist columnist-commentator.

■ The Rev. Robert Schuller, whose culturally conservative sermons are aired nationally from the Crystal Cathedral.

■ Kurt Schmoke, the black mayor of Baltimore and one-time Rhodes scholar.

There are differences of opinion within this group on how best to deal   4
with drug addiction—but total agreement that what we have been doing for many years is wrong-headed. All think it's time for change. Radical change.

What's bothering them? Mounting evidence that the campaign against   5
drugs has proved no more successful than the ill-remembered Prohibition law aimed at alcohol in an earlier day. Indeed, comparisons seem ominous. As with Prohibition (which lasted only 13 years) our government's war on drugs has led to ever-widening abuse and a frightening increase in crime.

How is one to defend a federal enforcement program which has failed   6
so conspicuously as this one has done, yet finds more Americans today locked up on drug-related crimes alone than were imprisoned on *all* offenses just 12 years ago?

This, with no visible reduction of drugs on the streets.   7

Only one other industrialized nation now keeps a higher percentage of   8
its people behind bars. But there is a profound difference. Government

intent in South Africa has aimed to check a rising tide of black resent-
ment against apartheid. Jammed jails in this country reflect efforts to
deal with an addiction which reaches from the pinnacle of society down
to ghetto streets, where drug trafficking can mean instant riches for a
school dropout.

However worthy their intent, the framers of Prohibition failed to look   9
ahead. By making liquor illegal, they automatically scrapped all controls
over its manufacture, labeling and distribution. The 1920s became a
time of "rotgut" and bathtub gin.

The same is sadly true of banned drugs today. Beyond their addictive   10
peril, poisoning from contamination is widespread, as are overdoses
from drugs of unknown strength.

But Prohibition, with its Keystone Kops-style pursuit of bootleggers,   11
left a far more serious legacy. From the rum runners and mob violence of
that era came a blueprint for today's illegal drug business—for criminal
syndicates and cartel management reaching into supplier countries
whose deliveries we find almost impossible to interdict.

From her prior experience spanning four terms as a state prosecutor   12
in drug-porous Miami, Attorney General Reno says she questions the
effectiveness of massive federal spending aimed at interdiction. A study
by the General Accounting Office found that Air Force patrols with
sophisticated AWACS surveillance planes over a 15-month period
brought a grand total of eight drug seizures. Meanwhile combined
efforts of the Navy and Coast Guard, sailing 2,512 ship-days at a cost of
$40 million, resulted in the seizure of only 20 drug-carrying vessels.

"It's time we come up with hard data (on) whether or not interdiction   13
is efficient and effective," the attorney general concludes.

Drugs are easy to smuggle. The cash return on supplies getting through   14
more than justifies the risk of being caught. The actual transporters,
moreover, are not drug kingpins but well-paid hired hands eager to take
their chances.

The sky-high prices driving this traffic rest solely on its illegality. While   15
failing to keep an illicit product off the market, the effect of our laws is
to provide a subsidy as certain as the price supports legislated for wheat,
cotton and corn.

If that is not hypocrisy enough, consider a comment by the Rev. Joseph   16
P. Kane, S.J., for 20 years the chaplain to inmates at New York's Rikers
Island. He asks: "Is there not something dishonest about drug policies
in which lower-class drug users, labeled *criminals*, go to prison while
middle-class addicts, labeled *alcoholics*, go to therapy?"

National priorities seem skewed when we spend three or four times as much on the chase and on punishment as we do for drug treatment and rehabilitation. It costs more than $50,000 a year to keep someone in a federal prison. 17

President Clinton has named a highly regarded big-city police commissioner to be the nation's new drug "czar." 18

We must hope that Lee Brown, the first authentic cop to hold this job, has seen enough to know that more police and more jail sentences are not the answer. 19

From The San Diego Union Tribune, *May 14, 1993, B5. © 1993.*
Reprinted by permission of the author.

Best Remedy: Crack Down on Users

JOSEPH PERKINS

Joycelyn Elders is unfit to be surgeon general. A person who advocates legalized sale and use of cocaine, heroin, LSD, PCP and other deadly drugs clearly does not have the nation's best health interests at heart. 1

In an appearance this week at the National Press Club in Washington, Elders revealed her ignorance of the nature of America's drug problem. "I do feel that we would markedly reduce our crime rate if drugs were legalized," she said. 2

What was she smoking? All she had to do was call her colleague Louis Freeh, over at the FBI, and he would have told her that 75 percent of crimes in America are committed by substance abusers—in many cases to support their habit. Making drugs even more freely available than they are now hardly would make America's streets safer. 3

Elders also wildly claimed that "some of the countries that have legalized drugs" have shown "no increase in their drug use rate." Yeah? Which ones? 4

For the surgeon general's information, no country in the world has actually legalized drugs. As to the handful of European nations that have effectively decriminalized drugs, their social experiments have been anything but successful. 5

In Zurich, Switzerland, for instance, a public park was turned over to drug users in 1989. By 1991, drug-related deaths were up 80 percent. Half the drug-takers in the park were under age 22. A fifth were infected with the AIDS virus. 6

Amsterdam has been a haven for drug users since 1976, when the   7
Netherlands liberalized its narcotics laws. In the ensuing 17 years, the
country's population of heroin addicts has more than tripled.

These are the models that Elders would have this country emulate.   8

President Clinton was right to rebuke his surgeon general for betraying   9
the nation's continuing war on drugs. He is the first man to sit in the
Oval Office who has ever had a family member known to be addicted to
drugs. Clinton often has noted that if drugs were more widely available—
as Elders would have it—his brother Roger probably would be dead
by now.

Clearly, there is no pathology that exacts a heavier toll on American   10
society than illegal drug use. This was well documented in a 1991 tract
by Mitchell Rosenthal, in the *UC Davis Law Review*.

"The fastest rising costs of drug abuse today are associated, not with   11
crime," wrote Rosenthal, "but with homelessness, chronic mental illness,
adolescent suicide and runaways, the spread of [AIDS], domestic violence, child abuse, and the number of new drug-impaired, addicted and
abandoned infants."

Rosenthal presented evidence showing that 60 percent of the nation's   12
homeless are drug abusers. He noted that in New York State, up to
50 percent of patients admitted to hospitals through emergency services
are mentally ill drug users.

In California, as many as 75 percent of teen-age runaways use drugs.   13
And, in general, drug-abusing youth are three times as likely to commit
suicide as kids who do not use drugs.

Largely because of drug abuse, there was a nearly 30 percent rise in   14
the number of foster care children in the United States between 1987 and
1990. In 1988, more than 10 percent of first-time mothers used drugs
during their pregnancies. That means that as many as 375,000 newborn
babies experienced prenatal exposure to drugs—a 300 percent increase
from 1985.

It seems clear that legalization of drugs would neither reduce the level   15
of drug-related crime and violence nor ameliorate other drug-related
social pathologies. The only viable approach to attaching America's drug
problems is to crack down on users.

The 12.5 million Americans who use an illegal narcotic once a month   16
provide a fertile market for drug merchants. A kilogram of cocaine costs
roughly $15,000 to deliver to the United States. It fetches $250,000
when sold on the streets in one-ounce packets. With that kind of return
on investment sellers will go to almost any lengths to provide product.

So what if the occasional cache of drugs is interdicted? There's always   17
more where it came from. So what if this drug lord or that one is gunned
down? There is always someone ready to take that person's place.

The only way to bring down the drug cartels is to deprive them of their   18
customers and, thus, their tremendous profits. This hardly would be
achieved by legalizing drugs (which would only provide drug merchants
with an even larger market for their deadly product). The key is zero tol-
erance of drug use.

A national strategy to reduce demand for drugs should employ a carrot-   19
and-stick approach. The government ought to provide drug treatment on
demand to users who need help to overcome their habit. Meanwhile, the
emphasis of drug enforcement should shift from the supply to the
demand side.

Anyone caught buying or using drugs ought to be given mandatory jail   20
time, if only a day or two. First-time offenders should not be excused (as
the shock of spending a night behind bars would be an excellent deter-
rent to future use).

Arrests for repeated drug use should carry progressively stiffer jail   21
sentences. As time passed, a clear message would be sent to users that if
they are caught, they will face swift and sure punishment.

America's drug users must be made to understand that they are as   22
responsible as drug dealers for the rise in drug-related crime and violence
and pathology that afflicts our society today. By legalizing drugs, as
Elders and other social nihilists suggest, drug users would be absolved of
this responsibility.

From The San Diego Union Tribune, *December 10, 1993, B5.*
Reprinted by permission.

We're Losing the Drug War Because Prohibition Never Works

HODDING CARTER III

There is clearly no point in beating a dead horse, whether you are a   1
politician or a columnist, but sometimes you have to do it just the
same, if only for the record. So, for the record, here's another attempt to
argue that a majority of the American people and their elected representatives can be and are wrong about the way they have chosen to wage the
"war against drugs." Prohibition can't work, won't work, and has never

worked, but it can and does have monumentally costly effects on the criminal justice system and on the integrity of government at every level.

Experience should be the best teacher, and my experience with prohibition is a little more recent than most Americans for whom the "noble experiment" ended with repeal in 1933. In my home state of Mississippi, it lasted for an additional thirty-three years, and for all those years it was a truism that the drinkers had their liquor, the preachers had their prohibition, and the sheriffs, made the money. Al Capone would have been proud of the latitude that bootleggers were able to buy with their payoffs of constables, deputies, police chiefs, and sheriffs across the state.

But as a first-rate series in the *New York Times* made clear early last year, Mississippi's Prohibition-era corruption (and Chicago's before that) was penny ante stuff compared with what is happening in the United States today. From Brooklyn police precincts to Miami's police stations to rural Georgia courthouses, big drug money is purchasing major breakdowns in law enforcement. Sheriffs, other policemen, and now judges are being bought up by the gross. But that money, with the net profits for the drug traffickers estimated at anywhere from $40 billion to $100 billion a year, is also buying up banks, legitimate businesses and, to the south of us, entire governments. The latter becomes an increasingly likely outcome in a number of cities and states in this country as well. Cicero, Illinois, during Prohibition is an instructive case in point.

The money to be made from an illegal product that has about 23 million current users in this country also explains why its sale is so attractive on the mean streets of America's big cities. A street salesman can gross about $2,500 a day in Washington, which puts him in the pay category of a local television anchor, and this in a neighborhood of dead-end job chances.

Since the courts and jails are already swamped beyond capacity by the arrests that are routinely made (44,000 drug dealers and users over a two-year period in Washington alone, for instance), and since those arrests barely skim the top of the pond, arguing that stricter enforcement is the answer begs a larger question: Who is going to pay the billions of dollars required to build the prisons, hire the judges, train the policemen, and employ the prosecutors needed for the load already on hand, let alone the huge one yet to come if we ever get serious about arresting dealers and users?

Much is made of the costs of drug addiction, and it should be, but the current breakdown in the criminal justice system is not one of them. That breakdown is the result of prohibition, not addiction. Drug addiction, after all, does not come close to the far vaster problems of alcohol and tobacco addiction (as former Surgeon General Koop correctly noted, tobacco is at least as addictive as heroin). Hard drugs are estimated to kill 4,000 people a year directly and several tens of thousands a year indirectly. Alcohol kills at least 100,000 a year, addicts millions more and costs the marketplace billions of dollars. Tobacco kills over 300,000 a year, addicts tens of millions, and fouls the atmosphere as well. But neither alcohol nor tobacco threatens to subvert our system of law and order, because they are treated as personal and societal problems rather than as criminal ones.

Indeed, every argument that is made for prohibiting the use of currently illegal drugs can be made even more convincingly about tobacco and alcohol. The effects on the unborn? Staggeringly direct. The effects on adolescents? Alcoholism is the addiction of choice for young Americans on a ratio of about one hundred to one. Lethal effect? Tobacco's murderous results are not a matter of debate anywhere outside the Tobacco Institute. 7

Which leaves the lingering and legitimate fear that legalization might produce a surge in use. It probably would, although not nearly as dramatic a one as opponents usually estimate. The fact is that personal use of marijuana, whatever the local laws may say, has been virtually decriminalized for some time now, but there has been a stabilization or slight decline in use, rather than an increase, for several years. Heroin addiction has held steady at about 500,000 people for some time, though the street price of heroin is far lower now than it used to be. Use of cocaine in its old form also seems to have stopped climbing and begun to drop off among young and old alike, though there is an abundantly available supply. 8

That leaves crack cocaine, stalker of the inner city and terror of the suburbs. Instant and addictive in effect, easy to use and relatively cheap to buy, it is a personality-destroying substance that is a clear menace to its users. But it is hard to imagine it being any more accessible under legalization than it is in most cities today under prohibition, while the financial incentives for promoting its use would virtually disappear with legalization. 9

Proponents of legalization should not try to fuzz the issue, nonetheless. Addiction levels might increase, at least temporarily, if legal sanctions were removed. That happened after the repeal of Prohibition, or so at least some studies have suggested. But while that would be a personal disaster for the addicts and their families, and would involve larger costs to society as a whole, those costs would be minuscule compared with the costs of continued prohibition. 10

The young Capones of today own the inner cities, and the wholesalers   11
behind these young retailers are rapidly buying up the larger system
which is supposed to control them. Prohibition gave us the Mafia and
organized crime on a scale that has been with us ever since. The new
prohibition is writing a new chapter on that old text. Hell-bent on learning nothing from history, we are witnessing its repetition, predictably
enough, as tragedy.

Should Drugs Be Legalized?

WILLIAM J. BENNETT

Since I took command of the war on drugs [as director of National   1
Drug Control Policy in Washington, D.C.], I have learned from
former secretary of state George Shultz that our concept of fighting
drugs is "flawed." The only thing to do, he says, is to "make it possible
for addicts to buy drugs at some regulated place." Conservative com-
mentator William F. Buckley, Jr., suggests I should be "fatalistic" about
the flood of cocaine from South America and simply "let it in."
Syndicated columnist Mike Royko contends it would be easier to sweep
junkies out of the gutters "than to fight a hopeless war" against the narcotics that send them there. Labeling our efforts "bankrupt," federal
judge Robert W. Sweet opts for legalization, saying, "If our society can
learn to stop using butter, it should be able to cut down on cocaine."

Flawed, fatalistic, hopeless, bankrupt! I never realized surrender was   2
so fashionable until I assumed this post.

Though most Americans are overwhelmingly determined to go toe-to-   3
toe with the foreign drug lords and neighborhood pushers, a small
minority believe that enforcing drug laws imposes greater costs on society than do drugs themselves. Like addicts seeking immediate euphoria,
the legalizers want peace at any price, even though it means the inevitable
proliferation of a practice that degrades, impoverishes, and kills.

I am acutely aware of the burdens drug enforcement places upon   4
us. It consumes economic resources we would like to use elsewhere. It is
sometimes frustrating, thankless, and often dangerous. But the consequences of *not* enforcing drug laws would be far more costly. Those consequences involve the intrinsically destructive nature of drugs and the toll

they exact from our society in hundreds of thousands of lost and broken lives . . . human potential never realized . . . time stolen from families and jobs . . . precious spiritual and economic resources squandered.

That is precisely why virtually every civilized society has found it necessary to exert some form of control over mind-altering substances and why this war is so important. Americans feel up to their hips in drugs now. They would be up to their necks under legalization.   5

Even limited experiments in drug legalization have shown that when drugs are more widely available, addiction skyrockets. In 1975 Italy liberalized its drug law and now has one of the highest heroin-related death rates in Western Europe. In Alaska, where marijuana was decriminalized in 1975, the easy atmosphere has increased usage of the drug, particularly among children. Nor does it stop there. Some Alaskan schoolchildren now tout "coco puffs," marijuana cigarettes laced with cocaine.   6

Many legalizers concede that drug legalization might increase use, but they shrug off the matter. "It may well be that there would be more addicts, and I would regret that result," says Nobel laureate economist Milton Friedman. The late Harvard Medical School psychiatry professor Norman Zinberg, a longtime proponent of "responsible" drug use, admitted that "use of now-illicit drugs would certainly increase. Also casualties probably would increase."   7

In fact, Dr. Herbert D. Kleber of Yale University, my deputy in charge of demand reduction, predicts legalization might cause a "five-to-sixfold increase" in cocaine use. But legalizers regard this as a necessary price for the "benefits" of legalization. What benefits?   8

1. *Legalization will take the profit out of drugs.* The result supposedly will be the end of criminal drug pushers and the big foreign drug wholesalers, who will turn to other enterprises because nobody will need to make furtive and dangerous trips to his local pusher.   9

But what, exactly, would the brave new world of legalized drugs look like? Buckley stresses that "adults get to buy the stuff at carefully regulated stores." (Would you want one in *your* neighborhood?) Others, like Friedman, suggest we sell the drugs at "ordinary retail outlets."   10

Former City University of New York sociologist Georgette Bennett assures us that "brand-name competition will be prohibited" and that strict quality control and proper labeling will be overseen by the Food and Drug Administration. In a touching egalitarian note, she adds that "free drugs will be provided to government clinics" for addicts too poor to buy them.   11

Almost all legalizers point out that the price of drugs will fall, even though the drugs will be heavily taxed. Buckley, for example, argues that somehow federal drugstores will keep the price "low enough to discourage a black market but high enough to accumulate a surplus to be used for drug education." 12

Supposedly, drug sales will generate huge amounts of revenue, which will then be used to tell the public not to use drugs and to treat those who don't listen. 13

In reality, this tax would only allow government to *share* the drug profits now garnered by criminals. Legalizers would have to tax drugs heavily in order to pay for drug education and treatment programs. Criminals could undercut the official price and still make huge profits. What alternative would the government have? Cut the price until it was within the lunch-money budget of the average sixth-grade student? 14

2. *Legalization will eliminate the black market.* Wrong. And not just because the regulated prices could be undercut. Many legalizers admit that drugs such as crack or PCP are simply too dangerous to allow the shelter of the law. Thus criminals will provide what the government will not. "As long as drugs that people very much want remain illegal, a black market will exist," says legalization advocate David Boaz of the libertarian Cato Institute. 15

Look at crack. In powdered form, cocaine was an expensive indulgence. But street chemists found that a better and far less expensive— and far more dangerous—high could be achieved by mixing cocaine with baking soda and heating it. Crack was born, and "cheap" coke invaded low-income communities with furious speed. 16

An ounce of powdered cocaine might sell on the street for $1200. That same ounce can produce 370 vials of crack at $10 each. Ten bucks seems like a cheap hit, but crack's intense ten- to fifteen-minute high is followed by an unbearable depression. The user wants more crack, thus starting a rapid and costly descent into addiction. 17

If government drugstores do not stock crack, addicts will find it in the clandestine market or simply bake it themselves from their legally purchased cocaine. 18

Currently crack is being laced with insecticides and animal tranquilizers to heighten its effect. Emergency rooms are now warned to expect victims of "sandwiches" and "moon rocks," life-threatening smokable mixtures of heroin and crack. Unless the government is prepared to sell these deadly variations of dangerous drugs, it will perpetuate a criminal black market by default. 19

And what about children and teenagers? They would obviously be barred from drug purchases, just as they are prohibited from buying beer and liquor. But pushers will continue to cater to these young customers with the old, favorite come-ons—a couple of free fixes to get them hooked. And what good will antidrug education be when these youngsters observe their older brothers and sisters, parents, and friends lighting up and shooting up with government permission? 20

Legalization will give us the worst of both worlds: millions of *new* drug users *and* a thriving criminal black market. 21

3. Legalization will dramatically reduce crime. "It is the high price of drugs that leads addicts to robbery, murder, and other crimes," says Ira Glasser, executive director of the American Civil Liberties Union. A study by the Cato Institute concludes: "Most, if not all 'drug-related murders' are the result of drug prohibition." 22

But researchers tell us that many drug-related felonies are committed by people involved in crime *before* they started taking drugs. The drugs, so routinely available in criminal circles, make the criminals more violent and unpredictable. 23

Certainly there are some kill-for-a-fix crimes, but does any rational person believe that a cut-rate price for drugs at a government outlet will stop such psychopathic behavior? The fact is that under the influence of drugs, normal people do not act normally, and abnormal people behave in chilling and horrible ways. DEA agents told me about a teenage addict in Manhattan who was smoking crack when he sexually abused and caused permanent internal injuries to his one-month-old daughter. 24

Children are among the most frequent victims of violent, drug-related crimes that have nothing to do with the cost of acquiring the drugs. In Philadelphia in 1987 more than half the child-abuse fatalities involved at least one parent who was a heavy drug user. Seventy-three percent of the child-abuse deaths in New York city in 1987 involved parental drug use. 25

In my travels to the ramparts of the drug war, I have seen nothing to support the legalizers' argument that lower drug prices would reduce crime. Virtually everywhere I have gone, police and DEA agents have told me that crime rates are highest where crack is cheapest. 26

4. Drug use should be legal since users only harm themselves. Those who believe this should stand beside the medical examiner as he counts the thirty-six bullet wounds in the shattered corpse of a three-year-old who happened to get in the way of his mother's drug-crazed boyfriend. They should visit the babies abandoned by cocaine-addicted mothers— infants who already carry the ravages of addiction in their own tiny 27 bodies. They should console the devastated relatives of the nun who worked in a homeless shelter and was stabbed to death by a crack addict enraged that she would not stake him to a fix.

Do drug addicts only harm themselves? Here is a former cocaine addict describing the compulsion that quickly draws even the most "responsible" user into irresponsible behavior: "Everything is about getting high, and any means necessary to get there becomes rational. If it means stealing something from somebody close to you, lying to your family, borrowing money from people you know you can't pay back, writing checks you know you can't cover, you do all those things—things that are totally against everything you have ever believed in." 28

Society pays for this behavior, and not just in bigger insurance premiums, losses from accidents, and poor job performance. We pay in the loss of a priceless social currency as families are destroyed, trust between friends is betrayed, and promising careers are never fulfilled. I cannot imagine sanctioning behavior that would increase that toll. 29

I find no merit in the legalizers' case. The simple fact is that drug use is wrong. And the moral argument, in the end, is the most compelling argument. A citizen in a drug-induced haze, whether on his backyard deck or on a mattress in a ghetto crack house, is not what the founding fathers meant by the "pursuit of happiness." Despite the legalizers' argument that drug use is a matter of "personal freedom," our nation's notion of liberty is rooted in the ideal of a self-reliant citizenry. Helpless wrecks in treatment centers, men chained by their noses to cocaine—these people are slaves. 30

Imagine if, in the darkest days of 1940, Winston Churchill had rallied the West by saying, "This war looks hopeless, and besides, it will cost too much. Hitler can't be *that* bad. Let's surrender and see what happens." That is essentially what we hear from the legalizers. 31

This war *can* be won. I am heartened by indications that education and public revulsion are having an effect on drug use. The National Institute on Drug Abuse's latest survey of current users shows a 37 percent *decrease* in drug consumption since 1985. Cocaine is down 50 percent; marijuana use among young people is at its lowest rate since 1972. In my travels I've been encouraged by signs that Americans are fighting back. 32

I am under no illusion that such developments, however hopeful, mean the war is over. We need to involve more citizens in the fight, increase pressure on drug criminals, and build on antidrug programs 33 that have proved to work. This will not be easy. But the moral and social costs of surrender are simply too great to contemplate.

Reprinted by permission from the Reader's Digest, *March 1990.*
© *1990 by* The Reader's Digest Association, Inc.

After You Read

Work with other students to develop responses to these questions or to compare responses that you have already prepared.

1. As in most debates, you should be able to find reasonable arguments on both sides of the issue. Make a list of the arguments for and against the legalization of drugs.

2. As you evaluate the arguments and take a stand, consider also your own experiences or the experiences of people you know. How would the arguments you have read in these articles affect them?

COMPETITION: HOW DOES IT AFFECT US?

Before You Read

1. In what ways has competition influenced you or your life? Do you see it as a positive or a negative influence in your life—or as a blend of both?

2. List whatever benefits and drawbacks you would expect to find when people argue about the nature of competition.

Is Winning Everything?

KATHERINE MARTIN

In the thick of a heated baseball game a young umpire is verbally harassed by two vehement coaches. The boy tries his best on the next play but gets more abuse from a parent restrained only by a hurricane fence. Exasperated, he flops down on the ground while the coaches and a referee go at it with each other.

A young boy afraid of batting is forced to stand at home plate while his father deliberately throws pitches that hit him.

During a Little League game a mother storms down to the dugout and belts her son across the head for being tagged out.

1

2

3

A football coach grabs the face mask of a youngster, yanks him spit-   4
close and screams obscenities at him.

A father beats his exhausted son to keep him running laps around   5
a track.

Twenty million children between the ages of eight and sixteen play   6
organized sports outside of school, and their experience in ballparks and
on playing fields has enormous impact on their physical, emotional, and
social development. Most of us believe that there's nothing more basic to
the American way of rearing young people than sports, but many have
come to realize that the world of sports for youth is not an entirely innocent or happy one. In recent years adults have imposed unchildlike standards on children's sports. In our zeal, we've overorganized, overregi-
mented, overstructured, and overtrained our kids. We've claimed their
games for the serious business of adult competition.

"That wasn't the case when there was a lot more spontaneous play,"   7
says Barry Goldberg, M.D., associate clinical professor of pediatrics at
Yale University and pediatric consultant at the Institute of Sports
Medicine and Athletic Trauma at Lenox Hill Hospital in New York City.
"Our society has changed a great deal in the last twenty years. The small
community is vanishing and there's less open space. People have to trek
to playing fields. As a result, organized teams have become a way to get
kids together and, often, they're patterned after professional and college
sports.

"As adults intervene in children's games," warns Goldberg, echoing a 8
growing concern among youth sports experts, "we have to accept the
responsibility for the end product."

That end product isn't always pretty. Over the past ten years, there   9
have been reports of children paralyzed and killed from "spearing" during football games, and passing out from dehydration. One coach
reportedly injected oranges with amphetamines to get his ten- to twelve-
year-old football players "up" for a game.

Many parents are transformed—and often not for the better—when   10
they see their youngsters in the thick of athletic competition. "When you
first go out to watch your child play sports, you see this biological exten-
sion of yourself on the field and you feel some powerful emotions," says
Rainer Martens, Ph.D., founder of the American Coaching Effectiveness
Program (ACEP) and author of *Joy and Sadness in Children's Sports*
(Human Kinetics Publishers). "Parents just aren't prepared for that.
Suddenly, they find themselves acting in ways they'd never think of at

home—standing up and screaming, 'You dummy! Catch the ball!' Behavior like this has a potentially severe effect on children."

Speaking of these effects, psychologist Thomas Tutko, a leading authority on youth sports and coauthor of the sobering book, *Winning Is Everything And Other American Myths* (Macmillan), comments. "I'm concerned about how many good athletes are scarred by injury or burned out psychologically by the time they are fifteen because they are unable to meet the insatiable needs of their parents, their coach, their fans, or their own personal obsession. And I am concerned, too, about those kids who feel rejected because of their limited athletic prowess.

"The effects may not be physically evident," continues Tutko, "but failure in sports, or heavy-handed approaches by parents and coaches, can destroy a child's self-esteem, turn him away from a lifelong involvement in physical activity, foster negative attitudes toward authority figures, and encourage hostile, aggressive behavior."

Our unfettered responses to our children as athletes can create insidious pressures. In her twelve years of extensive research on the sociopsychological aspects of competitive youth sports, Tara Scanlan, Ph.D., associate professor of kinesiology at the University of California, Los Angeles, found that children experience intense stress when they perceive they're being pressured to participate in an activity and when they worry about the performance expectations and evaluations of their parents and coaches. "Kids are very dependent on adults for feelings of their own competence and sense of self," says Scanlan. "It may not always seem so, since they may try to be stoic, tough little athletes who don't cry, but they process everything."

The implications for parents are clear. "As parents, we all have to walk a very fine line between caring and creating pressure, between enthusiasm and going overboard," comments Bob Chandler, former all-pro football player, in the recent film, *The Winning Trap: Sports and Our Kids.* "We have to answer the question, What's in it for us? as honestly as we can, because unless we know what we want out of kids' sports we can't be truly effective in helping our children get what they want."

Before involving our children in team sports we need to look at our own feelings about winning and losing, which may be colored by frustrations we feel in other areas of our lives, in our careers, or marital relationships. Our attitudes about sports may be charged, moreover, with memories of our own experiences as children, of our early successes or humiliations on the playing field.

"Before involving your child," says pediatrician Nathan Smith, a   16
sports medicine specialist at the University of Washington in Seattle and
coauthor of *Kidsports* (Addison-Wesley), "ask yourself whether you're
ready to be the parent of a loser, of a bench warmer. How would your
responses differ if your child struck out or made a home run in a tie
game? Would you be embarrassed if your child broke into tears after a
tough loss or after making a mistake? Can you tolerate becoming a target for your child's displaced anger and frustration when there is no
other outlet for disappointment and hurt?"

Or how would you feel if your child was benched during an important   17
game so that a child with less ability would have a chance to play? How
would you react if an official made a questionable call against your child?

If we understand our own expectations and motivations, we can help   18
our children explore theirs. We will be ready to hear what they are saying, rather than what we want them to say. Why do they want to play?
What do they expect the sport they have chosen to be like?

Although children learn very early the high value placed on sports by   19
society, when they play on their own, they tend to have a different per-
spective on sports than adults. They want to win, but winning is not
their exclusive goal. In a ten-year study of more than a thousand children, sports psychologist Terry Orlick discovered that 90 percent of his
young respondents would rather play on a losing team than warm a
bench on a winning team. In fact, winning was at the bottom of their
list. They wanted fun and excitement, and they wanted to improve their
skills and be with friends.

"If sides are unequal, if rules give an advantage to one team, children   20
will negotiate to make it possible for either side to win," says another
youth sport expert, Vern Seefeldt, Ph.D., director of the Youth Sports
Institute at Michigan State University. "That thrill of the unexpected
is a major part of why children play sports. As adults we try to set up
a distinct advantage for our team. We want to remove the element of
uncertainty.

"When we were kids," Seefeldt continues, "we used to make up all   21
kinds of modifications to games, because we didn't always have the right
number of people for a team, or the use of a baseball diamond or a basketball court. Now, as adults, we organize our children's games right
down to the letter of the rule, leaving them very little opportunity for
innovation and creativity, and depriving them of the process of arbitrat-
ing, negotiating, finding solutions."

According to Tutko, "We actually cripple children psychologically 22 when we set up all the plays. They feel like machines. Sport can be a medium to train children to be more responsible, but we have made winning take precedence over learning. That's so shortsighted. We could be teaching them leadership skills by having them take turns running the team's calisthenics and drills. We could teach them how to set up and run their own plays by alternating team captains every practice."

To guide our children's involvement with sports, we must recognize 23 that they have different needs at different ages and that, at each stage, success should be seen as an ongoing process of achieving potential.

The Winner Instinct

ROSS WETZSTEON

My wife used to hate playing cards with me. "You're too competi- 1 tive," she kept saying. "You get so intense, you can't just have fun—you always have to win."

That didn't have anything to do with the way I felt, but try telling her 2 that. All I could do was deny that I'm competitive.

Then one rainy weekend in the country we played a vicious, back-and- forth game of rummy, and when Kay finally edged me by three points, I 3 could see that her pleasure in winning was jeopardized by her fear that I'd sulk.

"Now, don't get mad just because you lost," she said. 4

"Mad? That was the closest game I've ever played!" 5

"You're just trying to prove you're not competitive." 6

"Not competitive? Then why was the game so much fun?" 7

She smiled cautiously as she gathered in the cards. "Now you're just 8 trying to pretend you don't care whether you won or lost."

"Of course I care, damn it, but don't you see? It's not winning or 9 losing that matters—it's the competition itself!"

I suddenly realized that when the subject had come up before, the only 10 reason I'd always denied being competitive was that Kay had made it seem like such a dirty word. "Sure, women are just as ambitious and aggressive as men," she had said once, "but we've been inhibited from expressing competitiveness. We were told when we were young that the only way we could compete was for the attention of men—to compete in any other way was 'unfeminine.' But society defines competitiveness as a brutal, winning-is-everything attitude. So if by competition you mean imitating the macho way men behave—no, thanks."

My wife just couldn't see that competitiveness means a lot more to men than that win-at-any-cost ethic. Listen to New York Mets' pitcher Tom Seaver, one of the most thoughtful athletes in America. "When we finally won the World Series, I realized I'd been wrong since boyhood. I'd always believed the thrill was in celebrating the victory. Now I saw that the thrill was in competition for its own sake." So I finally decided to admit that, yes, I'm very competitive, and what's more, I'm proud of it. 11

Now, I'm not going to deny that there are elements of adolescent insecurity or latent hostility or sexual rivalry in a lot of competition between men—all I'm saying is that there's another side to the story. Take male kidding around, for instance. I always tell my friend Arthur that he exaggerates so compulsively, he'll even tell people his summer house is at Six-Mile Harbor instead of Three-Mile Harbor. He comes right back at me: "You're putting on so much weight, pretty soon they'll have to give you your own zip code." 12

We indulge in so much of this typically male insulting humor that our wives can be forgiven for thinking that beneath our surface joking there must be bitter rivalry. Believe me, we see the "oh-you-men" way they roll their eyes, but what we actually hear when we insult each other like this is one of the most reassuring things a friend can say: "I know all your faults—you can't hide a thing from me—but I like you anyway. I accept you the way you are." Still skeptical? Just let some guy who's not a close friend try to get away with that kind of one-upmanship. 13

Male competitiveness in our professional lives is often a way to show our mutual respect. Sure, no one needs to be told that many men adopt a to-hell-with-the-bastards attitude in business; but far more often men also experience rivalry as a spur to achievement, as a means of being drawn to perform at the top of our abilities. I testified in a lawsuit a couple of years ago, and you would have thought the opposing attorneys would kill rather than let the other get the upper hand. But I overheard them talking after the decision. "I enjoy trying a case against you," one of them said. "You really keep me on my toes." 14

"Going up against you isn't any picnic," the other one answered. "I know I've got to do my best just to stand a chance." 15

Can you tell which one won the case? 16

I've heard other men express the same feelings in any number of highly   17
competitive professions. "It's really sad," the owner of a newspaper
where I once worked told me when a competing publication suddenly
folded. "I ran a much better paper because of them. Now I'm afraid I'll
get lazy." And while I'm not going to argue that men regret pulling off a
deal against a competitor, their gratification is often less if they don't feel
they were seriously challenged.

In sports the image of "winning is everything" is even more misleading.   18
Most men I know get their real kick in sports not from winning but from
the fact that the playing field is one of the few places where companionship and challenge come together. In bowling or touch football or softball, stiff competition not only brings men closer together, it also encourages them to do their best. This paradox at the heart of sports allows
men to feel both friendship and self-satisfaction, to share moments of
pride. Of course, there are nonstop competitors like John McEnroe, but
there are also competitors like my friends Josh and Michael—anyone
watching them play tennis would think their lives were riding on the outcome. But after the match is over, you can't tell who won—they both feel
great. Competition has pushed them to the limits of their abilities;
they've done as well as they possibly could; they've done something well
together.

Still think winning is everything to men? Take my friend Fred, who   19
finally managed to beat his weekly tennis partner after losing something
like ten sets in a row. "You must feel terrific," I said.

"Yeah, I suppose so," he said offhandedly.   20

"What's wrong?" I asked.   21

"Well, to tell the truth," Fred said, "he was so far off his game, it   22
wasn't much fun."

I knew exactly how he felt—I play tennis so competitively that my   23
friends call my game "Death in the Afternoon," but I'd much rather play
way over my head and lose 2–6 than hack around and win 6–love.

So when my wife says that men can't relate to one another except   24
competitively, that it's a way to disguise their animosity or assert their
superiority—no more apologies from me. I now argue that there's much
more going on, that men just as often use competition as a means of
expressing acceptance or respect or sharing.

Take it from me—busting your butt to win has its own rewards,   25
whether you win or not. I came home from a tennis match one day
absolutely glowing. "You must have won," Kay remarked.

"Why do you say that?"   26

"You look so happy."   27

"Well, actually I lost," I said. "But he was so good, he made me play   28
better than I've ever played in my life."

From Redbook *magazine, March 1984. Reprinted by permission of the author.*

Competition as a Mixed Good

RICHARD W. EGGERMAN

"Competition by its very nature is always unhealthy. Rivalry of any   1
kind is both psychologically disastrous and philosophically unjustifiable." These claims made by Alfie Kohn in "Why Competition?" (*The
Humanist*, January/February 1980) are too strong to be defensible.
Although competition has certain negative features, there are positive
aspects which should be noted. Competition is neither an unqualified
evil, as Kohn would claim, nor an unqualified good, as a Vince Lombardi
would have it. But it is on balance more likely to be a good than an evil.

The competitive person is one who, through his or her actions, indi-   2
cates a keen concern for succeeding in situations that measure relative
worth or excellence in an area. This usually involves attempting to beat
another person, although it is possible to speak of persons competing
against standards rather than persons. Furthermore, not every attempt at
beating another person counts as competition in the sense at issue here.
We are interested in assessing the merits of rivalry when the rivalry is
more for its own sake than for the sake of some essential good, such as
one's life or the lives of loved ones. When two soldiers fight to the death
in hand-to-hand combat, there is clearly rivalry, but it would unnecessar-
ily obscure issues to regard this as competition in the same sense that
rivalry for its own sake is competition.

It may be unwise to assess in one category competition for children   3
and competition for adults. It is reasonable to suppose that children may
be peculiarly liable to dangers of comparisons of relative worth in a way
that adults are not, just as it is reasonable to suppose that children
should not be exposed to pornography, violence, and so forth. One cannot presume that, if competition is a healthy activity on balance for the
normal adult, it will also be a healthy activity for the child. In order to
avoid blurring what may be significantly different categories, I shall
restrict this assessment of competition to only adults.

Some claims against competition are valid. It can lead to cheating, whether by tempting one to fabricate sources in the course of a debate or to improve one's lie on the golf course. This does not, of course, show that it must or even usually does lead to cheating, nor does it show that cheating in the context of sport makes a person more apt to cheat in noncompetitive areas, as in filing an income tax return. Nonetheless, cheating, even when done only occasionally and in the context of a sport, is still morally wrong. If competitive pressure tends to incite people to commit such a wrong, then this is a mark against competition.

A particularly insidious aspect of cheating is the tendency of competition to obscure the very wrongness of certain actions as long as everyone is doing them. For instance, dishonest practices in college athletic recruiting have gone on for so long as the result of pressures to win that the ability of the persons involved to recognize the difference between right and wrong seems largely to have withered. It is now perceived by some schools as a part of the game to entice would-be players with cars, female companionship, no-work jobs, and even altered high school transcripts. Cheating where one is aware of the wrongness of it is bad enough, but cheating to such an extent that one's moral sensibilities become anesthetized is surely worse.

Some suggest that competition leads one to regard opponents with suspicion and contempt. This happens often enough to be noteworthy. The tactic of "psyching up" by developing an artificial contempt or hatred has been publicized in some notable cases; Muhammad Ali in his earlier years, the "Mad Hungarian" relief pitcher, Al Hrabosky, and tennis stars John McEnroe and Ilie Nastase come immediately to mind. The situation is surely out of hand when the contempt becomes contagious and causes fans also to treat rivals with contempt, leading to incidents of violence. Competition sometimes leads persons to such behavior; whether such attitudes in fact make victory more likely is debatable.

Another questionable aspect of competition is its tendency to lead persons to perform under conditions which threaten long-term impairment to their health. "Playing while injured" is seen as meritorious rather than silly. It is an indictment of competition that it could tempt persons to risk permanent disability for the sake of the big game.

Closely allied is the phenomenon of using drugs to improve one's performance artificially, whether it be by blocking pain, increasing endurance beyond nature's limits, or increasing aggressiveness. Such chemical stimulation risks long-term injuries, but the pressures of competition cause persons to disregard this.

Other claims made against competition are without serious merit. 9
Kohn, for example, suggests that competition is anti-humanistic because
in it one person's success depends upon another person's failure. But it
is not always true that A's succeeding must involve B's failing. And,
even when this is the case, it does not follow that the situation is anti-
humanistic (if one assumes this word to mean something like "at odds
with the development of one's desirable human potential").

In competition, losing should not necessarily be seen as failing. If a 10
runner finishes behind Bill Rogers in the marathon but runs the race
twenty minutes faster than he has ever before, one cannot say that he has
failed. If a person enters a city tennis tournament and is eliminated in the
third round, he cannot be said to have failed if neither he nor anyone
else expected him to survive the first round. The point is simple: failure
in competition is not to be identified with losing *per se* but rather with
performing below reasonable expectations. Only when one could reasonably have expected to win does losing mean failing. In most competition
someone wins and someone or many lose, but this does not mean that
many (or even *any*) have performed below reasonable expectations and
have, therefore, failed.

Even when two persons of equal ability, both with strong expectations 11
of winning, are competing in an important contest, it does not follow that
the situation is anti-humanistic. In some cases, loss (when seen as failure)
may lead to a deterioration of the personality in some important way,
but it is flagrantly wrong to imply that it must do so. Psychological studies indicate that competitive persons are apt to be self-assertive, tough-
minded, self-sufficient, forthright, emotionally detached, and cheerfully
optimistic with an absence of severe mood swings. Failures simply do not
lead in a consistent way to deleterious effects upon the psyche of the competitor, for he or she realizes that competition (perhaps unlike real life)
will provide him or her with another day and a second chance. Failure
will cause short-term disappointment, but only a hedonist of a very simplistic sort would equate short-term disappointment with anti-humanism.

Kohn suggests that the competitor is caught on a treadmill, never able 12
to enjoy real satisfaction because there are always others who are, or soon
will be, better than he or she. But this also ignores the matter of reasonable expectations. The awareness that others are better is not *per se* a
source of dissatisfaction unless the competitor can reasonably expect to
be the very best; the awareness that others may become better is surely
not a source of dissatisfaction, since no one can reasonably expect to
remain the best forever. Such a claim would come closer to being defensi-

ble if it were to suggest that competitors seldom enjoy real satisfaction because they seldom are realistic in their expectations. But even this is quite dubious, for competitors, in spite of brief periods of heady and unreasonable expectations, usually do entertain fairly realistic impressions of what they are capable of and usually realize that even if they are "the best" they are not going to win all the time.

The "agony of defeat" approach to sport may give the opposite impression, but it probably has more to do with television's attempt to hype than with a genuine feature of competition. This is not to suggest that there are no keen disappointments involved in competition but rather that the view of the competitor as *perpetually* insecure or unsatisfied is generally quite fictional.   13

What are the virtues of competition? Frequently persons attempt to defend it by pointing to various good results that allegedly follow from it, such as character building, cooperation, and catharsis of anti-social tendencies. Most psychological studies, however, indicate that these consequentialist approaches to defending competition are doubtful if not simply false.   14

The virtue of competition is more likely to be intrinsic in character. Competition is enjoyable to most persons who participate in it. This is confirmed by the increasing numbers of persons who participate in city softball, tennis, and golf leagues. Such hedonistic reasons should not be considered alone but should be considered.   15

More importantly, competition offers an opportunity for deep pride to those who move beyond the level of casual involvement. The serious competitor who has worked to master his or her sport feels real accomplishment at what he or she can do. Competitors find that it is the competitive situation which routinely leads them to new levels of performance, often feats they did not know they were capable of. Runners frequently discover that a tough race leads them to performances they never dreamed possible, performances far superior to anything they can push themselves to in training. In such situations, one feels completely invigorated, very much in contrast to much of the humdrum routine of daily life. Perhaps under harsher conditions persons would not feel the pride which is generated from excelling at artificial challenges presented by competition, for the necessities of survival would provide sufficient feelings of accomplishment. But for many persons today the task of providing shelter and food has become too easy to provide feelings of real accomplishment. In the absence of such natural sources of pride, persons seek substitutes, and competition fits the bill excellently.   16

This is not, of course, to suggest that competition is the only way in which one can obtain a sense of pride in accomplishment today, nor that everyone who so competes will receive such benefits. But it is a plausible source, and this recommends it highly. Nor am I claiming that the virtues of competition in this regard should take priority over other activities which have more fundamental claims upon the person. It would be wrong for a person to neglect his children while "fulfilling" himself continuously on the golf course. Competitive rewards are basically self-centered, a fact which places them behind most moral *obligations* in any reasonable ranking of priorities. But they are still valuable, personal rewards—a fact too often overlooked by critics of competition.   17

Do competition's liabilities outweigh its assets, or vice versa? I am inclined to claim that *most* persons who engage in competition benefit from the experience and, further, that if a minimal amount of consideration were given to the true nature of competitive activity, almost everyone who tried it would benefit. Let us imagine the case of enlightened competitors—persons who take a bit of time to assess what they want from competition and how best to achieve it.   18

Enlightened competitors have reasonable expectations about their performances. They are not frustrated at the mere perception that others are better, as long as they can see themselves as making reasonable improvement. They are not terribly upset by an occasional lapse in performance, for they know that it is unreasonable to expect to play one's best game every time out. They will upon reflection see that cheating is antithetical to their goals of deep pride, rather than a means to it, for cheating vitiates their reward. It destroys the possibility of pride at performing well and thwarts the goal at drawing out maximal levels of performance. With a bit more reflection, they see that playing while injured or drugged is at odds with the most effective pursuit of their goals of maximal long-term development, for victories purchased today at the expense of risking permanent damage are too much of a risk. And, finally, they regard worthy rivals with gratitude and respect, rather than contempt, for they realize that it is only through their pushing themselves to the limit that they discover what those limits are.   19

The enlightened competitor may seem a rather utopian character, especially against the backdrop of competition as usually witnessed in professional or major college sports. This fact has more to do with the corruption of genuine competition at such levels of sport than with intrinsic problems of competition. When persons perform for a paycheck or scholarship rather than for intrinsic pride and achievement, cheating, intimidation, risk of debilitating injury, and the like may make sense—   20 but only then. The enlightened competitor seems less utopian when one looks at the level of city league play, local tennis and running clubs, and so forth. Persons approaching the enlightened competitor exist in large numbers at this level, where personal monetary gain is not a factor. Their competition is to them a source of pride, without the slightest desire to cheat or hold opponents in contempt.

Competition is a mixed good; it does have its risks. Competition   21
makes some persons anything but enlightened competitors. But critics such as Kohn have painted a far too bleak picture of it. The suspicious, contemptuous, deceitful, and insecure competitor—too often portrayed as typical—is far more the exception than the rule at the level of sport where persons still rival simply for the sake of the rivalry.

From The Humanist, *July/August 1982. Reprinted by permission of the American Humanist Association. © 1982.*

Who Wins? Who Cares?

MARIAH BURTON NELSON

Competition can damage self-esteem, create anxiety and lead to cheat-   1
ing and hurt feelings. But so can romantic love. No one suggests we do away with love; rather, we must perfect our understanding of what love means.

So too with competition. "To compete" is derived from the Latin   2
competere, meaning "to seek together." Women seem to understand this. Maybe it's because we sat on the sidelines for so long, watching. Maybe it's because we were raised to be kind and nurturing. I'm not sure why it is. But I've noticed that it's not women who greet each other with a ritu-alistic, "Who won?"; not women who memorize scores and statistics; not women who pride themselves on "killer instincts." Passionate though we are, women don't take competition that seriously. Or rather, we take competition seriously, but we don't take winning and losing seri-ously. We've always been more interested in playing.

In fact, since the early part of this century, women have devised ways   3
to make sport specifically inclusive and cooperative. Physical educators of the 1920s taught sportswomanship as well as sport skills, emphasizing health, vigor, high moral conduct, participation, respect for other players and friendship. So intent were these women on dodging the pitfalls of men's sports that many shied away from competition altogether.

Nowadays, many women compete wholeheartedly. But we don't buy   4
into the "Super Bull" mentality that the game is everything. Like
Martina Navratilova and Chris Evert, former "rivals" whose rapport has
come to symbolize a classically female approach to competition, many
women find ways to remain close while also reaching for victory. We
understand that trying to win is not tantamount to trying to belittle; that
winning is not wonderful if the process of play isn't challenging, fair or
fun; and that losing, though at times disappointing, does not connote
failure. For women, if sports are power plays, they're not about power
over (power as dominance) but power to (power as competence). Sports
are not about domination and defeat but caring and cooperation.

"The playing of a game has to do with your feelings, your emotions,   5
how you care about the people you're involved with," says University of
Iowa basketball coach C. Vivian Stringer.

Pam Shriver has said of Steffi Graf, "I hope in the next couple of years   6
that I get to be friends with her because it's just easier. It's more fun. I
don't think it affects the competitive side of things."

Friendship has been a major theme of my sporting life as well, along   7
with physical competence, achievement and joy. Though I've competed
in seven sports from the high school to the professional level, I have few
memories of victories or losses. I don't think winning taught me to be a
gracious winner. I don't think losing readied me for more serious losses
in life. Rather, my nearly 30 years of competition have taught me how to
play, with empathy, humor and honesty. If another player challenges me
to row harder, swim faster or make more clever moves toward the basket, the games take on a special thrill. But the final score is nearly irrelevant. Chris Evert once said the joy of winning "lasts about an hour."

I'm choosy about whom I compete with, and how. I don't participate   8
in games in which "losers" are no longer allowed to play. Monopoly,
poker, musical chairs, and single-elimination tournaments are a few
examples. If playing is the point, then exclusion never makes sense. I also
eschew competitions that pit women against men; they only serve to
antagonize and polarize. I no longer injure myself in the name of victory.
Nor, as a coach, will I allow players to get that carried away.

Some women, scarred by childhood exclusion, shamed by early   9
"defeats," or sickened by abuses such as cheating and steroid use, still
avoid competition. They're right to be wary. Although these things are
more visible in men's sports, female athletes and coaches can also suc-
cumb to the "winning is the only thing" myth, committing myriad ethical and personal offenses, from recruiting violations to bulimia, in the
name of victory.

But once one understands the spirit of the game, it's not a matter of   10
believing that winning and losing aren't important, it's a matter of noticing that they're not. Women seem to notice. Most women can play soccer, golf or run competitively and enjoy themselves, regardless of outcome. They can play on a "losing" team but leave the court with little
or no sense of loss. They can win without feeling superior.

I think it's the responsibility of these women—and the men who   11
remain unblinded by the seductive glow of victory—to share this vision
with young players. Children, it seems to me, naturally enjoy comparing
their skills: "How far can you throw the ball? Farther than I can? How
did you do it? Will you show me?" It's only when adults ascribe undue
importance to victory that losing becomes devastating and children
get hurt.

Adults must show children that what matters is how one plays the   12
game. It's important that we not just parrot that cliche, but demonstrate
our commitment to fair, participatory competition by paying equal attention to skilled and unskilled children; by allowing all children to participate fully in games, regardless of the score; and by caring more about
process than results. This way, children can fully comprehend what they
seem to intuit: that competition can be a way to get to know other people, to be challenged, and to have fun in a close and caring environment.
To seek together.

Some of my best friends are the women and men who share a court   13
or pool or field with me. Together we take risks, make mistakes, laugh,
push ourselves and revel in the grace and beauty of sports. Who wins?
Who cares? We're playing *with*, not *against* each other, using each
other's accomplishments to inspire.

At its best, competition is not divisive but unifying, not hateful but   14
loving. Like other expressions of love, it should not be avoided simply
because it has been misunderstood.

Reprinted by permission of the author.

After You Read

Work with other students to develop responses to these questions or to compare responses
that you have already prepared.

1. Consider you own personal experience in light of the articles you have read. What
   points in the articles confirm your experiences? What points contradict them?

2. Make a list of the benefits and drawbacks of competition as they are presented in these
   articles. Do any of these benefits or drawbacks affect your initial opinion about the
   nature of competition?

Writing Assignments

Note: Working with several sources can be substantially more difficult than working with only one source. As you respond to one of these assignments, consider working with other students to help you clarify and organize your ideas.

1. Write an essay in which you argue for or against the legalization of drugs. To support your thesis, use arguments and evidence both from the articles you have read and from whatever relevant experiences you or people you know may have had.

2. Write an essay that argues a point about the effects of competition, drawing on the articles you have read and on experiences of your own or of people you know. If you want to, you can focus your argument on one particular area, such as competitive sports in high school or competitive attitudes among fellow students. (For additional arguments about the nature of competition, see Alfie Kohn's article "Why Competition?" on pages 182–186.

3. Read the articles in Part Four pertaining to "English as the 'Official' Language of the United States." Using arguments and evidence from those articles and from your own experience, argue for or against the concept of establishing English as the official language of the U.S.

4. Use the articles in Chapter 7 pertaining to the toy weapon debate, the effects of television, or the benefits and drawbacks of part-time jobs for students to develop an argument on one of those subjects.

Evaluating Sample Papers

Argument Essay

1. Introduction

Does the first paragraph employ an effective lead-in to introduce the topic? Does the thesis take a definite stand and make it clear that the author intends to support a debatable point?

1   2   3   4   5   6

2. Unity

Does each paragraph have a clear and specific topic sentence that introduces an argument in support of the thesis? Does the material in each paragraph clearly relate to its topic sentence?

1   2   3   4   5   6

3. Support

Is the argument within each paragraph supported with facts, examples, statistics, and/or references to authority?

1   2   3   4   5   6

4. Coherence

Are transitions used between paragraphs? Are they used within paragraphs, especially when the writer is moving from one type of support to another?

1   2   3   4   5   6

5. References to the Text

Are direct quotations and paraphrases correctly introduced and smoothly incorporated into the text? Do they reflect the articles' points accurately?

1   2   3   4   5   6

6. Tone and Attitude

Has the writer recognized that other responses to this topic are possible? Has he or she raised and responded to obvious objections?

1   2   3   4   5   6

7. Sentence Structure

Do the sentences combine ideas that are related, using coordination, subordination, verbal phrases, or parallelism when appropriate? Are there too many brief, choppy main clauses?

1   2   3   4   5   6

8. Mechanics, Grammar, and Spelling

Does the paper contain a distracting number of errors of these kinds?

| 1 | 2 | 3 | 4 | 5 | 6 |

9. Overall Ranking of the Essay

| 1 | 2 | 3 | 4 | 5 | 6 |

Using the above criteria, evaluate the following student essays. These essays were written in response to the following assignment:

> Using the articles in Chapter 7 as well as your own experiences or the experiences of people you know, write an essay that argues a point about the harmful or beneficial effects that television has on its viewers.

Student Essay 1

Yesterday, when I came home from a late afternoon class that I'm taking, my two kids were watching a rerun of *Wings*. They both looked up as I stepped over them, said "Hi Mom!" and then returned to their show. I suppose I should have been bothered because we always hear that television is taking over our children's lives, but I just don't believe that television is really so bad. I enjoy watching television. I know it can be abused, but so can any good thing. On the whole, it seems to me that television watching has far more benefits than drawbacks.

One of its most obvious benefits is that it provides people with entertainment. It lets you sit down, catch your breath, and relax. I'm a busy person. I hold down a job, attend college, and raise two children. And my kids are active ten and thirteen year olds. So it's nice to be able to sit down at the end of a day for an hour or two. In the article "TV Can't Educate," Paul Robinson says how effectively television entertains. Although I don't agree with him when he says that television can't educate, I do agree when he says that television provides valuable entertainment. He points out that television "provides an escape from the world and from ourselves . . . . and gives us sense of union with humanity, if only in its foibles" (212–213).

In addition to entertaining us, tv also can also educate its viewers and can even help you to become a better thinker. In "The Meaning of TV" William Henry III states that children learn the alphabet on *Sesame Street* (208). I know that my own children's education has been helped by television. Last month we watched *Gone with the Wind*, and that movie led to all sorts of questions about the Civil War and slavery. Later in the week, when my kids were watching *The Cosby Show*, my youngest child asked if Bill Cosby was a slave. That led to a long talk about the roles of African-Americans in today's world. It is true that I am helping here, but it's also true that television causes my kids to ask questions.

I think one the most important benefits of television is what it shows my kids about their world. It's not that I only let them watch educational shows. They watch everything from *Roseanne* to reruns of *I Love Lucy*. But they notice the differences between Roseanne's attitude and how naive Lucy is. These shows are not "educational" by any stretch of the imagination, but they do show different types of American women that I can talk about with my children. Daniel Anderson, a psychologist at the University of Massachusetts at Amherst, says that children watching tv "do not merely absorb words and images. Instead they muse upon the meaning of what they see, its plausibility and its implications for the future—whether they've tuned in to a news report of a natural disaster or an action show" (qtd in Drexler 216). My experiences with my children make me agree with Anderson.

In spite of what I see as the benefits of television, there are still major objections that people raise about television. For instance, in "Shadows on the Wall," Donna Woolfolk Cross claims that many people end up preferring the fantasy world of television to the real world that they live in (214). She's right. Television can be abused, and one way is to treat it as a babysitter. However, as Daniel Anderson points out, when parents and children talk about what they watch, children learn to expect "that TV will require thought [and] they spend more time thinking" (qtd. in Drexler 217). Also, many people believe that television hurts education because it replaces reading, but I don't think so. My kids read a lot, even though we also watch a lot of television. I think Anderson's right when he states that kids will read if their parents do. (Drexler 216–217).

I suppose I don't really think the television is the source of our problems. The problems start with parents who do not talk to their children. It is amazing what children can understand when people talk to them. If too much violence or poor morality is pointed out to them on one show, they will think about such violence and immorality on other shows when the parent is not there. Children are young and impressionable, but they are not stupid. Let's not blame the television for the poor performance of so many parents.

Student Essay 2

. . . a burglar . . . broke into a home and killed the father of three children, aged nine, eleven, and twelve. The crime went unnoticed until ten hours later, when police entered the apartment after being called by neighbors and found the three children watching television just a few feet away from the bloody corpse of their father. (Cross 215)

Doesn't this scene read like an unbelievable script for a bad movie? Unfortunately, according to Donna Woolfolk Cross in "Shadows on the Wall," it is a real-life situation, reported by United Press International. It illustrates the powerful hold that television has over young minds, and it points out how television can draw attention away from the real world, replacing reality with its own distorted fantasy world. I have to admit that I am one of the 1980's generation that grew up glued to the television, but I still think that in many ways the TV is one of the most dangerous devices invented in the last century.

One reason it's so dangerous is that it does exactly what the above quotation suggests—it replaces reality with illusion. Ms. Cross gives several studies to prove this point. One of them involved a group of children in a room where two people started to yell at each other and fight. The fight was projected on video screens, and rather than reacting to what was happening, the kids all sat and watched the screens. It was as if the video were more important than the people themselves (215). I've seen other situations that make me believe that television causes children to confuse reality and illusion. For instance, when I started high school, shows like *Beverly Hills 90210* had me thinking that all the kids there would look cool and be going to bed with each other. I was so worried that I would never fit in that for the first month I didn't even talk to anybody. Luckily, I finally figured out that real life was different from what I'd seen on TV, but I sure went through a lot of misery for nothing.

I think that TV is also dangerous because it pretends to be educational when it's really not. According to Paul Robinson in "TV Can't Educate," television cannot provide the time that is needed for a person to really think about an issue. Instead, all it can do is present bits and pieces of facts that ignore all sorts of more involved questions (211). I think this is really true. I remember watching *Sesame Street* as I grew up, and I can't remember ever really learning anything from it. I just liked Big Bird and Cookie Monster. I thought they were funny, but mostly I ignored or already knew all the things they did with the alphabet and numbers. Also, I practically never watch the news or shows like *Nightline* because I like to relax when I watch television, so for the most part the television is not really very educational for me.

The worst part about television is the violence and sex that are becoming so common, even during early evening hours. It seems to me that there is no way children can avoid being affected by all of the negative things they see every day and evening on television. Even the writers who argue in favor of TV admit how damaging this part of it can be. In "Don't Touch That Dial," Madeline Drexler refers to the "violence of primetime shows . . . . the sexism of MTV . . . . [and] the materialism of commercials" (218). Also, in "The Meaning of TV," William Henry III admits that without TV we might have a less violent society and a more restrained world where "premarital pregnancy and divorce were still treated with distaste rather than with sympathy" (209).

Some people think that TV doesn't cause as many problems as I have listed, but I don't see how they can really think that. Television is entertaining, and I have to admit that I watch it for that reason, but it's not educational, and it really does cause people to make bad judgments about what reality is like. When I have children, I don't think I'll want them to sit and stare at the TV all day, but I will let them watch shows that are entertaining and amusing.

Sentence-Combining Review

In the first seven chapters of this text, you have practiced using a variety of techniques to combine related ideas. In the paragraphs that follow, combine the related sentences using whichever techniques seem most appropriate. Here is a brief summary of the sentence-combining ideas you have studied.

Chapter 1:	Embed adjectives, adverbs, and prepositional phrases in related sentences.
Chapter 2:	Use coordination to combine sentences or parts of sentences that are grammatically alike.
Chapter 3:	Use subordinate clauses to indicate the relative importance of related ideas.
Chapter 4:	Use present participial phrases, past participial phrases, and infinitive phrases to combine related ideas.
Chapter 5:	Use appositives when nouns or pronouns are used to rename other nouns and pronouns.
Chapter 6:	Use parallel sentence structure to join items in a series or with correlative conjunctions.
Chapter 7:	Vary the length and structure of your sentences to achieve sentence variety.

EXERCISES   **1** Roger Williams was the great seventeenth-century religious emancipator. **2** He died in 1683. **3** He was buried in a poorly marked grave in the backyard of his home in Providence, Rhode Island. **4** Fifty-six years later, in 1739, a workman was excavating a nearby grave. **5** He accidentally broke into the coffin and exposed the bones. **6** Years after that, in 1860, a descendant of Williams ordered workmen to exhume the remains. **7** He wanted to transfer them to a more suitable tomb. **8** When the coffin was opened, no bones were found. **9** Instead, the coffin contained the root of a nearby apple tree. **10** It was exactly where the body should have been. **11** It was in the exact shape of Williams's body, from head to toe. **12** Apparently the root had entered the coffin when it was broken open in 1739. **13** It encountered Williams's skull. **14** Then it followed the path of least resistance. **15** It inched down the side of his head, backbone, hips, and legs. **16** It molded itself closely to the contours of his body. **17** The corpse itself was gone. **18** It had been absorbed into the tree through the roots. **19** The human-shaped root was removed for safekeeping. **20** Today it is on display at the Rhode Island Historical Society in Providence.

1 Many actors and actresses are superstitious people. **2** They rely not only on their talent, looks, and charm. **3** They also rely on rabbits' feet and a whole host of other superstitions. **4** Some stage superstitions are purely personal. **5** Others have been picked up from tradition. **6** They are treasured by those who have no idea how or why the superstitions originated. **7** For example, real flowers are welcome after a performance. **8** They are unlucky for stage decorations. **9** Of course, real flowers would fade and have to be replaced regularly. **10** The superstition probably derives from a very practical concern. **11** An artist might slip and fall if he stepped on a petal or leaf that had fallen from a vase. **12** There are other common stage superstitions. **13** A fall on stage is the sign of a long run. **14** Wishing an actor good luck will bring bad luck. **14** Performing or even quoting from *Macbeth* is unlucky. **15** Tradition also has it that something going wrong during dress rehearsal means the opening night's performance will be a success. **16** In fact, many actors have a firm belief. **17** A bad dress rehearsal heralds a smash opening night. **18** The list of superstitions goes on and on. **19** Flowers should be handed over the footlights instead of delivered backstage. **20** One should never mention the exact number of lines he has in a show. **21** Congratulatory telegrams should not be read during a run. **22** One should not write on the dressing room mirror. **23** If someone whistles in the dressing room, one should go outside. **24** Then one should turn around three times and spit before re-entering.

1 Ever since 1966, a scientific controversy has raged. **2** The controversy is about whether apes actually exhibit signs of human intelligence. **3** In 1966, a chimpanzee named Washoe first began to use American Sign Language, or AMESLAN. **4** Apes that have been taught sign language have developed significantly large vocabularies. **5** They recognize nouns, like "fruit," "candy,'" and "banana." **6** They also recognize verbs, such as "give," "hug," and "take." **7** Sometimes they combine these words in creative ways. **8** One chimp did not know the term for citrus fruit. **9** It called them "smell fruit." **10** Others called watermelons "candy drink" and cucumbers "banana which is green." **11** Apes apparently recognize the meaning of certain words. **12** They seem able to string together some words into meaningful sentences. **13** Critics of ape research assert that supposed ape "language ability" is due solely to drill, imitation, or mere conditioned response. **14** These critics claim that ape trainers misinterpret ape "language." **15** They say that the trainers are too eager to believe that apes are truly displaying human-type intelligence. **16** In addition to language ability, researchers have discovered evidence that apes also possess self-awareness. **17** Self-awareness has long been considered an exclusive trait of the human race. **18** For example, apes can learn to recognize themselves in mirrors. **19** No primate other than humans seems able to do that. **20** It is suspected that other species with large brains, such as whales, porpoises, and elephants, may also be self-aware.

Editing Skills

Effective writing requires care and precision, much more so than speaking does. When speaking, we always have the opportunity to stop and explain ourselves further. When we write in college, business, and the professions, we make hundreds, even thousands, of separate choices, even in relatively brief pieces of writing. Some of the choices are large, such as those concerning the overall organization of our writing, and some of the choices are small, such as those concerning the placement of an apostrophe or comma. Other choices involve sentence patterns, words, and punctuation.

Skillful editing can enhance the quality of your writing and allow you to express yourself in the way that you desire. Not only does it allow you to write effectively, but it also gains you the confidence of your readers. Poor grammar and usage can cause your readers to feel that you have not thought carefully about both the form and the content of your writing. In this section, we will present the basic editing skills of a good writer. We begin with a few important definitions.

CHAPTER NINE

Some Basic Editing Terms

Clause

A **clause** is a group of words that contains at least one subject and one verb. Here are some clauses:

       S   V
Harvey cares about Beatrice.

          S   V
The train was late.

            S   V
Almost all cats hate dogs.

Here are some groups of words that are not clauses:

To find out the cause of the problem.
Trying out for the team.

To find out the cause of the problem is not a clause because it does not contain a subject and a verb. It does contain a form known as an infinitive ("to find"), but the infinitive is a **verbal**, and verbals cannot be used as the verb of a sentence.

Trying out for the team also lacks a subject and verb. This phrase contains another verbal—the "-ing" form of the verb. However, the "-ing" form cannot be used as the verb of a clause unless it is accompanied by a helping verb, as in the following clause:

   S   V
I <u>was trying</u> out for the team.

Clauses come in two types—main and subordinate.

Main Clause

A **main clause** expresses a complete idea. Here are some main clauses:

Cromwell was a serious man.
Have some red beans and rice. (Here, the understood subject is *you.*)
What have I done wrong?

Subordinate Clause

A **subordinate clause** begins with a word that prevents it from expressing a complete idea. Here are some subordinate clauses.

    S V
When I arrive at the airport. . .

       S V
. . . which Joe kept for himself.

    S V
After you inspect the kitchen. . .

The words that begin the above subordinate clauses are called subordinators. They come in two types—**subordinating conjunctions** and **relative pronouns**.

Subordinating Conjunctions

after	so that
although	than
as	though
as if	unless
as long as	until
because	when
before	whenever
even though	where
if	wherever
since	while

Relative Pronouns

that	who(ever)
which	whom(ever)
(and sometimes when, as, or where)	

Subordinate clauses may appear at the start, at the end, or in the middle of a sentence.

After he had passed the bar exam, Eduardo was ready to join a law firm.
Sarah was angry at her coach because he refused to listen to her excuses.
The movie that I rented last night was really boring.

(See pages 91–94 for a further discussion of subordinate clauses.)

Sentence

A **sentence** is a group of words that contains at least **one main clause**.

(not a sentence) *Just staring into the sky.*

(not a sentence) *Because he was so angry.*

(sentence) *He just stared into the sky.*

(sentence) *Because he was so angry, he just stared into the sky.*

EXERCISE   Indicate whether the following are main clauses (MC), subordinate clauses (SC), or neither (N).

1. Gordon forgot his sunscreen. _____

2. Shifting into warp speed. _____

3. Griffins are scary creatures. _____

4. If you say that one more time. _____

5. Why don't you understand? _____

6. To point his pistol at the intruder. _____

7. Charles and Ann are proud of the magazine. _____

8. Because Suzanne likes to ride horses. _____

9. Having already made up his mind. _____

10. He ordered a Spam-and-okra pizza. _____

11. Because Sam Lucas gave him such good advice. _____

12. Even though Jack had to use a cane. _____

13. He never missed one meeting. _____

14. Play it again, Sam. _____

15. When Brent fakes out the point guard. _____

16. To watch Charles and Louis comparing hatchets. _____

17. When Steve and Marste are chatting. _____

18. They do not want to be interrupted.   _____

19. And I want an answer immediately.   _____

20. It is a double pleasure to deceive the deceiver.   _____

Coordinating Conjunction

The **coordinating conjunctions** are *and, but, or, nor, for, so* and *yet*. An easy way to learn the coordinating conjunctions is to remember that their first letters can spell **BOYSFAN** (*But Or Yet So For And Nor*). These words join parts of a sentence that are grammatically equal. For example, they may join two subjects, two verbs, or two adjectives. They may also join two similar phrases, two subordinate clauses, or two main clauses.

Two subjects	<u>Fred</u> **and** <u>Ethel</u> own this building.
Two verbs	Lucy <u>stared</u> at the wallpaper **and** <u>started</u> to cry.
Two adjectives	Alicia felt <u>awkward</u> **and** <u>uncomfortable</u> in the dentist's office.
Two similar phrases	Jaime wanted <u>to win the marathon</u> **or** <u>to place in the top three finishers.</u>
Two subordinate clauses	<u>After they ate the dessert</u> **but** <u>before they washed the dishes</u>, Dan and Roseanne yelled at the kids.
Two main clauses	<u>I have mockingbirds in my backyard</u>, **and** <u>they mimic the sounds of the neighborhood's car alarms.</u>

(See pages 55–56 for a further discussion of coordinating conjunctions.)

Conjunctive Adverb

A **conjunctive adverb** is a word or phrase that serves as a transition, usually between two main clauses. When a conjunctive adverb joins two main clauses, it is preceded by a semi-colon and followed by a comma.

Percival enjoyed artichoke hearts; **however,** *Consuela could not stand them.*

Here is a list of the most common conjunctive adverbs:

accordingly	for example	however
as a result	for instance	indeed
consequently	furthermore	in fact
first	hence	instead

likewise	next	therefore
meanwhile	otherwise	thus
moreover	second	unfortunately
nevertheless	still	

Do not use a semicolon before a conjunctive adverb that does not begin a main clause. For example, in the following sentences, the conjunctive adverbs are not immediately preceded by semicolons.

*The man on the left, **meanwhile**, studied his bus schedule.*

*The cat yowled all night long; none of the neighbors, **however**, seemed to mind.*

(See pages 58–59 for a further discussion of conjunctive adverbs.)

EXERCISE

In the following sentences, identify all main clauses by underlining them once and all subordinate clauses by underlining them twice. Identify all coordinating conjunctions by labeling them CC, all subordinating conjunctions by labeling them SC, all relative pronouns by labeling them RP, and all conjunctive adverbs by labeling them CA.

1. While Wally worked on his bicycle, Beaver watched television.

2. The CDs that I had bought were stolen from my car.

3. The pelicans skimmed the water as the sun came up.

4. The group of men kept shouting loudly; consequently, we moved to another part of the stadium.

5. The *Reader* comes out every Thursday, and it has a great deal of handy information.

6. Duke Ellington wrote many beautiful pieces, but my favorite is "Concerto for Cootie."

7. Cootie Williams played trumpet for the Duke Ellington orchestra; next, he formed his own band.

8. Some great blue herons have nested in some trees near our house, so we often see them flying majestically overhead.

9. Walter Benjamin occupied Brent's mind much of the time when he was pondering the meaning of the life that spooled out endlessly before him.

10. At other times, he worked on his jump shot, or he prepared burritos and broccoli for Kyle.

11. My friend named his German shepherd Beethoven because he admired the composer so much.

12. If Ludwig were alive, he might be insulted.

13. The soldiers that fought for the South during the Civil War did not wear gray; in fact, they wore butternut.

14. Joseph Campbell taught us much about myth, but Louis Armstrong taught us to swing.

15. Leda had a phobia about swans; therefore, she refused to ride the swan boats in Boston.

16. Although red beans and rice is my favorite dish, I would not mind some hushpuppies right now.

17. Sometimes Hamlet could not stop talking; consequently, he hardly got any work done.

18. Homer is a heroic eater because he eats sushi; moreover, he eats snails.

19. Jazz may be the United States' only original art form although, according to some people, the short story was also developed here.

20. The manual for my VCR is unreadable, so I have never recorded a program.

CHAPTER TEN

Sentence Fragments

The easiest way to identify a **sentence fragment** is to remember that *every sentence must contain a main clause*. If you do not have a main clause, you do *not* have a sentence. You can define a fragment, then, as follows: A **sentence fragment** occurs when a group of words that lacks a main clause is punctuated as a sentence.

Using this definition, you can identify almost any sentence fragment. However, you will find it easier to locate fragments in your own writing if you know that fragments can be divided into three basic types.

The Three Types of Sentence Fragments

1. **Some fragments contain no clause at all.** This type of fragment is simple to spot. It usually does not even sound like a sentence because it lacks a subject or a verb or both.

    The child in the park.

2. **Some fragments contain a verbal but still no clause.** This fragment is a bit less obvious because a verbal can be mistaken for a verb. But remember, neither a participle nor an infinitive is a verb. (See Chapter 9 if you need to review this point.)

    The child <u>playing</u> in the park.   (participle)

    <u>To play</u> on the swings in the park.   (infinitive)

3. **Some fragments contain a subordinate clause but no main clause.** This type of fragment is perhaps the most common because it does contain a subject and a verb. But remember, *a group of words without a main clause is not a sentence.*

    As *the child played in the park.*
    Because *the swings in the park were wet.*

Repairing Sentence Fragments

Once you have identified a fragment, you can repair it in one of two ways:

1. Add words to give it a main clause.

(fragment)	*The child in the park.*
(sentence)	*The child <u>played</u> in the park.*
(sentence)	*The child in the park <u>looked worried</u>.*

(fragment)	*The child playing in the park.*
(sentence)	*The child <u>was</u> playing in the park.*
(sentence)	*The child playing in the park <u>ran toward the swings.</u>*

| (fragment) | *Because the swings in the park were wet.* |
| (sentence) | *<u>The child played on the slide</u> because the swings in the park were wet.* |

2. Join the fragment to a main clause written before or after it.

| (incorrect) | *I saw a ball rolling down the walk. And a child playing on the swings.* |
| (correct) | *I saw a ball rolling down the walk and a child playing on the swings.* |

| (incorrect) | *A dog chased a cat into the bushes. As a child played on the swings.* |
| (correct) | *A dog chased a cat into the bushes as a child played on the swings.* |

Of the two possible ways to correct fragments shown above, try to use the second method of joining fragments to nearby main clauses as often as possible. Doing so will help you to avoid writing a string of short, choppy sentences, and it will help to clarify the relationship between the ideas you are joining.

One final point might help you identify and correct sentence fragments. Remember that we all speak in fragments every day. (If a friend asks you how you are, you might respond with the fragment "Fine.") Because we speak in fragments, you may find that your writing seems acceptable to you even though it contains fragments. When you work on the exercises in this chapter, do not rely on your "ear" alone. Look at the sentences. **If they do not contain main clauses, they are fragments, no matter how correct they may sound.**

EXERCISE   Underline any fragment you find. Then correct it either by adding new words to give it a main clause or by joining it to a main clause next to it.

1. Sarah stared at the cotton candy. Wondering if she could eat the whole thing.

2. The dog that had been barking all night long.

3. After visiting the dentist. Zelda stopped at the ice cream store. Where she ate two hot fudge sundaes and a banana split.

4. Sit in the chair by the door. Until your number is called.

5. While visiting his cousins in France where he had spent all of his childhood and most of his teenage years.

6. The word *mutant* might be considered redundant in the name *Teenage Mutant Ninja Turtles*.

7. Because Fabio had kissed her hand. Andrea did not wash it for three weeks.

8. Disgusted with the performance of his new Corvette. Which he had just purchased for $30,000. Heathcliff threw his car keys into the lake.

9. To prevent Lois from discovering his true identity. Clark told her that he was afraid of heights.

10. A mouse scampered across the floor. Stopped to stare at the cat in the chair. And then disappeared into a crack in the wall.

11. From where she stood, Myna was able to hear every word. She kept repeating whatever the speaker said.

12. The recent earthquake caused all the dishes to fall out of the cupboard. And the microwave oven to crash to the floor.

13. Some skiers like to take unnecessary risks. Jumping from high ledges above steep slopes. They seem to enjoy the danger.

14. Turning restlessly from side to side. Henry dreamed about Walden Pond. Which he knew would soon freeze over.

15. Even though Huck had never painted a fence before. Tom assured him that he could do a good job.

16. Dorothy stared at the Munchkins and then looked at the dead witch. She knew that she wasn't in Kansas anymore.

17. Tomorrow we will experience a full solar eclipse. For the last time in this decade. It should be rather exciting.

18. Whenever Sam and Ella visit a restaurant. All of the patrons scream and run away.

19. My neighbor down the street, who needs to make more money to support his family but who has never held a steady job, even though several have been offered to him.

20. The deep blue skies. The rich green grass. The gentle afternoon breezes. The smell of the ocean. Karen missed them all.

CHAPTER ELEVEN

Fused Sentences and Comma Splices

The **fused sentence** and the **comma splice** are serious writing errors that you can correct with little effort. Either error can occur when you write a sentence that contains two or more main clauses.

Fused Sentences

The **fused sentence** occurs when two or more main clauses are joined without a coordinating conjunction and without punctuation.

(fused)   *Chelsea jumped into the pool she waved at her father.*

As you can see, the two main clauses in the above fused sentence (*Chelsea jumped into the pool* and *she waved at her father*) have been joined without a coordinating conjunction and without punctuation of any kind.

Comma Splices

The **comma splice** is a similar error. The comma splice occurs when two or more main clauses are joined with a comma but without a coordinating conjunction.

(comma splice)   *The rain soaked all of the campers, they wondered when it would finally stop.*

In this comma splice, the two main clauses (*The rain soaked all of the campers* and *they wondered when it would finally stop*) are joined by a comma, but a comma alone is not enough to join main clauses.

One of the most frequent comma splices occurs when a writer joins two main clauses with a comma and a conjunctive adverb rather than with a semicolon and a conjunctive adverb.

(comma splice)   *I saved enough money to take a trip to Hawaii, however, at the last minute I had to change my plans.*

Repairing Fused Sentences and Comma Splices

Because both fused sentences and comma splices occur when two main clauses are joined incorrectly, you can correct either error using one of five methods. Consider these two errors:

(fused)   *Leroy won the lottery he decided to buy a car.*

(comma splice)   *Leroy won the lottery, he decided to buy a car.*

Both of these errors can be corrected in one of five ways:

1. **Use a comma and a coordinating conjunction.** (See page 287 for a list of coordinating conjunctions.)

   Leroy won the lottery, **so** *he decided to buy a car.*

2. **Use a semicolon.**

   *Leroy won the lottery**;** he decided to buy a car.*

3. **Use a semicolon and a conjunctive adverb.** (See pages 287–288 for a list of conjunctive adverbs)

   Leroy won the lottery; **therefore,** *he decided to buy a car.*

   Do not use a semicolon before a conjunctive adverb that does not join two main clauses. For example, in the following sentence, however does not need a semicolon.

   The person in the blue raincoat, **however,** *has not seen this movie.*

4. **Change one of the clauses to a subordinate clause by beginning it with a subordinating conjunction or relative pronoun.** (See page 285 for a list of subordinating conjunctions and relative pronouns.)

   When *Leroy won the lottery, he decided to buy a car.*

5. **Punctuate the clauses as two separate sentences.**

   Leroy won the lottery. He decided to buy a car.

Sometimes the two main clauses in a fused sentence or comma splice are interrupted by a subordinate clause. When this sentence pattern occurs, the two main clauses must still be connected in one of the five ways.

(fused)   *Roberta sold her house even though she had thought she would always live there she could not afford the payments.*

(comma splice)   *Roberta sold her house even though she had thought she would always live there, she could not afford the payments.*

(possible correction)   *Roberta sold her house even though she had thought she would always live there; unfortunately, she could not afford the payments.*

EXERCISE   Identify the following sentences as fused (F), comma splice (CS), or correct (C). Then correct each incorrect sentence using one of the five methods discussed above.

_____ **1.** Samantha turned sadly away from the window it had started to rain.

_____ **2.** The pilot said that he was not superstitious, nevertheless, he always avoided the Bermuda Triangle.

_____ **3.** Two alley cats climbed over the fence then they began to yowl.

_____ **4.** Halfway through the first act, the prima donna's voice began to waver and crack.

_____ **5.** Mickey told Pluto to fetch the stick, Pluto told Mickey to forget it.

_____ **6.** Suddenly a message appeared on the computer screen, it said that the hard drive had crashed.

_____ **7.** Don Quixote stared at the windmill he raised his lance and attacked it.

_____ **8.** The miner threw his helmet into the air and gave a victorious shout because he had finally found the Lost Dutchman's Mine.

_____ **9.** Mother Abigail stared toward Las Vegas she knew she would win all of the money that she needed.

_____ **10.** All of the wiring had been installed correctly, however, the lights still would not turn on.

_____ **11.** After visiting Earth, the extraterrestrials headed for home, disappointed by their failure to discover any intelligent life.

_____ **12.** Michael refuses to drink diet soft drinks also he hates coffee.

_____ **13.** Ahmed knew it was time to leave even though he was not ready he picked up his bags and boarded the plane.

_____ **14.** The German shepherd down the street, however, is quite gentle.

_____ **15.** Although it was nearly 2:00 A.M., the party was still going strong, then one of the neighbors called the police.

_____ **16.** Clive has some rather unusual eating habits, for instance, yesterday morning he ate Frosted Flakes and mayonnaise for breakfast.

_____ **17.** A deranged-looking man claimed giant grasshoppers were living in the sewers of Los Angeles nobody believed him.

_____ **18.** Leonardo's knock-knock jokes were rather dumb, consequently, all Mona Lisa would do was smile politely.

_____ **19.** The sun had reached its zenith Doc Holliday and the Earp brothers entered the O.K. Corral.

_____ **20.** After fifteen years of hard labor, Jackson wondered if he would ever again see his home and family, but little did he know that his brother, Seymour, had decided to rescue him and was about to make his move.

CHAPTER TWELVE

Consistency in Verb Tense and Verb Voice

Shifts in Verb Tense

Like almost all English speakers and writers, you use verb tenses quite unconsciously. If you are discussing something that happened in the past, you use the past tense without giving it a second thought *(I **ate** that entire turkey!).* If you are writing about future events, you very naturally shift to future tense *(I **will eat** that entire turkey!).* Sometimes, however, writers accidentally shift from one tense to another when there is no reason to do so. Such unnecessary shifts occur most commonly between the past and present tenses:

> past   present
> *When Joel <u>saw</u> the lion at the circus yesterday, he <u>sits</u> right in front of its cage*
>
> present
> *and <u>starts</u> to tease it.*

Would you agree that there is no reason for the writer to shift to the present tense in the above example? All three actions occurred in the past, so all three should be written in the past tense. Of course, you *should* shift tenses if the meaning requires such a shift, as in the following example:

> present   future   past
> *Alex <u>hopes</u> that he <u>will win</u> tonight's lottery because last weekend he <u>lost</u> all of his rent money in Las Vegas.*

Past-Tense Verbs Ending in -*d* and -*ed*

Sometimes you might mistakenly write a past-tense verb in its present-tense form by leaving off a -*d* or -*ed* ending. This problem is particularly common for students who do not pronounce those endings when they speak. If such is the case in your writing, you need to look closely at each of your verbs as you proofread your papers. If you are discussing an event that occurred in the past, add -*d* or -*ed* where such endings are needed.

(incorrect)   *After the party last night, Mark <u>thank</u> Fiona for giving him a ride home.*

(correct)   *After the party last night, Mark <u>thanked</u> Fiona for giving him a ride home.*

Supposed to, Used to

Two verbs that are often incorrectly written without the -*d* ending are *suppose* and *use* when they are followed by the word *to*. Don't leave the -*d* off the ending just because you don't hear it. (It tends to be combined with the *t* in *to*.)

(incorrect)   *Calvin is <u>suppose to</u> be on a diet, but he can't get <u>use to</u> skipping his usual dessert of chocolate chip ice cream.*

(correct)   *Calvin is <u>supposed to</u> be on a diet, but he can't get <u>used to</u> skipping his usual dessert of chocolate chip ice cream.*

Verb Tense When Discussing Someone Else's Writing

Throughout this text, you are asked to respond to what other writers have written. You should use the present tense when you write about someone else's writing—whether it be nonfiction, fiction, or poetry—or when you write about film. Be careful not to inadvertently shift to the past tense.

(incorrect)   *In "Why I Won't Buy My Sons Toy Guns," Robert Shaffer <u>claims</u> toys are teachers. He <u>said</u> that toy guns will teach children to solve problems with violence.*

(correct)   *In "Why I Won't Buy My Sons Toy Guns," Robert Shaffer <u>claims</u> toys are teachers. He <u>says</u> that toy guns will teach children to solve problems with violence.*

EXERCISE   Revise the following paragraphs to correct any unnecessary shifts in verb tense.

1 In "The Thin Grey Line," Marya Mannes says that the difference between right and wrong is becoming blurred. 2 She wrote that today's society was losing its moral fiber. 3 I agreed with many of the points that Mannes makes.

4 One point I agree with was that the parents of today's children cross the "thin grey line" many times a day. 5 When I was a child, my parents use to hide my brother and me on the floor of our Pinto so they would not have to pay for us when we go to drive-in movies. 6 And when I am too old for a Kids' Meal at McDonald's, they would lie and get me one anyway. 7 As I grew older, these things do not seem wrong to me. 8 I thought that as long as I didn't get caught there is nothing wrong.

9 Mannes also wrote, "Your son's friend admitted cheating at exams because 'everybody does it.'" 10 I have to admit that I also have cheat on an exam or two and that many people I know have done the same. 11 In the eleventh grade a student I know manage to get a copy of the exam we were suppose to take the next day. 12 He then proceeds to distribute it to his friends, and no one ever was caught. 13 Did we all learn a lesson? 14 We sure did. 15 We learn how easy it is to cheat.

16 All in all, the morality of the nation was headed in the wrong direction. 17 And if this generation is bad, what will the next generation be like? 18 Mannes's solution was a good one. 19 We use to be a moral nation, and we can be one again if we educate people. 20 We should start with the children before they became corrupt in their thinking.

Shifts in Verb Voice

Verb voice refers to the relationship between the subject and the verb of a sentence. If the subject is *performing* ("doing") the action of the verb, the sentence is in the **active** voice. If the subject is *receiving* the action of the verb, the sentence is in the **passive** voice. Note that the subject is the "doer" in the following active-voice sentence:

                                     S   V

(active voice)   *A red-tailed hawk seized the unsuspecting rabbit.*
                (The subject—the hawk—*performs* the action.)

Now compare the above active-voice sentence with its passive-voice counterpart:

                                     S   V

(passive voice)   *The unsuspecting rabbit was seized by a red-tailed hawk.*
                (The subject—the rabbit—*receives* the action.)

Identifying Verb Voice

To distinguish between active and passive voice, first identify the verb itself, and then ask the following questions:

1. Does the subject perform the action of the verb, or does it receive the action? If the subject performs the action, the sentence is in the active voice; if the subject receives the action, the sentence is in the passive voice.

2. Does the verb consist of a form of *to be* and a past participle? The forms of *to be* are *am, are, is, was, were, be, being,* and *been. Any* verb consisting of one of these verb forms *and* a past participle is in the passive voice. All of the following verbs, therefore, are automatically passive: *has been eaten, is passed, was purchased, might be seen, were stolen.*

Choosing the Active Voice

Most writers prefer the active voice, so they try not to shift to the passive voice unless there is a good reason to do so. One reason writers prefer the active voice is that it requires fewer words than the passive. In the above examples about the hawk and the rabbit, for instance, the active voice requires only seven words while the passive voice requires nine. Two extra words don't seem excessive, do they? But over the course of an entire essay, those needless words begin to add up, creating a sense of looseness and wordiness that can detract from the effectiveness of your writing.

Another reason writers choose active voice is that passive-voice verbs, as the word *passive* implies, lack the forcefulness of active-voice verbs. Because the subject in the passive voice *receives* the action rather than *performs* it, there is a sense that the sentence is not moving forward. In fact, too many passive-voice verbs can make your writing dull and lifeless.

Finally, the passive voice often obscures the real performer of the action, either by placing that performer in a prepositional phrase following the verb or by omitting the performer altogether. Who, for example, is the person who denies the building permit in the following sentence?

After serious consideration, your request for a building permit has been denied.

Not all verbs must be either active or passive. For example, when a form of to be (am, are, is, was, were, be, being, been) is the main verb of a sentence, no action is shown at all, so the verb is neither active nor passive. Verbs of this type are called linking verbs. Although these verbs are not passive, you can often improve your writing by replacing them with active-voice verbs.

S   V

(linking verb)   *Mrs. Mallard's driving is quite reckless.*

              S   V

(active voice)   *Mrs. Mallard <u>drives</u> quite recklessly.*

Choosing the Passive Voice

If the above discussion has left you with the impression that you should write in the active voice, it has achieved its purpose. But don't be misled—the passive voice does have a place in good writing, particularly in the following situations:

1. Use the passive voice when the performer of an action is unimportant or when the receiver of the action needs to be emphasized.

     S   V

   <u>All</u> of the buildings <u>had been inspected</u> by noon yesterday.
   (Who did the inspecting is not important.)

2. Use passive voice when the performer of the action is unknown.

                 S   V

   Last night my <u>car was stolen</u> from the Wal-Mart parking lot.
   (Who stole the car is not known.)

3. Use passive voice when the receiver of the action needs to be emphasized.

                            S   V

   During the Holocaust, <u>Jewish people were executed</u> by the hundreds of thousands.
   (The receiver of the action—Jewish people—is being emphasized.)

Changing the Passive Voice to the Active Voice

Some people write too many sentences in the passive voice merely because they cannot figure out how to change them to the active voice. Use these suggestions to help you revise your passive sentences to active ones:

1. If the performer of the action is an object (usually following the verb), reverse the subject and the object.

                                  S   O

   (passive voice)   *The CD-ROM drive was purchased by John for $200.*

                          S   O

   (active voice)   *John purchased the CD-ROM drive for $200.*

2. If the performer of the action has been left out of the sentence, write it in as the subject.

                               S   V

   (passive voice)   *Every official transcript was destroyed last night.*

                 S   V

(active voice)   *Last night's fire destroyed every official transcript.*

3. Change the verb.

                                 V

(passive voice)   *Stephen Spielberg was given an Academy Award for directing* Schindler's List.

                                V

(active voice)   *Stephen Spielberg received an Academy Award for directing* Schindler's List.

EXERCISE   Rewrite the following sentences so that they use the active voice. When necessary, supply the missing performer of the action. Some of the sentences may already use the active voice.

1. Alice was invited to play croquet by the Queen of Hearts.

2. Several trees were uprooted during the recent storm.

3. Mario had been training for the marathon for six months.

4. Janet was not allowed to watch the movie because her homework was not yet completed.

5. Hundreds of oil workers were flown to Kuwait to help put out oil fires.

6. Airline passengers are routinely checked by security guards to make sure no weapons are being carried on board.

7. Many scenes of American life in the 1950s were painted by Norman Rockwell.

8. Fireworks are considered dangerous by many people and have been outlawed by many cities.

9. The check from her employer had been mailed to Ms. McCormick on Friday.

10. The algebra rules were read over and over until they were finally memorized.

11. The strong wind bent the newly planted birch tree to the ground.

12. Blue skies and warm weather are hoped for by everyone who has been invited to the picnic.

13. Darnell is studying to be a doctor even though he does not know how his tuition will be paid.

14. Herman started to worry when he was told that wasps had been seen flying into his bedroom.

15. A llama and an aardvark were chased from one end of the park to the other by six worried zookeepers.

CHAPTER THIRTEEN

Subject-Verb Agreement

Subject-verb agreement refers to the need for the form of the verb you have used in a sentence to match the form of its subject. If the subject of your sentence is singular, your verb must be singular. If the subject is plural, your verb must be plural.

You need to pay special attention to subject-verb agreement when you use present-tense verbs. **Most present-tense verbs that have singular subjects end in s. Most present-tense verbs that have plural subjects do not end in s.** Here are some examples:

Singular	**Plural**
The bird flie**s**.	The birds fly.
He sing**s**.	They sing.
It i**s**.	They are.
The child ha**s**.	The children have.
She doe**s**.	They do.

Notice that in each case the verb ends in *s* when the subject is singular. This rule can be confusing because an *s* at the end of a *noun* almost always means that the noun is plural, but an **s at the end of a *verb* almost always means it is singular.**

Problem Areas

Almost all subject-verb agreement errors occur for one of two reasons: Either the writer has identified the wrong word as the subject of the verb or the writer has mistaken a singular subject for a plural one (or vice versa). The following points address these two problems.

1. **Subjects are never part of a prepositional phrase.** Prepositional phrases often occur between the subject and the verb. Do not confuse the object of the prepositional phrase with the subject of the verb.

       S   V

One of our neighbor's dogs <u>*barks*</u> *every night.*

The subject is *One*, not *dogs*, because *dogs* is part of the prepositional phrase *of our neighbor's dogs.*

Here is a list of common prepositions to help you identify prepositional phrases:

about	because of	except	of	toward
above	before	for	on	under
across	behind	from	onto	until
after	below	in	over	up
among	beside	in spite of	past	upon
around	between	into	through	with
as	by	like	till	without
at	during	near	to	

2. **The order of the subject and verb is reversed in sentences that begin with *there* or *here* and in questions.**

         V   S

There were several people in the park this morning.

        V   S

Here is the person with the keys.

      V   S

Is the plane on time?

      V   S

Was the photo album in the box in the attic?

3. **Only the subject affects the form of the verb.**

              S   V

Our least concern is the people next door.

The singular verb form is correct here because the subject is the singular noun *concern*. The plural noun *people* does not affect the form of the verb.

4. **Two subjects joined by *and* are plural.**

          S   S   V

The puppet and the grasshopper were an unusual pair.

      S   S   V

Steak and eggs sound good to me.

5. **If a subject is modified by *each* or *every*, it is singular.**

          S   S   V

Every *can and bottle on the beach was picked up.*

S   S   V
Each driver and bicyclist is eligible to enter the contest.

6. **Indefinite pronouns are usually singular.** See page 312 for a list of indefinite pronouns.

S   V
Each of the contestants is on the stage.

S   V
Everyone in the stadium has a white flag.

7. **A few nouns and indefinite pronouns, such as *none, some, all, most, more, part,* and *half* (and other fractions), may sometimes be considered plural and sometimes singular, depending on the prepositional phrase that follows them.**

                    S   V
(singular)   *Some of the food is missing.*

                    S   V
(plural)   *Some of the cars were stolen.*

8. **When the subjects are joined by *either/or, neither/nor, not only/but also,* or just *or,* the verb agrees with the subject closer to it.**

              S   S   V
Neither Maria ***nor*** her sisters want to leave the house.

Of course, if you reverse the order of the subjects above, you must change the verb form.

              S   S   V
Neither her sisters ***nor*** Maria wants to leave the house.

This rule also applies to questions.

   V   S   S   V
*Does Maria **or** her sisters want to leave the house?*

   V   S   S   V
*Do her sisters **or** Maria want to leave the house?*

Note: When you have helping verbs in a sentence, as in the example above, the helping verb—not the main verb—changes form.

9. **Collective nouns usually take the singular form of the verb.** Collective nouns represent groups of people or things, but they are considered singular. Some common collective nouns are *audience, band, class, committee, crowd, family, flock, group, herd, jury, society,* and *team.*

S V
The jury was told to reach its verdict quickly as possible.

S V
My family goes to Yellowstone National Park every summer.

10. **The relative pronouns *that, which,* and *who* may be either singular or plural.** When one of these pronouns is the subject of a verb, you will need to know which word it refers to before you decide whether it is singular or plural.

                                        S   V
(singular)   *I bought the peach that was ripe.*

                                        S   V
(plural)   *I bought the peaches that were ripe.*

                                                S   V
(plural)   *Colleen is one of the students who are taking flying lessons.*

                                                S   V
(singular)   *Colleen is the only one of the students who is taking flying lessons.*

11. **A few nouns end in *s* but are considered singular; they take the singular form of the verb.** These nouns include *economics, gymnastics, mathematics, measles, mumps, physics,* and *politics.*

                        S   V
International politics is not my favorite field of study.

            S   V
Mathematics has been difficult for me.

12. **When units of measurement for distance, time, volume, height, weight, money, and so on are used as subjects, they usually take the singular verb form.**

            S   V
Two teaspoons of sugar was all that the cake recipe called for.

            S   V
Five dollars is too much to pay for a hot dog.

EXERCISE   Circle the subjects and underline the correct verb form (in parentheses) for each one.

1. Someone with too many children (has)(have) been turned away from the theater.

2. (Do)(Does) the guard at the gate or the people waiting in line know whether or not the concert is canceled?

3. His dream of success and his fear of failure always (keep)(keeps) Joe feeling frustrated.

4. The audience attending last night's premiere (was)(were) disgusted by the performance.

5. Even though many people do not think so, measles (is)(are) a serious illness.

6. A coffee table along with two chairs and a sofa (cost)(costs) $1,000 at Jerome's Furniture.

7. Five hundred miles (is)(are) a long way from home.

8. Here (is)(are) the lawn food and snail bait that you ordered.

9. Every man, woman, and child attending the recent Padres baseball games (has)(have) wondered if things can get much worse.

10. Neither his sisters nor his wife (visit)(visits) Mr. Parker in the rest home very often.

11. One of the children who (live)(lives) on our street has green hair.

12. Politics (seem)(seems) to be all that Mr. Washington ever wants to discuss.

13. A group of anti-lepidopterists (has)(have) recently started to demand equal rights for butterflies.

14. Anyone from the nearby apartment houses along with any relatives (is)(are) allowed to use the recreation room.

15. There (was)(were), according to every report that Salvatore had ever read, only one reason to reduce the tuna fishing fleet.

EXERCISE

Correct any subject-verb agreement errors in the following sentences. If a sentence is correct, do nothing to it. To check your answers, circle the subjects.

1. Either the telephone book or the encyclopedia have enough weight to press that flower.

2. After last night's concert, everyone who had attended were praising the quality of the orchestra.

3. Every book and magazine in the library has been attacked by bookworms.

4. No matter how hard he studied, mathematics were Albert's worst subject.

5. In the past two weeks, there has been a fistfight and a mugging in the walkway near the cafeteria.

6. Marge, along with her friend Leona, send letters to the editor every week.

7. A herd of buffalo cross the stream behind my house every evening.

8. Does the Del Mar Fair or the Pomona County Fair make the most money?

9. Mr. Gadget is one of the people who applies for a new patent nearly every year.

10. On the roof of the business across the street stands a large wooden chicken and a gigantic ax.

11. Each of the fifteen applicants from the three different cities were presented with a bowl of fruit.

12. My family, together with the people next door, help to clean up the street every month.

13. Elmer's main concern was the flies and bugs that kept invading his house.

14. Everyone who knows the Delgados think that they should have been asked to lead the parade.

15. Fifteen minutes have passed since we received our last telephone solicitation.

CHAPTER FOURTEEN

Pronoun Agreement and Reference

Pronoun-Antecedent Agreement

Because pronouns stand for or take the place of nouns, it is important that you make clear in your writing which pronouns stand for which nouns. The noun that the pronoun takes the place of is called the **antecedent.** The term **pronoun-antecedent agreement** refers to the idea that a pronoun must match, or "agree with," the noun that it stands for in **person** and **number.**

Person

Person, in describing pronouns, refers to the relationship of the speaker (or writer) to the pronoun. There are three persons: **first person, second person,** and **third person.**

1. **First-person** pronouns refer to the person speaking or writing:

Singular	Plural
I	we
me	us
my, mine	our, ours

2. **Second-person** pronouns refer to the person spoken or written to:

Singular	Plural
you	you
you	you
your, yours	your, yours

3. **Third-person** pronouns refer to the person or thing spoken or written about:

Singular	Plural
he, she, it	they
him, her, it	them
his, her, hers, its	their, theirs

Because nouns are almost always in the third person, pronouns that refer to nouns should also be in the third person. Usually this rule poses no problem, but sometimes writers mistakenly shift from third to second person when they are referring to a noun.

> When _a person_ first enters the Department of Motor Vehicles, _you_ might feel overwhelmed by the crowd of people.

In this sentence, y*o*u has mistakenly been used to refer to _person_. The mistake occurs because the noun _person_ is in the third person, but the pronoun _you_ is in the second person. There are two ways to correct the sentence:

1. You can change the second-person pronoun _you_ to a third-person pronoun.

> When _a person_ first enters the Department of Motor Vehicles, _he or she_ might feel overwhelmed by the crowd of people.

2. You can change the noun _person_ to the second-person pronoun _you_.

> When _you_ first enter the Department of Motor Vehicles, _you_ might feel overwhelmed by the crowd of people.

Here is another incorrect sentence.

> Most _visitors_ to the Wild Animal Park will have a good time if _you_ follow the signs and do not stray off the marked path.

One way to correct this sentence is to change _you_ to _they_ so that it agrees with _visitors_.

> Most _visitors_ to the Wild Animal Park will have a good time if _they_ follow the signs and do not stray off the marked path.

Number

Errors in number are the most common pronoun-antecedent errors. To make pronouns agree with their antecedents in **number,** use singular pronouns to refer to singular nouns and plural pronouns to refer to plural nouns. The following guidelines will help you avoid errors in number:

1. When you use a pronoun to refer to words joined by _and_, you should use a plural pronoun unless the words are modified by _each_ or _every_.

> _Benjamin Franklin_ and _Thomas Edison_ were both known for _their_ work with electricity.
> **Every** _dog_ and _cat_ in the kennel had lost _its_ appetite.

2. Because the following indefinite pronouns are singular, you should use singular pronouns to refer to them.

anybody	either	neither	one
anyone	everybody	nobody	somebody
anything	everyone	no one	someone
each	everything	nothing	something

> _Everything_ that he said seemed to have _its_ own secret meaning.

Neither of the contestants wanted to trade *her* prize for an unmarked door.
One of the children was staring sadly at *his* broken toy.

Note: In spoken English, the plural pronouns *they, them*, and *their* are often used to refer to the antecedents *everyone* or *everybody*. However, in written English the singular pronoun is still more commonly used.

Everybody on the men's hockey team determined to do *his* best.

3. **You should use singular pronouns to refer to collective nouns.** Some common collective nouns are *audience, band, class, committee, crowd, family, flock, group, herd, jury, society*, and *team*.

   The *class* decided to skip *its* scheduled break in order to review for the test.
   The *family* next door spent *its* summer in the Grand Canyon last year.

4. **When antecedents are joined by the following words, you should use a pronoun that agrees with the closer antecedent.**

   either/or
   neither/nor
   nor
   or
   not only/but also

   Neither *Mr. Snead* nor the *golfers* remembered to bring *their* golf shoes.

   The plural pronoun *their* agrees with the plural noun *golfers* because *golfers* is the closer noun.

Sexist Language

In the past it has been traditional to use masculine pronouns when referring to singular nouns whose gender could be either masculine or feminine. A good example is the sentence *A **driver** should slow down whenever **he** approaches a blind intersection*. Although the noun *driver* could be either masculine or feminine, traditionally only masculine pronouns like *he* or *his* have been used in a case like this one.

Because females make up over 50 percent of the English-speaking population, many of them have been justifiably dissatisfied with this tradition. The problem is that the English language does not contain a singular personal pronoun that can refer to either sex at the same time in the way that the forms of *they* can.

The solutions to this problem can prove awkward. One of the solutions is to use feminine pronouns as freely as masculine ones to refer to singular nouns whose gender could be masculine or feminine. Either of the following sentences using this solution is acceptable.

A driver should slow down whenever she approaches a blind intersection.
A driver should slow down whenever he approaches a blind intersection.

Another solution is to change the *he* to *he or she*. Then the sentence would look like this:

A <u>driver</u> should slow down whenever <u>he or she</u> approaches a blind intersection.

As you can see, this solution does not result in a very graceful sentence. Still another alternative is to use *she/he*, but the result would be about the same as the one above. Sometimes a better solution is to change a singular antecedent to a plural one and use the forms of *they*, which can refer to either gender. Doing so would result in a sentence like this:

<u>Drivers</u> should slow down whenever <u>they</u> approach a blind intersection.

This sentence is less awkward and just as fair. Finally, in some situations, the masculine pronoun alone will be appropriate, and in others the feminine pronoun alone will be. Here are two such sentences:

<u>Each</u> of the football players threw <u>his</u> helmet into the air after the victory.
(The football team is all male.)

One member of the Arabian swim team passed <u>her</u> opponent ten yards before the finish line.
(The swim team is all female.)

Whatever your solutions to this problem, it is important that you be logical and correct in your subject-verb agreement in addition to being fair.

EXERCISE   Choose the pronoun (in parentheses) that agrees with the antecedent. When you choose a pronoun, you may also need to change the verb.

1. If a motorcyclist rides without a helmet in California, (you)(he or she)(they) will be given a ticket.

2. Everybody who attended the Fourth of July party brought (their)(his or her) own food.

3. When a person is first learning to work with a computer, (you)(they)(he or she) might feel a little intimidated.

4. While the jury delivered (their)(its) verdict, the defendant stood and stared at the floor.

5. Neither Oliver nor Stanley visited (his)(their) mother on Mother's Day.

6. The zookeeper was stunned when he realized that not only an orangutan but also three monkeys had managed to escape from (its)(their) enclosure.

7. Last year the most successful company in the county refused to give (its)(their) employees a raise.

8. Although Esther likes to visit Lake Arrowhead, the drive up to the lake tends to make (you)(her) nervous.

9. Someone keeps calling me on the phone, but (she)(they) won't say anything.

10. A noisy patron of that library will sometimes be asked to lower (their)(his or her) voice.

11. Each of the members of Footwear Anonymous vowed to throw all of (their)(his or her) shoes into the garbage.

12. After the humiliating defeat, the team boarded (their)(its) bus and headed for home.

13. Skinner could tell that either the pigeon or the mouse would soon learn to signal for (its)(their) food.

14. Leona grabbed her scuba gear and headed for the beach, even though she knew that (you)(she) shouldn't dive without a partner.

15. Andrea, who moved here from Vermont, and Charlie, who used to live in Australia, were distressed when (they)(he or she) first saw all the smog.

Unclear Pronoun Reference

Sometimes, even though a pronoun appears to agree with an antecedent, it is not clear exactly which noun in the sentence is the antecedent. And sometimes a writer will use a pronoun that does not clearly refer to any antecedent at all. The following two points will help you to use pronouns correctly.

1. A pronoun should refer to a specific antecedent.

> _The principal_ told _Mr. Aldonado_ that _his_ son had been arrested by the police.

In this sentence, _his_ could refer to the _principal_ or to _Mr. Aldonado_. To correct this problem, you can eliminate the pronoun.

> _The principal_ told _Mr. Aldonado_ that _Mr. Aldonado's_ son had been arrested by the police.

Or you can revise the sentence so that the pronoun clearly refers to only one antecedent.

> _The principal_ told _Mr. Aldonado_, "Your son has been arrested by the police."

2. Pronouns should not refer to implied or unstated antecedents. Be especially careful with the pronouns _this, that, which,_ and _it_.

> In the paper _it_ says that the weather will be rainy for the next two months.
> The game was canceled even though we had driven five hundred miles to see it; _this_ was unfair.

In these sentences, there are no specific antecedents for the pronouns *it* and *this* to refer to. The following sentences clarify the pronoun reference.

<u>The weather report</u> in the paper says that the weather will be rainy for the next two months.

The game was canceled even though we had driven five hundred miles to see it; <u>canceling the game after we had driven so far</u> was unfair.

Sometimes a pronoun refers to a noun that is only implied in the first part of the sentence.

Mr. Brouillard is a fisherman, <u>which</u> he does every weekend.

In this sentence, the *which* apparently refers to *fishing*, which is implied in the noun *fisherman*; however, there is no specific noun for the pronoun *which* to refer to. The faulty pronoun reference can be cleared up in several ways.

Mr. Brouillard is a fisherman, <u>and he goes fishing</u> every weekend.
Mr. Brouillard is a fisherman <u>who fishes</u> every weekend.

EXERCISE

Correct all errors in pronoun-antecedent agreement as well as in pronoun reference in the following sentences. If a sentence is correct, do nothing to it.

1. Juan had planned to visit his uncle last weekend, but he was not feeling well.

2. Mr. Baurmeister missed his bus three days in a row, which frustrated him.

3. When someone is blindfolded and turned in a circle, you can easily lose your sense of direction.

4. That flock of pigeons seems to think that the roof of my house is their home.

5. Anybody who responds to this questionnaire will receive a free trip to the country of her choice.

6. The health department recently closed down a local restaurant because it found rats in the kitchen, and this distressed the people who usually eat there.

7. The rock group at last night's concert must know that their performance was absolutely terrible.

8. If a person is rude to retail clerks, you shouldn't be surprised if they are rude back.

9. Last summer, Mr. Smith kept burning garbage in his backyard, which caused my neighbors to sell their house and move away.

10. Just as the police officer was about to write my mother a ticket for speeding, she fainted.

11. Whenever one of Jethro's sisters tastes his homemade beer, they shudder from head to toe.

12. Will you please take either the grapes on the counter or the watermelon in the refrigerator and put it into the picnic basket?

13. On the news it said that last night's fire was started by an arsonist.

14. Whenever a driver hears a siren, you should pull to the side of the road until the emergency vehicle has passed.

15. Estella knew that she had to get out of the freezing snow, which was making her feet turn numb.

CHAPTER FIFTEEN

Pronoun Case

Pronouns, like verbs, can appear in a variety of different forms, depending on how they function in a sentence. For example, the pronoun that refers to the speaker in a sentence may be written as *I, me, my*, or *mine*. These different spellings are the result of what is called **pronoun case**.

The three pronoun cases for English are the **subjective**, the **objective**, and the **possessive**.

Subjective Case

Singular	Plural
I	we
you	you
he, she, it	they
who	who

Objective Case

Singular	Plural
me	us
you	you
him, her, it	them
whom	whom

Possessive Case

Singular	Plural
my, mine	our, ours
your, yours	your, yours
his, her, hers, its	their, theirs
whose	whose

Subjective Pronouns

The subjective pronouns are *I, we, you, he, she, it, they*, and *who*. They are used in two situations:

1. **Subjective pronouns are used as subjects of sentences.**

   S
   I will take the test next week.

   S
   They have stolen my car.

2. **Subjective pronouns are used when they follow linking verbs.** Because the linking verb *identifies* the pronoun with the subject, the pronoun must be in the same case as the subject.

   S
   It was he who found the missing link.
   (The subjective pronoun *he* is identified with the subject *it* by the linking verb *was*.)

   S
   That was I you heard speaking on the phone.

   S
   It was they who won the final game of the series.

Objective Pronouns

The **objective pronouns** are *me, us, you, him, her, it, them,* and *whom*. They are used in three situations:

1. **Objective pronouns are used as objects of prepositions.**

   Oliver stared at the birthday card that Stanley had given to him.
   The disagreement between Shayla and me was not really very serious.

2. **Objective pronouns are used as direct objects of action verbs.** The noun or pronoun that receives the action of the action verb is called the **direct object.** For example, in the sentence *Tuan visited Serena yesterday*, the verb is *visited*, an action verb. The direct object of *visited* is *Serena* because *Serena* receives the action of the verb *visited*. If you substitute a pronoun for *Serena*, it must be the objective pronoun *her: Tuan visited* **her** *yesterday*.

   Tyrone insulted her at the party last night.
   After we ate dinner, Juanita took me to the mall.
   Mr. Kong picked up all of the banana peels and threw them out the window.

3. **Objective pronouns are used as indirect objects.** The **indirect object** indicates **to whom or for whom (or to what or for what) an action is directed,** but the prepositions *to* and *for* are left out.

(prepositional phrase)   *He gave the flowers <u>to her</u>.*

(indirect object)   *He gave <u>her</u> the flowers.*

In the first sentence, *her* is the object of the preposition *to*. In the second sentence, the *to* is omitted and the pronoun is moved, making *her* the indirect object. In both sentences, the direct object is *flowers*. Here are other examples:

She had already told <u>him</u> the secret password.
My sister showed <u>them</u> a baseball that had been autographed by Babe Ruth.

Possessive Pronouns

The **possessive pronouns** are *my, mine, our, ours, your, yours, his, her, hers, its, their, theirs,* and *whose.* They are used in two situations:

1. **Possessive pronouns are used as adjectives to indicate possession.**

   Mrs. Cleaver could not believe what <u>her</u> ears had just heard.
   Lumpy and Eddie looked sheepishly at <u>their</u> feet.
   Wally looked at the car and wondered who had stolen <u>its</u> tires.

   Note: the contraction *it's* means "it is." The word *its* is the only possessive form for *it.* (In fact, you do not use apostrophes with any of the possessive pronouns.)

2. **Some possessive pronouns indicate possession without being used as adjectives.** In this case, they may be used as subjects or objects.

   I used my father's watch because <u>mine</u> was broken.
   (Here the possessive pronoun *mine* is the subject of its clause.)

   Maria's room is neat, but <u>yours</u> is a mess.
   (In this example, *yours* is the subject of its clause.)

   Arlo rented a car because he had sold <u>his</u>.
   (Here the possessive pronoun *his* is a direct object.)

Common Sources of Errors in Pronoun Case

Compound Constructions

Compound subjects and objects often cause problems when they include pronouns. If your sentence includes a compound construction, be sure you use the correct pronoun case.

(compound subject)	_Melissa and she_ own a fifty-acre ranch.
(compound after linking verb)	_That was <u>Leslie and I</u> whom you spoke to last night._
(compound object of a preposition)	_After the fire, the police took statements from <u>my brother and me</u>._
(compound direct object)	_Julio saw <u>Mark and him</u> at the racetrack._
(compound indirect object)	_She gave <u>him and me</u> a reward when we found her lost dog._

In most cases, you can use a simple test to check whether you have chosen the right pronoun case when you have a compound construction. Simply remove one of the subjects or objects so that only one pronoun is left. For example, is this sentence correct? _Our host gave **Erin and I** a drink_. Test it by dropping **Erin and**. _Our host gave **I** a drink_. Now you can see that the _I_ should be _me_ because it is an object (an indirect object). The correct sentence should read: _Our host gave **Erin and me** a drink_.

Who *and* Whom

When to use _who_ or _whom_ is a mystery to many writers, but you should have no problem with these pronouns if you remember two simple rules:

1. Use the subjective pronoun _who_ or _whoever_ if it is used as the subject of a verb.

2. Use the objective pronoun _whom_ or _whomever_ if it is not used as the subject of a verb.

   While standing in line at the bus depot, I saw someone <u>who</u> looked like my long-lost brother.
   (_Who_ is the subject of _looked_.)

   The position will be given to the person <u>whom</u> the committee finds most qualified.
   (_Whom_ is not the subject of a verb.)

   This wallet should be returned to <u>whoever</u> lost it.
   (_Whoever_ is the subject of _lost_.)

Comparisons

When a pronoun is used in a comparison, you often need to supply the implied words in order to know what pronoun case to use. For example, in the sentence _My brother cannot_ *skate as well as I*, the implied words are the verb *can skate*: *My brother cannot skate as well as I* [*can skate.*]

When we visited the petting zoo, the animals seemed to like my brother more than <u>me</u>.

You can tell that *me* is the correct case in this sentence when you supply the implied words:

When we visited the petting zoo, the animals seemed to like my brother more than <u>[they liked]</u> <u>me</u>.

Appositives

An appositive is a word group containing a noun or pronoun that renames another noun or pronoun. When the appositive contains a **pronoun** that does the renaming, be sure that the pronoun is in the same case as the word it renames. (For more discussion of appositives, see pages 162–165.)

Three employees—Miguel, Pierre, and <u>I</u>— were fired for insubordination.

Here *I* is in the subjective case because the appositive *Miguel, Pierre, and I* renames the word *employees*, the subject of the sentence.

This report is the responsibility of only two people, Mark and <u>her</u>.

Here *her* is in the objective case because the appositive *Mark and her* renames *people*, the object of the preposition *of*.

EXERCISE   In each sentence, underline the correct pronoun form (in parentheses).

1. Just between you and (I)(me), do you really think we should eat this entire gallon of ice cream?

2. A small striped kitten is drinking (its)(it's) milk from a green bowl.

3. The tram took Bill and (he)(him) on a ride through Universal Studios.

4. It was (she)(her) (who)(whom) your cousin met at the party last night.

5. The Leonards next door bought many more fireworks for the Fourth of July than (we)(us).

6. Ask Amy and (she)(her) to water our lawn while we are on vacation.

7. The hunters (who)(whom) had exceeded their limit drove slowly down the dark road.

8. Do Tiffany and (her)(she) have any extra money with them?

9. Two skiers, Alberto and (he)(him), have a chance to win the gold medal.

10. Was it (they)(them) (who)(whom) we saw coming out of the House of Mirrors?

11. The prize goes to (whoever)(whomever) can eat this 5-gallon jar of pickles in the least amount of time.

12. Sam wondered why his parents would not buy a new jet ski for his sister and (he)(him).

13. The instructor knew that three students—Marcia, Fred, and (I)(me)—had not studied for the test.

14. Horace complained that the judges gave the other participants more attention that (he)(him).

15. (It's)(Its) loud, grinding sound frightened Steve and (she)(her).

EXERCISE   Correct any errors in pronoun case in the following sentences. Some sentences may not contain errors.

1. Mr. Livingston loves to visit Africa, but his sister is much less fond of that country than him.

2. Where have Orville and he put the parachute?

3. Henrietta was sure that it was George who she saw on the Ferris wheel.

4. On the camping trip, our guide told Armando and I a terrifying story.

5. Karen was irritated when the guard gave passes to only two people, Jodi and she.

6. Its too bad that your dog hurt it's neck when its chain became caught in the tractor.

7. The giraffe stared at Yolie and I as we crept into its enclosure.

8. Until he insulted our daughter, Oscar and we have always been good friends.

9. Yvonne and Eunice, whom were passengers on the *Titanic*, feel uncomfortable whenever they take a bath.

10. Although Frank and Joe spoke to all of the neighbors, the Bobbsey twins still sold more tickets than them.

11. Between Ramona and he stood a huge marble column covered with mysterious inscriptions.

12. Show the guest of honor and them to the table.

13. Both Mary and Jorge were seriously ill, but the doctor gave Mary more medication than him.

14. The flight attendant who Salvatore kept harassing finally dumped a cup of coffee on his lap.

15. To the winners of the marathon, Hal and him, the judges gave blister ointment and bandages.

CHAPTER SIXTEEN

Misplaced and Dangling Modifiers

Misplaced Modifiers

Misplaced modifiers are exactly what their name says they are—modifiers that have been "misplaced" within a sentence. But how is a modifier "misplaced"? The answer is simple. If you remember that a modifier is nearly always placed just before or just after the word it modifies, then a misplaced modifier must be one that has been mistakenly placed so that it causes a reader to be confused about what it modifies. Consider the following sentence, for example:

A police officer told us <u>slowly</u> to raise our hands.

Does the modifier *slowly* state how the officer told us, or does it state how we were supposed to raise our hands? Changing the placement of the modifier will clarify the meaning.

A police officer <u>slowly</u> told us to raise our hands.
(Here the word modifies the verb *told*.)

A police officer told us to raise our hands <u>slowly</u>.
(Here the word modifies the infinitive *to raise*.)

Misplaced Words

Any modifier can be misplaced, but one particular group of modifiers causes quite a bit of trouble for many people. These words are *only, almost, just, merely*, and *nearly*. Consider, for example, the following sentences:

By buying her new waterbed on sale, Maureen <u>almost</u> saved $100.
By buying her new waterbed on sale, Maureen saved <u>almost</u> $100.

As you can see, these sentences actually make two different statements. In the first sentence, *almost* modifies *saved*. If you *almost* saved something, you did *not* save it. In the second sentence, *almost* modifies *$100*. If you saved *almost* $100, you saved $85, $90, $95, or some other amount close to $100.

Which statement does the writer want to make—that Maureen did *not* save any money or that she *did* save an amount close to $100? Because the point was that she bought her waterbed on sale, the second sentence makes more sense.

To avoid confusion, be sure that you place all of your modifiers carefully.

(incorrect)   *Her coach told her <u>often</u> to work out with weights.*

(correct)   *Her coach <u>often</u> told her to work out with weights.*

(incorrect)   *Kara <u>nearly</u> ate a gallon of ice cream yesterday.*

(correct)   *Kara ate <u>nearly</u> a gallon of ice cream yesterday.*

Misplaced Phrases and Clauses

Phrases and clauses are as easily misplaced as individual words. Generally, phrases and clauses should appear immediately before or after the words they modify. Notice how misplaced phrases and clauses confuse the meaning of the following sentences.

A bird flew over the house <u>with blue wings</u>.
The irritated secretary slapped at the fly <u>typing the report</u>.
They gave the food to the dog <u>left over from dinner</u>.
Lucia smashed the car into a telephone pole <u>that she had borrowed from her sister</u>.

Obviously, misplaced phrases and clauses can cause rather confusing (and sometimes even humorous) situations. However, when such clauses are placed close to the words they modify, their meaning is clear.

A bird <u>with blue wings</u> flew over the house.
The irritated secretary <u>typing the report</u> slapped at the fly.
<u>Typing the report,</u> the irritated secretary slapped at the fly.
They gave the food <u>left over from dinner</u> to the dog.
Lucia smashed the car <u>that she had borrowed from her sister</u> into a telephone pole.

Whether the modifier appears before or after the word it modifies, the point is that you should place a modifier so that it clearly refers to a specific word in the sentence.

Dangling Modifiers

A **dangling modifier** is usually an introductory phrase (usually a verbal phrase) that lacks an appropriate subject to modify. Since these modifiers usually represent some sort of action, they need a **doer** or **agent** of the action represented.

For example, in the following sentence, the introductory phrase "dangles" because it is not followed by a subject that could be the "doer" of the action represented by the phrase.

Singing at the top of his voice, the song was irritating everybody at the party.

The phrase *Singing at the top of his voice* should be followed by a subject that could logically perform the action of the phrase. Instead, it is followed by the subject *song*. Was the song *singing*? Probably not. Therefore, the modifying phrase "dangles" because it has no subject to which it can logically refer. Here are some more sentences with dangling modifiers.

Completely satisfied, the painting was admired.
(Was the *painting* satisfied?)

After reviewing all of the facts, a decision was reached.
(Did the *decision* review the facts?)

To impress the judges, Cecil's mustache was waxed.
(Did the *mustache* want to impress the judges?)

As you can see, you should check for dangling modifiers when you use introductory phrases.

Correcting Dangling Modifiers

You can correct a dangling modifier in one of two ways.

1. **Rewrite the sentence so that its subject can be logically modified by the introductory modifier.**

   Completely satisfied, Vincent admired the painting.
   (*Vincent* was completely satisfied.)

   After reviewing all of the facts, I reached a decision.
   (*I* reviewed all of the facts.)

   To impress the judges, Cecil waxed his mustache.
   (*Cecil* wanted to impress the judges.)

2. **Change the introductory phrase to a clause.**

   When Vincent was completely satisfied, he admired the painting.
   After I reviewed all of the facts, I reached a decision.
   Because Cecil wanted to impress the judges, he waxed his mustache.

   Note: Do not correct a dangling modifier by moving it to the end of the sentence. In either case, it will still "dangle" because it lacks a "**doer**," or **agent**, that could perform the action of the modifier.

   (incorrect)   *After missing three meetings,* the request was denied.
                   (There is no "doer" for *missing*.)

   (still incorrect) The request was denied *after missing three meetings.*
                   (There is no "doer" for *missing*.)

(still incorrect) *After missing three meetings,* Alfredo's request was denied.
(Adding the possessive form Alfredo's does not add a "doer" of the action.)

(correct) *After Alfredo had missed three meetings, his request was denied.*
(Here the "doer" of the action is clear.)

(correct) *After missing three meetings,* Alfredo was told that *his request was denied.*
(Here *Alfredo* is clearly the person who missed the meetings.)

EXERCISE

Identify and correct any misplaced or dangling modifiers in the following sentences. Some of the sentences may be correct.

1. Waiting impatiently in the car, the party had already started.

2. The painting was found in a pawnshop that had been stolen from the museum.

3. Amber only decided to study after she had received poor grades on her first two tests.

4. Whistling under her breath, Julissa walked her dogs down the street and into the park.

5. Disappointed by his poor performance, Eli's eyes stared at the ground.

6. The dog groomer put the collie on the table with the shaggy tail and began to clip its fur.

7. After almost eating three strawberry pies, Oscar felt a bit woozy.

8. Slowly sinking toward the horizon, Bonnie and Clyde held hands and admired the sunset.

9. Butch Cassidy pulled out his pistol and shot at a coyote riding his favorite horse.

10. After robbing dozens of trains, Jesse James's luck finally ran out.

11. Sara Lee finally decided to serve the dessert to her guests that she had been keeping in the refrigerator.

12. The doctor performing the autopsy carefully recorded her findings.

13. Stepping into the living room, the television blared at me.

14. Herman will only eat vegetables if they are covered in cheese sauce.

15. While camping in the desert, a snake crawled next to my sister with a triangular head.

CHAPTER SEVENTEEN

Comma Usage

The comma is probably more troublesome to writers than any other punctuation mark. Long ago commas were used to tell readers where to put in a slight pause. Although the placement of the comma does affect the rhythm of a sentence, today it also conveys many more messages than when to pause.

Comma use can be broken down into four general rules:

1. **Use commas before coordinating conjunctions that join main clauses.**

2. **Use commas between elements in a series.**

3. **Use commas after introductory elements.**

4. **Use commas before and after interrupting elements.**

Commas Before Coordinating Conjunctions that Join Main Clauses

1. **When you join two main clauses with one of the coordinating conjunctions, place a comma before the conjunction.**

   Richard Pryor is a hilarious comedian, **and** *Robin Williams is also great in his own unique way.*

   Hercules had to shovel a huge amount of horse manure, **or** *he would never complete his task.*

2. **When conjunctions join other parts of a sentence, such as two words, two phrases, or two subordinate clauses, do not put commas before the conjunctions.**

   Every morning Charlie shaves with his favorite cleaver **and** *then goes down to breakfast with his family.*

   No comma is needed before *and* because it does not join two main clauses. It joins the verbs *shave* and *goes.*

   You can find good coffee **and** *conversation at Kafana Coffee House* **or** *at Spill the Beans.*

   No comma is required before *and* because it joins the nouns *coffee* and *conversation.*

   No comma is required before *or* because it just joins the names of the coffee shops.

Commas with Elements in a Series

1. **When you list three or more elements (words, phrases, clauses) in a series, separate them with commas.** When the last two elements are joined by a coordinating conjunction, a comma before the conjunction is optional.

   (words)   *The film* The Piano *was **intriguing, puzzling, and controversial.***

   (phrases)   *Omar enjoyed **cooking okra and Spam for his friends, competing in the Spam cooking contest at the fair, and betting on horses with strange names at the racetrack.***

   (clauses)   *While shopping at the mall, **Quinlan bought pants that were much too big, his brother bought him a hat that he could wear backwards, and his girlfriend bought some Doc Marten black boots.***

2. **When you use two or more adjectives to modify the same noun, separate them with commas if you can put *and* between the adjectives without changing the meaning or if you can easily reverse the order of the adjectives.**

   *The bear waded into the **shallow, swift** river after the salmon.*
   *The **witty, gregarious** comedian kept us laughing for hours with her stories.*

   Note that you could use *and* between the adjectives. (The river is *shallow* and *swift*; the comedian is *witty* and *gregarious*.) You could also reverse the adjectives (the *swift, shallow* river or the *gregarious, witty* comedian).

3. **On the other hand, if the adjectives cannot be joined by *and* or are not easily reversed, no commas are necessary.**

   *The computer technician wore **white cotton** gloves as she worked.*

   Notice how awkward the sentence would sound if you placed *and* between the adjectives (the *white and cotton* gloves) or if you reversed them (the *cotton white* gloves).

Commas with Introductory Elements

1. **Use a comma after introductory words and phrases.**

   Introductory Words

next	third	similarly	indeed
first	nevertheless	moreover	yes
second	therefore	however	no

Introductory Phrases

on the other hand	for example	in addition
in a similar manner	for instance	as a result
in other words	in fact	

Next, *Persephone made the mistake of eating a pomegranate.*

In addition, *Charles purchased a remote electronic noise device to embarrass his colleagues.*

2. **Use a comma after introductory prepositional phrases of five words or more.** However, you may need to use a comma after a shorter introductory prepositional phrase if not doing so would cause confusion.

Before the famous main attraction, *a very good harmonica band entertained the audience.*

In the film, *actors kept changing into androids.*

Without the comma, this last sentence might look as if it begins *in the film actors.*

Use a comma after all introductory infinitive and participial phrases.

(Infinitive phrase)	*To eat a hot dog,* *Ambrose had to forget his diet.*
(Present participial phrase)	*Running in the marathon,* *Sam finally achieved his goal.*
(Past participial phrase)	*Congregated in the student union,* *the students planned their protest.*

(See pages 122–124 for a further discussion of infinitive and participial phrases.)

3. **Use a comma after a subordinate clause that precedes a main clause.**

Because Ulysses was bored, *he wanted to go fishing again.*

Although I am an English major, *I sometimes say "Ain't."*

(See pages 93–94 for a further discussion of punctuating subordinate clauses.)

Commas with Interrupting Elements

Sometimes certain words, phrases, or clauses will interrupt the flow of thought in a sentence to add emphasis or additional information. These **interrupting elements** are enclosed by commas.

1. **Use commas to set off parenthetical expressions.** Common parenthetical expressions are *however, indeed, consequently, as a result, moreover, of course, for example, for instance, that is, in fact, after all, I think,* and *therefore.*

*A new baseball glove was, **after all,** a luxury.*

*Her old one**, therefore,** would have to do for another season.*

Note: Whenever a parenthetical expression introduces a second main clause after a semicolon, the semicolon takes the place of the comma in front of it.

*Colin was looking forward to his vacation**; moreover,** he was eager to visit his family in England.*

2. **Use commas to set off nonrestrictive elements. Nonrestrictive** elements are modifying words, phrases, or clauses that are *not* necessary to identify the words they modify. On the other hand, **restrictive** elements are those that *are* necessary to identify the words they modify. Restrictive elements are not set off with commas. **Adjective subordinate clauses, participial phrases,** and **appositives** require that you decide whether they are nonrestrictive or restrictive.

Adjective Subordinate Clauses

Adjective subordinate clauses begin with one of the relative pronouns: *who, whom, whose, which, that,* and sometimes *when* or *where.* They follow the nouns or pronouns that they modify. An adjective clause is **nonrestrictive** when it *is not necessary to identify the word it modifies.* It is enclosed in commas.

(nonrestrictive)   *Dizzy Gillespie, **who helped to develop the form of jazz known as bebop,** played an unusual trumpet.*

Because Dizzy Gillespie is named, the adjective clause *who helped to develop the form of jazz known as bebop* is nonrestrictive. It is not needed to identify Dizzy Gillespie.

(restrictive)   *One of the people **who helped to develop the form of jazz known as bebop** was Dizzy Gillespie.*

Because *who helped to develop the form of jazz* is needed to identify the "people" you are referring to, it is restrictive and is not set off with commas.

Here is another example of a nonrestrictive clause:

*My youngest sister**, who is a paleontologist,** showed me her collection of skulls.*

Because a person can have only one youngest sister, the adjective clause *is not needed to identify her,* making it nonrestrictive.

(See pages 93–94 for a further discussion of punctuating adjective clauses.)

Participial Phrases

The present participle is the "-ing" form of the verb (*eating, writing*); the past participle is the form of the verb that you would use after "have," has," or "had" (*eaten, written*).

Participial phrases that *do not contain information necessary to identify the word they modify* are nonrestrictive and are therefore set off by commas. Restrictive participial phrases do not require commas.

(nonrestrictive)   *Van Gogh,* **seeking something to paint,** *looked up into the night sky.*

Because Van Gogh is named, the participial phrase *seeking something to paint* is nonrestrictive. It is not needed to identify Van Gogh.

(restrictive)   *The man* **painting in the middle of the night** *called the work Starry Night.*

Because the man is not named, the participial phrase *painting in the middle of the night* is restrictive.

(See pages 122–124 for a further discussion of participial phrases.)

Appositives

An **appositive** is a noun or pronoun, along with any modifiers, that **renames** another noun or pronoun. The appositive almost always follows the word it refers to, and it is usually set off by commas.

The computer, **an extremely useful tool,** *has advanced a long way in just a few years.*
(The noun *tool* renames the noun *computer*.)

On the street, the Yugo, **the one with the rusty doors,** *is an eyesore.*
(The pronoun *one* renames the noun *Yugo*.)

(See pages 162–165 for a further discussion of appositives.)

3. **Use commas to set off words of direct address.** If a writer addresses someone directly in a sentence, the words that stand for that person or persons are set off by commas. If the words in direct address begin a sentence, they are followed by a comma. If they end a sentence, they are preceded by a comma.

What if, **Charlie,** *you were to hurt someone with one of your weapons?*
Brent, *you are hogging the ball.*
I am sorry if I hurt your feelings, **Aaron***.*

4. **Use commas to set off dates and addresses.** If your sentence contains two or more elements of a date or address, use commas to set off these elements. The following sentences contain two or more elements:

We went to Magic Mountain on **Thursday, November 18, 1993,** *because children were admitted free that day.*

Concepcion had lived at **4590 Portello Street, San Francisco, California,** *for twelve years.*

In 1992 she move to **1754 Pacific Court, Vista, California 92083,** *to be near her mother.*

Note: The state is not separated from the zip code by a comma.

EXERCISE   Add commas to the following sentences where necessary.

1. Even though she had such a hard time she is greatly admired as a person and artist.

2. I have always enjoyed driving up the coast of California so we will leave for Big Sur on Saturday.

3. Alberto opened his first restaurant in San Diego in 1987 with only $300.

4. Chico in fact had never even heard of okra.

5. Tomorrow Oedipus intends to go to the foot doctor talk to the Sphinx eat lunch with his wife and ponder his fate.

6. The salesperson's considerate kind attention impressed Mr. Gutierrez.

7. The melodious soothing sound of the flute helped Favio to relax.

8. Homer liked the collard greens yet avoided the beets.

9. Craig's mother who doubted he could swim very well asked him to be careful.

10. Sunday June 4 1994 was an important day in Jose's life.

11. Billie Holiday who is one of the greatest jazz singers lived a hard life.

12. King Lear a stupid old man finally saw the errors that he had committed.

13. Suzanne called Brent packed her belongings said her goodbyes and moved to her new place.

14. The man who corrupted Hadleyburg just disappeared.

15. Carlos did not want to go to Disneyland nor did he want to go fishing.

16. Send the feathers and wax to 8965 Maze Way Minotaur Ohio 09999 and make it quick Otto.

17. Crying for help the people in the first raft went over the falls.

18. To force the owners of factories to listen to their demands they threw shoes into the machinery.

19. Friar Laurence did you say that Juliet was just sleeping?

20. Beginning on June 1 1883 the Civil War battle that took place at Gettysburg Pennsylvania was probably the most decisive battle of the war.

EXERCISE   Add commas to the following sentences where necessary.

1. Yes Icarus flew like a bird but he lived to regret it.

2. Remember Carlos to bring a flashlight a compass a sleeping bag and some matches.

3. Ken's bicycle had a flat near Taos New Mexico so he camped there overnight.

4. Because it had been almost a year Bruce had to perform one of his most feared tasks a trip to the dentist.

5. On July 9 1898 Torvald refused to do the dishes or change the baby's diapers.

6. Nora enraged by his behavior told him how she felt; moreover she packed her bags and left.

7. Torvald a notoriously insensitive man did not understand her feelings.

8. The rugged dependable DC-3 passenger plane served in World War II and it is still in service all over the world.

9. Putting her finger to her lips Olga pointed to their mother who was placing presents under the tree.

10. In the middle of a serious speech on poverty the senator suddenly recited a tasteless poem a bawdy limerick.

11. Of course Scylla liked eating at Greek restaurants but she liked attacking the various ships that came by more.

12. Grabbing his wallet and sword Achilles headed for Troy New York to join his friends.

13. When he arrived they had already started building a large wooden horse.

14. Joy feeling quite contented just sat and watched all of the birds at her bird feeders.

15. New Orleans for instance is my favorite city because of the music the food the coffee and the wide variety of people who like to have fun.

16. June 24 1981 was a special day for Michelle for on that day she saw sunshine clouds and sky for the first time.

17. Soaked by the rain the cat ran under the small green table outside the resort hotel in Naples Italy and curled up.

18. Josefina completely exasperated by her car's performance painted the word *lemon* all over it in bright yellow paint.

19. Dr. Nguyen teaches her psychology class in unique ways; for instance she has her students act out parts of the plays *Hamlet* and *Oedipus Rex* to illustrate the Oedipus complex and manic depression.

20. In fact Katie included most of the characters from *Alice in Wonderland* in her "Alice" paintings which are now being shown at the Museum of Modern Art.

CHAPTER EIGHTEEN

Semicolons and Colons

The Semicolon

1. **A semicolon is used to join two main clauses that are not joined by a comma and a coordinating conjunction.** Sometimes a conjunctive adverb follows the semicolon. (See page 287–288 for a list of conjunctive adverbs.)

   The generals checked Hitler's horoscope; it told them when to attack.

   Nancy wanted to check her horoscope; however, Ron advised against it.

2. **A semicolon can be used to join elements in a series when the elements require further internal punctuation.**

   By the time Guillermo reached home, he had worked for eighteen hours, which tired him out; he had had a car accident, which depressed him; he had drunk too much coffee, which made him jittery; and he had yelled at his partner, which made him remorseful.

3. **Do not use a semicolon to separate two phrases or two subordinate clauses.**

   (incorrect)   *Sonia is going to Little Vietnam because she likes the spring rolls; and because she likes the atmosphere.*

   (correct)   *Sonia is going to Little Vietnam because she likes the spring rolls and because she likes the atmosphere.*

   (See pages 58–60 for further discussion of semicolon usage.)

The Colon

1. **A colon is used to join two main clauses when the second clause is an example, an illustration, or a restatement of the first clause.**

The party had been a great success: everyone had had fun and had gotten safely home.

This incident is the same as all of the others: Wolfgang never agrees with any of our ideas.

2. **A colon is used when a complete sentence introduces an example, a series, or a list.**

The magazine covered a number of subjects related to biking: racing bicycles, touring bicycles, mountain bicycles, and safety equipment.

The list on the refrigerator included the following requests: clean the kitchen, wash the car, make reservations at Jake's, and take a shower.

3. **A colon is generally not used after a verb.**

(incorrect)   *My favorite foods are: red beans and rice, catfish, and pasta carbonara.*

(correct)   *My favorite foods are red beans and rice, catfish, and pasta carbonara.*

EXERCISE   Add semicolons or colons where necessary.

1. Form a line then walk to the cafeteria.

2. Describe one of the following characters Hamlet, Captain Ahab, Emma, Roseanne, Joan of Arc, Holden Caulfield, or Iago.

3. The elves enjoyed the shade of the mushroom however, they lamented the lack of dew.

4. Here is the equipment that I will need a laptop computer, a printer, paper, envelopes and stamps.

5. Raul was unable to solve the puzzle therefore, he sent for a book of hints.

6. You take the high road I will take the low road.

7. Mabel desperately wanted to visit her favorite aunt, who lived in Denver, Colorado, to spend some days gambling in Deadwood, South Dakota, and to tour Graceland, where Elvis had lived.

8. The ingredients are pink beans, ham hocks, hominy, and okra.

9. The dog whined because of the scratch on his nose meanwhile, the cat sauntered away.

10. The burglar took the following items two old lottery tickets, chewing gum, a telephone book, and my Hank Williams record collection.

CHAPTER NINETEEN

The Apostrophe

1. **Apostrophes are used to form contractions.** The apostrophe replaces the omitted letter or letters.

it is	it's	cannot	can't
I am	I'm	were not	weren't
they are	they're	is not	isn't
would have	would've	does not	doesn't

2. **Apostrophes are used to form the possessives of nouns and indefinite pronouns.**

   ■ Add *'s* to form the possessive of all singular nouns and indefinite pronouns.

   (singular nouns)   *The <u>boy's</u> bicycle was new.*
                        <u>Louis's</u> courage was never questioned.

   (indefinite pronouns)   *<u>Someone's</u> horn was honking.*

   (compound words)   *My <u>father-in-law's</u> car had a flat.*

   (joint possession)   *<u>Julio and Maria's</u> mountain cabin is for rent.*

   ■ Add only an apostrophe to form the possessive of plural nouns that end in *s*. However, add *'s* to form the possessive of plural nouns that do not end in *s*.

   (plural nouns   *Both <u>teams'</u> shoes were lined up on the field.*
   that end in *s*)   *The <u>Smiths'</u> house was on fire.*

   (plural nouns that   *The <u>women's</u> cars were parked in front of the house.*
   do not end in *s*)

   ■ Expressions referring to time or money often require an apostrophe.

   Sheila asked for a <u>dollar's</u> worth of candy.
   The player was given three <u>days'</u> suspension.

3. Do not use apostrophes with the possessive forms of personal pronouns.

Incorrect	Correct
her's	hers
our's	ours
their's	theirs

Note: *It's* means "it is." The possessive form of *it* is *its*.

Add apostrophes (or 's) to the following sentences where necessary.

1. That is Barrys baseball glove; he wont mind if you use it.

2. Do think Charles tie goes well with his socks?

3. Mel Gibsons portrayal of Hamlet was lively, but Ive seen better.

4. In two hours time the mechanic had the clutch fixed.

5. People thought that Bridgets monologue on roadkill at the dinner table wasnt in good taste.

6. Its customary for the female black widow spider to kill her mate.

7. Were all going for coffee after the meeting, and youre invited.

8. The childrens bicycles shouldnt have been left out in the rain.

9. I dont want to hear anyones excuses after the game.

10. My mother-in-laws visits to her five relatives homes were a pleasant surprise.

CHAPTER TWENTY

Quotation Marks

1. **Quotation marks are used to enclose direct quotations and dialogue.**

   As Oscar Wilde once said, "Fashion is a form of ugliness so intolerable that we have to alter it every six months."

   Will Rogers said, "Liberty doesn't work as well in practice as it does in speeches."

2. **Quotation marks are not used with indirect quotations.**

   (direct quotation)   *Tony said, "I'll play trumpet in the band."*

   (indirect quotation)   *Tony said that he would play trumpet in the band.*

3. **Place periods and commas inside quotation marks.**

   Eudora Welty wrote the short story "A Worn Path."

   "I am a man more sinned against than sinning," cried Lear.

4. **Place colons and semicolons outside quotation marks.**

   The class did not like the poem "Thoughts on Capital Punishment": it was silly, sentimental, and insipid, and the rhythm was awkward and inappropriate.

   The local newspaper ran a story entitled "Mayor Caught Nude on the Beach"; it was just a joke for April Fools' Day.

5. **Place the question mark inside the quotation marks if the quotation is a question. Place the question mark outside the quotation marks if the quotation is not a question but the whole sentence is.**

   Homer asked, "What is for dinner, my dear Hortense?"

   Did Hortense really reply, "Hominy, okra, and barbecued Spam"?

6. **Place the exclamation point inside the quotation marks if the quotation is an exclamation. Place it outside the quotation marks if the quotation is not an exclamation but the whole sentence is.**

   "I have a dream!" yelled Martin Luther King, Jr.

   I insist that you stop calling me "dude"!

(See pages 136–137 for a further discussion of quotation marks.)

EXERCISE Add quotation marks and semicolons to the following sentences where necessary.

1. Hal said, Squid tentacles are my favorite snacks.

2. Will you get the tickets for the concert? asked Georgette.

3. Oscar said that he would clean up his house.

4. Michelle said to her teacher, I'll see you next year then she left on her vacation.

5. Did Bob Dylan really sing Moon River?

6. Dive, dive! yelled the captain of the submarine.

7. Mark Twain once muttered that a classic was a book that everyone praised, but no one read.

8. Gloria Steinem stated, Some of us are becoming the men we wanted to marry.

9. Did the Cyclops actually believe him when he said, My name is No Man?

10. Bill yelled across the lobby, I hated that movie!

11. Camilla said, I am going to write a short story about an aardvark in Ireland; afterwards, she changed her mind.

12. Are we there yet? asked the children over and over.

13. *Star Trek* fans used to say, Beam me up, Scotty.

14. Willy told his boys that they needed to be well liked.

15. Send in the clowns, sang the frustrated coach.

CHAPTER TWENTY-ONE

Titles, Capitalization, and Numbers

Titles

1. **Underline or place in italics the titles of works that are printed separately, such as books, periodicals, and plays.**

   - Books: *Moby Dick, Bartlett's Familiar Quotations*
   - Plays: *The Glass Menagerie, A Doll's House*
   - Pamphlets: *Grooming Your Labrador, Charleston's Ten Best Restaurants*
   - Long musical works: Mozart's *String Quartet in C Major*, Miles Davis's *Sketches of Spain*
   - Long poems: *Howl, The Faerie Queene*
   - Periodicals: *The Washington Post, Time*
   - Films: *The Flintstones, When a Man Loves a Woman*
   - Television and radio programs: *60 Minutes, Masterpiece Theater*
   - Works of art: El Greco's *Saint Matthew, Nike of Samothrace*

2. **Use quotation marks to enclose the titles of works that are parts of other works, such as articles, songs, poems, and short stories.**

   - Songs: "The Sweetest Days," "Friends"
   - Poems: "My Last Duchess," "Dover Beach"
   - Articles in periodicals: "Three-Headed Snake Born As Two-Headed Brother Looks On," "The Last Stand"
   - Short stories: "A Jury of Her Peers," "Resurrection"
   - Essays: "Male Fixations," "A Custody Fight for an Egg"
   - Episodes of radio and television shows: "What's in a Name?"
   - Subdivisions of books: "The Cassock" (Chapter 29 of *Moby Dick*)

Capitalization

1. **Capitalize the personal pronoun *I*.**

2. **Capitalize the first letter of every sentence.**

3. **Capitalize the first letter of each word in a title except for *a*, *an*, and *the*, coordinating conjunctions, and prepositions.**

   > **Note:** The first letter of the first or last word of a title is always capitalized.

   Dictionary of Philosophy and Religion
   "A Good Man Is Hard to Find"

4. **Capitalize the first letter of all proper nouns and adjectives derived from proper nouns.**

   - Names and titles of people: President Clinton, William Shakespeare, Uncle Christopher, Ms. Hohman
   - Names of specific places: Chicago, Smoky Mountains, Tennessee, The Armenian Cafe, Saturn, the South

     Note: Do not capitalize the first letter of words that refer to a direction (such as *north, south, east,* or *west*). Do capitalize such words when they refer to a specific region.

     Alabama and Mississippi are among the states in the <u>South</u>.
     Turn <u>south</u> on Hill Street and go four blocks to the end of the street.

   - Names of ethnic, national, or racial groups: Native American, British, French, Canadian, Hispanic, Russian
   - Names of groups or organizations: National Organization for Women, Girl Scouts of America, Methodists
   - Names of companies: General Motors, Nordstrom, Pepsi-Cola Bottling Company, R. J. Reynolds
   - Names of the days of the week and the months of the year but not the seasons: Saturday, April, winter, spring
   - Names of holidays and historical events: the Gulf War, Christmas, the Battle of Concord
   - Names of *specific* gods and religious writings: God, Zeus, Buddha, Koran, Yahweh, Bible

   The names of academic subjects are not capitalized unless they refer to an ethnic or national origin or are the names of specific courses. Examples include *mathematics, history, Spanish,* and *Physics 100.*

Numbers

The following rules about numbers apply to general writing rather than to technical or scientific writing.

1. **Spell out numbers that require no more than two words. Use numerals for numbers that require more than two words.**

   Ninety-three people attended the dean's retirement party.
   We have now gone 125 days without rain.

2. **Spell out numbers at the beginning of sentences.**

   Two hundred thirty-five miles is a long distance to rollerblade.

3. **Use numerals in the following situations:**

   - Dates: June 24, 1981; 55 B.C.
   - Sections of books or plays: Chapter 26, page 390; Act 5, scene 2, lines 78–90
   - Addresses: 3245 Sisyphus Street
                     Stonewall, Nebraska 90345
   - Decimals, percentages, and fractions: 7.5; 75%, 75 percent; 1/8
   - Exact amounts of money: $10.86; $6,723,001
   - Scores and statistics: Padres 10, Reds 0; a ratio of 4 to 1
   - Time of day: 5:23; 12:45

   Note: Round amounts of money that can be expressed in a few words can be written out: *thirty cents, twelve dollars, three hundred dollars.* Also when the word *o'clock* is used with the time of day, the time of day should be written out: *eight o'clock.*

4. **When numbers are compared, are joined by conjunctions, or occur in a series, either consistently use numerals or consistently spell them out.**

   For the birthday party we needed one hundred fifteen paper hats, two hundred twenty napkins, one hundred fifteen paper plates and forks, eight gallons of ice cream, three cakes, forty candles, and eight cases of soda.

   OR

   For the birthday party we needed 115 paper hats, 220 napkins, 115 paper plates and forks, 8 gallons of ice cream, 3 cakes, 40 candles, and 8 cases of soda.

EXERCISE

The following sentences contain errors in the use of titles, capitalization, and numbers. Correct any errors you find.

1. Holly Hunter won an academy award for the film the piano even though she spoke only in the last scene.

2. The character of edgar in the play king lear and the character of iago in the play othello are two of shakespeare's worst Villains.

3. 375 cats were believed to have been killed in the city of pompeii when mount vesuvius erupted in seventy-nine A.D.

4. The Principal of imperial valley high school canceled classes when the Temperature reached 100 degrees.

5. Yesterday, the houston rockets beat the new york knicks eighty-six to 84.

6. When the japanese fishing boat was attacked by a Whale, 7 sailors were seriously injured.

7. My fine was three dollars and seventy-five cents when i returned the book the hero with a thousand faces to the Library.

8. Before he closed up, amador ordered 2 new computers, one hundred fifty reams of paper, 90 gallons of ink, and two hundred boxes of staples and paper clips for his copy shop.

9. Brent likes to listen to the radio program fresh air on national public radio.

10. One of my favorite Essays, entitled smoking ads: a matter of life, is written by ellen goodman, a syndicated columnist whose work appears in many Newspapers, including the kansas city star.

11. On their album kiko, the band los lobos included a song called arizona skies.

12. The works of many great mystery writers, including p. d. james, appear on the television show mystery.

13. A psychologist, dr. john gavion, claims that as many as fifty percent of the homeless people are vietnam veterans.

14. Andre took notes as professor guerra talked about south american art in his hispanic studies 120 class.

15. All 30 of the students were able to recognize the painting madonna and child by fra lippo lippi.

Additional Readings for Writing

The reading selections on the following pages present opinions on a range of topics. The articles in the section entitled "Our Changing Society" discuss sexism, bigotry, violence, and personal values. The section "Two Proposals" presents an argument in favor of establishing a voluntary national youth service and an argument in support of abolishing the grading system. The section "Flag Burning and Freedom of Speech" presents two argumentative selections pertaining to the proposed constitutional amendment to prohibit the burning of the American flag. The sections "Ethics: Cheating, Lying, and Breaking the Law" and "English as the 'Official' Language of the United States" consist of related articles that you can use as sources for your own synthesis or argumentative essays.

As you read these selections, consider the "Steps in Evaluating a Text" from Chapter 6:

1. Read the text actively.
   - Determine its intended audience and purpose
   - Identify its thesis
   - Identify its main points
2. Determine how well the main points are supported.
   - Distinguish between facts and opinions
   - Distinguish between specific support and generalizations
   - Identify statistics, examples, and references to authority
3. Test the article's points against your own knowledge and experience.
4. Consider any obvious objections that have been ignored.

OUR CHANGING SOCIETY ·

Kids in the Mall: Growing Up Controlled

WILLIAM SEVERINI KOWINSKI

Butch heaved himself up and loomed over the group. "Like it was different for me," he piped. "My folks used to drop me off at the shopping mall every morning and leave me all day. It was like a big free baby-sitter, you know? One night they never came back for me. Maybe they moved away. Maybe there's some kind of a Bureau of Missing Parents I could check with."

RICHARD PECK, SECRETS OF THE SHOPPING MALL (A NOVEL FOR TEENAGERS)

From his sister at Swarthmore, I'd heard about a kid in Florida whose mother picked him up after school every day, drove him straight to the mall, and left him there until it closed—all at his insistence. I'd heard about a boy in Washington who, when his family moved from one suburb to another, pedaled his bicycle five miles every day to get back to his old mall, where he once belonged. 1

These stories aren't unusual. The mall is a common experience for the majority of American youth; they have probably been going there all their lives. Some ran within their first large open space, saw their first fountain, bought their first toy, and read their first book in a mall. They may have smoked their first cigarette or first joint, or turned them down, had their first kiss or lost their virginity in the mall parking lot. Teenagers in America now spend more time in the mall than anywhere else but home and school. Mostly it is their choice, but some of that mall time is put in as the result of two-paycheck and single-parent households, and the lack of other viable alternatives. But are these kids being harmed by the mall? 2

I wondered first of all what difference it makes for adolescents to experience so many important moments in the mall. They are, after all, at play in the fields of its little world and they learn its ways; they adapt to it and make it adapt to them. It's here that these kids get their street sense, only it's mall sense. They are learning the ways of a large-scale, artificial environment; its subtleties and flexibilities, its particular pleasures and resonances, and the attitudes it fosters. 3

The presence of so many teenagers for so much time was not something mall developers planned on. In fact, it came as a big surprise. But kids became a fact of mall life very easily, and the International Council 4 of Shopping Centers found it necessary to commission a study, which they published along with a guide to mall managers on how to handle the teenage incursion.

The study found that "teenagers in suburban centers are bored and come to the shopping centers mainly as a place to go. Teenagers in suburban centers spent more time fighting, drinking, littering and walking than did their urban counterparts, but presented fewer overall problems." The report observed that "adolescents congregated in groups of two to four and predominantly at locations selected by them rather than management." This probably had something to do with the decision to install game arcades, which allow management to channel these restless adolescents into naturally contained areas away from major traffic points of adult shoppers.

The guide concluded that mall management should tolerate and even encourage the teenage presence because, in the words of the report, "The vast majority support the same set of values as does shopping center management." *The same set of values* means simply that mall kids are already preprogrammed to be consumers and that the mall can put the finishing touches to them as hard-core, lifelong shoppers just like everybody else. That, after all, is what the mall is about. So it shouldn't be surprising that in spending a lot of time there, adolescents find little that challenges the assumption that the goal of life is to make money and buy products, or that just about everything else in life is to be used to serve those ends.

Growing up in a high-consumption society already adds inestimable pressure to kids' lives. Clothes consciousness has invaded the grade schools, and popularity is linked with having the best, newest clothes in the currently acceptable styles. Even what they read has been affected. "Miss [Nancy] Drew wasn't obsessed with her wardrobe," noted the *Wall Street Journal*. "But today the mystery in teen fiction for girls is what outfit the heroine will wear next." Shopping has become a survival skill and there is certainly no better place to learn it than the mall, where its importance is powerfully reinforced and certainly never questioned.

The mall as a university of suburban materialism, where Valley Girls and boys from coast to coast are educated in consumption, has its other lessons in this era of change in family life and sexual mores and their economic and social ramifications. The plethora of products in the mall, plus the pressure on teens to buy them, may contribute to the phenomenon that psychologist David Elkind calls "the hurried child": kids who are exposed to too much of the adult world too quickly and must respond with a sophistication that belies their still-tender emotional development. Certainly the adult products marketed for children—form-fitting designer jeans, sexy tops for preteen girls—add to the social pressure to look like an adult, along with the home-grown need to understand adult finances (why mothers must work) and adult emotions (when parents divorce).

Kids spend so much time at the mall partly because their parents allow 9 it and even encourage it. The mall is safe, doesn't seem to harbor any unsavory activities, and there is adult supervision; it is, after all, a controlled environment. So the temptation, especially for working parents, is to let the mall be their baby-sitter. At least the kids aren't watching TV. But the mall's role as a surrogate mother may be more extensive and more profound.

Karen Lansky, a writer living in Los Angeles, has looked into the sub- 10 ject, and she told me some of her conclusions about the effects on its teenaged denizens of the mall's controlled and controlling environment. "Structure is the dominant idea, since true 'mall rats' lack just that in their home lives," she said, "and adolescents about to make the big leap into growing up crave more structure than our modern society cares to acknowledge." Karen pointed out some of the elements malls supply that kids used to get from their families, like warmth (Strawberry Shortcake dolls and similar cute and cuddly merchandise), old-fashioned mothering ("We do it all for you," the fast-food slogan), and even home cooking (the "homemade" treats at the food court).

The problem in all this, as Karen Lansky sees it, is that while families 11 nurture children by encouraging growth through the assumption of responsibility and then by letting them rest in the bosom of the family from the rigors of growing up, the mall as a structural mother encourages passivity and consumption, as long as the kid doesn't make trouble. Therefore all they learn about becoming adults is how to act and how to consume.

Kids are in the mall not only in the passive role of shoppers—they also 12 work there, especially as fast-food outlets infiltrate the mall's enclosure. There they learn how to hold a job and take responsibility, but still within the same value context. When *CBS Reports* went to Oak Park Mall in suburban Kansas City, Kansas, to tape part of their hour-long consideration of malls, "After the Dream Comes True," they interviewed a teenaged girl who worked in a fast-food outlet there. In a sequence that didn't make the final program, she described the major goal of her present life, which was to perfect the curl on top of the ice-cream cones that were her store's specialty. If she could do that, she would be moved from the lowly soft-drink dispenser to the more prestigious ice-cream division, the curl on top of the status ladder at her restaurant. These are the achievements that are important at the mall.

Other benefits of such jobs may also be overrated, according to Laurence D. Steinberg of the University of California at Irvine's social ecology department, who did a study on teenage employment. Their jobs, he found, are generally simple, mindlessly repetitive and boring. They don't really learn anything, and the jobs don't lead anywhere. Teenagers also work primarily with other teenagers; even their supervisors are often just a little older than they are. "Kids need to spend time with adults," Steinberg told me. "Although they get benefits from peer relationships, without parents and other adults it's one-sided socialization. They hang out with each other, have age-segregated jobs, and watch TV."

Perhaps much of this is not so terrible or even so terribly different. Now that they have so much more to contend with in their lives, adolescents probably need more time to spend with other adolescents without adult impositions, just to sort things out. Though it is more concentrated in the mall (and therefore perhaps a clearer target), the value system there is really the dominant one of the whole society. Attitudes about curiosity, initiative, self-expression, empathy, and disinterested learning aren't necessarily made in the mall; they are mirrored there, perhaps a bit more intensely—as through a glass brightly.

Besides, the mall is not without its educational opportunities. There are bookstores, where there is at least a short shelf of classics at great prices, and other books from which it is possible to learn more than how to do sit-ups. There are tools, from hammers to VCRs, and products, from clothes to records, that can help the young find and express themselves. There are older people with stories, and places to be alone or to talk one-on-one with a kindred spirit. And there is always the passing show.

The mall itself may very well be an education about the future. I was struck with the realization, as early as my first forays into Greengate, that the mall is only one of a number of enclosed and controlled environments that are part of the lives of today's young. The mall is just an extension, say, of those large suburban schools—only there's Karmelkorn instead of chem lab, the ice rink instead of the gym: It's high school without the impertinence of classes.

Growing up, moving from home to school to the mall—from enclosure to enclosure, transported in cars—is a curiously continuous process, without much in the way of contrast or contact with unenclosed reality.

Places must tend to blur into one another. But whatever differences and dangers there are in this, the skills these adolescents are learning may turn out to be useful in their later lives. For we seem to be moving inexorably into an age of preplanned and regulated environments, and this is the world they will inherit.

Still, it might be better if they had more of a choice. One teenaged girl 18 confessed to *CBS Reports* that she sometimes felt she was missing something by hanging out at the mall so much. "But I'm here," she said, "and this is what I have."

A Generation of Bigots Comes of Age

RICHARD COHEN

There's hardly a politician in the land who, when children are mentioned, does not say they are our future. That's true, of course—and nothing can be done about it—but the way things are going we should all be worried. A generation of bigots is coming of age.

The evidence for that awful prognostication can be found in a recent 2 public opinion survey conducted for the Anti-Defamation League by the Boston polling firm of Marttila & Kiley—two outfits with considerable credentials in the field of public opinion research.

For the first time, a trend has been reversed. Up to now, opinion polls 3 have always found that the more schooling a person has, the more likely he is to be tolerant. For that reason, older people—who by and large have the least education—are the most intolerant age group in the nation.

But no longer. The ADL found a disturbing symmetry: Older and 4 younger white Americans share the same biases. For instance, when white people were asked if blacks prefer to remain on welfare rather than work, 42 percent of the respondents 50 years old and over said the statement was "probably true." Predictably, the figure plummeted to 29 percent for those 30 to 49. But then it jumped to 36 percent for respondents under 30.

Similarly, a majority of younger respondents thought blacks "complain 5 too much about racism (68 percent) and "stick together more than others" (63 percent). For both statements, the young had a higher percentage of agreement than any other age category.

The pattern persisted for the other questions as well—questions designed to ferret out biased attitudes. In the words of Abraham Foxman, the ADL's national director, the generation that's destined to run this country is either racist or disposed to racism to a degree that he characterized as "a crisis." It's hard to disagree with him.   6

What's going on? The short answer is that no one knows for sure. But some guesses can be ventured and none of them are comforting. The first and most obvious explanation has to do with age itself: The under-30 generation is pathetically ignorant of recent American history.   7

Younger people apparently know little about—and did not see on television—the civil rights struggles of the 1950s and 1960s, everything from the police dogs of Birmingham to the murder of civil rights workers. They apparently do not understand that if blacks tend to see racism everywhere, that's because in the recent past, it was everywhere and remains the abiding American sickness.   8

But historical ignorance is not the only factor accounting for the ADL's findings. Another, apparently, is affirmative action. It has created a category of white victims, either real or perceived, who are more likely than other whites to hold prejudicial views.   9

For instance, when the ADL asked "Do you feel you have ever been a victim of reverse discrimination in hiring or promotion," only 21 percent said yes. But the percentage rose to 26 percent for college graduates and 23 percent for people with post-graduate degrees. Since the ADL found that "about one-third" of the self-described victims of reverse discrimination fell into the "most prejudiced" category, these numbers are clearly worth worrying about.   10

Too many of the American elite are racially aggrieved—although possibly some of them were bigoted in the first place.   11

One could argue that not all of the statements represent proof of bigoted attitudes. For instance, white college students who witness voluntary self-segregation on the part of black students—demands for their own dorms, for instance—have some reason to think that blacks "stick together more than others."   12

Nevertheless, the data strongly suggests that progress on racial attitudes is being reversed—with contributions from both races. Worse, this is happening at a time when the economic pie is shrinking and competition for jobs increasing. If the economic trend continues, racial intolerance is likely to grow.   13

It's nothing less than a calamity that a generation has come of age with-   14
out a deep appreciation of the recent history of African-Americans. At
the same time, black leaders who advocate or condone separatism had
better appreciate the damage they are doing.

And finally, affirmative action programs, as well-intentioned as they   15
may be, need to be re-examined—and without critics automatically
being labeled as racist. No doubt these programs have done some good.
But there's a growing body of evidence—of which the ADL poll is only
the latest—that they also do some bad.

The Changing Face of America

OTTO FRIEDRICH

Reina came from El Salvador because of "horrible things." She says   1
simply, "I got scared." When she finally reached Los Angeles and
found a job as a housekeeper at $125 a week, her new employer pointed
to the vacuum cleaner. Vacuum cleaner? Reina, 24, had never seen such a
thing before. "She gave me a maid book and a dictionary," says Reina,
who now writes down and looks up every new word she hears. "That's
how I learn English. I don't have time to go to school, but when I don't
speak English, I feel stupid, so I must learn. . . ."

Lam Ton, from Viet Nam, is already a U.S. citizen, and he did well   2
with a restaurant, the Mekong, at the intersection of Broadway and
Argyle Street in Chicago. "When I first moved in here, I swept the sidewalk after we closed," he recalls. "People thought I was strange, but
now everyone does the same." Lam Ton's newest project is to build an
arch over Argyle Street in honor of the immigrants who live and work
here. "I will call it Freedom Gate," he says, "and it will have ocean
waves with hands holding a freedom torch on top. It will represent not
just the Vietnamese but all the minorities who have come here. Just look
down Broadway. That guy is Indian, next to him is a Greek, next to him
is a Thai, and next to him is a Mexican."

They seem to come from everywhere, for all kinds of reasons, as indeed   3
they always have. "What Alexis de Tocqueville saw in America," John F.
Kennedy once wrote, "was a society of immigrants, each of whom had
begun life anew, on an equal footing. This was the secret of America: a

nation of people with the fresh memory of old traditions who dared to explore new frontiers." It was in memory of Kennedy's urging that the U.S. in 1965 abandoned the quota system that for nearly half a century had preserved the overwhelmingly European character of the nation. The new law invited the largest wave of immigration since the turn of the century, only this time the newcomers have arrived not from the Old World but from the Third World, especially Asia and Latin America. Of the 544,000 legal immigrants who came in fiscal 1984, the largest numbers were from Mexico (57,000 or more than 10%), followed by the Philippines (42,000) and Viet Nam (37,000). Britain came in ninth, with only 14,000. . . .

In addition to the half-million immigrants who are allowed to come to the U.S. each year, a substantial number arrive illegally. Estimates of the total vary widely. The Immigration and Naturalization Service apprehended 1.3 million illegal immigrants last year and guessed that several times that many had slipped through its net. . . . 4

The newest wave raises many questions: How many immigrants can the country absorb and at what rate? How much unskilled labor does a high-tech society need? Do illegals drain the economy or enrich it? Do newcomers gain their foothold at the expense of the poor and the black? Is it either possible or desirable to assimilate large numbers of immigrants from different races, languages and cultures? Will the advantages of diversity be outweighed by the dangers of separatism and conflict? 5

When asked about such issues, Americans sound troubled; their answers are ambiguous and sometimes contradictory. In a *Time* poll taken by Yankelovich, Skelly & White Inc., only 27% agreed with the idea that "America should keep its doors open to people who wish to immigrate to the U.S. because that is what our heritage is all about." Two-thirds agreed that "this philosophy is no longer reasonable, and we should strictly limit the number." Some 56% said the number of legal immigrants was too high, and 75% wanted illegal immigrants to be tracked down. On the other hand, 66% approved of taking in people being persecuted in their homelands. 6

"One of the conditions of being an American," says Arthur Mann, professor of history at the University of Chicago, "is to be aware of the fact that a whole lot of people around you are different, different in their origins, their religions, their life-styles." Yet most Americans do not know exactly what to make of those differences. . . . Much of the concern comes from people who favor continued immigration, but who fear 7 the consequences if a slowdown in the economy were to heighten the sense that immigrants, especially illegal ones, take jobs away from Americans. . . .

The number of newcomers is large in itself, . . . but their effect is height-   8
ened because they have converged on the main cities of half a dozen states. Nowhere is the change more evident than in California, which has become home to 64% of the country's Asians and 35% of its Hispanics. Next comes New York, followed by Texas, Florida, Illinois and New Jersey. Miami is 64% Hispanic, San Antonio 55%. Los Angeles has more Mexicans (2 million) than any other city except metropolitan Mexico City, and nearly half as many Salvadorans (300,000) as San Salvador.

These population shifts change all the bric-a-brac of life. A car in Los   9
Angeles carries a custom license plate that says *Sie sie li*, meaning, in Chinese, "Thank you." Graffiti sprayed in a nearby park send their obscure signals in Farsi. A suburban supermarket specializes in such Vietnamese delicacies as pork snouts and pickled banana buds. The Spanish-language soap opera *Tu o Nadie* gets the top ratings among independent stations every night at 8.

Such changes require adaptation not only in the schools and the mar-   10
ketplace but throughout society. The Los Angeles County court system now provides interpreters for 80 different languages from Albanian and Amharic to Turkish and Tongan. One judge estimates that nearly half his cases require an interpreter.

These changes do not represent social decline or breakdown. The new-   11
comers bring valuable skills and personal qualities: hope, energy, fresh perspectives. But the success stories should not blot out the fact that many aliens face considerable hardships with little immediate chance of advancement. Avan Wong, 20, came from Hong Kong in 1983 and hoped to go to college. She lives in the Bronx with her aged father, com-mutes two hours by bus to a job of up to twelve hours a day in a subur-ban restaurant. "I don't even read the newspapers," she says. "You don't have time. Once you go home, you go to sleep. Once you get up, you have to go to work. The only thing I'm happy about is that I can earn money and send it back to my mother. Nothing else. You feel so lonely here." College is not in sight. . . .

Even with the best intentions on all sides, the question of how to fit all   12
these varieties of strangers into a relatively coherent American society remains difficult. Linda Wong, a Chinese-American official of the Mexican-American Legal Defense and Education Fund, sees trouble in

the racial differences. "There is concern among whites that the new immigrants may be unassimilable," says Wong. "Hispanics and Asians cannot melt in as easily, and the U.S. has always had an ambivalent attitude toward newcomers. Ambivalent at best, racist at worst."

Many historians disagree. Hispanics, says Sheldon Maram, a professor   13
of history at California State University at Fullerton, "are moving at about the same level of acculturation as the Poles and Italians earlier in the century. Once they've made it, they tend to move out of the ghetto and melt into the rest of society." Asians often have it easier because they come from urban middle-class backgrounds. "They are the most highly skilled of any immigrant group our country has ever had," says Kevin McCarthy, a demographer at the Rand Corp. in Santa Monica, Calif. . . .

How long, how complete and how painful the process of Americaniza-   14
tion will be remains unclear. It is true that ethnic elitists have bewailed each succeeding wave of Irish or Germans or Greeks, but it is also true that the disparities among Korean merchants, Soviet Jews, Hmong tribesmen, French socialites and Haitian boat people are greater than the U.S. or any other country has ever confronted. On the other hand, Americans are probably more tolerant of diversity than they once were. . . .

The question is not really whether the new Americans can be assimi-   15
lated—they must be—but rather how the U.S. will be changed by that process.

The Warfare in the Forest Is Not Wanton

BROOKS ATKINSON

After thirty-five years the forest in Spruce Notch is tall and sturdy. It   1
began during the Depression when work gangs planted thousands of tiny seedlings in abandoned pastures on Richmond Peak in the northern Catskills. Nothing spectacular has happened there since; the forest has been left undisturbed.

But now we have a large spread of Norway spruces a foot thick at the   2
butt and 40 or 50 feet high. Their crowns look like thousands of dark crosses reaching into the sky.

The forest is a good place in which to prowl in search of wildlife. But   3
also in search of ideas. For the inescapable fact is that the world of civilized America does not have such a clean record. Since the seedlings were

planted the nation has fought three catastrophic wars, in one of which the killing of combatants and the innocent continues.[1] During the lifetime of the forest 350,000 Americans have died on foreign battlefields.

Inside America civilized life is no finer. A President, a Senator, a man of God have been assassinated. Citizens are murdered in the streets. Riots, armed assaults, looting, burning, outbursts of hatred have increased to the point where they have become commonplace.

Life in civilized America is out of control. Nothing is out of control in the forest. Everything complies with the instinct for survival—which is the law and order of the woods.

Although the forest looks peaceful it supports incessant warfare, most of which is hidden and silent. For thirty-five years the strong have been subduing the weak. The blueberries that once flourished on the mountain have been destroyed. All the trees are individuals, as all human being are individuals; and every tree poses a threat to every other tree. The competition is so fierce that you can hardly penetrate some of the thickets where the lower branches of neighboring trees are interlocked in a blind competition for survival.

Nor is the wildlife benign. A red-tailed hawk lived there last summer— slowly circling in the sky and occasionally drawing attention to himself by screaming. He survived on mice, squirrels, chipmunks and small birds. A barred owl lives somewhere in the depth of the woods. He hoots in midmorning as well as at sunrise to register his authority. He also is a killer. Killing is a fundamental part of the process. The nuthatches kill insects in the bark. The woodpeckers dig insects out. The thrushes eat beetles and caterpillars.

But in the forest, killing is not wanton or malicious. It is for survival. Among birds of equal size most of the warfare consists of sham battles in which they go through the motions of warfare until one withdraws. Usually neither bird gets hurt.

Nor is the warfare between trees vindictive. Although the spruces predominate they do not practice segregation. On both sides of Lost Lane, which used to be a dirt road, maples, beeches, ashes, aspens and a few red oaks live, and green curtains of wild grapes cover the wild cherry trees. In the depths of the forest there are a few glades where the spruces stand aside and birches stretch and grow. The forest is a web of intangible tensions. But they are never out of control. Although they are wild they are not savage as they are in civilized life.

---

[1] The Vietnam War.

For the tensions are absorbed in the process of growth, and the clusters 10 of large cones on the Norway spruces are certificates to a good future. The forest gives an external impression of discipline and pleasure. Occasionally the pleasure is rapturously stated. Soon after sunrise one morning last summer when the period of bird song was nearly over, a solitary rose-breasted grosbeak sat on the top of a tall spruce and sang with great resonance and beauty. He flew a few rods to another tree and continued singing: then to another tree where he poured out his matin again, and so on for a half hour. There was no practical motive that I was aware of.

After thirty-five uneventful years the spruces have created an environ- 11 ment in which a grosbeak is content, and this one said so gloriously. It was a better sound than the explosion of bombs, the scream of the wounded, the crash of broken glass, the crackle of burning buildings, the shriek of the police siren.

The forest conducts its affairs with less rancor and malevolence than 12 civilized America.

Bikini Team: Sexism for the Many

RONALD K. L. COLLINS

When a single voice badgers or degrades women in the workplace 1 because of their gender, we call it sexual harassment. When that voice is amplified for millions of people by millions of dollars, we call it advertising. The former is a legal wrong, the latter a legal right. Yet, both acts exploit women, injure them and attempt to impose male power over them. Why then do we tolerate a dichotomy that makes the larger harm the lesser evil?

Five women in St. Paul, Minn., turned to a court of law to get an 2 answer to this question. To borrow a thought from noted feminist Catharine MacKinnon, these women are asking the law to "adjust a bit to accommodate the realities of sexual harassment." The everyday reality is that women's sexuality is used to sell things, their commodified bodies are plastered on advertising to stimulate men to buy things. Their very identity as autonomous persons is electronically transformed into media images of marketable chattel.

What the company voice says outside of the office carries into it as 3 well. That's part of what the St. Paul women were saying when they filed a lawsuit against their employer, Stroh Brewing Co. In Stroh's "It Does Not Get Better" television ad, bikini-clad young Swedish women parachute into a male campsite bearing six-packs of beer. (Tellingly, the "Swedish bikini team" will be featured on the cover of the January issue of *Playboy* magazine.) Buxom women convey the same message in the company's promotional posters. The advertising fantasy is that men can have both the beer and the "broads."

A spokesman for Stroh says that the company has a "very definite and strong policy" against sexual harassment and other forms of sex discrimination. It "simply won't tolerate it." But the very thing that it purports not to tolerate in the workplace, it promotes in the marketplace. 4

Men get mixed messages. The law tells the men at Stroh not to treat women as sex objects, while company ads tell them to revel in the thought. The law says that they must be sexually civil, while Madison Avenue says that they must be sexually uncivil. The five women of St. Paul have turned to the courts to reaffirm a single message—sexual oppression in all of its forms is an affront to civilized society. 5

If Stroh's management displayed its girlie posters at its work sites and if it broadcast its Swedish fantasy ads on company monitors, few would deny that such messages create an environment conducive to sexual harassment. But Stroh's "very definite and strong policy" does not pertain to its openly sexist ads. The five women in the lawsuit claim that it should. When, in an overt way, men verbally and physically confront women in the workplace, as is alleged in this case, their behavior only actualizes the fantasies in mass advertising that feature women as sex objects. In this sense, sexist advertising compounds the injury against women. 6

Culturally speaking, the key point is not whether any particular ad or ads directly caused Stroh's workmen to act in ways allegedly degrading and injurious to women. What is important is the infrastructure of sexism, the systematic and unjust exercise of male power over women. In this system of commercial exploitation, Stroh is one of many players. Its voice is part of a chorus of commercial forces using women to sell everything from booze to batteries. In a larger sense, what is really being sold and bought is a sexual image of subservient women. Such ad-porn shapes men's conception of women, and to that extent influences their behavior at work. 7

If not in the St. Paul case, then in the next, those who champion the commercial exploitation of women in advertising will wrap themselves in the First Amendment's flag. Any government action on this issue (like 8 the Ontario, Canada, campaigns to outlaw sexist liquor ads) is incompatible, they claim with our system of freedom of expression. Here, again, we confront a paradox. The constitutional guarantee does not categorically protect the worker's sexist voice in the workplace, but the same guarantee is said categorically to protect the company's sexist voice when it is amplified for the marketplace.

In a more noble First Amendment tradition, the women of St. Paul summon us to begin a dialogue about an ideal of gender equality free of the shackles of commercial exploitation. It is high time that we amplify their voices and their message.

9

From The Los Angeles Times, *Nov. 20, 1991, B7.*
Reprinted by permission of the author.

Some Reasons for "Wilding"

SUSAN BAKER AND TIPPER GORE

"Wilding." It's a new word in the vocabulary of teenage violence. The crime that made it the stuff of headlines is so heinous, the details so lurid as to make them almost beyond the understanding of any sane human being.

1

When it was over, a 28-year-old woman, an investment banker out for a jog, was left brutally beaten, knifed and raped by teenagers. She was found near an isolated road in New York's Central Park, covered with mud, almost dead from brain damage, loss of blood and exposure.

2

"It was fun," one of her suspected teenage attackers, all between 14 and 17 years old, told the Manhattan district attorney's office. In the lockup, they were nonchalantly whistling at a policewoman and singing a high-on-the-charts rap song about casual sex: "Wild Thing."

3

Maybe it's the savagery, the remorseless brutality that brought the national attention to this crime. We all heard about this one, either directly or from a friend or family member who would end the story with an "I can't believe it."

4

Believe it. Because it's happening elsewhere too.

5

In 1987, in Brooklyn, N.Y., three teenagers methodically set fire to a homeless couple. When at first rubbing alcohol wouldn't ignite the couple, they went to a local service station for gasoline. It worked.

6

In 1988, in rural Missouri, three teenagers killed a friend—partly out of curiosity! They just wanted to know what it would feel like to kill

7

someone. One of the teenagers claimed the fascination with death began
with heavy-metal music. When the victim asked "Why?" over and over
as his friends brutally attacked with baseball bats, the answer was
"Because it's fun."

In 1988 a record 406 people died in the county of Los Angeles alone   8
in teen-gang-related attacks. One victim who survived was a pregnant
woman who was shot, allegedly by a 16-year-old as a gang initiation rite.

This is truly a "generation at risk." Indeed, the statistics reflect its pain   9
and confusion:

- The three leading causes of death among adolescents are drug- and   10
alcohol-related accidents, suicide and homicide.

- Every year 1 million teenagers run away from home.

- Every year 1 million teenagers get pregnant:

- Every year over half a million—600,000 teenagers—attempt suicide; 5,000 succeed.

- Alcohol and drug abuse are so prevalent among the young that a
Weekly Reader survey recently reported that 10-year-olds often feel
pressure to try alcohol and crack.

- According to the Department of Education, 81 percent of the victims of violent crime are preteens and teenagers, 19 or younger. For
the first time, teenagers have topped adults in the percentages of serious crimes committed per capita.

There are many complex reasons for this sad litany. Divorce and work-   11
ing parents strain the family's ability to cope. Latchkey kids are the rule
more than the exception. Our schools and neighborhoods have become
open-air drug markets. But it is not enough to excuse these children as
products of a bad environment.

As a society, we must take full responsibility. Our music, movies and   12
television are filled with images of sexual violence and killing. The message to our kids is: it's OK to enjoy brutality and suffering: "It's fun."

The American Academy of Pediatrics released a national policy state-   13
ment on the impact of rock lyrics and music videos on adolescents last
November. In it, they noted that some lyrics communicate potentially
harmful health messages in a culture beset with drug abuse, teenage
pregnancy, AIDS and other sexually transmitted diseases.

The No. 2 album in the country this week is "GN'R Lies" from the   14
very popular group. Guns N'Roses. This band is a favorite of sixth

through 12th graders. It contains the following lyrics: "I used to love her but I had to kill her, I had to put her six feet under, and I can still hear her complain."

Teen "slasher" films, featuring scenes of graphic, sadistic violence against women are so popular that characters like Jason from "Friday the 13th" and Freddie from "Nightmare on Elm Street" are considered cult heroes, and now there are spinoff television shows.   15

As parents, it is our responsibility to teach our children to make wise decisions. This responsibility is not only to feed and clothe their bodies, but also to feed and nurture their spirits, their minds, their values. The moral crisis facing our nation's youth requires that we *all* share the responsibility, parents and the entertainment industry.   16

Too often, those who produce this violence evade any discussion of their own responsibility by pretending the entire debate begins and ends with the First Amendment. We are strong advocates of its protections of free speech and free expression. We do not and have not advocated or supported restrictions on those rights: we have never proposed government action. What we are advocating, and what we have worked hard to encourage, is responsibility.   17

For example, producers and songwriters don't consider putting out songs, movies or videos that would portray racism in a positive way. They could. The First Amendment provides that freedom. But they don't. In part, perhaps it's because they think those products wouldn't sell. But in part, they recognize it would be irresponsible. Why is there no similar reticence when the issue is glorifying violence, generally against women?   18

The same sense of responsibility should be brought to a marketplace so saturated with violence that it legitimizes it for our children. It's time to stop the spilling of blood both as "entertainment" and in real life.   19

From Newsweek, *May 29, 1989. Reprinted by permission of Susan Baker.*

Deliberate Living, Not Spontaneity, Is the Heart of Freedom

RICHARD KIRK

Thoreau went into the woods, he said in "Walden," to "live deliberately," to live, in other words, with careful premeditation, methodically weighing actions in his mind's eye in order to get, as he put it, to life's "marrow."   1

Almost a century and a half later the most touted goal of American   2
pop culture is to live spontaneously, to act, in other words, on one's
instincts, impressions or feelings—to "be oneself," in the jargon of the
day. This somewhat oxymoronic ideal, "achieving spontaneity," essentially amounts to the annihilation of deliberation.

Why, one might ask, would anyone want to do away with the charac-   3
teristic Thoreau so prized? Answer: because it is considered an impedi-
ment to "freedom"—the term denoting in this case the indulgence of
feeling.

A young man rises late in the morning and does not feel like making   4
the bed upon which he slept. The voice of modernity intones, "No matter, let it slide. What's the big deal? You're free to do as you please." The
same late riser has chores to perform but again isn't feeling up to the
tasks. "So what," the internal voice again whispers, "if you aren't really
motivated"—meaning if you're not enthusiastically anticipating these
activities—"the work can wait."

Our young friend receives word that a neighbor is in need of help.   5
He is able to provide assistance but isn't that excited about the prospect.
"Oh, well"—so goes the rationalization provided by his unseen Zeit-
geist—"it doesn't really do any good to help if your heart isn't in it,
does it?"

These are examples, small and large, of the way the doctrine of spon-   6
taneity, of following one's feelings, plays out in specific cases. An implicit
assumption of this ideology is that I am most "me" when I follow the
urges that immediately present themselves in any situation—as if these
initial passions, appetites or desires are quintessentially "me." The voices
of restraint, deliberation and discipline, on the other hand, which are
regularly drowned out by the aforementioned rush of emotions, are
viewed skeptically as representatives of "society" or "parental authority" and thus not authentically "me."

"Do what you *feel* is right"—not "do what you think is right"—and   7
"go with your feelings" are creedal affirmations of the ego-equals-id mentality. The paradoxical result of following this gospel is that one becomes
a slave to his own emotions, bound like Ixion to the flaming wheel of
desire, tossed at one moment whimsically this way and the next in the
contrary direction. No pilot guides this ship, no rudder keeps it on course
since its direction is dictated by the unpredictable winds of emotion.

These affective elements—name your poison, but do not forget the   8
seven deadly sins—turn out to be less benign than advertised and belat-

edly reveal themselves as distinct from the "me" perched on the verge of annihilation. I find myself addicted, enslaved to . . . myself?

Thoreau is wiser. He does not ask which of the feelings seeking expression through my body is "me." He rather latches on to a capacity that he possesses—deliberation—and exercises it. This intention-laden capacity allows a human being to gain some leverage over bodily instincts.   9

It is superfluous in 1995 to assert that the body has its virtues. For us, the body has become the very essence of virtue. Rarely, however, does one hear it proposed that gaining "leverage" over bodily instincts is necessary or that simply identifying the "self" with bodily passions puts one at a subhuman level.   10

Civilization is not the result of exterminating passions, but it is the product of directing and asserting control over them. Puritans, Victorians and the medieval church are depicted by modern proponents of spontaneity as repressive party-poopers who disparage the body. A fairer, more accurate assessment is that they were yeomen laborers facilitating the emergence of a distinctive human spirit from the bondage of bodily passion. The "ego" that psychologists pamper and often claim to enhance by indulging bodily desires is today vanishing into the vortex of passion out of which it, with heroic effort, emerged.   11

Michelangelo's "Boboli Captive" is constructed of stone. Yet it is by cutting away and molding this stone that the image itself emerges. No cutting, no molding, no sculpture. Only thus does the character imprisoned within the stone emerge. The same can be said, *mutatis mutandis*, of the"I" ("the spirit") in its relation to the body. Am I my body? Yes and no.   12

"I" exist only to the extent that I am distinguished from the body and its passions to which I am joined. "I" am "free" only to the extent that I can exercise control over "my" passions, can shape and direct them. "I" exist in the discipline of setting goals, as opposed to the passive enactment of imperatives originating in the spleen.   13

"I," in reality, means character, and character is achieved, not given. It is a product of regimen, discipline and intention.   14

"Spontaneity" and "freedom" are the deceptive ideological labels modernity has given to the ascendancy of the id, to the rule of Plato's hydra-headed monsters that animate the spirit but can give it no integrity. "True freedom" comes, paradoxically, not from indulging the whims of desire but from "living deliberately."   15

Reprinted by permission of the author.

TWO PROPOSALS

Our Youth Should Serve

STEVEN MULLER

Too many young men and women now leave school without a well-developed sense of purpose. If they go right to work after high school, many are not properly prepared for careers. But if they enter college instead, many do not really know what to study or what to do afterward. Our society does not seem to be doing much to encourage and use the best instincts and talents of our young.

On the other hand, I see the growing problems of each year's new generation of high-school graduates. After twelve years of schooling—and television—many of them want to participate actively in society; but they face either a job with a limited future or more years in educational institutions. Many are wonderfully idealistic; they have talent and energy to offer, and they seek the meaning in their lives that comes from giving of oneself to the common good. But they feel almost rejected by a society that has too few jobs to offer them and that asks nothing of them except to avoid trouble. They want to be part of a new solution; instead society perceives them as a problem. They seek a cause; but their elders preach only self-advancement. They need experience on which to base choice; yet society seems to put a premium on the earliest possible choice, based inescapably on the least experience.

On the other hand, I see an American society sadly in need of social services that we can afford less and less at prevailing costs of labor. Some tasks are necessary but constitute no career; they should be carried out, but not as anyone's lifetime occupation. Our democracy profoundly needs public spirit, but the economy of our labor system primarily encourages self-interest. The Federal government spends billions on opportunity grants for post-secondary education, but some of us wonder about money given on the basis only of need. We ask the young to volunteer for national defense, but not for the improvement of our society. As public spirit and public services decline, so does the quality of life. So I ask myself why cannot we put it all together and ask our young people to volunteer in peacetime to serve America?

I recognize that at first mention, universal national youth service may sound too much like compulsory military service or the Hitler Youth or the Komsomol. I do not believe it has to be like that at all. It need not require uniforms or camps, nor a vast new Federal bureaucracy, nor vast new public expenditures. And it should certainly not be compulsory.

A voluntary program of universal national youth service does of course require compelling incentives. Two could be provided. Guaranteed job training would be one. Substantial Federal assistance toward post-secondary education would be the other. This would mean that today's complex measures of Federal aid to students would be ended, and that there would also be no need for tuition tax credits for post-secondary education. Instead, prospective students would *earn* their assistance for post-secondary education by volunteering for national service, and only those who earned assistance would receive it. Present Federal expenditures for the assistance of students in post-secondary education would be converted into a simple grant program, modeled on the post–World War II GI Bill of Rights.

But what, you say, would huge numbers of high-school graduates do as volunteers in national service? They could be interns in public agencies, local, state and national. They could staff day-care programs, neighborhood health centers, centers to counsel and work with children; help to maintain public facilities, including highways, rail beds, waterways and airports; engage in neighborhood renewal projects, both physical and social. Some would elect military service, others the Peace Corps. Except for the latter two alternatives and others like them, they could live anywhere they pleased. They would not wear uniforms. They would be employed and supervised by people already employed locally in public-agency careers.

Volunteers would be paid only a subsistence wage, because they would receive the benefits of job training (not necessarily confined to one task) as well as assistance toward post-secondary education if they were so motivated and qualified. If cheap mass housing for some groups of volunteers were needed, supervised participants in the program could rebuild decayed dwellings in metropolitan areas.

All that might work. But perhaps an even more attractive version of universal national youth service might include private industrial and commercial enterprise as well. A private employer would volunteer to select a stated number of volunteers. He would have their labor at the universally applied subsistence wage; in return he would offer guaranteed job training as well as the exact equivalent of what the Federal government would have to pay for assistance toward post-secondary education. The inclusion of volunteer private employers would greatly amplify

5

6

7

8

job-training opportunities for the youth volunteers, and would greatly lessen the costs of the program in public funds.

The direct benefits of such a universal national-youth-service program would be significant. Every young man and woman would face a meaningful role in society after high school. Everyone would receive job training, and the right to earn assistance toward post-secondary education. Those going on to post-secondary education would have their education interrupted by a constructive work experience. There is evidence that they would thereby become more highly motivated and successful students, particularly if their work experience related closely to subsequent vocational interests. Many participants might locate careers by means of their national-service assignments.

No union job need be lost, because skilled workers would be needed to give job training. Many public services would be performed by cheap labor, but there would be no youth army. And the intangible, indirect benefits would be the greatest of all. Young people could regard themselves as more useful and needed. They could serve this country for a two-year period as volunteers, and *earn* job training and/or assistance toward post-secondary education. There is more self-esteem and motivation in earned than in unearned benefits. Universal national youth service may be no panacea. But in my opinion the idea merits serious and imaginative consideration.

A Proposal to Abolish Grading

PAUL GOODMAN

Let half a dozen of the prestigious universities—Chicago, Stanford, the Ivy League—abolish grading, and use testing only and entirely for pedagogic purposes as teachers see fit.

Anyone who knows the frantic temper of the present schools will understand the transvaluation of values that would be effected by this modest innovation. For most of the students, the competitive grade has come to be the essence. The naïve teacher points to the beauty of the subject and the ingenuity of the research; the shrewd student asks if he is responsible for that on the final exam.

Let me at once dispose of an objection whose unanimity is quite fascinating. I think that the great majority of professors agree that grading hinders teaching and creates a bad spirit, going as far as cheating and plagiarizing. I have before me the collection of essays *Examining in Harvard College*, and this is the consensus. It is uniformly asserted, however, that the grading is inevitable; for how else will the graduate schools, the foundations, the corporations *know* whom to accept, reward, hire? How will the talent scouts know whom to tap?

By testing the applicants, of course, according to the specific task 4 requirements of the inducting institution, just as applicants for the Civil Service or for licenses in medicine, law, and architecture are tested. Why should Harvard professors do the testing *for* corporations and graduate schools?

The objection is ludicrous. Dean Whitla, of the Harvard Office of Tests, 5 points out that the scholastic aptitude and achievement tests used for *admission* to Harvard are a super-excellent index for all-around Harvard performance, better than high-school grades or particular Harvard course grades. Presumably, these college entrance tests are tailored for what Harvard and similar institutions want. By the same logic, would not an employer do far better to apply his own job aptitude test rather than to rely on the vagaries of Harvard section men? Indeed, I doubt that many employers bother to look at such grades; they are more likely to be interested merely in the fact of a Harvard diploma, whatever that connotes to them. The grades have most of their weight with the graduate schools—here, as elsewhere, the system runs mainly for its own sake.

It is really necessary to remind our academics of the ancient history of 6 examination. In the medieval university, the whole point of the grueling trial of the candidate was whether or not to accept him as a peer. His disputation and lecture for the Master's was just that, a master-piece to enter the guild. It was not to make comparative evaluations. It was not to weed out and select for an extramural licensor or employer. It was certainly not to pit one young fellow against another in an ugly competition. My philosophic impression is that the medievals thought they knew what a good job of work was and that we are competitive because we do not know. But the more status is achieved by largely irrelevant competitive evaluation, the less will we ever know.

(Of course, our American examinations never did have this purely 7 guild orientation, just as our faculties have rarely had absolute autonomy; the examining was to satisfy Overseers, Elders, distant Regents— and they as paternal superiors have always doted on giving grades, rather than accepting peers. But I submit that this setup itself makes it impossible for the student to *become* a master, to *have* grown up, and to commence on his own. He will always be making A or B for some over-seer. And in the present atmosphere, he will always be climbing on his friend's neck.)

Perhaps the chief objectors to abolishing grading would be the students 8 and their parents. The parents should be simply disregarded; their anxiety has done enough damage already. For the students, it seems to me that a primary duty of the university is to deprive them of their props, their dependence on extrinsic valuation and motivation, and to force them to confront the difficult enterprise itself and finally lose themselves in it.

A miserable effect of grading is to nullify the various uses of testing. 9 Testing, for both student and teacher, is a means of structuring, and also of finding out what is blank or wrong and what has been assimilated and can be taken for granted. Review—including high-pressure review—is a means of bringing together the fragments, so that there are flashes of synoptic insight.

There are several good reasons for testing, and kinds of test. But if the 10 aim is to discover weakness, what is the point of downgrading and punishing it, and thereby inviting the student to conceal his weakness, by faking and bulling, if not cheating? The natural conclusion of synthesis is the insight itself, not a grade for having had it. For the important purpose of placement, if one can establish in the student the belief that one is testing *not* to grade and make invidious comparisons but for his own advantage, the student should normally seek his own level, where he is challenged and yet capable, rather than trying to get by. If the student dares to accept himself as he is, a teacher's grade is a crude instrument compared with a student's self-awareness. But it is rare in our universities that students are encouraged to notice objectively their vast confusion. Unlike Socrates, our teachers rely on power drives rather than shame and ingenuous idealism.

Many students are lazy, so teachers try to goad or threaten them by 11 grading. In the long run this must do more harm than good. Laziness is a character defense. It may be a way of avoiding learning, in order to protect the conceit that one is already perfect (deeper, the despair that one *never* can be). It may be a way of avoiding just the risk of failing and being downgraded. Sometimes it is a way of politely saying, "I won't." But since it is the authoritarian grown-up demands that have created such attitudes in the first place, why repeat the trauma? There comes a time when we must treat people as adult, laziness and all. It is one thing courageously to fire a do-nothing out of your class; it is quite another thing to evaluate him with a lordly F.

Most important of all, it is often obvious that balking in doing the   12
work, especially among bright young people who get to great universities, means exactly what it says: The work does not suit me, not this subject, or not at this time, or not in this school, or not in school altogether.
The student might not be bookish; he might be school-tired; perhaps his
development ought now to take another direction. Yet unfortunately, if
such a student is intelligent and is not sure of himself, he *can* be bullied
into passing, and this obscures everything. My hunch is that I am
describing a common situation. What a grim waste of young life and
teacherly effort! Such a student will retain nothing of what he has
"passed" in. Sometimes he must get mononucleosis to tell his story and
be believed.

And ironically, the converse is also probably commonly true. A student   13
flunks, and is mechanically weeded out, who is really ready and eager to
learn in a scholastic setting, but has not quite caught on. A good teacher
can recognize the situation, but the computer wreaks its will.

FLAG BURNING AND FREEDOM OF SPEECH

The American Flag: A Symbol We Should Protect

PAUL GREENBERG

The flag amendment is back. And well on its way to becoming the   1
28th Amendment to the Constitution of the United States. What's
this? It was supposed to be dead a couple of years ago, remember?

But now the House of Representatives has voted in favor of a simple   2
declaration that, once upon a common-sense time, would scarcely have
attracted notice, let alone controversy: "The Congress and the States
shall have the power to prohibit the physical desecration of the flag of
the United States." The vote was 312 to 120, easily more than the two-
thirds' vote (280) required to propose a constitutional amendment. The
prospect for Senate approval is good, and the states are primed to ratify.

But didn't our intelligentsia explain to us yokels again and again that   3
burning the flag of the United States isn't an action, but speech, and therefore a constitutionally protected right? That's what the Supreme Court
decided, too, if only in one of its confused and confusing 5-to-4 splits.

But the people don't seem to have caught on. They still insist that 4
burning the flag is burning the flag, not making a speech. Stubborn lot,
the people. Powerful thing, public opinion, Congress certainly seems to
be reflecting it.

It isn't the *idea* of desecrating the flag that the American people pro- 5
pose to ban. Any street-corner orator who takes a notion to should be
able to stand on a soapbox and bad-mouth the American flag all day
long—and apple pie and motherhood, too, if that's the way the speaker
feels. It's a free country.

It's actually burning Old Glory, it's defacing the Stars and Stripes, it's 6
the physical desecration of the flag of the United States that ought to be
against the law. And the people of the United States just can't seem to be
talked out of that notion—or orated out of it, or lectured out of it, or
condescended and patronized out of it.

Maybe it's because the people can't shut their eyes to homely truths 7
as easily as our Advanced Thinkers. How many legs does a dog have,
Abraham Lincoln once asked, if you call its tail a leg? And he answered:
still four. Calling a tail a leg doesn't make it one. Not even a symbolic
leg. The people have this stubborn notion that calling something a constitutional right doesn't make it one, despite the best our theorists and
pettifoggers can do.

The people keep being told that their flag is just a symbol. 8

Just a symbol. 9

"We live by symbols," said a justice of the United States Supreme 10
Court (Felix Frankfurter) when the standards for appointees, whether
liberals or conservatives or neither, were considerably higher. And if a
nation lives by its symbols, it also dies with them.

To turn aside when the American flag is defaced, with all that the flag 11
means—yes, all that it *symbolizes*—is to ask too much of Americans.

There are symbols and there are Symbols. There are some so rooted in 12
history and custom, and in the heroic imagination of a nation, that they
transcend the merely symbolic; they become presences.

Many of us may not have the words to express it (which is why nations 13
wave flags instead of computer printouts), but we know it's right to protect the flag—by law. To do nothing when that flag, that presence, is desecrated is not simply to let the violent bear it away; it is to join the mob,
to aid and abet it by our silence, our permission, our unnatural law. It is
to become one more accessory to the general coarsening of society, to the
desensitizing of America, to the death of the symbolic.

No, this is not an argument over who loves the flag more. Patriots can   14
disagree; American ones almost have an obligation to. This Republic was
not conceived as some kind of factory for manufacture of robots. And
those on the other side of this issue have every right to resent it if somebody wants to turn this disagreement over law and the role of the symbolic in American life into some kind of loyalty test. No one political
persuasion has a monopoly on the American flag. May it long wave over
every kind of political rally.

But this also isn't a fight over who loves the Bill of Rights more. And   15
those of us who favor a simple constitutional amendment to protect the
flag have every reason to resent it when others try to monopolize the Bill
of Rights, or confuse it with the Supreme Court's confused reading of the
First Amendment where the flag is concerned.

Burning the flag is no more speech than vandalizing a cemetery, or   16
scrawling slogans on a church or synagogue, or spray-painting a national
monument—all of which are *acts* properly forbidden by the laws of a
civilized country. Not to mention public decency.

Even if no flag were ever burned, or no cemetery or church ever   17
defaced, laws against such acts would be proper, and should be constitutional. Because the law is a great teacher, and one thing it needs to teach
a less-and-less-civil society is a little respect.

The great Italian—what? historian? philosopher? moralist? philoso-   18
pher of history? proto-anthropologist?—Giambattista Vico spoke of a
barbarism of the intellect that confuses concept with reality (speech with
action?) and so loses touch with the *sensus communis*, the common-
sense values of language and custom in which nations are rooted.
Today's strange arguments from our best-and-brightest against protecting the national emblem are not symptomatic of any kind of treason-of-
the-intellectuals, but of a different malady: an isolating intellectualism
cut off from a sense of reverence, and so from the historical memory and
heroic imagination that determines the fate of any nation.

Reprinted by permission.

Flag Burning and The First Amendment

CHARLES LEVENDOSKY

Click on Internet's Flag Burning Page, and you can flick a virtual Bic   1
and burn a virtual American flag. Is that desecration?

Members of the House of Representatives, in a stampede to show us just how super patriotic they are, overwhelmingly passed a proposed amendment to the Constitution which would allow Congress and the states "to prohibit the physical desecration of the flag of the United States."   2

As they rushed to vote, their heels stomped all over the core meaning of the First Amendment. Reason couldn't head them off. Argument couldn't. Not even the Constitution can halt a herd of congressmen when they want to prove to voters they are patriotic.   3

If the Senate doesn't stop this proposed amendment, free speech will have another exception carved out. One that impacts political speech.   4

The First Amendment is clear and decisive: "Congress shall make no law . . . abridging the freedom of speech . . ." But once again Congress is mucking about with our liberties.   5

Some say that flag burning isn't speech. Then why are these folks so upset about the flag being burned? Obviously, the act does communicate something. It expresses a profound disagreement with the policies of the federal government.   6

The "not speech" ploy is an attempt to persuade us that the proposed amendment would not limit the First Amendment.   7

Of course, there is symbolic speech.   8

And some acts are eloquent speech.   9

The U.S. Supreme Court recognized that more than 60 years ago when it ruled that raising a red flag to show support for worker unity was protected speech. And again 25 years ago, when the high court protected the right of students to wear black armbands to protest our role in Vietnam.   10

Even silent sit-ins to protest racial segregation were recognized as symbolic speech and thus protected by the court.   11

Burning the flag is the act of someone who has little or no political power.   12

It is an act of someone who desperately wants to communicate a disagreement with U.S. policy. It shocks us into paying attention to those who could not otherwise command the interest of the media. It presents a grandstand forum in order to express political dissent. Our dissidents are then heard.   13

This is a profound First Amendment issue for the powerless.   14

It is easy for those in the power structure to ignore this side of the issue. A member of Congress can call a news conference whenever he or she wishes. The media will be there. The little guy, the working class stiff, commands no such attention.   15

The flag proposal is another piece of elitism parading in the guise of patriotism.   16

Nothing in our Constitution could be more significant than protecting the right of the ordinary citizen to express his or her disagreement with the government—so that the dissent will be heard. This is a profound First Amendment issue for our nation.   17

Political speech must have the broadest protection—even to include burning the American flag—for us to be able to contend that We the People govern ourselves.   18

We protect waving the flag or displaying it as a statement of political assent. The First Amendment means that we must protect burning the flag as a counter-statement, a statement of political dissent. That is the essence of freedom of speech.   19

What your congressmen aren't telling you is that, if they wished—even if the amendment is ratified—they could burn the American flag on the floor of either house of Congress during congressional debate and not be taken to court for it.   20

Read Article I, sec. 6 of the U.S. Constitution: they cannot be held legally accountable for any speech while in debate on the floor of Congress.   21

So, We the People, who by inalienable right should have the most expansive reading of the First Amendment, will have a narrower one, while our political servants have the greater. Seems backward, doesn't it?   22

That's because this amendment is flagrantly, deeply un-American.   23

And where will this erosion of liberty stop? Will a few ministers begin a movement to stop people from burning the cross—after all can't the cross be considered a more important symbol than the flag?   24

What does physical desecration of the flag mean? Does it mean you can be arrested if you wear a bikini with a representation of the flag on it? The U.S. Code defines the American flag as "any substance" that shows the colors, stars and stripes, and could be considered a clear representation.   25

Will the flag be desecrated if you sit down while wearing your flag pants?   26

Will a frosting flag on a Fourth of July cake be desecrated if you eat the cake?   27

Is burning a virtual flag in the cyberspace of Internet desecration?   28

Confused? That's because we are dealing with a symbolism. Symbolism has few boundaries in the real world. But liberty is tangible in our daily lives.   29

Our Congress seems willing to protect the symbol of our liberties—at 30 the expense of those liberties. Our representatives have sworn to protect the Constitution, yet in this proposal they violate the very essence of it.

Clearly, our stampeding congressmen have charged off the edge—just 31 to prove they are patriotic. What sad irony.

Reprinted by permission of the author.

ETHICS: CHEATING, LYING, AND BREAKING THE LAW

Why Most Students Cheat: It's Not What You Think

MICHAEL MOORE

Three-quarters of all college students have cheated at least once. And 1 that may be a conservative estimate. A 1990 survey, conducted at the University of Miami, Ohio, found that 9 of 10 students there cheated by methods ranging from copying a classmate's answers during an exam to plagiarizing term papers.

Every day, we hear and read that America is losing its competitive edge. 2 One explanation is that American students are graduating without getting an education. Anyone who has spent some time in a college classroom can hardly disagree. But this is not entirely the fault of the undergraduate.

Many people find it hard to sympathize with students who cheat. If 3 undergraduates, or their parents, are financing a college education, they have a responsibility to attend class, learn the subjects and complete assignments. But our institutions of higher learning also have a responsibility: to provide the kind of education that is not only interesting but stimulating. They have largely failed in this mission by choosing to become diploma mills.

The dynamics of the "system" are to blame. A majority of students 4 don't cheat because they are lazy, or hung over. They mostly cheat in classes they are forced to take. They mostly cheat in classes that are boring. Instead of using stimulating techniques to present their subjects, professors simply teach at students. An unmotivated professor sends a distressing signal to students—it's easier for them to cheat, since they can blame their lack of intellectual interest on an uninspiring professor. Why should a student be any more interested in learning than a professor is in teaching?

Professors are the primary reason that cheating continues. If students are getting away with cheating, it's usually the result of a lack of vigilance on the part of the professor. Ask any administrator. A lot of professors refuse to enforce academic integrity codes, thereby signaling students that they have little to lose by cheating. Indeed, if more professors looked forward to class day as much as they do to payday, the incidence of cheating would dramatically diminish. They should wake up.

Still, the American college professor must contend with administrators and college boards of trustees who have traditionally placed great pressure on them to produce research, attract federal, state and private grants, and get published. These pressures ultimately shortchange the student. The "publish-or-perish" mentality relegates educating to a secondary status. And these factors, combined with traditional professional laziness (read: tenure), have distorted priorities.

So where is the student in all of this? Students will continue to cheat until "the system" is reformed. One reason I wrote *Cheating 101* was to let outsiders in on college's dirty little secret. Cheating in itself isn't that bad, when compared with a system that tolerates—even encourages—cheating. Higher education clearly needs reforming.

One reform would be to promote greater interest in learning. Cheating is a paradox. Students cheat when they are not interested in a course or there is no mutual respect between student and professor.

Honor codes can discourage cheating. At the University of Virginia, which has the nation's oldest code, student cheating is rare and does not go unpunished. The value of honor codes is that they encourage a student to be responsible. Statistics prove this approach works.

A related reform is to provide incentives for professors to be more vigilant in the classroom. Instead of simply acknowledging that cheating exists, they should push for honor codes where they don't exist, and enforce them where they do. And administrators need to be prepared to back up their professors, rather than running scared from the mere threat of lawsuits. A University of Pittsburgh professor, for example, brought charges against a student after he found evidence that the student had copied exams, quizzes and lab reports. When the student's father, a lawyer, threatened to sue, the case went nowhere.

No wonder cheating in college is hard to combat.

The Truth About Our Little White Lies

KAREN S. PETERSON

Gail Safeer, a graduate student in suburban Washington, D.C., doesn't   1
let on to people that two of her three children were born during a
previous marriage. "I don't correct people when they assume all three
are my husband's," she says. "It's nobody's business. It's a little white
lie of omission, like not telling somebody her husband is running
around. . . . White lies are not daily currency in my life," adds Safeer.
"But we all do it."

Indeed we do. Each of us fibs at least 50 times a day, says psychologist   2
Jerald Jellison of the University of Southern California in Los Angeles,
who has spent a decade musing on the truth about our lies. He says we
lie most often about the Big Three—age, income and sex—areas where
our egos and self-images are most vulnerable. To protect them we even
lie non-verbally with our gestures, silences, inactions and body language.
"You can even lie with your emotions," says Jellison. "The smile you
don't mean, or the classic nervous laugh. A man asks a woman, 'Your
place or mine?' and then chuckles. If she's offended, he can always elaborate on that laugh by saying, 'Can't you take joke? I was only kidding.'"

These types of lies are what Jellison calls "little white lies," the kind   3
we throw around as casually as old sneakers but which he claims are our
"social justifications." "We lie because it pays," he says. "We use [lies] to
escape punishment for our small errors. . . . Also, our social justifications
help us avoid disapproval. 'I gave at the office,' or 'I'm sorry.'"

Our most common reason for lying is to spare someone else's feelings,   4
says Jellison. "We often tell ourselves that, but usually we're trying to
protect our own best interests. I'll feel that if I tell you the truth, you'll
get mad." Adds B. L. Kintz, a psychology professor at Western
Washington University in Bellingham: "We lie so often, with such regu-
larity and fluency, so automatically and glibly that we're not even aware
we're doing it. The little self-serving deceptions, the compliments we
don't mean, stretching the point in a social situation—they are part of
reality. Lying is simply something that is."

Jellison couldn't agree more. He believes that white lies are the oil for   5
the machinery of daily life. "Society actually functions fairly well on many
small deceptions. They contribute the little, civilized rituals that comfort
us. . . . The idea that we must always tell the truth is too simplistic," he
says. "'Is lying right or wrong?' is an impossible question to answer."

Be it right or wrong, we have become so accustomed to lying and being 6
lied to that we only see it as harmful in daily life when we don't realize
that it's happening to us. "We take for granted some degree of lying from
politicians, government, business, advertising," says psychiatrist Dr.
Irving Baran of the USC San Diego Medical School. "We don't get
excited about the ad that hypes some product in a way we know isn't
true. But the rub comes when we go to someone we need and trust and
are deceived. A banker for a loan who says he's got the best interest rate
going. A real estate agent who convinces us his is the best package available. An insurance agent pushing an unsound policy. An auto dealer who
doesn't tell you the product's safety record. Then our backs go up, and
what isn't true—hurts."

Copyright 1983, USA Today. *Reprinted with permission.*

Most Americans Admit Lying, But Who's Being Fooled?

SANDI DOLBEE

Most Americans believe in God, brush their teeth before going to 1
bed and lie regularly. Nine out of 10 Americans think lying has
become commonplace, say pollsters who surveyed the country last year
for a book about what people really think.

Why should we care? 2

"It's unraveling our society," warns Jim Walls, an ethicist and author 3
based in Washington, D.C.

Lying has made us sick, says the Rev. John Cobb Jr., a retired professor 4
from the Claremont School of Theology.

And it is only the beginning of other bad things, adds Joe Sprecco, an 5
El Cajon court marshal who for 11 years has watched witnesses and
defendants swear to be truthful and then proceed to "lie their butts off."

What they've seen breathes life into the numbers crunched by pollsters 6
who questioned 5,700 people in 50 cities for the book *The Day America
Told the Truth.*

Lying is what drove Susan Van Zant out of a job processing unemploy- 7
ment claims two decades ago.

"They were supposed to be looking for work," says Van Zant. "I knew 8
they weren't looking for work. They knew they weren't."

Still, she processed the forms and the applicants got their checks. 9

"I realized that children don't lie and that's why I'm in education," 10
says Van Zant, who is principal at Morning Creek School, a campus of
456 kindergarteners through fifth graders in the Poway Unified district.

Ask a child a question and wait long enough, she says, "and they'll tell 11
you the truth. But our society, we're not rewarding that any more."

Trickle-Down Theory

The moral bonds of society have broken down, says Wallis, who edits 12
Sojourner magazine, a nondenominational publication that focuses on
the impact of faith, politics and culture on modern life.

Wallis just returned from working on a book about the nation's lack 13
of social vision—or moral conscience. He cites Proverbs from the Old
Testament: "Where there is no vision, the people perish."

"Which I think," Wallis adds, "is what is happening to us." 14

Wallis and Cobb talk about lying in medical terms. Wallis calls it a 15
symptom; Cobb says it has made us sick as a society.

"And the 'medicine' that has made us sick seems to be what people 16
think we need more of," says Cobb, who founded the Center for Process
Studies in Claremont, which is affiliated with the School of Theology
there.

Cobb and Wallis blame materialism. 17

People are always moving to find a better job. Companies close or 18
relocate. Turnover is constant in the community. And all this makes it
harder for people to develop loyalties, relationships and care about their
community, they say.

Wallis singles out politics and advertising for sanctioning lying as a 19
way of life.

"Advertising is basically institutionalized lying. . . . Believability or 20
credibility has replaced truth telling."

Wallis recalls a panel discussion of journalists discussing the Clarence 21
Thomas–Anita Hill hearings.

"They were all talking about lying and one of them said, 'It's just 22
political lying that they're doing. . . . political lying is something that
everybody does.'"

And so it trickles down. 23

"It's very basic and simple that telling the truth to each other, in some 24
sense, life depends on it," Wallis adds.

But do we really want to hear the truth? 25

"We are torn between what we want and what we need," says John 26
Quiring, a staff member at Cobb's Center for Process Studies. "What we

need is the truth. We need to know the facts about our job, our relationship, what other people think . . . but what we want is to be comfortable."

Good People Lie, Too

People lie for all sorts of reasons. They don't want to hurt someone's feelings. They fear the reaction they'll get. They don't want to be unpopular. They don't want to get in trouble.   27

Sprecco, the court marshal, is an expert on this last reason.   28

In the courtrooms he monitors, Sprecco says, the slogan appears to be: the bigger the lie, the better.   29

He recalls a case in which two men were arrested for possession of marijuana after a sheriff's deputy found a big bag of it in their truck. The bag was sitting on the floorboard in the front seat, brimming over. "You couldn't miss it," Sprecco said.   30

But the two men told the jury that they had borrowed the truck and didn't see the marijuana until a deputy tried to pull them over. They said they ran because they feared the deputy would think the marijuana was theirs.   31

"The jury thought nobody would make up a story like that—so they skated," Sprecco said.   32

He adds, "It scares me. I used to think people were good and society could make them screwed up. I'm no longer so sure of that."   33

Is it ever OK to lie?   34

Although religions universally do not condone lying, their leaders also admit that there may be certain situations where it may be OK.   35

"Basically we are against lying, but I ask, 'What is the condition?'" says the Rev. Akio Miyaji of the Buddhist Temple of San Diego.   36

A parent may be sick and he does not yet want the children to know, so he lies. "That's lying, but we don't call it a real lie," Miyaji says.   37

But Buddhism believes you have to take responsibility for whatever you say, even the small lies. "And maybe I'm going to get punished in the future," he adds.   38

You have to look at the degree of seriousness of the lie and how it affects people, says the Rev. Bernard Filmyer, communications director of the San Diego County Ecumenical Conference.   39

While lying is a sin, he says, there are varying degrees of sinfulness. Telling someone your mother isn't home when she is may be lying, "but it really doesn't have that much affect on anybody else."   40

Gary Gehring may be relieved to hear that.   41

Gehring, a bartender at the Alibi bar in San Diego, argues that a lot   42
of the lying he sees on the job is just "harmless fun." Someone trying to
impress someone else. Someone trying to look good.

And when a wife calls up and the husband asks Gehring to lie for him?   43
He'll probably do it. "That's why we call it the Alibi."

Can We Stop Lying?

So how do we get back to telling the truth?   44

Wallis and Cobb aren't so sure it is possible without significant   45
changes in society.

Principal Van Zant thinks perhaps it's not too late for the children. But   46
there have to be some changes.

"We know that children spend more time watching TV than they do   47
in school," she says. "And we know that morality on television is 'get by
any way you can.'

"There's no Beaver Cleaver on television any more," she adds. "We're   48
not giving them any role models."

Outside forces need to change—but so does the inner self.   49

"We just need to toughen up and accept hard facts and not be so insis-   50
tent on our own security," Quiring says.

Meanwhile, Sprecco watches with dismay and a touch of fear the   51
parade of people in court.

"I used to think the only difference between me and them was the   52
way I was raised. Then I see these people from good families. . . . There's
a thin line there somewhere and I haven't crossed it—thank God. And it
scares me."

Sprecco doesn't separate lying from other bad behavior.   53

"Once you start, where do you stop? Lying is a start—the same as   54
skimming $15 off drug raid money because nobody would miss it."

From the San Diego Union-Tribune, *February 15, 1992.*
Reprinted by permission of the publisher.

A Red Light for Scofflaws

FRANK TRIPPETT

Law-and-order is the longest-running and probably the best-loved   1
political issue in U.S. history. Yet it is painfully apparent that millions of Americans who would never think of themselves as lawbreakers,

let alone criminals, are taking increasing liberties with the legal codes
that are designed to protect and nourish their society. Indeed, there are
moments today—amid outlaw litter, tax cheating, illicit noise and motor-
ized anarchy—when it seems as though the scofflaw represents the wave
of the future. Harvard sociologist David Riesman suspects that a majority of Americans have blithely taken to committing supposedly minor
derelictions as a matter of course. Already, Riesman says, the ethic of
U.S. society is in danger of becoming this: "You're a fool if you obey the
rules."

Nothing could be more obvious than the evidence supporting Riesman. 2
Scofflaws abound in amazing variety. The graffiti-prone turn public sur-
faces into visual rubbish. Bicyclists often ride as though two-wheeled
vehicles are exempt from all traffic laws. Litterbugs convert their communities into trash dumps. Widespread flurries of ordinances have failed
to clear public places of high-decibel portable radios, just as earlier laws
failed to wipe out the beer-soaked hooliganism that plagues many parks.
Tobacco addicts remain hopelessly blind to signs that say NO SMOKING.
Respectably dressed pot smokers no longer bother to duck out of public
sight to pass around a joint. The flagrant use of cocaine is a festering
scandal in middle- and upper-class life. And then there are (Hello, everybody!) the jaywalkers.

The dangers of scofflawry vary wildly. The person who illegally spits 3
on the sidewalk remains disgusting, but clearly poses less risk to others
than the company that illegally buries hazardous chemical waste in an
unauthorized location. The fare beater on the subway presents less threat
to life than the landlord who ignores fire safety statutes. The most immediately and measurably dangerous scofflawry, however, also happens to
be the most visible. The culprit is the American driver, whose lawless
activities today add up to a colossal public nuisance. The hazards range
from routine double parking that jams city streets to the drunk driving
that kills some 25,000 people and injures at least 650,000 others yearly.
Illegal speeding on open highways? New surveys show that on some
interstate highways 83% of all drivers are currently ignoring the federal
55 m.p.h. speed limit.

The most flagrant scofflaw of them all is the red-light runner. The flout- 4
ing of stop signals has got so bad in Boston that residents tell an anecdote
about a cabby who insists that red lights are "just for decoration." The
power of the stoplight to control traffic seems to be waning everywhere.
In Los Angeles, red-light running has become perhaps the city's most
common traffic violation. In New York City, going through an intersection is like Russian roulette. Admits Police Commissioner Robert J.

McGuire: "Today it's a 50-50 toss-up as to whether people will stop for a red light." Meanwhile, his own police largely ignore the lawbreaking.

Red-light running has always been ranked as a minor wrong, and so   5
it may be in individual instances. When the violation becomes habitual, widespread and incessant, however, a great deal more than a traffic management problem is involved. The flouting of basic rules of the road leaves deep dents in the social mood. Innocent drivers and pedestrians pay a repetitious price in frustration, inconvenience and outrage, not to mention a justified sense of mortal peril. The significance of red-light running is magnified by its high visibility. If hypocrisy is the tribute that vice pays to virtue, then furtiveness is the true outlaw's salute to the force of law-and-order. The red-light runner, however, shows no respect whatever for the social rules, and society cannot help being harmed by any repetitious and brazen display of contempt for the fundamentals of order.

The scofflaw spirit is pervasive. It is not really surprising when schools   6
find, as some do, that children frequently enter not knowing some of the basic rules of living together. For all their differences, today's scofflaws are of a piece as a symptom of elementary social demoralization—the loss by individuals of the capacity to govern their own behavior in the interest of others.

The prospect of the collapse of public manners is not merely a matter   7
of etiquette. Society's first concern will remain major crime, but a foretaste of the seriousness of incivility is suggested by what has been happening in Houston. Drivers on Houston freeways have been showing an increasing tendency to replace the rules of the road with violent outbreaks. Items from the Houston police department's new statistical category—freeway traffic violence: (1) Driver flashes high-beam lights at car that cut in front of him, whose occupants then hurl a beer can at his windshield, kick out his tail lights, slug him eight stitches' worth. (2) Dump-truck driver annoyed by delay batters trunk of stalled car ahead and its driver with steel bolt. (3) Hurrying driver of 18-wheel truck deliberately rear-ends car whose driver was trying to stay within 55 m.p.h. limit. The Houston Freeway syndrome has fortunately not spread everywhere. But the question is: Will it?

Americans are used to thinking that law-and-order is threatened mainly   8
by stereotypical violent crime. When the foundations of U.S. law have actually been shaken, however, it has always been because ordinary law-abiding citizens took to skirting the law. Major instance: Prohibition. Recalls Donald Barr Chidsey in *On and Off the Wagon*: "Law-breaking

proved to be not painful, not even uncomfortable, but, in a mild and perfectly safe way, exhilarating." People wiped out Prohibition at last not only because of the alcohol issue but because scofflawry was seriously undermining the authority and legitimacy of government. Ironically, today's scofflaw spirit, whatever its undetermined origins, is being encouraged unwittingly by government at many levels. The failure of police to enforce certain laws is only the surface of the problem: they take their mandate from the officials and constituents they serve. Worse, most state legislatures have helped subvert popular compliance with the federal 55 m.p.h. law, some of them by enacting puny fines that trivialize transgressions. On a higher level, the administration in Washington has dramatized its wish to nullify civil rights laws simply by opposing instead of supporting certain court-ordered desegregation rulings. With considerable justification, environmental groups, in the words of *Wilderness* magazine, accuse the administration of "destroying environmental laws by failing to enforce them, or by enforcing them in ways that deliberately encourage noncompliance." Translation: scofflawry at the top.

The most disquieting thing about the scofflaw spirit is its extreme infec-   9
tiousness. Only a terminally foolish society would sit still and allow it to spread indefinitely.

© 1983, Time, Inc. Reprinted by permission.

ENGLISH AS THE "OFFICIAL" LANGUAGE OF THE UNITED STATES

English Should Be Official

BRADLEY S. O'LEARY

No other country has been able to assimilate so many people, from   1
so many backgrounds, for so long a time as the USA.

What draws immigrants to America's shores today is the same as it   2
was in the days of Ellis Island: religious, political and economic freedom—all of which are possible because there are more ties that bind us than misunderstandings that divide us. The strongest of those ties is a common language. That language is English.

Many Americans are surprised to learn that English is not our official   3
language. English is the official language of 14 other countries, yet not ours. English also is the language that 90 percent of immigrants' children

speak. It is the language of 80 percent of the world's electronic databases and communications networks. Yet some politicians oppose making our common language our official language. English has been our common language for more than 200 years, but its future as our common language is threatened by those who court ethnic groups by spending tax dollars to Balkanize our language.

Making English official wouldn't mean: "If you can't speak the language, get out." It would mean the government encourages the learning of English, and stress that it's vital to speak English to reap the benefits of American life and contribute to America.   4

A common language fosters growth and understanding. We can be taught by others only if we can understand what they say.   5

With out-of-control government costs in the news, we must address the exorbitant price of multilingualism. Last year, politicians in L.A. spent $900,000 to translate voting documents into seven languages.   6

Just look north for an example of how expensive multilingualism is. Canada, with one-tenth our population, spends $6 billion a year translating into two languages. The USA, with nearly 150 ethnic languages, could see the costs of multilingualism reach many billions of dollars more. The costs of civil fragmentation defy economic calculations.   7

The USA has become the planet's oldest democracy because of its ability to absorb, rather than accommodate, immigrants. We should accept legal immigrants only if they accept the responsibility of learning our laws, our language and our way of life.   8

From USA Weekend, *Oct. 22, 1993. Reprinted by permission of the author.*

English Shouldn't Be Official

Victor Kamber

If "English-only" proponents would put half their resources into increasing opportunities for immigrants to learn English, rather than into oppressive, pointless legislation, they would solve whatever problems non-English speakers may cause society.   1

But that isn't the point. They aren't interested in solving problems. They are cynically using "English only" to whip up anti-immigrant frenzy for political gain, exploiting our ugliest instincts.   2

We don't need a law formalizing what already is a fact: English is the language in which this nation's business is conducted. English somehow   3 has maintained this status through endless immigration. In spite of the hysteria of the "English-only" Chicken Littles, the sky hasn't fallen and the republic hasn't collapsed.

Any immigrant smart enough to get into this country is smart enough   4
to realize that a good command of English is essential to success. Immigrants work hard to learn the language. But we lack the resources to accommodate the high demand. In New York City this year, 35,000 to 40,000 students were enrolled in adult English classes, but 50,000 had to be put on the waiting list. This is the real scandal.

Making English our official language won't help. And it would do real   5
damage. For example: The testimony of crime victims who can't yet speak English might be prohibited in court. Police officers and doctors might be left without the interpreters they rely on to protect people who don't speak English. Schools might find it more difficult to communicate with pupils' parents.

A failure to pass "English-only" laws would benefit all, because multi-   6
lingualism will help the USA compete in the new global economy. While we must give every immigrant access to English classes, let's not inhibit the use of other languages. In most of the rest of the world, educated people speak more than one language. The more Spanish speakers in the USA, the better we can compete in Latin America. The more speakers of Asian languages, the better we can compete in the Pacific Rim.

Immigrants are a resource for economic development, not a burden.   7
They should be cultivated, not bashed.

From USA Weekend, *Oct. 22, 1993. Reprinted by permission of the author.*

Does America Need an "Official" Language?

RUBÉN G. RUMBAUT AND ALEJANDRO PORTES

During the last 10 years, U.S. English, the Federation for American   1
Immigration Reform (FAIR), and similar organizations have gained national attention by denouncing the impending demise of the English language in the wake of massive Latin and Asian immigration to the United States.

In a book called *The Immigration Time Bomb*, a former Colorado   2
governor accused Hispanic immigrants of not wanting to assimilate and deplored their arrival, which, in his opinion, is leading to the "fragmenting of America."

U.S. English has not yet succeeded in dictating how people should   3
speak, but it has succeeded in defining the terms of the debate. By planting the concern that today's immigrants do not want to assimilate, it has
focused the discussion on the survival of English as the nation's only language and as its cultural centerpoint.

Perhaps we're missing something. We are, after all, Latin immigrants   4
ourselves and still speak Spanish when allowed to. But we find the
"problem" to be as illusory as the solutions that the nativist organizations propose. For a quarter of a century—since 1965 to be exact—the
United States has received a growing number of newcomers from all over
the world. But after these 25 years of accelerated immigration, 90 percent of the population speak English and most of the remainder speak
English and another language.

How is this possible? A first reason is that the vast majority of the   5
population is still native-born of native parentage. A second, and more
important, reason is that children of immigrants give up their language
in one or two generations.

Most first-generation immigrants learn English in order to survive and   6
typically combine it with their home language. Some even forget that
language after a while. But it is among their children that the real shift
takes place. The typical second-generation adolescent makes a concerted
effort *not* to speak anything other than English. Despite parental
entreaties to preserve their "heritage," these kids are far more interested
in rock, rap, clothing, and peer acceptance than in the latest news from
Thailand.

The available census figures tell the story in stark terms. Ninety-three   7
percent of native-born Americans speak only English at home. Among
immigrants with less than 10 years in the country the figure is only
16 percent, but it reaches 75 percent among their children. This last figure is actually an average. The lowest point is found among children of
European immigrants (71 percent), the highest among Filipino-
Americans (95 percent).

By the third generation, however, virtually no one recalls how their   8
ancestors talked to each other. This process explains why the United
States has been called a "language graveyard." Literally dozens of languages spoken by the foreign-born have disappeared in the course of
50 years or less.

The threat that the self-appointed guardians of English agitate today   9
may yield juicy donations, but it is illusory. Immigration has never challenged the absolute dominance of English, nor is it doing so today.

The question, in fact, may be reversed. If every second-generation child   10
is going to speak English, does this mean that he or she should speak
English *only*? Is it really necessary that youth who could grow up speaking English and another language be compelled to give up bilingualism
as the price of full assimilation? Is knowledge of two languages incompatible with good citizenship?

As the United States finds itself more enmeshed in global economic   11
competition, the need of pools of Americans who can speak foreign languages fluently becomes compelling. The second generation now growing up in many cities could fulfill such a need.

Unfortunately, the available evidence suggests that the combined   12
weight of peer pressures, school programs to "mainstream" children of
immigrants as soon as possible, and the generalized absence of support
for bilingualism leads to rapid English acquisition *and* the equally rapid
loss of the home language.

U.S. English, FAIR, and like-minded organizations contribute to a   13
peculiar paradox. While thousands of children of immigrants lose the
treasure of knowing another language, thousands of young Americans
enroll in high school and college courses to acquire a halting command
of Spanish, French, Chinese, etc.—the very tongues that immigrants are
told to forget. Apparently, for these nativist organizations, the only
acceptable way of speaking a foreign language is poorly and with an
accent.

This enforced linguistic homogeneity is not a desirable goal in a coun-   14
try that prides itself on being at the center of the international economy.
While English undoubtedly will remain the language of the land, the
presence of pockets where other languages are spoken fluently enriches
the nation's culture and strengthens its international standing.

From the San Diego Union-Tribune, *November 10, 1991.*
Reprinted by permission of the authors.

Language Cements Nationhood

RON SAUNDERS

Why do we need to designate English as the nation's official lan-   1
guage of government? The United States has never had an official
language. Why do we need one now?

Government deals with issues as they arise. Day care, education   2
reform, and term limits are relatively new to our national agenda. Just
because we've never faced these issues before doesn't mean we don't
need to now. Language policy also has evolved into an issue of national
concern.

U.S. English is a national, multi-ethnic group of almost 500,000   3
Americans. We believe that maintaining the tie of common language is
crucial for the unity and stability of this country.

The central issue is communication. Democracy, more than any other   4
system of government, depends upon communication. Our democracy
could not function if the people could not communicate with their
elected representatives. Through our common language, we argue,
debate, and reach compromises.

That our democracy works is a tribute to our ability to communicate.   5
As a people, Americans have little in common. For more than 200 years,
we have come with every cultural heritage, religious belief, nationality,
and race to share in the riches of this country. More than 150 languages
are represented within our borders, yet we live together in peace and
freedom. Our common language unites us and promotes understanding
through communication.

Although our people are diverse, we share a common culture, heritage   6
and, of course, language. As a nation, Americans must strive to preserve
those things that unite us because unity is more difficult than diversity to
achieve and maintain. Unity must be nurtured, encouraged and affirmed;
diversity comes naturally.

U.S. English opposes the segregation of our country along language   7
lines. Our central argument is for unity—not uniformity. We believe
attempts to make our country officially multilingual are expensive and
divisive. Bills supporting official multilingualism have been introduced in
at least 12 states and passed in three. And in Congress bills have been
presented that would require local education offices and private businesses to operate in Spanish—even if they don't serve Spanish-speaking
communities.

Language-of-government legislation is often misrepresented and misin-   8
terpreted. Official language is language of government. Period. It says
that the business of the legislative, executive, and judicial branches of
government will be conducted in English. Official language does not
affect the home, the community, the church, the private business. It does
not affect essential government services in other languages, such as 911
calls for emergency assistance.

The Language of Government Act establishes a common-sense policy   9
where today there is none. Multiple language usage is subtly expanding
in government bureaucracies. We must establish a government policy
that puts the focus and the money back where it belongs: on teaching
our new citizens English. We need a policy that says: English is important in the United States. To benefit fully from the social, political, and
economic opportunities our country offers, you should know the English
language.

Language is at the core of nationhood. More than half the nations of   10
the world have official languages, many of them in our own hemisphere.
Venezuela, for instance, is a democracy with Spanish as its official language. Spanish is not the only language used in Venezuela, but government business is conducted in Spanish and elections are conducted in
Spanish. If you travel or move to Venezuela, you would be wise to know
Spanish.

Every viable nation fosters a common culture to survive. When we   11
speak of "multiculturalism," we should be aware that American culture
is constantly changing, like a kaleidoscope, making this country unique
among nations. We could not be a truly multicultural society without a
common language because we would be unable to share our diverse traditions and heritages. Instead we would be divided into enclaves separated by language and ethnic barriers—segregated and apart.

English is the logical choice as our nation's official language, not   12
because it is "better" than other languages but because it is our common
language. English is the only language that crosses all ethnic, racial, and
religious lines in our country. With our common language, we have dis-
solved mistrust and fear and drawn up understandings that make our
society possible.

Around the world—in Yugoslavia, Sri Lanka, Canada, Estonia,   13
Cyprus—countries without a common language are in turmoil, illustrating that language can divide as well as unite. In this country there is a
need for logical, well-constructed, long-term language policies that take
care of legitimate needs. We must strengthen the strongest and most
durable bond that we as Americans share, through passage of the
Language of Government Act.

Reprinted by permission.

Subject Index

Author/Title Index

WE'D LIKE TO HEAR FROM YOU

Thank you for using *Reading-Based Writing.* We care a lot about how well you liked this book. Please let us know how we can improve the next edition! Return this page with your comments, using the postage-free label on the other side. Or send a letter. Either way, we'd like to hear your thoughts.

Overall, how valuable was the book as part of your course? _____

_____

_____

Circle each chapter that you used as part of your course assignments.

1	Writing with a Central Idea	12	Consistency in Verb Tense and Verb Voice
2	Reading for the Central Idea	13	Subject-Verb Agreement
3	Supporting the Central Idea	14	Pronoun Agreement and Reference
4	Unity and Coherence	15	Pronoun Case
5	Summarizing and Responding to Reading	16	Misplaced and Dangling Modifiers
6	Evaluating Reading	17	Comma Usage
7	Synthesizing Ideas from Reading	18	Semicolons & Colons
8	Arguing from Several Reading Selections	19	The Apostrophe
9	Some Basic Editing Terms	20	Quotation Marks
10	Sentence Fragments	21	Titles, Capitalization, and Numbers
11	Fused Sentences and Comma Splices		

Mark an X by any chapter that you read in addition to the course assignments. Mark an O by any other chapter that your class didn't cover but you wish it *had.*

Did you find some parts or exercises particularly helpful? Which? _____

_____

_____

Are there any parts or exercises that you think should be changed? _____

_____

_____

Are there any topics not covered in this book that you think should be added? _____

_____

_____

How else can we improve *Reading-Based Writing?* _____

_____

_____

Thanks and good luck!

Stephen McDonald   William Salomone

Your name _____ School _____

Your address _____

City/State _____ Zip _____

Your instructor's name _____

FOLD HERE

TEAR PAGE OUT

FOLD HERE

BUSINESS REPLY MAIL
FIRST CLASS   PERMIT NO. 34   BELMONT, CA

POSTAGE WILL BE PAID BY ADDRESSEE

Stephen McDonald / William Salomone
Reading-Based Writing
^{c}/o Angela Gantner Wrahtz
Wadsworth Publishing Company
10 Davis Drive
Belmont, CA 94002-9801